UNIVERSALS OF PSYCHOANALYSIS IN THE
TREATMENT OF PSYCHOTIC AND BORDERLINE STATES

CW00819172

HENRI REY is Former Consultant Psychotherapist, Maudsley Hospital, London.

JEANNE MAGAGNA is Consultant Psychotherapist, Hospitals for Sick Children, Great Ormond Street, London.

JOHN STEINER is a training analyst of the British Psycho-Analytical Society and Consultant Psychiatrist at the Tavistock Clinic, London.

UNIVERSALS OF PSYCHOANALYSIS IN THE TREATMENT OF PSYCHOTIC AND BORDERLINE STATES

FACTORS OF SPACE–TIME AND LANGUAGE

HENRI REY

Edited by Jeanne Magagna

Foreword by John Steiner

'an association in which the free development of
each is the condition of the free development of all'

Free Association Books / London

Published in 1994 by
Free Association Books Ltd
Omnibus Business Centre
39–41 North Road
London N7 9DP

ISBN 1 85343 370 5

A CIP catalogue record for this book is available from the
British Library.

Produced for Free Association Books Ltd by
Chase Production Services, Chipping Norton.
Typeset by Archetype, Stow-on-the-Wold.
Printed in the EC by The Cromwell Press, Broughton Gifford.

CONTENTS

Acknowledgements   vi

Credits   vii

Foreword by Dr John Steiner   ix

1   Universals of Psychoanalysis   1

2   The Schizoid Mode of Being and the Space–Time Continuum (Before Metaphor)   8

3   Intrapsychic Object Relations: The Individual and the Group   31

4   Anorexia Nervosa   47

5   A Group of Anorexic and Bulimic Patients   76

6   Manic-Depressive Psychosis   86

7   Psycholinguistics, Object Relations Theory and the Therapeutic Process   136

8   Chronic Schizophrenia: A Group Illustration   151

9   Basic Schizoid Structures and Space–Time Factors   163

10   The Psychodynamics of Psychoanalytic and Psycholinguistic Structures   176

11   The Psychodynamics of Depression   190

12   Reversibility, Depression and the Therapeutic Process   199

13   Reparation   207

14   That Which Patients Bring to Analysis   229

15   On Ignacio Matte-Blanco

     Part 1: A Critical Review of *The Unconscious as Infinite Sets: An Essay in Bi-Logic*   249

     Part 2: Notes on Matte-Blanco   256

16   Femininity, Sexuality and Inner Space   263

17   Awake, Going to Sleep, Asleep, Dreaming, Awaking, Awake: Comments on W. Clifford M. Scott   277

18   The Scapegoat Motif in Society and its Manifestations in a Therapeutic Group (with F.K. Taylor)   288

Bibliography   307

List of Publications of Henri Rey   311

Index   313

ACKNOWLEDGEMENTS

Dr Robert Young of Free Association Books contacted me and suggested writing the book. Jeanne Magagna assisted me as an editor in London. There is no way adequately to recognize her efforts in the task of reading, correcting and suggesting how to improve the articles.

I am grateful to Jason Aronson, Stratton International, Medical Book Corporation, the *Journal of the Melanie Klein Society* and the Institute of Psycho-Analysis for permission to use articles published by them.

Mrs Michelle Plummer and Mrs Rosanna Koplowicz did all the typing and deserve all my gratitude. I do not forget my friends and colleagues from the Maudsley Hospital, the British Psycho-Analytical Society, and the Universities of Montreal, Cape Town and Perth for their encouragement over the years. A special thought for my old friend, Dr Murray Jackson, for his constant support.

It remains for me to thank my wife for her kind help, especially during the years of travelling and teaching abroad.

All names of patients have been changed.

Henri Rey

CREDITS

I am grateful to the following publications, which have granted me permission to use previously published articles in this book:

'The schizoid mode of being', first presented at the British Institute of Psycho-Analysis in 1977; 'Schizoid phenomena in the borderline' (1979), in eds J. LeBoit and A. Capponi, *Advances in the Psychotherapy of the Borderline Patient*, New York: Jason Aronson, pp. 449–84; 'The schizoid mode of being' (1988), *Journal of the Melanie Klein Society* 6: 12–52; and in ed. E. Spillius, *Melanie Klein Today*, vol. 1, Routledge, 1988, pp. 203–29.

'Intrapsychic object relations: the individual and the group' (1975), in ed. Wolberg, *Group Psychotherapy*, New York: Jason Aronson.

'Anorexia nervosa', permission generously granted by Alice Friedman (née Rouah) to reproduce her personal account in this chapter.

'Psycholinguistics, object relations theory and the therapeutic process' (1986), *Journal of the Melanie Klein Socety*, 4: 53–73.

'Psychoanalytic and psycholinguistic structures' (1986), lecture given to University College London.

'Basic schizoid structures and space–time factors' (1986), *Cahiers pédagogiques* V: 47–62, Dept. de Psych., Université de Montréal.

'The psychodynamics of depression' (1986), *Cahiers pédagogiques* V: 78–88, Dept. de Psych., Université de Montréal; and *Journal of the Melanie Klein Society* 4: 93–104.

'Reparation' (1986), *Journal of the Melanie Klein Society* 4: 5–36.

'That which patients bring to analysis' (1988), *International Journal of Psycho-Analysis* 69: 457–70.

'A critical review of Matte-Blanco's *The Unconscious as Infinite Sets* (1975), *International Journal of Psycho-Analysis* 49.

'Awake, going to sleep, asleep, dreaming, awaking, awake: comments on W. Clifford M. Scott', (1992) *Free Associations* no. 27: 439–54.

'Fémininité, sexualité et espace intérieur' (1986), *Cahiers pédagogiques* V: 88–111, Dept de Psych., Université de Montréal.

Rey, H. and Taylor, F. K. 'The scapegoat motif in society and its manifestations in a therapeutic group' (1953), *International Journal of Psycho-Analysis* 34: 1–12.

FOREWORD

Dr John Steiner

Until now the work of Henri Rey has been less known than it should be, and it is to be hoped that this book will enable a wider public to become acquainted with some of the most original and creative ideas to be found in the interface between psychoanalysis, psychiatry and other disciplines. Henri Rey rightly thinks of himself first as a psychoanalyst, but having spent much of his professional life at the Maudsley Hospital, he knows and shares many of the ways psychiatrists think, and he has a unique knowledge of psychotic and borderline patients.

Henri Rey has a special affection for the Maudsley, which he would refer to as 'the brick mother', and this is partly because of his gratitude for the shelter and opportunity it gave him early in his career. He saw how important the hospital was as a place of safety for patients who were afraid of breaking down, and that it offered a kind of continuity and stability. He also recognized that this kind of 'brick mother' could be cold and unresponsive, but this was often compensated for by his personal warmth and enthusiasm. In this setting, Rey was always reminded of the terrible suffering experienced by psychotic and borderline patients, and he remained distressed by patients for longer and in a deeper way than most of his hardened colleagues. Despite this personal involvement, or perhaps because of it, he was able to think about the problems his patients were facing, and to enlarge his understanding of the mental mechanisms they used.

He is one of the first analysts to have described the anxieties and the thinking of borderline patients, whom he has understood particularly well. He recognizes that they find choices so difficult that they inhabit an area between two alternatives. This is particularly true when issues which give rise to a feeling of identity are involved. The borderline patient feels he is not fully male or female, neither large nor small, neither inside nor outside, but on the border between these states.

These patients have helped Rey to recognize the essentially spatial structure of the mind and to see how this evolved in relation to objects who are also represented spatially. The self may in this way be felt to reside in an object, and the process of differentiations requires a specific disengagement and emergence from the object. Rey writes in an original and enlightening way about such spatial relationships. For example, he describes how psychological birth need not correspond with biological birth since the infant often feels he retains so close a dependence on his mother that he lives in a kind of marsupial space, like the newborn kangaroo in his pouch, and true psychological birth requires a further process of separation, loss and mourning. A knowledge of these processes is essential for the understanding of phobic patients who feel they have discovered a safe haven, and consider that they have been forced prematurely to emerge from the maternal space into a world for which they are not yet ready.

Rey also, however, understands that such agoraphobic reactions to the thought of emergence are always accompanied by a claustrophobic reaction if the patient fears that his escape route is blocked. This leads to what he has called a claustro-agoraphobic dilemma in which the patient feels trapped inside his objects and tries to escape. Once outside, however, he is afraid he will lose the object on which he depends, and becomes agoraphobic. As a result he is able to find security neither with objects nor away from them; this is one of the factors which leads him to prefer a situation on the border between inside and outside. Henri Rey thus understood the term 'borderline' in a much broader sense than has been usual: certainly as a diagnostic category of patients who fall roughly between psychosis and neurosis, but also as a metaphor describing the way such patients structure their mental space and the position they occupy in it.

He himself has a particular affinity for borderline areas, which fascinate him because they allow him to make contact with territory on either side of the divide. Unlike his patients, he is able to enter and move freely about neighbouring fields such as medicine, physiology, linguistics, psychology, mathematics and literature. It is not that he puts himself forward as an authority in each of these fields, but rather that his enthusiasm, curiosity and respect for his scientific colleagues has enabled him to look into them and take what he needs to expand and clarify a psychoanalytic idea.

It was these discoveries in the field of space-and-time relationships which led Rey to study Piaget. Later he saw how symbolism and language are the tools through which mastery over mental space is acquired by the developing child, and he taught himself linguistics, mathematics and the physics of relativity. He was particularly engrossed by the work of René Thom and of Matte-Blanco, whose application of mathematics to mental problems impressed him. It is through the study of transformations that Rey is led to re-examine the process of mourning through which symbolic function is restored. Once this is achieved, experiences can become represented as images, memories and symbols, which are then available for use in thinking, dreaming and in the making of relationships. He shows how some patients are unable to make such transformations and are destined to remain in a persecutory world peopled by concrete objects; others can experience loss, and through their suffering enable a symbolic residue of the lost object to remain. In one of his papers he has illustrated this movingly through the poem of Paul Valéry entitled 'Le Cimetière Marin', in which it is the melting of fruit in the mouth which leads to an experience of absence as the shape dies leaving behind only an experience.

With the realization of the importance of symbolic function Rey could address the problems which face a patient who is unable to symbolize properly, and here he was struck by the failure of such patients to make reparation. Because of their concrete thinking, the damage which they have done to their objects is experienced as real and actual, and as a result the repair which the damaged object demands is equally real and actual. Such concrete repair is mostly beyond the means of any individual, and Rey shows how this is one of the factors which encourages omnipotence and a shift towards manic pseudo-reparation. The understanding of such failures in reparation led Rey to pay close attention to what it was his patients specifically wanted from their treatment, and he was able to discover that it was often the repair of an object which they had damaged or felt they had damaged which was the primary purpose of their analysis. Only after the object had been dealt with did they feel that they were able to ask for anything for themselves.

In these and other areas Rey shows how influenced he has been through his psychoanalytic work by Melanie Klein and her followers. He had his training analysis with Herbert Rosenfeld, and was also very influenced by Joan Rivière, who was one of his supervisors, and by Hanna Segal, whose pioneering work on symbol-formation helped him to look at this from his own original point of view.

Henri Rey arrived at the Maudsley to study psychophysiological relationships between the menstrual cycle and psychiatric illness. He progressed from this field to some of those areas itemized above, but always remembered the importance of the body and of the body schema in the mental organization. Until his retirement he continued to work and teach at the Maudsley, where he inspired many young psychiatrists to develop their own individual interests, and helped several, myself included, to begin training as psychoanalysts. Following his retirement he settled in France but travelled extensively, especially to Canada, South Africa, and Australia, where his teaching was much valued and sought after. The good friends he made while abroad enabled him to extend his clinical observations, and these led to a number of papers, some of which appear in the present book.

Rey's skill and enthusiasm as a teacher became legendary, and the reader will gain much from this book if he treats some of the chapters as clinical seminars in which Rey, with his uniquely French appetite for good things, shows us the way his patients are prevented from participating in life by their anxieties and their demand for revenge and withdrawal into negativity. It is this kind of clinical focus which has enabled Henri Rey to study the deepest areas of human responses, and to link the tragic self-destructiveness of borderline and psychotic patients with problems of revenge, guilt and forgiveness. Many of the themes to be found in this book are of fundamental importance, and all psychoanalysts as well as many in those neighbouring fields will find it fascinating to read, and will emerge enriched and also encouraged to broaden their own points of view.

1   UNIVERSALS OF PSYCHOANALYSIS

The term 'Universals' in the title refers to very primitive mechanisms and structures of the mind relevant to psychoanalysis, such as *in utero* processes as well as early baby–mother relationships, to such paranoid-schizoid structures, part-object relationships, depressive processes and also the early elaboration of inner space, consisting of inner and external objects. It is only after years of clinical practice that I venture to develop some ideas in which I have been interested. First of all, I have often thought about two notions which could be expressed fairly simply, in spite of the complexities of psychoanalytic processes. The first is that the human race could not have existed without sex. Second, temporariness and death are our lot. For this reason, both the consequences of the life and death instincts govern our life.

In order to account for the emergence and elaboration of the inner part of our mind in the course of evolution, Freud postulated that the early primitive activities of the mind, which he called 'phantasy', gradually evolved from sensori-motor schemas to higher representations. These representations, occurring first as phantasies, imagination and symbols, led to interiorizations, introjections and identifications, which contributed to the formation of a more developed inner world. Gradually, as the mind became more complex, these were more elaborated, leading to new interpretations of the world and human behaviour. When a person was awake, the first and most primitive representations became less apparent with other, more advanced thoughts taking their place. But the repressed phantasies were not dead; they remained dynamically active in what Freud called the 'Unconscious'. The task was how to find a 'royal road to the Unconscious', and Freud discovered it in the language of dreams, in symbols and free associations.

Freud called the driving force of those repressed phantasies Instincts. At first, he only considered the life instincts, but later, in 1920, he called certain aspects of the instincts the death instinct. In doing this, he postulated that part of the aggressive impulses remained inside, and part turned towards the outside world.

I want to consider the term 'death instinct' not only in terms of physical death, but in terms of the death of thought. As the mind evolved to higher levels, more sophisticated representations became possible. The question is how to deal with the death of thoughts selectively. One cannot kill thoughts, one can only try to block them, which would be equivalent to killing them in thought. Thus arose such mechanisms as repression, denial, memory suppression, as well as integration of primitive thoughts into higher levels of thought. In some ways, these are mechanisms deriving from the death instinct. Similarly, in the physical sphere, Freud postulated some physical substance in each cell of the body, whose action would lead to cellular death. For instance, we know now from modern biochemical and neurological research that certain cells of the brain not used at birth are abolished, which is known as apoptosis. The undoing and abolition of somatic and psychological structures are vital for a more advanced structure to evolve in the course of evolution and during the maturation of the individual. For this reason, the death instinct involving the death of thought serves both the human race and the individual.

The next aspects to investigate are the structures of space and time. I have attempted whenever possible to make an analysis of those structures, their elaborations and their dynamic mechanisms. Psychoanalysis has thrown an amazing light on the manifestations, conscious and unconscious, of the psychodynamics of human behaviour. But from the beginning of psychoanalysis, little had been said of the step-by-step development of man's sense of reality in its detailed external reality. Forty years ago when I began studying psychoanalysis this gradually struck me and I began to study Piaget's work and his attempts to give to the cognitive process the same impetus as psychoanalytical studies had given to the life and death instincts and to phantasies. Without Piaget's contributions I could not have written papers on space and time, which described the gradual emergence of space-centred thought, the early spatial thinking, followed by progress through displacement and the notion of speed, which leads to the emergence of time structures in the mind. Freud, in his usual moments of genius, had been able to understand that primary processes, dreams and certain other processes partially ignored time restrictions and contradictions.

Freud analysed adults and deduced and hypothesized the steps that the adult had gone through to reach adulthood. Melanie Klein showed by her methods that Freud's hypotheses could be ~~treated~~ TESTED through the analysis of children. Her own emotions, feelings of aggression, for instance, would be affected. I have described some of these effects in this book.

In early schizoid processes and borderline syndromes, the 'border' is not only between the paranoid-schizoid and the depressive positions, but also between the various states of part-objects and part-spaces and domains to

Her own work was then tested by the direct observation of infants. Now because of new methods even in utero behaviour can be used to check on the continuity of in-utero to after-birth processes The which they belong in the course of development and in terms of hierarchical structuration. 'Borderline' means the absence of communication or defective communication between those dynamic structures which go on functioning separately and are incapable of integrating. The interplay between those parts and their disintegration is what I have tried to describe. I have described in detail claustro-agoraphobia and claustro-agoraphobia-philia, which result from that state of affairs.

Claustro-agoraphobia-philia not only concerns objects and their domains but also words and their domains. This leads to my interest in psycholinguistics. At a meeting years ago of the Curriculum Committee of the London Institute of Psycho-Analysis, I mentioned that the main therapeutic tool for psychoanalysts was language, and I thought we ought to consider a course on the subject. This was well received, but when the question was raised who would conduct the course, there was nobody available. I was told, 'It looks as if you have to do it yourself, or else . . . ' I was most unprepared for this task and said, 'Well, the students and myself will have to learn together.' The part that most interested me was the relationship of early sensori-motor schemas, early representations and their linking with schizophrenic disorders of thought, representations and their linking with words. It became extremely helpful to understand schizoid and schizophrenic disorders of thought, representations and symbol formation. Some attempts at these have been included in the present book. A number of psycholinguistic writers have been quoted, specially some of the very original ideas of René Thom on the semantic density of words. However, I have attempted to discuss more fully the concrete and spatial nature of words used as containers for projective identification, giving them meaning and life, that is to say, as object structures with inner and external domains in intercommunications.

In the first part of this introduction, consideration has been given to the step-by-step evolution of the reality principle, somewhat in the same sense as happened for the pleasure–pain principle. However, the main aspect of this book is about clinical considerations, for which clinical examples are given to enable the reader to make direct observations of mental states. Thus, for manic-depressive psychosis a verbatim account of sessions is included, and only afterwards is there a commentary on their interpretations; also for anorexia nervosa a written account by the patient is presented, including what she called her '*in utero* phantasies', and acting out of pregnancy. There is also a full paper on feminine identity and inner space. The treatment of a schizophrenic patient is described, as well as numerous clinical examples of various psychopathologies. Further, examples of group therapy of borderlines, schizophrenics and anorexia nervosa have been described as near as possible to the clinical events. This is an attempt to show how in small groups, psychotic thinking can be talked about with understanding by the patients, and intercommunications and transference situations can develop.

research into dream structures + symbolism has also advanced our appreciation of Freud's hypotheses. This has helped enormously to understand the phantasies of patients + human beings in general

It was impossible to write without mentioning reparation. This is one of the basic contributions of Melanie Klein to psychoanalysis. The papers on the subject illustrate the importance of psychic inner objects that need reparation to achieve a well-integrated mental life. This reparative drive, basic to Kleinian psychodynamic theory, is linked with the paper on depression (Chapter 11) and the paper entitled 'That Which Patients Bring to Analysis' (Chapter 14).

The concepts of instincts and drives have been reconsidered in more modern and appropriate terms using Lawrence Kubie's views of a unit consisting of a biochemical substrate, a neuronal net and a psychological structure in search of an appropriate object. This new definition is of great help when it comes to psychosomatic structures and sensori-motor schemas, and even to the consideration of the genetic components of behaviour.

Since part-objects and part-spaces or domains have been assessed as very important, there are examples of their functions. For instance, the structure of local units are contrasted with more sophisticated wholes. Included are descriptions of the role of the sexual organs not only as to the discharge of sexual tension or in reproduction, but as a psychophysical bridge, that is, the vagina as an entrance to the inner space and the inner world, or the penis and its use as a container for the projection of the breast, ensuring for the infant a continuation from mother to father.

Later I refer to some of the new ideas of Matte-Blanco, which appeared to me to be most interesting. They open a new vista on the development of part-objects and of the concepts of the infinitely small and the infinitely big. Matte-Blanco's work is connected with the ideas on space-centred thought and to the relevance of relative spatial dimensions of objects and impulses, as well as to the ideas about symmetrical and asymmetrical thinking.

Like all psychoanalysts, I have a particular attraction to dreams and their use in theory and practice. The paper entitled 'Awake, Going to Sleep, Asleep, Dreaming, Awaking, Awake' (Chapter 17) is making use of Dr Clifford Scott's ideas expressed in his paper 'Repairing broken links between the unconscious, sleep and instinct; and conscious, waking and instinct' (1988).

The vital process that drives men and women to each other, to love each other and then create life, and thus achieve the continuation of the human race Freud called the Oedipus complex. In a way he has created a double-edged problem, for this life activity was thus not only described as the most important psychobiological undertaking of human beings, but also it was transferred to the realm of mythology around the Oedipus complex. As such it was made to be part of the great mythologies of the world, as part of the heritage of the great timeless beliefs of the human race. But at the same time it had become a myth, or something beyond ordinary understanding. I wonder what problems this has resulted in for psychoanalytic theory. Was it a so-called scientific theory, or had it become part of mythology? Or was it both? Is not something similar applicable to the concept of narcissism? Of course, I have no answers, but the questions have come to my mind. To remain in touch with examples, we have: the classical Oedipus complex, the precursors of the Oedipus complex, the early Oedipus complex, and there is also the male Oedipus and the female Electra complexes. If we take narcissism, we have narcissism proper, primary narcissism and secondary narcissism. Other examples can be provided.

Something else has appeared to me of great importance. The question can be put as follows: what other process simultaneously takes place during all baby's early phase of temporary identification with father? I think it is the role that father plays during that period of intense progress in representation, symbol- and language-formation. As father gradually becomes an important object, symbol-formation becomes in part linked with father, or, in Lacanian terms, with 'the name of the father'. This new object, father, is considered to be 'pregnant with logos'; that is to say, the collection of phallic masculine attributes such as knowledge of the world, thinking and reasoning which we subsume under the classical term logos.

I have mentioned earlier that to ease the move from mother to father, the breast in phantasy is projected into the penis so that something of mother is transferred to father. The penis thus becomes the container and the breast the contained; that is to say, the penis becomes the first primitive symbol. Needless to say, the penis acquires at that time some of the characteristics of the breast and of the mother. The practice of fellatio is an example. The relationship of the struggle to achieve final sexual identity and the elaboration of language can be seen in what happens in schizophrenia and manic-depressive psychosis, for instance. In schizophrenia, the disorder of language, or so-called schizophrenic jargon, is most prominent, as well as symbolic distortions of one kind or another which frequently occur together with most important failures of identity. It is during the manic phase that logorrhoea and other such disturbances are also most frequent.

It is relevant to mention here the work of Jost (1947, 1953) in France. If at the appropriate time *in utero* both male and female mammalian foetuses are castrated, they will develop as females. Therefore, the male foetus has to evolve from its female beginnings and succeed in its male identification. The female, after a temporary male identification, must return to its original femaleness. I have linked all these with the phase of attempting to identify with father and not fully succeeding. Clinical examples are provided.

The depth and primitiveness of symbolic and language abnormalities are more or less proportionately related to the periods that correspond for Kleinians to the paranoid-schizoid and the depressive positions. You may remember Schreber, whom Freud described as having difficulties with his sexual identity and language, as well as experiencing a frightful upbringing and 'soul murder'. The depressive position belongs to a more advanced state of representational maturation and is a metasystem to the paranoid-schizoid position. Intermediate between the paranoid-schizoid positions and the depressive positions there are the schizoaffective disorders in which there is a pendulum shift from one state to the other. Similarly we have the shift in manic-depressive psychosis. In both cases the metasystems fail to establish themselves and there is a failure to progress. Since I have fairly extensively used the concept of metasystems and hierarchical structures, the Gödel Theorem must be mentioned, especially in reference to the evolution of higher systems during maturation.

Finally, the question of genetics should be referred to. It is futile to argue incessantly about the relative contribution of genetic inheritance and of the environment: both are contributors; both must be considered. It is necessary to try to make use of discoveries in the domain of genetic research and of physical methods of treatment in psychiatry as derived from new knowledge about brain mechanisms.

Similarly, one cannot ignore the revolutionary contributions of psychoanalysis to the deeper and most primary understanding of the mind. Even in the domain of genetics, the minute and detailed investigations of psychoanalysis in the course of treatment may provide a clue to the period when a constitutional abnormality has occurred and provide the direction for research.

Another point that deserves to be mentioned is some of the progress due to research connected to the question of chaos. Chaos, in the original sense of the word, means total disorder. Now it is suggested that there are at least two kinds of chaos – chaotic chaos and deterministic chaos. This means that from time to time a repetitive order is found in the systems investigated. However, when haphazard changes multiply themselves too quickly, then deterministic chaos becomes chaotic chaos. This implies also a new discovery known as 'sensitive dependence on initial conditions', referred to as the 'butterfly effect'. That is to say, at the very beginning of similarly developing processes, small differences between them will turn into very different results. As Lorenz (1988) puts it, 'Does the flap of a butterfly's wings in Brazil set off a tornado in Texas?'

It is impossible to avoid thinking that as the human infant evolves and matures, he never relinquishes his sensitive dependence on initial conditions. Further, as deterministic chaos progresses towards order, we have to think of biological rhythms and recurrent mental illnesses, for instance, the shift from depression to mania or from depression to schizophrenia, or vice versa in schizoaffective disorders. When doing research on psychophysical relationships the question of recurrent mental illnesses interested me, but it was only later, when learning about deterministic chaos and sensitive dependence on initial conditions, that I realized these ideas could be applied to psychoanalysis.

I have given here an introduction to some ideas of the subjects considered in this book. In doing so, I have tried to keep an open mind about changing views, starting with adult analysis, on to infant observation, and finally to intra-uterine observations. My own developing consciousness of the structures of states can be summed up as: what part of the subject is in what state, situated where in space and time, with what consequences for the object and the subject?

does what, with what motivation to what part of the object, in what state, situated where in space and time,

2   THE SCHIZOID MODE OF BEING AND THE SPACE-TIME CONTINUUM (BEFORE METAPHOR)

THE SCHIZOID MODE OF BEING

The period that followed the Second World War revealed a remarkable change in the kind of patients seen by, or referred to, the psychotherapist and the psychoanalyst. The bulk of patients seemed to consist of a certain kind of personality disorder which defied classification into the great divisions of neurosis and psychosis. We now know them as having a borderline, narcissistic, or schizoid personality organization. This simplification is the result of a long process of attempts at classification of all kinds.

An attempt has been made in this essay to extract aspects of human behaviour and mental processes that seem to constitute the core of what we now know as schizoid or borderline personality organization. It can be found not only in those people with such a personality as will be described, but also in people who may break down into schizophrenia, depression or mania, or as the underlying core of personality in people with hysterical or obsessional personality. By studying the schizoid traits in these various states, I hope to be able to define the schizoid personality and the schizoid mode of being in its more or less pure form, and to distinguish it from the other states of which it may form part. It seems that those people represent a group who have achieved a kind of stability of personality organization in which they live a most limited and abnormal emotional life which is neither neurotic nor psychotic, but a sort of frontier state.

Schizoid and/or borderline patients when seen by the psychiatrist are usually in their early twenties. They complain of an inability to make contact with others, and find it impossible to maintain any warm and steady relationship. If they actually manage to enter into a relationship it rapidly becomes intensely dependent and results in disorders of identity. They rapidly and transiently form an identification with their objects, and experience a loss of their sense of identity with the self. They seldom establish a firm sexual identity, and vacillate in their experience of maleness and femaleness. They are not homosexuals but have fears that they may be, and their choice of love objects, or attempts at choice of love objects, are just as vacillating. They are demanding, controlling, manipulating, threatening and devaluing towards others. They accuse society and others for their ills and are easily persecuted. This may be associated with grandiose ideas about themselves. In fact, their feelings are dominated by phantasies of relative smallness and bigness. When threatened by feeling small and unprotected and in danger they may defend themselves by uncontrollable rages and various forms of impulsive behaviour.

Other aspects of their abnormal affectivity are reflected in the sense of futility they complain of and which is characteristic of them. This is reflected as well in the special kind of depression from which they suffer, a form of depersonalized depression, that is, boredom, uselessness, lack of interest, with a marked deadening of the pain aspect of true depression. Together with this deadness there is a search for stimulants and production of sensory experience by means of alcohol, drugs, hashish, cutting themselves, perversions, promiscuity. They often complain of various abnormal sensations, body-image disturbance of various kinds, as well as depersonalization and derealization experiences. Their body ego is no more structured and stable than their personality, ego or self. Their underlying state of perplexity and confusion is frequently apparent.

Their work performance varies a great deal. Often when they come to treatment they have given up their studies or their work or they are doing some form of manual or low-level occupation, although they may have achieved university standards. However, their working capacity may be preserved if they work in a structured situation.

There is one difference in my personal experience in the way the two sexes present themselves, with many more men responding to the description I have given than women. In the case of women, hysterical manifestations – that is, hysterical mechanisms of defence – mark the underlying personality structures, and they show more often than men histrionic behaviour, acting out, hysterical fits, and overtly the claustro-agoraphobic syndrome. The claustro-agoraphobic syndrome, however, is basic to both sexes; only certain manifestations of it are different. As Guntrip (1968) has so clearly described, the schizoid person is a prisoner: he craves love but is prevented from loving because he is afraid of the destructive force of his love so far as his object is concerned; he dares not love for fear that he will destroy. He finds himself enclosed in a dilemma, enclosed in a limited space, and with limited objects and limited relationships.

It is the mechanism at work in this 'limitation state' that I intend to describe. Kindness and support in the transference situation are not enough to treat these patients. A thorough knowledge of their mental processes, phantasies, and underlying structures subtending their behaviour is essential, in combination with affective understanding.

I will begin with internal part-objects and their language – projective identification – because we must begin somewhere in this Tower of Babel which makes up the schizoid structure. I mean this expression literally because these part-objects whose structure we need to understand speak to each other and speak to us in a confusion of languages which demand special interpretation.

In normal interpersonal relationships one or another aspect of the whole ego corresponds with one or another aspect of the ego of the other person. It is a relationship at the level of the integrated ego. Moreover, in normal conduct, apart from certain aspects of love and hate, when we tend to be concrete, the ego makes use of conventional signs which are conscious and of symbols which may be conscious or unconscious, both, however, existing at a representational level.

Schizoid communication by contrast often takes place at a level of 'merchandise', a sort of barter agreement in which the subject feels himself to be given 'things', made to accept 'things', and where 'things' are done to him. Thus, after weeks or even months of refusing to speak of her intimate feelings a patient said, 'You don't understand. If I speak to you I hit you. I poison you with the rotting and mouldy things which I am full of.' She had previously simulated a suicide attempt in order to get her stomach washed out, to clean out some of these contents. Another patient said, 'When you speak to me and ask me questions you bite me and tear out a piece of my flesh. I won't speak any more, I won't listen.' It is a well-accepted fact for psycholinguists that at first the utterances of the mother are considered to be experienced by the child as perceptual parts of mother like any other parts.

Moreover, more or less normal people think in terms of persons, not objects placed somewhere in a container. In contrast, this is just how schizoid thought functions: thoughts are material objects contained somewhere and expelled into something or other; even the containing object is itself contained somewhere. It is thus that the schizophrenic is the patient who most concretely shows the true problem of claustrophobia and agoraphobia. In the consulting-room he sits near the door or the window even if this cannot be opened sufficiently for him to escape. He feels himself to be engulfed, immured in one object or another, and feels that he does the same thing with the objects which are inside him.

A schizophrenic patient illustrated this by explaining why he was frightened to lie on the couch. He was afraid of becoming engulfed in it, and, being so tall that his feet overlapped the couch, he feared that his father would see his legs poking out and cut them off. He could not distinguish between the couch and his mother in his unconscious phantasy, and felt himself caught inside his mother with only his feet showing. This is concrete thinking, where the idea is equivalent to the object and where these idea-objects are always contained or containing.

We must now consider the characteristics of these objects and their fate when they are displaced. This will lead us to examine the notion of partial objects, and of splitting and denial. It is remarkable that these ideas, which took on an increasing importance in Freud's thought, remained unused, or almost so, by the adherents of classical psychoanalysis. To quote Laplanche and Pontalis:

> It is of some interest to note that it was in the field of psychosis – the very area where Bleuler too, from a different theoretical standpoint speaks of *Spaltung* – that Freud felt the need to develop a certain conception of the splitting of the ego. It seemed to us worth outlining this conception here even though few psychoanalysts have adopted it; it has the merit of emphasizing a typical phenomenon despite the fact that it does not provide an entirely satisfactory explanation of it. (1973, p. 429)

Similar comments could be applied to the concept of partial objects and of denial since these concepts are interdependent. I think it is necessary to make an important distinction between a pathological part-object and a normal part-object, which is only partial in the sense that it forms one of the parts of an object which is capable of being assembled into a whole. Thus the maternal breast is a part-object only by comparison with the whole mother formed by the integration of her various parts, and functions in an infant phantasy like an object endowed with capacity for action, love and hate.

Splitting plays a part in normal development also, for example, splitting of good and bad aspects of the object as well as of the subject, and also the splitting of one object from others. But the schizophrenic behaves differently. Under the sway of persecutory anxiety and the fear of catastrophic dissolution of the ego – primitive and elemental anxieties which arise from the beginning of life – he proceeds to use splitting repetitively and intensively to get rid of bad parts of himself, which leads to a fragmentation of the object and of the fragmented parts of the ego, as well as fragmented parts of internal objects. The impulses and anxieties belonging to these fragments are projected into his objects, which acquire by projective identification these split-off aspects of the self, now projected and denied. These objects become persecutors and are introjected, but cannot be assimilated. They are in turn projected into an external object – or even into an internal object in an intrapsychic relation – and the vicious circle continues. These objects, some of which Bion has called 'bizarre objects', are important as elements in the thinking not only of the schizophrenic but also of the schizoid patient. These processes do not only apply to bad aspects of the object or of the self: from fear of destruction, the good parts of the object or the ego are also split off and projected in the same manner into objects which are expected to look after them while they contain them, preserving and protecting them.

In the course of psychotherapy the schizoid, having projected his good parts into the therapist in order to preserve them, as if depositing them in a bank, becomes frantic if he cannot find his therapist, which would mean also the loss of elements of the self and of his objects. Moreover, since the reparative activity of the schizoid is based on concrete reparation, as if he were rebuilding a house with its bricks, the loss of the 'bricks' contained in the therapist makes reconstruction impossible. This, in my opinion, is one of the fundamental reasons for the schizoid's refusal to form an ordinary transference relationship with the therapist. Unless one can interpret this mistrust, which is fundamentally justified and which the therapist needs to understand, it is extremely difficult ever to obtain the confidence of the schizoid patient. Concurrently with these internal splits, the therapist too is split into good and bad objects, and the transference relationship changes constantly and remains unstable and fragmented for a long time, changing not only from day to day, but from minute to minute during the session.

Thus, a young schizophrenic whom I treated in hospital perceived me either as an object whom she could not do without – from whom she could not separate, and to whom she wanted perpetually to adhere – or, within an instant, as an object which she attacked so vigorously that I had to defend myself from her by force. One day she illustrated the change from a neurotic transference to a psychotic transference in a remarkable way: she spoke to me about her life at home in a reasonable manner and in contact with reality, and then, all of a sudden, with astonishing rapidity, she went to the door and with piercing eyes and voice trembling with emotion she said, 'Get down here in front of me. Obey. You know how for years you have mistreated my mother and me, the cruelties and torture that you have done, when you came to my room at three o'clock in the morning.'

External reality had disappeared and only psychic reality remained. The image of the father and of me had become one. I had become her father with his partly real characteristics and those partly attributed to him by the patient by that same process of projective identification. At the end of five minutes, which seemed as long as five centuries, when I wondered what was going to happen, she became calm and resumed a more or less normal conversation. But she remained mistrustful, close to the door, as if she might await the return of the 'feared ones' which she called 'they', and which would come to take her away to a hellish fate. She could not be friends with me because 'they' became angry and punished her. It was best to be on good terms with 'they'. She asked if she could kill me to convince 'they' that she did not love me. On the other hand, the idea of losing me was intolerable: after she let down the tyres of my car so that I would be killed in an accident, she hid herself to watch me, and ran after me to warn me that if I went in the car I was in great danger, without telling me why.

The fear of separation from the object and the desire to penetrate into it and fuse with it into a primal unity can be so intense that it surpasses human understanding. Thus, a paranoid and persecuted patient complained ceaselessly with years of virulent reproaches full of rage and despair because I did not love her, after having seduced her by my interpretations and having led her to believe that she was loved. She found proof of my wish to torture her in the fact that I did not let her penetrate into me physically and fuse with me. On this subject she lost all contact with reality and insisted that such a fusion was possible. One proof of my refusal, which made the analysis almost impossible, consisted in reproaching me as often as she could that I was not in agreement with what she was saying. This produced two people, not one person, and I became a monster which, at least at that moment, she hated.

It is clear from what I have just said that the question of his or her identity is a major problem for the schizoid. The enormous difficulty of acquiring a stable ego is the result of faulty introjective identification, made very difficult by persecutory feelings and a fear of the object created by the projection of destructive, envious, and insatiable impulses, which can become incredibly violent. They are neither heterosexual nor homosexual, not even bisexual. This arises from the fact that their identifications depend both on an internal object which is not assimilated, and on a containing external object in which they live; hence this identity depends on the state of the object and varies with it, its identity and its actions. They have an external shell or carapace, but no vertebral column. They live as parasites in the shell which they seem to have borrowed or stolen, and this creates a feeling of insecurity.

Thus, an extremely schizoid young man, who during his treatment went through a breakdown diagnosed by all the psychiatrists except me as totally schizophrenic, would dress himself at night in clothes typical of a London businessman. He would enter his parents' bedroom at three o'clock in the morning, wake them and say to his father, 'Am I now the person you wanted me to be?' Previously he had dressed himself in his mother's clothes for a number of years. Under the pressure of the psychotherapeutic group where he received treatment, which attempted to confront him with his lack of initiative and his failure to leave home and go to work, he decided to become a man.

One day, some workmen happened to be working on road-works in front of his house; he urinated into a bottle, which he put at the front door as a gesture of contempt. He looked at himself in a mirror, brushed his hair in the style of Wellington, and in a military manner marched around the courtyard. He then took some of his neighbour's washing, which was drying on the hedge between their houses, and threw it into her garden. He invited the workers to tell him who gave them permission to be there, and then returned to his house. Since it was the first of May, a special day for workers, he sang a patriotic anti-Communist song. Then he convinced himself that he was in danger because the workers were Communists and would attack him. Moreover, the BBC would begin to talk about him, and the Irish rebels would come to get him. He had become important, but persecuted, and his homosexual passivity and his feminine identification entered into the conflict as a passive defence. Finally, to separate himself, to undo the identification with his parents, he became irritable, oppositional and aggressive. They could no longer look after him, and he was admitted to the hospital as an in-patient.

During individual sessions with me he sat on the floor to look up at me from a lower position as a sign of respect, like a baby. Then he said that if he lay down, or sat down, he would, like a baby, fail to orientate himself in relation to the things around him. Later, he became preoccupied with multiple aspects of his personality: he no longer knew which parts of his parents he was made of, and each piece had a nationality: his father English, his mother German/Polish, now living in England. Each 'piece' had a special and separate characteristic. His father is a professor, but in addition was a military man through family tradition, but at the same time a pacifist; he is upper- and lower-class, conservative and socialist, and so on. He began to believe that his mother was Jewish. He gave a nationality to a large variety of 'pieces' including one 'piece' of him that was Prussian, and very rigid, one 'piece' that was English, and one 'piece' Polish. Then he wanted to become a Jew, and soon after he changed his mind. First he admired them, then he criticized them. Finally, he explained to me why he wanted to become Jewish: it was because the Jews were fragmented, dispersed, persecuted and dispossessed, living in a Tower of Babel of languages and of different nationalities, and yet found their unity and their identity by the fact that they were Jewish, a fact that could transcend and unite all these fragments into an integrated whole.

What a marvellous unconscious description of the integrative functions of the object! He had to have this schizoid regression, this dissociation of parts which had been assembled in a faulty way in order to separate out the elements and to reconstruct the edifice. This example illustrates clearly the problem which integration of the ego poses for the schizophrenic or schizoid person.

SCHIZOPHRENIC BREAKDOWN

I have had the occasion to treat a young schizophrenic who had an attitude resembling catatonia, and very interesting rituals in which a gesture of her limbs or face was always annulled by an opposing gesture controlling and undoing the preceding one. I eventually understood that these gestures were either sexual or aggressive and needed to be controlled. After the death of her father she adopted typically catatonic postures and said she could not move because she would come into collision with her father, who was enclosed inside her.

Later, with other patients, I came to understand that the opposite of immobility could be seen in paroxysmal movements such as those of an epileptic fit, which by contrast results in the projection of internal contents outside, where they can be attacked and destroyed. Then I came to understand the extreme mental rigidity of the schizoid who has to control all his objects, both internal and external. The anxiety of his sexual persecutory and destructive impulses is so great that no autonomy can be allowed to his objects. The fear of fragmentation is catastrophic. Thus, a schizoid man could alter nothing of his life or his attitudes, and said he could never live anywhere else than at his home because if he moved he would have to take with him his room with all his furniture and things as they were, without changing anything.

TRANSFORMATION, REPRESENTATION AND SYMBOLIZATION

The second fact to consider with the schizoid is the mental apparatus necessary for the transformation of sensory or sensori-motor experience into representations, into images, into symbols and signs, and into memories – such transformations being essential both for the maintenance of ordinary human relationships, and for the construction of a normal mental apparatus for thinking.

We have seen that the elements of thought in the schizoid have a concrete character which Freud himself described as one of the essential qualities of the system Unconscious, namely, the representation of things instead of the representation of words. This defect in the function of transformation seems to be a basic defect in the schizoid. But at the same time we know that the schizoid is in many cases capable of great intelligence – even though he treats people as things, thus removing the affectivity which for him is dangerous and persecuting. The coexistence of a schizoid type of personal relationship and of a highly developed intelligence can only be explained by a split in the ego which results in a partial ego, which is intellectual and highly developed such as Piaget or Hartmann would describe, and another part of the ego in which the development has been arrested at the schizoid stage, and where the depressive position has not been worked through.

During psychotherapy with the schizoid, progress in treatment depends on the possibility of undoing this schizoid structure and of allowing normal symbolization of bizarre objects and of sensory experiences to occur; that is to say, to make other modes of communication possible. It is sometimes possible to achieve this without a catastrophic reaction – without the coherent parts of the ego disintegrating. In other cases this is impossible and the patient needs to go through a frankly schizophrenic episode. For some this is a good thing because it is the only way of returning to the point of bifurcation between normal and abnormal development where the growth of a paralysed affectivity, previously enslaved and rigidly controlled, may be resumed. If this happens I believe no one can predict whether the patient will become a chronic schizophrenic or will progress towards new horizons.

The same situation applies to the schizophrenic in a clinically obvious schizophrenic state: does he have the potential to resume his development or not? This chiefly depends on the capacity of his mental apparatus for symbolic transformation and on the stage he has reached in relation to the depressive position. Indeed, there is a group of patients for whom the schizoid state is a regression and constitutes a defence against the suffering and pain of the depressive state; these patients have a better outlook than those who are true schizophrenics, those who have never reached the depressive state. A schizoaffective state, whereby the patient oscillates between a state of schizophrenia and depression, is also well known, and these cases again have a more favourable outcome with psychotherapy. We also know of cases which without treatment change from schizophrenia to depression or vice versa in the course of time.

Among those who have studied the function of transformation and representation in the mental apparatus, the work of Bion (1965) stands out as especially significant. I would like to give an example of defective transformation. Bion says, 'In psychoanalytic theories statements by patients or by analysts are representations of an emotional experience. If we can understand the process of representation this will help us to understand the representation and that which is represented.'

A patient told me the following dream:

> I am dining with friends and get up from the table. I am thirsty and I start to drink. I realize that the bottle in my mouth has a neck shaped like a feeding bottle; there is no teat, but I think I can feel the flange which normally holds the teat in place. While I think of this I begin to see the bottle more clearly. I hold it in front of my face and see that it has the shape of a feeding bottle. In the bottle I see water. The level of the water falls and bubbles of air mount through the liquid, and because of this I am aware that some of the water has become part of me; but I cannot feel this thing that becomes part of me. I am anxious because I can neither understand nor feel the water passing from a state separate from me to become an intimate part of me. While I am thinking thus, the bottle becomes bigger. I see at that moment that on the inside of the bottle facing me, words are engraved on the surface in raised letters which give instructions on how to wean an infant.

In this dream the subject failed to transform the experience of the movement of water from the exterior to the interior of his body into a good experience in the form of a representation and a memory. He did not participate in the experience; he did not understand what happened; he tells us that he lacks the experience of the change. This can only be the experience in the mouth where the presence of water produces a sensation, a sensation which is needed to make the work of transformation possible. One part of the experience is lacking; it is as if he had been fed through a tube. But he tells us what was lacking – it was the teat and it was the experience of weaning, and of suckling from a mother. He took the bottle himself and gave himself a drink. The teat no doubt represents a maternal breast and a mother whose presence and whose bodily contact is absolutely necessary for the awareness and recording of the experience. It seems that in the absence of the good object, part of the work of assimilation did not take place.

REPARATION

In addition to structural mechanisms of the schizoid phase and its mechanisms of defence I would like to consider a fundamental aspect of schizoid mentality. This is the law of the talion and the absence of the capacity for reparation which governs the whole behaviour of the schizoid. By the law of the talion I mean: an eye for an eye and a tooth for a tooth; let the punishment fit the crime; if I have stolen, my hand will be cut off, if I have transgressed I will be punished, you have stolen and I will cut off your hands. It is this law of vengeance which is responsible through its incredible power in the schizoid not only for the stunted mental structure, but also for its lack of humanity. There is no forgiveness, no compassion, no reparation. There is only the terrible vengeance and anger of Jehovah as preached by the prophets of the Old Testament.

Reparation in the schizoid state also obeys the law of the inverse talion. Like everything I have already described, it has to be concrete. I call this *repair* to distinguish it from reparation; we could also perhaps call it reconstruction, which has some things in common with the restitution with which Freud was concerned. Reparation, on the other hand, is a notion unknown to Freud and plays a fundamental role in the work of Melanie Klein. Even Freud's ideas on restitution remained sketchy and far from complete, as were his ideas on splitting and denial. Almost all analysts have rejected the fundamentally new theme which appears in his work after 1920 in which the life instinct as a constructive force was contrasted with the death instinct as an instinct of disintegration. People have quarrelled about words and have forgotten that analysis is rooted in observation. The study of the schizoid personality structure has led us back to the observations of a master on splitting, projection and denial, which Freud's ultraconservative disciples had well buried. In reconstruction or repair, infantile omnipotence is retained and an attempt is made to reconstruct the damaged one. Reparation, by contrast, is not and cannot be an omnipotent act.

THE MANIC DEFENCE

We will now consider the role of the manic state. On the one hand its role is a defence against the anxiety of disintegration and of schizoid persecution, and on the other hand a defence against the pain of the depressive state. One can observe this from the point of view of psychiatry in the clinical syndrome of hypomania, but also as a potential psychodynamic state during psychotherapy. We must not forget that the manic state can represent an exaggeration of a normal phase of maturation and of reparation. I believe that in all depressive states the object with which the subject has a relationship is, contains, or symbolically represents the maternal breast, which as a partial object represents the mother who is destroyed, emptied, or poisoned, and thus is in a depressed state. The subject feels this is his fault, becomes identified with this depressed object, and consequently depressed himself.

In manic states or in the manic defence we are no longer concerned with the maternal breast but with the penis. The object of the manic state is the penis which is needed by the subject for the task of reparation: through it he can regain the destroyed object either as a direct substitute by identification or by recreating the contents of the mother, for example, by making her pregnant by filling her empty breasts and so on. The more the maternal object is destroyed by the subject's attacks, the more must the penis become omnipotent, and the subject by identification becomes omnipotent also. In this manner the destroyed state of the object is denied. There is no reparation proper, and after the manic phase the subject returns to his depression or his schizoaffective state at the level of maturation which he had previously reached.

A very schizoid patient dreamed that on his nose he was balancing a long pole which reached right to the sky with a baby balanced on the end. As he awakened he said to himself, 'This fucking penis is good for nothing, it's so big that it's useless.' On the couch, the patient (of whom I have already spoken) had identified his whole body with a phallus, and felt himself to enlarge physically and be invaded by delusions of grandeur. In the manic state we have a pseudo-penis which repairs nothing; it serves to deny the reality of destroyed objects, and presents itself as the universal substitute, which leads to the formation of a false self. Meanwhile, the aggressive impulses continue to destroy the object.

Manic reactions can actually represent a pathological deviation of a normal phase of development. I believe that when the separated fragments of the ego reunite, whether in a mosaic or in a fusion, it is done with the help of the phantasied action of the phallus. This is achieved on the one hand by an identification with the penis, adopting its characteristics and functions; and, on the other hand, because, although a partial object, it usually functions, as we have explained, as a representation of the whole object – the father – and enters into the relationship with the maternal breast, the partial object representing the mother. We have here the prototypes of the sexual identity of the two sexes and the prototype of the relationship between them. The role of the penis as a creator integrating and repairing through reproduction becomes clear in this model.

However, in the manic state there is a partial identification with the immeasurably grandiose aspect of the erect penis. The manifestations of this aspect are omnipotent, contemptuous, and persecutory as well. It is always present in a latent form in the schizoid, and, when seen clinically as delusions of grandeur in paranoid states or as a feature of the depression of the manic-depressive, illustrates the role of the phallus in the grandiosity seen in these conditions.

The patient referred to earlier, who felt himself to vary in size both physically and mentally, explained that he felt he had a permanent personality for the first time when he experienced the presence inside him of a hard column extending from his anus to his mouth, which could resist all attacks. Later, in his grandiose state, he identified with Jesus Christ, grew a beard and became a carpenter, designed religious motifs and wanted to preach in church.

THE DEPRESSIVE POSITION

It will not be possible to go into the mechanism by which a depressive state develops, even though this forms an essential phase in treatment. This is work about which much has been written, and I want to concentrate on schizoid states. Suffice that we remember that in this process destructive impulses lose their intensity and loving impulses play a fundamental role. The good and the bad parts of the ego and also of the object unite gradually into a whole, and the law of the talion loses its virulence. Primitive compassion begins to take over from the total egocentricity characteristic of the beginnings of life. The object achieves a life of its own, and the subject becomes an object related to like any other object.

FROM SCHIZOID STATES TO SCHIZOPHRENIA

These phases of development belong to the preverbal period. Instead of the basic development, we have here to understand a triphasic evolution: first an archaic preverbal phase and an archaic verbal phase where the distinction can be thought of as an example of ontogeny repeating phylogeny; then, after the age of six, seven, eight, a phase in which external reality dominates. I take the view that non-verbal schemata give a structure to verbal thought, which in turn influences the pre-existing non-verbal schemata. This reciprocal relationship sheds light on the disorders of verbal thought which are seen when a schizoid individual becomes schizophrenic. The task of defining what happens when this change from a schizoid to a schizophrenic state occurs is not easy; the more I understand the language and structure of the schizoid the more I find the distinction difficult.

From the point of view of classical psychiatry it is quite simple: are there delusions or hallucinations? If there are, it is schizophrenia, if not, it is not. But when one works not only longitudinally but simultaneously in depth as the psychoanalyst does, the situation is quite different. We can see this if we compare material from schizoid patients with the delusional ideas of some-one floridly schizophrenic.

Let us take an extreme case, a patient who had four schizophrenic breakdowns, each presenting a different clinical picture. In his hebephrenic-catatonic state, which began with an intense interest in the universe and the stars, he felt himself to be communicating with an extraterrestrial universe. As proof he took out of his briefcase some little oval- and circular-shaped pieces of ivory-coloured paper, and assured me that their extraterrestrial origin was obvious. Much later he admitted that although at first he had firmly believed this, he later came to realize that he himself had simply collected these pieces of paper from somewhere.

We see here the interplay of a number of schizoid mechanisms. First of all, the wish to be omnipotent, to participate in the universe, which he held very strongly. To achieve this wish without becoming mad he had to avoid destroying external reality and instead tried to transform it. With the external physical proof he could thus reinforce the internal psychic reality of his wish. For this he had transformed the pieces of paper through the phantasy of projective identification and obtained in this way a formal proof of his experience. He had thus decided not to abandon external reality completely, but grossly to transform it by a process of splitting, by omnipotent wishing, and by projective creation.

Some schizoid patients are past masters in the art of choosing objects which are precisely appropriate for their projections; that is, which have characteristics so similar to their projections that it becomes very difficult to make a distinction between the object and the projected phantasy.

It seems to me, then, that the schizophrenic goes further and does not concern himself with the existence of external reality, but declares and delusionally believes whatever he wishes, having made a regression to a very primitive, infantile stage where the distinction between psychic reality and external reality is almost non-existent and hardly concerns him. There is only one reality – the reality of the internal phantasy world. In the schizoid world we find various gradations of abnormality in the type of morbid processes I have just described.

THE SPACE–TIME CONTINUUM AND DISPLACEMENT IN THE BORDERLINE

An attempt will be made now to examine the clinical observations previously described, in terms of the organization of space and time as in any other branch of knowledge. Piagetian observations, ideas and constructs have been extensively used both explicitly and implicitly but by no means exclusively. The main source for this work is clinical observation during treatment and psychoanalytical psychotherapy supervisions, and interpretations of data. I have made use of Piaget only for the reason that psychoanalysis has never studied the structure of external reality – of space, displacement and time – as have he and his pupils.

During the treatment of patients, especially of claustrophobic and agoraphobic patients, it appeared more and more evident to me that a fundamental organization of objects in space (including the patient himself) was underlying the mode of behaviour observed. All sorts of physical and mental situations which claustrophobic and agoraphobic patients experience are very likely to refer to a primary situation which all the other secondary situations are substitutes for and symbolic of.

Claustrophobic persons are afraid to be in an enclosed situation: they develop extreme anxiety or panic and want to get out. The 'situation' may be a room, a traffic-jam, a marriage. When they are not contained, they become agoraphobic and develop anxiety or panic. Thus they may be housebound, or may only travel so far alone from the place of safety and no further, or have to be accompanied. The manifestations of those conditions are well known. However, it was when I made the observation that this condition is really a basic one in schizoid states and schizophrenia that I realized it had a very important meaning. By a basic condition I mean that whenever schizoid and schizophrenic patients are seen in the context of dynamic treatment they reveal claustro-agoraphobic basic fears not in the least evident when their behaviour is assessed from a purely phenomenological psychiatric approach. The mental and emotional disturbances of the schizoid state are disturbances in the early, primitive and basic organization of the human being, ontogenetically speaking. It is the importance that Piaget gives to the early structuralization of space that led me to attempt the explanation of the way of life of the schizoid in terms of the early organization of space, movement and time.

SPATIAL DEVELOPMENT OF THE INFANT AND HIS WORLD

The foetus is at first contained within the uterus, which is itself contained inside the mother. It is relatively deprived of freedom of movement and displacement, although a certain degree of movement is possible. It moves with the mother in the mother's external space. After birth, one could say that the mother through her care, feeding, warmth and support recreates partially this uterine state for the baby. Although restricted still, the baby's personal space allows him more freedom than in the womb. It could be called the marsupial space. The baby now moves in the mother's space, but only in that portion of her space which is the baby's personal space. As he or she grows up, the personal space increases until it has coincided with the maternal space. If the mother is normal, for instance, not claustro-agoraphobic, that space will coincide with general space, where the subject will be an object among objects. Simultaneously with this process a space internal to the subject is formed where psychic internal objects live in intrapsychic relationships. They are experienced very concretely at first, for example, as sensations, or elaborated later as representations of a very complex nature.

It would seem that everybody has an external personal space of some kind which persists, somewhat like the notion of territory in ethology, and in which our object relations are somewhat different from those in the universal space. However, as Piaget has pointed out and described so clearly, space is not a Newtonian absolute space, neither is time absolute time; they are both constructs. The infant and the child have to construct their objects and their space, space being the relative positioning of objects as in the Einsteinian model.

The idea, then, would be to look at some aspects and stages of those early constructions and how they appear either unevolved or distorted as structures underlying the schizoid mode of being. The pure Piagetian approach is unsatisfactory, for although emotions, affects, and drives are accepted as intrinsic parts of the cognitive structures, they are not referred to as such. I will therefore present my own psychoanalytical and Piagetian-inspired elaborations.

Objects that are familiarly looked upon and treated as individual wholes by adults are certainly not experienced as such for the infant. The child has to 'construct' them, linking parts by action schemas as described by Piaget, that is, by interiorized actions of the subject on the object. Piaget says the child co-ordinates

> . . . the actions among themselves in the form of practical schemas, a sort of sensori-motor preconcept, characterized by the possibility of repeating the same action in the presence of the same objects or generalizing it in the presence of analogous others. (Battro, 1973)

For Piaget more complex schemas are not just the association or synthesis of previously isolated elements. Thus, he writes of the sensori-motor scheme that

> . . . it is a definite and closed system of movements and perceptions. The schema presents, in effect, the double characteristics of being structures (thus structuring itself the field of perception or of understanding) and of constituting itself beforehand as totality without resulting from an association or from a synthesis between the previously isolated elements. (Battro, 1973)

For Piaget the 'sensori-motor schemas are not simply what we sometimes call patterns, that is to say, they have further power to generalize and further power to assimilate' (Battro, 1973).

As to schemas relative to persons, Piaget says that 'they are cognitive and affective simultaneously. The affective element is perhaps more important in the domain of persons and the cognitive element in the domain of things, but it is only a question of degree.' Thus, he says that an 'affective schema' means simply the affective aspect of schemas which are otherwise also intellectual.

For Piaget, action is at the very beginning the source of all manifestations of life. It precedes thought, it controls perception and sensation. It is by a process of combinations of actions of the subject on his object, followed by the internalization of these action schemas, that the precursors of thought are generated. Thus the infant puts his or her thumb in the mouth, then extends this action to other objects, then elaborates the action by using a rod or some such object to extend the reach of his or her arm to get to objects that will be taken to the mouth or elsewhere.

I do not know if a study has been made of such a way of thinking in Freud's writings apart from the structural theory itself. But it is interesting to note that in the Rat Man, for instance, Freud makes constant references to psychical structures. In fact, Part IIa is entitled 'Some General Characteristics of Obsessional Structures' (Freud, 1909). He says that 'obsessional structures can correspond to every sort of psychical act', and:

> In this disorder (obsessional neurosis) repression is affected not by means of amnesia but by a severance of causal connections brought about by a withdrawal of affect. These repressed connections appear to persist in some kind of shadow form (which I have elsewhere compared to an endopsychic perception) and they are thus transferred, by a process of projection, into the external world, where they bear witness to what has been effaced from consciousness. (p. 221)

This is as good a definition of mental structure as any structuralist could wish.

For the object-relations psychoanalyst, therefore, there exists in the behaviour of adults primitive object relationships or schemas, normal or pathological, which govern aspects of behaviour. Some of these primitive internalized object relations may have remained unintegrated and function autonomously. Part-object psychology, or the psychology of part-object, part-subject, part-states, relates to the study of the aspect of the genetic development of object relationships.

Starting with the need of the infant expressed as desire for gratification, there is little doubt that the infant wishes to make part of his endogenous space, that is, the precursor of the self, the gratifying objects he needs for survival and growth. His early discovery of the appearance and disappearance of the object in his space (early ego or self) will prompt him to desire the good objects as part of himself or of his good space in the only way he is capable – the concrete. The frustration of not being able always to keep the object in his spaces (that is, internal space and personal space) will increase the desire for the object to be his possession. The growth of this desire and the need for securing such objects, if it reaches great intensity, will become greed. The frustration, anger and anxiety resulting from the non-possession of the desired gratifying objects will lead to the desire to deprive it of the other space containing the desired objects, for the other space containing the objects is now in a state of no-pain or pleasure, a state previously experienced by the infant. The wish is not only to possess the object, but to deprive the other space as he is himself deprived. This is envy.

Further, the infant left in his self-space while waiting for the gratifying object will have to substitute objects of his own self-space, for example, parts of his own body or toys. Thus in the place of the breast-mother he will have thumb, excrements or genitals as part of his space. They may prove helpful in waiting for the appearance of the external breast-mother, and thus temporarily relieve anxiety or frustration following non-gratification. Non-gratification may lead to punishing the non-self space by putting frustrating objects, say faeces, into it, thus substituting them for the good breast or transforming it into a bad object. However, those parts of the self-space put into the non-self-space are still considered to be somehow part of the self-space, and a particular kind of bond is formed between self-space and non-self-space by displacement in or out of them – that is, by introjection and projection. This bond gives to early object relationships a quality of possessiveness and identification between objects which are at the roots of introjective and projective identification processes.

This process is by no means abnormal when it is concerned with displacement of objects for need gratification and communication purposes. Its persistence and distortions are, however, responsible for a large number of typical features of the schizoid way of experiencing. It creates the feeling of living in the object because part of oneself is in the object; it creates the need for never leaving the object out of control; it creates a sense of impending doom through the possible loss of part of the self if the object is lost. And it results in persecutory feelings if the projected or displaced part of the self is believed to have envious, greedy, and destructive impulses, and accounts for innumerable other schizoid manifestations.

We shall now proceed with the systematic examination of schizoid manifestations in terms of our space–time model, and illustrate this with examples. First of all, I will try to show how one must extend the claustro-agoraphobic syndrome from a specific syndrome to a basic universal organ-ization of the personality. A claustrophobic woman is seen for assessment for psychotherapy. She says she is afraid that something terrible will happen to her if she goes out. She insists she does not know what it is. I point out that there are only two possibilities, either it is something she will do to others, or something others will do to her. She says after a lot of hesitation, 'I'm afraid I'll do something mad.' After more hesitation, she says, 'I'll shout and people will think I'm mad.' I say, 'Shouting is something coming out of you. What else could come out of you?' She becomes extremely tense and nervous, and after a while asks to be allowed to leave. I say that, of course, she can leave if she so desires, but if she can have the courage to say what thought is making her so uncomfortable that she wants to leave, it might save her months of treatment and misery. She plucks up the courage and says, 'Urine and faeces.' I will leave out the rest of the interview. This is a routine happening in various forms.

What years of study of my own patients and patients treated by others has revealed I will put in schematic form. It will be noticed that the patient wanted to remove herself from the space where she was in contact with what she felt as a threatening object. She wanted to leave the room. However, we also know that phobics avoid certain situations, for instance, eating in public; they will not go to a restaurant, or to the cinema, or to shops. They restrict their outside space until they are housebound. It is important to understand what the ultimate space into which they retire corresponds to in the unconscious.

The outside world or outside space is in such an instance transformed by projective identification into the body or internal space of the subject him or herself, identified with the internal space of the mother. Thus entering and coming out of a room is coming out of that which the room stands for – ultimately – the mother's body. A primitive imprinted state of birth experiences persists in the hierarchies of transformation and representation of that early experience. What is fixed in the mind is not necessarily the original experience of birth, but one or another experience of a primitive similar state belonging to the hierarchy of space constructions, such as the marsupial space described previously. When something comes out of the body such as a shout, urine, faeces, semen, saliva, or vomit, it fires the system coming-out-of and produces the attached affect. The mechanism involved is the identification by projective identification of the subject with the contents of his own body, and of his body identified with that of the mother; he thus experiences himself coming out of mother.

As I have said, the primitive emotional experience, the affect, has been dominant in the structurization of the self- and the non-self-spaces. Displacement, then, of any kind of objects, including the subject himself from self-space to non-self-space or vice versa is experienced in a primitive manner. Space in certain circumstances is experienced as it was once experienced in a part of the personality, split off from the rest, and this way of experiencing space persists. The panic associated with that state and the bodily anguish and sensations are but the persistence of the experience when the ego was mostly body ego. The coming into activity of that split-off archaic part of the adult self takes over and paralyses the more adult ego. Thus adult methods of coping with danger are no longer available.

I realized the fundamental structure underlying all this when I came across the same experiences as a basic state with schizophrenics, for example: their difficulty lying on the couch from fear of merging and disappearing into it, and, out of the blue, expressing the same fear about mother; or their difficulty staying in the room with me unless they could be near the door or the window, even with bars; or the person who has to be by the door of a plane at 10,000 feet in the air to avoid panic. As I have said, it is not only the mother but the early spatial structures constructed to replace the mother's internal space that are suffused with primitive emotional experiences.

As those spaces are structured by objects and their displacement, the objects in these spaces are gratifying or non-gratifying, persecuting or protecting, good or bad. Here are two dreams from two very schizoid patients. One dreamt that he was quite happy inside mother. He then felt he wanted to find out about outside, so he got out and started enjoying himself sexually and also doing aggressive things. He then became anxious as he felt some people might be angry with him, and that he was outside in the open and unprotected. So he got back inside mother. Unfortunately, he realized that it was not much safer because he could do things to his mother from inside that would put him in danger just the same.

Another schizoid young man dreamt that he was living in a sort of tunnel-like building and he was moving about in the tunnel in a sort of trolley. At intervals there were openings from which he could see the outside world. Sometimes the trolley would stop and he would get out to mix in with this outside world, especially for sexual purposes. Then he would get back and resume the inside life. However, one day he was seized with panic at the thought that the tunnel might close and he would be enclosed forever, and he desperately wanted to get out. There is nowhere for the claustro-agora-phobic.

An example of coming out of a containing space and something coming out of the body and their linking together by a common experience is given by the following patient, who was the most severe claustro-agoraphobic I have come across. He dreamt that he had passed a stool several hundred feet long which was still attached to his anus, unseparated from him. We proceeded with the session, and when the end of the session approached he sat on the couch in a state of extreme terror saying, 'Help me, help me. If I come out of the room, outside I will only be a mass of liquefied shit.'

Here we can see that coming out of the room was associated with faeces coming out of him, and the identification with the faeces was complete as he felt he would be nothing other than the faeces. Further, he could not in the dream let the faeces be separate from him. As he was himself identified with the faeces so he was afraid to be in open space, unprotected after he left me. This patient could only go to the lavatory to defecate if somebody knew he was in the toilet. He thus also demonstrates the fear of fragmentation if a part of him separates from the rest, and a fear of dissolution of self by identification with another object, such as the faeces.

It is obvious that problems of identity – for example, being small or adult, being male or female, and so on – are understandable on the above basis of transient identification with objects. Demandingness, controlling impulses, possessiveness are all clearly connected with the fact that the parts of the self-space put into the non-self-space and vice versa cannot be allowed separateness, and dictate such behaviour to prevent catastrophic loss of parts of the self. To prevent loss of self, objects must be kept at a distance and vice versa. Thus a young schizoid man in an attempt to solve this problem would remain in his room and communicate with others by watching children play from his window and communicating with others at a distance by telephone. A woman attempted to live in my personal space by constantly walking near my residence or using the telephone to penetrate into my flat. When there was nobody there she would let the telephone ring and fall asleep, being in my personal space. So the schizoid person, to prevent pain, anxiety or depression, splits parts of him or herself, projects them and denies their existence. Immediately he or she experiences the opposite feelings: fear of loss, of fragmentation, and attempts to remake contact, and the vicious circle goes on.

Internal and personal spaces are not the same. Personal-space objects are transitional between universal space and internal space. There is a story about Voltaire that describes how he built himself a tomb half in the church and half outside to confound those who argued about whether or not he was an atheist. The relative positioning of objects in space is astonishing at times. We know of the preoccupation of obsessionals not to let objects touch each other, and the need for symmetry. But sometimes positioning is even more explicit. A very schizoid girl wondered if when objects were on top of each other, for example, a bird flying over her head, it meant sexual intercourse. After the death of her father she could not move because any movement would either hurt her father inside her or would have a sexual connotation. The relative positioning of objects was extremely meaningful to her. She would put her right foot on top of the left and do a short, quick tapping movement. This was sexual, and was undone by putting the right foot from forwards to backwards, and instead of tapping she then did a larger and wider movement in the opposite direction.

I will now consider how immature 'concepts' of time are involved in a similar way of being. A little autistic boy who wanted his sessions at the same time every day, which I could not do, would take my watch and set it at the time he wanted. The time was the time indicated by the watch face, watches being very special spatial devices. We had to play a game of going from London to Brighton, and returning by train. We had to go from station to station and then return through each station in reverse order. Any fault on my part and everything had to be started all over again. He had seriated space as Piaget has demonstrated but could not decentre from it. He could pass from A to B to C to D, and so on, but not from D to A to return to A. He had to move from each position to the next like Achilles and the tortoise, or like Zeno's arrow. These examples lead us to examine more closely the elements of displacement and movement, and of time.

Piaget describes a simple experiment carried out with children of various ages. There are two tunnels, one visibly longer than the other. Two dolls, each on a separate track and moving at a fixed speed, are made to enter their respective tunnels at exactly the same time, and to emerge at the distal end also at exactly the same time. Children of a certain age repeatedly say the two dolls moved at the same speed, although they agree that one tunnel is longer. The tunnels are removed and the experiment repeated. This time, the same children will say that the doll overtaking the other one goes faster. However, if the tunnels are put back again, they say that the dolls were going at the same speed. They are clearly basing their judgement on the relative positioning of the dolls, irrespective of length and time. In that way, and by combining a large number of delightfully simple experiments, it is possible to reconstruct the stages through which the growing child passes as he constructs his adult ideas of space, speed, and time. At least these notions are involved in the notion of time: seriation or the ordering of events in time, for example, B comes after A, C after B, and so on; then class inclusion, for example, if B comes after A and C after B, then A–C is greater than A–B, or a whole class is greater than the subclass; finally, there is the measurement of time.

Similarly, the notion of causality is developed in stages and depends on the emergence of other notions such as those of the permanent object, of space and of time, leading to an objective view of causality instead of a magico-phenomenal one.

A woman, a very intelligent woman patient at that, said to me very seriously that she knows she will be married to me and live with me in my country of origin; that she will be married and live with her husband in England; and it will be the same with many other men – all simultaneously, without seeing any contradiction. In fact, she was angry at my suggesting there could be some difficulty in realizing this project.

'Time past is time future which is time present', says T. S. Eliot. But this is obviously time inconsistent. Time as a seriation process makes it impossible to go back in time. To be in the same place years later is not the same as previously. But displacement and movement to the schizoid can be disastrous, as it may tear part of him away and leave him fragmented or empty or lost, and it can do the same to his objects. Therefore, movements may be very slow or immobility may set in, as in the case of the girl with her father in her internal space. Movement brings about separation and loss, and if it comes fast, catastrophe. Rigidity, fixity, frigidity, impotence – are all defences against that possibility.

A very severely ill woman one day revealed to her therapist that she could not leave the hospital immediately after her session, which would be incompatible with her not collapsing. To take the bus and disappear quickly was dreadful. She wandered on the hospital ground first, and then very slowly moved away, very gradually. The speed at which she moved from one place to another mattered very much. In depression, movements of the body and limbs become slower and slower until a state of depressive stupor is reached; ultimate non-movement is found in suicide. In mania the contrary takes place: the speed of every movement including speed is increased and the patient cannot keep in one place. The sense of the passage of time is greatly altered in both states.

Piaget says:

> Psychological time is the connection between work accomplished and activity (force and rapidity of action) or time is plastic; it expands according to the deceleration or contracts according to the acceleration of action . . . or time is conferred at its point of departure with the impression of psychological duration inherent in the attitudes of expectations, effort, and of satisfaction in brief in the activity of the subject. (Battro, 1973)

The schizoid patient, paralysed in his activities, empty of actions with objects, can only experience duration in relationships in a completely abnormal way.

It is necessary at this point to return to the relationship between localization of object and the most important notion of permanence of subject. Piaget describes frequently a little experiment showing how in the first half-year of mental life an infant who is about to grasp an object will stop his hands if the object is covered with a handkerchief. At a later stage the baby will try to lift the handkerchief to look for the object at the place A where it has just been covered. But, Piaget observes, if the object placed at A is displaced to B in front of the child watching the displacement, he will often look for the object at A, where he had been successful in finding it on previous occasions. It is only towards the end of the first year that the infant looks unhesitatingly for the object at the place to which it has been displaced; before this he ignores series of displacements, but is fixated on his own action on the object. Thus object permanence, says Piaget, is closely linked with its localization in space.

It is absolutely vital here to differentiate between the concept of object in Piaget and the libidinal object of psychoanalysis. Piaget describes an object as a permanent object at the end of the sensori-motor stage, at about eighteen months. Where the subject himself is an object among others, this concept applies to all objects and in no way considers the question of libidinal investment which renders an object meaningful and unique to the infant. The libidinal object is meaningful long before the completion of the sensori-motor object. Of vital interest for understanding distortions of self and object of the schizoid person are the stages of object formation described by Piaget, especially because of the specific use of objects of the physical world for identification purposes in schizoid mechanisms of defence.

Since the individual has also to construct his own body image as that of other bodies in space, and gradually to reach a sense of permanence of his identity, similar considerations apply here. As Marcel Proust has Swann say, if one wakes up in the night in the dark, not knowing the time or where one is, then one does not know who one is. It is extremely interesting that Piaget has demonstrated by lovely, simple little experiments that the concept of identity of matter takes place in definite stages, and that the concept of identity occurs, for instance, before the concept of conservation of quantity. Thus, by showing changing shapes of the same object, for instance, water, in differently shaped containers, it will take time before the child can say it is the same water. It will take more time before he is decentred from spatial ties such as believing there is more water in the tall thin tube than in the other. Only when able to co-ordinate two independent variables simultaneously, as width and height, will he achieve the right answer.

We now begin to understand the kind of level of organization of mental operations used by the schizoid patient when he feels instability, confusion of identity, disorder of body image, and fears of impermanence, since he is bound to experience himself differently in various localities, in various situations, with various objects.

The difficulty existing outside the space with which existence and permanence are so closely linked is enormous for the schizoid. Thus a young man only had a sense of existence when he drove his motor bike so long as there was a car in front of him or if his engine was going. If he passed the car or the engine stopped, he became depersonalized. A young woman, although she had changed greatly in analysis, could only be the person she was in her mother's head. A young man who lived alone for a considerable time in a room in a boarding house made progress, started studying, but had to move out of his room in order to have people about him, as he could not bear to be alone. So he sat in various public places like bars and cafés. Then he went through a phase when the place had to move with him, and so he sat on buses and wandered everywhere while studying. Was he being carried by mother everywhere? After months of this behaviour, he had a dream that he was standing in a bus holding a baby, his baby, and somewhat monstrous. Then the baby grew up and appeared normal, but he lost him. In his association he said the baby was also himself. Some phobics, and perhaps most, will go nowhere unless accompanied, and this can reach amazing extremes with some patients.

For this paper I have attempted to introduce concepts of space, movement and time as the basic elements, the weft and warp of primitive human behaviour. Primitive thought is centred on the first moves taken by the infant to structure space. This is done by the action of the subject on his objects and vice versa. Primitive notions of time then follow. Patterns of behaviour belonging to any stage may persist and become active at any time later.

3 INTRAPSYCHIC OBJECT RELATIONS: THE INDIVIDUAL AND THE GROUP

The group that is referred to here is a psychotherapeutic group. Its aim is to alter in each of its individual members the underlying 'structure' and phantasy systems that govern their way of thinking and feeling and their interpersonal relationships. Although the constellation of factors influencing structures and phantasies may be different in groups than in individual therapy, the actual processes of dissolution and reconstruction cannot differ fundamentally in the individual himself. Within the group, each individual is his own centre of psychic activity. It follows that, however perfect and ideal conditions are in a group, it is the personality organization of the individual that will decide changes in him. As in individual therapy, increasing knowledge of favourable and unfavourable aspects of the group setting will improve the possibility of achieving the goal of change in the individual within the group.

The aim of this paper is to attempt to describe a number of fundamental processes deriving from deep personality structures, which are believed to be always at work in groups. It is suggested that the link between those deep structures and apparent phantasies and behaviour is often masked and difficult to establish. One method of determining them is the study of groups of borderline patients. The main attempt is to evaluate how the existence of groups of inner objects and primitive intrapsychic object relations, as well as their role in determining interpersonal object relations, contribute to an understanding of group dynamics. Special attention will be paid to the very early processes by which objects and space are arranged, and the part they play in the structuring of groups.

THE INDIVIDUAL

It would seem that however one looks at theories of personality structures, there emerges in all of them a distinction between deep and surface aspects of experiencing, thinking and communicating.

This essay is based on the psychoanalytical model, but uses contributions from many other sources. Thus, in the Freudian model we have primary and secondary processes; in classical psychiatry, psychosis and neurosis; in Jung, archetypes of the collective unconscious and phantasies of the personal unconscious.

The Piagetian contribution has acquired more and more importance. It is distinguished by the fact that prelogical (now called sublogical) and logical structures and subdivisions are described in detail; this list could be considerably extended, but since language is used in all models, Chomsky's theory of deep and surface structures must be mentioned.

The systems underlying mental behaviour in any specific individual are hierarchically structured: ultrastable, stable, unstable; reversible, irreversible. Some structures are useful under certain conditions of the environment or to achieve certain aims. In other conditions, they are positively unfavourable or even obnoxious. The more fixed the structures, the less the degree of freedom of choice according to the demands of the environment, and the more restricted and pathological the behaviour. An important aim of treatment is to increase freedom of choice.

EARLY CONSTRUCTIONAL ACTIVITY AND PRIMITIVE INTRAPSYCHIC GROUPS

By constructional activity we mean that the infant 'constructs' his own body image as well as his objects; they are not passively given constructs. This constructional activity takes place against the background of an interaction between constitutional maturational processes and the activating environment. It is intended in this essay to make use of two main streams of thought. The first is the theory of paranoid-schizoid and depressive positions. Early object relationships, whatever their exact nature – for example, part-object psychology, the coming together of parts into a whole and the mechanisms used by the infant in achieving a world of inner objects in intrapsychic relationship – are considered to be of vital importance. The early introjections organized as internal objects constitute the most primary groups. The infant is not only structured by the environment, he also structures it. As an adult he will compulsively and repetitively structure his environment according to the structure of his internal groups. His success or failure in interpersonal relationships will depend on the nature of his intrapsychic object relations. It follows that an understanding of group dynamics will depend on understanding how intrapsychic groups work. However, the important point is that the person will not relate to external objects solely according to his already evolved intrapsychic relationships. It is suggested that he will attempt to restructure his external objects in the way his internal objects were structured. This also applies to a group of objects considered as part-objects, or grouped together as a whole object according to the person's own models. The more pathological, fixed and ultrastable his internal objects and groups of internal objects are, the more his external group constructs will tend to be fixed and pathological.

One controversial point must be clarified regarding object-relations theory. How early are early objects sufficiently cathected to be considered not simply as biological objects but to deserve consideration as having primitive mental representation? Certain analysts believe that very early in the infant's emotional life objects no longer are purely biological, and at each stage of development object relations are seen as a continuum from early beginnings to later, more sophisticated constructs. Thus Joan Rivière (1937) writes quite clearly on this point:

> There can be no such distinction (solution of continuity) since the 'beginnings' and so on are the object-relations appropriate and proper to the earliest stage of development. At each stage of instinctual primacy the character or degree of object-relations is proper to that stage. (Only if 'object-relation proper' were understood to mean fully developed adult object-relation could such a distinction be made.)

As to the character of this experience, Susan Isaacs (1952) writes that they are hardly distinguishable from sensory experiences. Thus, 'The first phantasied wish-fulfilment, the first "hallucination", is bound up with *sensation*.' These early constructs may remain unlinked with word representation and act autonomously, compulsively and repetitively; also, primitive mental processes are resorted to. In pathological states, excessive use is made of splitting, denial and projective identification to defend against profound anxiety. Rigidity, concrete thinking and fear of human feelings are marked characteristics.

The psychic organization of any individual, whether normal, neurotic, borderline or psychotic, cannot be completely free – and never will be – from the activity of autonomous intrapsychic primary-group formations. If so, in any form of treatment the individual will necessarily have to go through certain phases involving changes in the structures and activity of the primary intrapsychic groups, to the extent that this is possible for any given individual.

In view of the objections raised by many to the ideas expressed here, it does not seem out of place to recall that Freud also postulated stages of development that are in some ways not dissimilar from those later described by Klein. Thus, he postulated an order of development of the individual, beginning with an auto-erotic phase where parts are separate and unintegrated, and there is no reference to a unified body image. There is no external libidinal object, but parts of the body provide, so to say, their own gratification. The notion of auto-eroticism is extremely complex and cannot be discussed in detail here. But as Laplanche and Pontalis (1973) point out, the notion is clarified greatly by considering the next stage postulated by Freud, that of narcissism. They write:

> In narcissism it is the ego's unified image of the body which is the object of narcissistic libido, whilst auto-eroticism by way of contrast is defined as the anarchic stage preceding this convergence of the consistent theory about the construction of the object itself. If the self has to be put together, so must the object. (p. 46)

The idea of parts coming together is a constant one in Freud's thinking. Thus: 'The sexual drives, isolated up to now, have from now on come together in a state of unity and at the same time have found an object' (1895, p. 88).

But just as important is the fact that Freud maintained a double point of view about auto-erotic activity: as a genetic notion, a libidinal stage, and, also, as an activity which has its place in all phases of libidinal displacement. It is a most interesting exercise to determine at what point Freud later separated libido and aggression, and how he dealt with the stages of the aggressive impulse from the genetic developmental point of view, as seen in his theories of sadism and masochism. Until Klein, little was said about the state of the object as a consequence of aggressive attacks.

Similarly, when the work of Piaget is considered, definite stages of development are described in which schemas come together to form wholes.

The work of Spitz (1965) on child development shows similar paths of development, including part-object theory and separation anxiety of a severe depressive nature at about nine months. He refuses to call it depression despite the clinical picture, because depression means super-ego activity; he refuses to accept precursors of super-ego structures as being active at that age; therefore, depression cannot be depression. Having referred to the adult, sadistically cruel super-ego in depression, he writes, 'Nothing comparable exists in the infant, where at this stage even the precursors of the super-ego cannot be discerned.' It is only a superficial nosological picture, he states, and yet continues to refer to it as an anaclitic depression. Spitz insists on the prior existence of a good mother-relationship as opposed to a bad one. Presumably, then, the infant can distinguish between good and bad 'bits'. Here we have an example of the building up of early primitive and primary intrapsychic groups.

EVOLUTIONARY HIERARCHIES

It seems a fascinating exercise to compare manifestations of split-off activities of individuals within themselves and of themselves within the group with the activities of parts of a whole organism consisting of loosely connected autonomous parts or activities. What comes to mind is the hypothesis put forward by Eugène Marais in his now-famous book *The Soul of the White Ant* (1973), in which he suggests that the activities of similar members of each subgroup of the termitarium – the workers, the soldiers, the king and queen – are linked together like the parts of a higher organism functioning as a whole towards a single aim.

It is also an interesting fact that in an earlier book, *The Soul of the Ape* (1969), Marais writes about his ideas of the emergence of new behaviours in the evolutionary hierarchy. He compares the behaviour of a mare having lost her foal with that of a chacma, a species of ape, having lost her baby. Although more detailed studies have since been made, Marais was a great precursor of such studies, and, in the case mentioned, his comparison of the behaviour to loss is very striking, especially in relation to the emergence of the mourning reaction. Could we say: of the depressive position? Both the mare and the chacma showed great distress at the time of their loss. However, when confronted with her dead foal, the mare paid no attention to it at all, and kept on returning in great distress to the place where it had drowned. The chacma, on the other hand, when faced with the dead body, stopped her restlessness, touched the body, made sounds of endearment, put her face and lips close to her dead infant, uttered a succession of cries, and then went and sat in a corner. She then allowed the body to be taken away and buried. Later, she started again taking an interest in the environment.

SPACE, SENSORI-MOTOR SCHEMAS AND PIAGET

The second theme is that psychoanalytical views of whatever description are insufficient to understand fully the constructs just described. They are not enough because the external object, that is external reality, is considered as given, and only the making of emotional libidinal objects and of psychic reality are considered. Analysis of borderline and psychotic patients leaves the analyst in little doubt that this is wrong. To understand fully early emotional constructs and their psychopathology, it is also necessary to understand how external reality is constructed. It is the writer's belief that only one psychology of external reality can compare with psychoanalytic theory: the genetic developmental psychology of Jean Piaget. It stands as a unique monument of intellectual beauty, and has become indispensable to an understanding of the way in which the infant and the child construct their perceptual and intellectual worlds.

It is not irrelevant here to mention how Freud distinguished between neurosis and psychosis. In the former, an impulse is repressed; in the latter, a piece of external reality is denied. This statement speaks for itself as to the importance of early external reality constructs, that is, for the relevance of the sensori-motor stage of Piagetian psychology. Two concepts of Piaget will be especially referred to here: first, the spatial nature of very early thought; and second, the notion of early interiorized sensori-motor schemas as precursors of representational thinking. Also, the early beginnings of object formation are considered to be, in some way, prolongations of the action of the subject on the object. Assimilation and accommodation processes are the two pivotal mechanisms used. Their relationship to introjective and projective identification is obvious.

Primary processes, as best illustrated in dreams, are centred on spatial representations of a visual nature. The unconscious is repeatedly considered by psychoanalytical writers to be timeless. Events can take place in any order that does not respect sequence, duration or separation in time. A long time is a long space; the older generation is taller in size but when the child grows he may become taller than the elders and considers he has become older or is catching up. Condensation and displacement were seen by Freud as the two main mechanisms of the dream world. Psychoanalysis has never systematically considered how the child, step by step, constructs his notions of space, displacement and time. Yet the nature of thought, of personality organization and of intrapsychic and interpersonal relationships depends on these very processes, as well as the emotional, libidinal and aggressive factors so well studied by psychoanalysts.

Piaget systematically studied the ontogeny of thought since birth. He has demonstrated in a uniquely clear way the dominance of the spatial factor in the early constructs of the infant. It is only through displacement and co-ordination of action on objects in space that infantile thought gradually becomes spatially decentered and the concept of time emerges. Further, for Piaget the first 'structures' or schemas of the sensori-motor stage underlying behaviour are interiorized actions of the subject on the object, such as holding the object, taking it into the mouth, sucking it, putting it away, taking it up again. As more actions of the subject on the object, and vice versa, take place and are co-ordinated between themselves, increasingly complicated schemas and structures are interiorized. Piaget considers that the schemas are not available at first to the infant at the representational level, because it is not until the permanence and constancy (two different concepts) of objects are well established that the interiorized schemas can be evoked in the absence of the external object. However, when the external object is perceptually available, the schemas can become activated. We are here reminded of Winnicott's concept of the transitional object, and of his brilliant series of observations.

Although it is impossible to expand freely on Piagetian theory here, it was necessary to refer to this work because of its importance for the understanding of certain phenomena in groups, and for an explanation of some of the main trends in the evolution of group therapy. But so far as the present writer is aware, there is no work relating the importance of such factors as size of groups, arrangement in a circle, distance between members, position relative to the therapist, to the early and primitive stages of spatial organization of the body ego and of the objects both internal and external. Primitive identifications depend on the relative spatial position of objects to each

other. Freud linked together primitive introjection and primitive identification. People take the 'place' of others to acquire their possessions and
characteristics. Indeed, it is a very difficult task to convey by description,
analogy or metaphor the processes of transformation that are at work in
identification. A superimposition of two objects is not enough; one or both
objects must become part or all of the other.

DREAMS, SENSORI-MOTOR ACTIVITY, CHANGE AND ACTING OUT

In *The New Psychology of Dreaming* Richard Jones (1970), in a chapter on
Piaget and dreams (inspired by a yet unpublished work of Dr Peter Castle)
makes the point that:

> A dream can be characterized as a form of thought which is experienced
> as action. It thus occupies a unique place in the spectrum of symbolic
> functioning in that it seems to be what it is not, that is, action, and is what
> it does not seem to be, that is, thought.

The connection between this statement and the Piagetian concept of
schemas and structures being the interiorized action of the subject on the
object is obvious. This has to be considered in relation to processes involved
in changing early patterns of behaviour, with the concept of acting out, and
with some of the major trends in psychotherapy, especially group therapy,
in the past few years.

In a remarkable article, 'Language and Dreams', Edelson (1973) has
compared some of the views of Freud and Chomsky. In spoken language,
deep structures (meaning) are expressed in phonetic symbolism through
transformation into surface structures. Is it that in dreams the same deep
structures undergoing other transformations appropriate to visual symbolism are expressed in visual form? The interpretation of dreams in spoken and
written form implies an understanding of the coding systems that allows the
transfer from one system of representation and communication to the other.
Of course, all levels of ontogenic development of thought could be used by
the dreamer. Also, it is possible to suggest with Piaget that instead of the
association of ideas by contiguity, as in psychoanalytical theory, structure
represents the way in which parts are linked together as they were by the
action of subject on object, and vice versa, in the preverbal or sensori-motor
stages. Contiguity would be spatial but structural pathways would facilitate
a certain association rather than another.

The later considerations are important in understanding change and
theories of acting out. If in therapy the preverbal stages of interiorized action
schemas have to be undone, it may well be that to 'relive' the action, purely
verbal schemas are insufficient. It would mean attempting to alter the original

action schemas by approaching the task only at the level of phonetic symbolization, that is, in Freudian terms, at the level of secondary processes; in Chomsky's terms, not deep but surface structures; in Piagetian terms, as representation and not as sensori-motor schemas.

This takes us to the role of acting out in psychotherapy. Acting out was anathema in early psychoanalytic days. As treatment became longer, certain forms of action and life decisions could not possibly be postponed until the completion of treatment. Then came the treatment of children by play therapy and the treatment of borderline and psychotic cases and the emergent problem of how to analyse non-verbal structures. The concept of acting out within – as opposed to outside – therapy came into the picture. Eventually, the whole restricted concept blew up in a volcanic eruption. Abreaction techniques came in, as well as psychodrama, encounter groups, behaviour therapy and many more, all making use of concrete behaviour and acting out techniques. Further, in our permissive society it would be very difficult to control acting out in groups. Are we therefore reckoning with the possibility that early sensori-motor non-verbal structures play an important part at all levels of human behaviour and thought processes? That to change patterns of behaviour and thinking we have to find methods of changing those very early structures, often ultrastable (if not actually similar to imprints of the ethologists because of the sensitive or critical periods at which they were evolved), which are difficult to alter solely at the verbal level? The verbal level will always be necessary, but we do not know how far, in some cases, action has to be combined with verbal expression. The writer has no doubt that whatever can be achieved by purely verbal methods is preferable to non-verbal methods. However, the upsurge of non-verbal techniques makes it imperative to study the stability and reversibility of deep structures and their mode of action in influencing surface structures, as well as their connection with acting out. It is possible that the linking of preverbal material with words has to be done first in the mind of others before the patient can do the linking himself – linking that he was unable to do at the normal primary stages of development.

THE ROLE OF THE THERAPIST

Evolution in the group will never take place without the guidance of the therapist. He differs from the other members in two ways: his goal and task are not the same; he has the knowledge to interpret. The therapist is a special inner object of the group. He has the role of the privileged observer. He is the 'genius' of the group in the true primitive sense of the word: he generates. He is a metasystem with regard to the system of members. Group interpretations structure the group. Individual interpretations are needed to destructure the individual ultrastable structures. They produce 'chaos', confusion in the individual and the group. The group then restructures loosely according to a different blueprint. With the passage of time, the equilibrium is disturbed again. This very sequence of events itself acquires stability and increases the freedom to change in the group along an axis of change and in an ever-widening spiral. The system acquires new degrees of freedom from psychotic and neurotic restrictive processes.

With such a method of conducting the group, size becomes vitally important: it becomes a question of how many inner objects the group – itself considered as a structured whole – can contain and deal with for this task. Each member and the analyst are substructures of the group with their own inner world of internal objects. It follows that the number of psychic objects as opposed to the number of members, that is, the apparent size, must be the decisive factor. Experience seems to indicate a smaller number than the traditional eight.

CLINICAL EXAMPLE

Dreams and psychoses bring the primary processes to the surface and make them manifest. In the context of this study, it would seem reasonable to say that they make the primary groups manifest as well. Borderline or schizoid individuals are remarkably rewarding to treat from this point of view because they seem to function on the frontier of primary and secondary processes. They are integrated enough not to disintegrate easily into psychoses, and yet are consciously or preconsciously aware of primary processes at work within them. Such a group is now described.

The patients in the group were in their mid-twenties. They all came from a list of patients assessed as serious personality disorders, schizoid or borderline cases. In fact, the group represented the remnants of two such groups which had been joined together. There were three women and two men. The therapist (myself) was male.

One woman, Mrs A, was divorced and had just remarried at the time the group started. She was a very intelligent woman. At the initial assessment interview her complaint was that she had no head. Her story is too complex and her problems too intricate to be related in full. From childhood until age seventeen she had slept in her mother's bed, her father having opted out of the conjugal couch. According to the patient, her first husband, a business man, was highly abnormal. She thought he was bisexual, and he dressed in feminine clothes to make love to his wife. She was very afraid of the feelings he might have towards the children. Her first born, a severely retarded child, by arrangement between the mother of the patient and her husband, and without her being consulted, had been placed in an institution. They had also adopted a little boy of different racial origin. The patient lived in fear of what her ex-husband would do to her and the children. This she felt had started as a result of never being away from her mother.

The fact that she felt she had no head derived from two levels of experience. At one level it meant that she did not want her head as it was now, because it meant that she had lost the head she had when she was sixteen, when she had met her first husband and was pure, lovable and good-looking. She did not experience this as a denial and a psychological process, but was frightened that people would not believe the truth of her experience, that she had no head. At a deeper level, the physicality of this symptom was explained by her inability to feel separate from her mother. The latter had told the patient that when the patient was born her head had torn her mother's vagina; to the patient, her head was still stuck there. Furthermore, her mother had told her that she, the mother, also had no head, and that therefore there was no hope for the patient.

The primitiveness of the functioning of the patient's mind was reflected in her relationship with her children. She would never leave them alone, as she herself had never been alone or slept alone in her life. The experiences of the patient at the body ego and part-object levels seemed to be shared by the children in a conscious way. For instance, at age four the little boy who was racially different kept insisting that he wanted to go right into his mother's tummy in order to come out like the others, so that his mother would be really his mother. He did not know officially he was an adopted child. Needless to say, the patient was severely phobic. Yet she proved to be a marvellous patient from all points of view.

Of the two other female patients, Mrs B had been married and divorced. She had never been able to form any stable relationships of any kind whatsoever, and was totally immature. At the assessment interview she stated that she thought her difficulty could be related to her inability to decide whether she was a little boy or a little girl. She clung to any object she could put her hands on, and could not bear being alone. She would hitchhike at two o'clock in the morning to find her way to somebody she could talk to fifty miles away, and hitchhike back a few hours later. In an unsuccessful attempt to make contact, she talked incessantly. An artist with a vivid imagination, she suffered from LSD flashbacks, which terrified her and stimulated fears of a psychotic breakdown.

The other girl, Miss C, had one fixed idea. Her father, a poor man, had not been able to obtain a longed-for higher education. He had three daughters and no son. The patient, the youngest daughter, had been the brightest of the three daughters, and had felt she was the only one who could fulfil her father's wishes for higher education. She had tried and had given up. She was absolutely adamant that she had no right to be anything else than what she had decided her father wanted her to be. Therefore, she could not exist in the external world. She insisted that she must not relate to anybody, that the world was not for her, and that she had created her own phantasy world in which she lived. She furiously defended any intrusion into this private world. She did not at first reveal any of these phantasies, and was terrified that any happening in the group might lead to such an intrusion; therefore, she would leave the group precipitously. She often kept away from the group and the group wrote to her, requesting her return. But she kept coming.

It was only at a much later date when Miss C made her phantasies concretely real in external reality that a phantasy was revealed. At the time that this particular topic – the inversion of external and internal reality – was being analysed by me, she telephoned the hospital in a state of panic saying she did not know how to breathe any more and wanted to be told what to do about it. At the next session she explained that she could not any longer know what was in her mind and what was real. She was afraid she might have cancer of the breast (her father had died of cancer). When I interpreted that maybe she was saying she wanted to be examined physically to know if she had breast cancer, perhaps because she had found a lump there, she replied indignantly that I did not understand. I did not understand because, 'Can't you see, I am totally incapable of knowing if there is a lump because I would not know if it is in my breast or in my mind.'

Of the two men, Mr D was a tall, fair-haired man who did not seem to have any personality of his own, and who said so. He gave a strong impression of acting a role of one kind or another all the time, and insisted that this was what he himself felt. When he went to work (he had organized a cleaning unit and worked at night in order to avoid contact), he said his muscles felt strong and manly. When he came back home and made a cup of coffee for himself, he started feeling weak and feminine; by the time he sank into an armchair to drink the coffee, he was feeling quite feminine. Intellectually, he was capable of a much more sophisticated occupation. He was totally isolated and, as he said, the only relationship he ever had with a woman was with an inflatable rubber female contraption.

Mr E turned out to be a very complicated case indeed, and only the barest outline of his case will be given. He had been a promising boy at school, but in his last year did not function very well. He tried various jobs later and could not keep them. He had had psychiatric treatment before he was referred to me. In the initial interview Mr E kept saying, 'Sorry, doctor, I'm not with you. Could you repeat what you said, please?' This was to prove very important later. He had no friends and was living at home with his parents. He made little contact with other patients in the group at first.

When Mr E was asked, 'Where are you, or parts of you, if you are not here?', it was revealed that he wanted to be a woman and had dressed on a few occasions in his mother's clothes. That was where he was. On an earlier occasion, one night he had dressed as a London business man and entered his parents' bedroom at three o'clock in the morning and said, 'Father, is this what you want me to be?' Later in the treatment, when pressed by the other members to be less apathetic and complacent, and told that he would never get on unless he got a job, he broke down under pressure into a regressive mixture of schizophrenic and manic behaviour. He combed his hair à la Wellington, challenged the neighbours, and thought the BBC was mentioning him in their programmes. He had become important. Then he regressed to being like a baby. Later he went through all the phases of growing up. He became intensively preoccupied with Jews and then with blacks. His father was British, his mother Polish-German. He wanted to know if she was Jewish, the explanation of which came later. Mr E wanted to know the nature of the bits of which he was made, and gave a nationality to each bit. Jewishness meant the possibility of integrating all the bits because Jews of all nationalities are basically Jewish and one.

Mr E's negativism and apathy had a very interesting origin. When dressed as a man, he kept on feeling he could not understand the news on the television. However, he found out that when dressed as a woman he could. It seemed that any activity associated in his mind with making him a man was rejected. Later, he started to identify with his father in a manic way, calling himself an important soldier or a general; then he identified with me and attempted to do psychotherapy in the war. During all this period he had developed a language of physical signs which from time to time overcame verbal language and took over. Although he was tolerated by the group at first, after his breakdown I took him over for individual treatment. In fact, this patient showed all the levels of behaviour and mental processes mentioned in this paper, and went through the various developmental phases both in a regressive way at first and a progressive way afterwards.

It is now possible to discuss from this clinical material some of the statements made previously, and to consider new ones.

First, it is appropriate to consider how primitive, autonomous, internal psychic groups of primitive objects had survived in these patients through splitting, denial, projection and non-transformation of primitive part-objects into more advanced, more integrated and more adult objects. An aspect of this state of affairs is evident in the concreteness of the thoughts of these patients and their defective symbolization.

In one session, a patient had denied a sense of identity. Mrs A said she had no head, was not separate from her mother, would not feel she was a real woman until she had borne a normal child instead of a retarded one (one other child being adopted and the other felt as not normal), and exposed to the others her various bad bits and pieces. The others immediately started mentioning that it reminded them of similar experiences, and brought forward the unintegrated pieces of which they felt they were made, as described previously. I, as therapist, had the extraordinary experience that we were not six people in the room, but a whole crowd of people of all ages, sexes and statuses, speaking and acting in all sorts of ways. It was a real encounter with a very concrete projection of the autonomous primitive groups into a Tower of Babel, a crowd made up of an assembly of subgroups of unrelated part-objects.

When, added to this, such patients talk about real external people, however distorted by phantasy they are, the complication of human interpersonal relationships for them becomes flabbergasting. Further, objects and personal experiences exist side by side simultaneously at various levels and degrees of symbolization, representation and transformation, from the concrete or perceptual to the psychological. Thus, for example, Mrs A (the patient with no head), who concretely denied a split-off part of herself, was also able to express her feelings about what she did not want to be at a psychological level. Miss C knew there was a difference between a physical and a 'mental' cancer, but since she was unable to avoid experiencing both the primitive and higher levels simultaneously, she had to enter into a confusional state.

The difficulty of communicating adequately with words is enormous for these patients because words are experienced by them as objects. There is also the difficulty of describing experiences they feel are not shared by others in the outside world. An example of this was provided by Mr D in a most unexpected way. At the second session he said, more or less out of the blue, that it was difficult to attend two groups. I did not understand the remark, and I enquired to what he was referring. It turned out that through a clerical mistake his name had been left on the waiting list although he had already been taken into a group. I said I would enquire about what had happened. He said that he did not want to interfere or dictate his wish, but if possible he would like to stay in the present group. I found out that in the other group, of neurotic and less-ill patients, he had been a loner, unpopular, hardly saying anything, and, whenever he spoke, antagonizing the others. In a group of his peers he got on extremely well. Although each one of these patients lived in a complex world of his or her own, they all somehow felt some sort of similarity and capacity to be in the world of each other as one of the peculiar objects of their peculiar world.

Using Kleinian terminology, one could call that stage of group organization the paranoid-schizoid phase. The group is in bits and fragments. The therapist plays a role of immense importance: he must be active, pick up all the bits from each member individually, patiently put them together, and allow the group to remain functional despite the chaos.

In an ordinary neurotic group, it seems that the process through which the assembly of patients must go before it is a group is somewhat as follows. The therapist is praised and criticized in turn; in that way he is cathected and becomes emotionally meaningful. His introjection by the members gives them something in common: the person of the therapist, however distorted by the members and however precarious the state of the introject (one is reminded of the Last Supper). It is obvious that this process of introjection of the therapist in patients of the kind described above is a very long and difficult process. Nevertheless, each member of the group progressively becomes more of a person to the other members; they start caring more for each other, and become anxious to help. Feelings of compassion and depression begin slowly to appear and replace threats of dissolution of the self, panicky anxieties and persecutory feelings. Feelings of despair of ever getting better, as well as hopes to do so, are voiced. Group members become anxious if a member misses a session; they offer to help. The group acquires the qualities of a part-object or of a much more complicated organism. It is treated like a breast or a mother (sometimes a pregnant mother), or may be experienced as a threatening object. All this may be revealed by the phantasies of the patients, consciously or in their dreams.

There were various changes in the inner world of inner objects of the patients as they progressed from their original fragmented and persecuted state. Miss C, who also received help individually, has now accepted the existence of the external world and her being separate from her father. After the cancer panic she developed hypochondriacal pains in various parts of her body, which in our view represented localized, concretely experienced internal objects. She recognized spontaneously that she was so jealous and envious of any woman 'from infancy to old age' (her words) that she had to deny their existence. She established a good relationship with an older married sister, but not yet with her mother, whom she visited. She worked part-time in a hospital and babysat to earn her living. Reparation at a semi-concrete level started with the introjection of better, less split-off, more integrated objects deriving from a more integrated group.

Mrs B, who was so terrified of her lack of proper capacity for communication and deep feelings and of not being a proper woman, acted out on an extensive scale. She tried to force a number of men to love her, including members of the group. Complaining of being empty and not a real woman, she talked of her desire for a baby and got herself pregnant twice. Again, reparation at a concrete level. As an artist she specialized in animation drawing (a similar desire to recreate life) for films, and won several scholarships. All of these false attempts at reparation were gradually analysed, until she realized the futility of this acting out as a method of reparation. She became depressed on several occasions, showed concern for other members of the group, and became less demanding of the therapist's total attention. There was a vast reduction in her egocentric and demanding behaviour.

Mrs A was the patient who showed the greatest change. She became more real, and very slowly accepted the various parts of her body as her own. At first, in order to become separate from her mother, she had to stop seeing her physically. Simultaneously, her children became separate from her and were not actually felt as having to be part of herself as proof of her love for them. She demanded constant reassurance from the therapist that she would not die, nor would her children. The spectre of her first husband started fading into the background; her present husband became an important person in her life. Instead of believing she had physically to create a normal child in the place of her mentally abnormal first one, she found the courage to visit him. Her travelling phobias started to diminish. She is a very intelligent woman with a university degree. She started in a school as a teacher of children on a small scale, and ended by doing all the teaching for the retarded children in the school. By then she decided to leave the group, but kept in touch by occasional visits, and wrote two letters which were most touching and grateful to the group and myself; they revealed in the most simple language a woman with the deepest human feelings. Her second letter was about the death of her retarded son, leaving no doubt about her capacity to mourn.

Mr D became less and less of an actor. In such a group it was extremely difficult to maintain this defence. Instead, he had to talk about the phantasies about himself, which he acted as an actor acts a part. The real Mr D started to come to the surface. His was an extremely arid soul. It was then that he revealed that his only relationship to a woman had been the inflated rubber model. An attempt by Mrs B to seduce him physically left him with an utter feeling of repulsion. However, he became less passive and more aggressive in the group and towards the therapist. Mr D joined an encounter group, and criticized the therapeutic group. Then he became disillusioned with the encounter group, and said he realized he had to persevere with the present group. He gave up the night cleaning job, and started to work for an advertising firm and to produce his own weekly paper with a partner, which was a failure. By the time he left the group, Mr D had acquired some feelings of identity and good superficial relationships with others, but he had not established any deep relationship with a woman.

Mr E, as mentioned, is still in treatment and showed as clearly as Mrs A the bringing together of parts, first at a concrete level, then symbolically. Only after a number of regressions and a manic episode was he able to show feelings of compassion, sadness and depression. The concreteness of his thoughts and the passage to warm feelings was shown in a touching way on one occasion. It was winter and there was an oil crisis and no heating. I kept my overcoat on during a session. He was then very concerned with the language of signs he thought he had invented. A week later, as he was recovering, he said to me that he had felt very sad indeed during that session because wearing my coat had proved to him that his feelings for me were not warm enough to keep me warm. He is now working at a humble job, but reads and studies for a better one.

All these patients showed strong disorders of personality; a confusion of sexual identity; a confusion of a very concrete nature as to the various parts of their body and their respective functions; an equally strong confusion as to whether they were children or adults; and a severe defect of symbolization. This internal inadequacy reflected itself in their failure at interpersonal relationships, their incapacity to find an adult group in society, either family or work group, in which they could function. They could not distinguish between father, mother, brothers and sisters, children or adults, familiar or strange people, inferiors or superiors, persecutors or friends. They had to cling to whatever they could. Primitive anxiety dominated their relationships. They did not know how to care and mind. In our view, the failure of their intrapsychic organization reflected itself completely in a failure to organize their lives in a setting of adult, interpersonal relationships within the social group. Their external worlds were crumbling to pieces, as was the state of their inner worlds. The group, in part kept together by the therapist, was a new world where reorganization was made possible.

SUMMARY

The aim of a therapeutic group is primarily to bring change in the individual. The individual can be considered as having an inner space 'inhabited' by inner objects in intrapsychic relationships. Inner objects are constructs of the subject corresponding to various levels of development from the most primitive to the most sophisticated stages. The subject tends to interpret and structure his environment in terms of these groups of internal objects. The more pathological the early stages of structuration of the inner world, the more autonomous primary groups will be, and the more they will impose their structure on the external environment.

Pathological structural activities of each individual in the group will determine the structure of the group, will eventually become manifest, and can become available for conscious working through. Early constructional activity is considered to be centred on spatial activity and on the action of the subject on its objects. Non-verbal structures are thought to be of primary importance in determining ultrastable patterns of behaviour, especially pathological behaviour. Since they might be responsible for acting out, special consideration is given to them in this essay.

The size of groups suitable for deep analytical work is important. The following questions are asked: How many inner objects can a person deal with? How many members considered as inner objects within the group taken as a whole can be held within a group?

The evolution of the group in some ways will be similar to the evolution of the individual from part- to whole-object relationships, and from paranoid-schizoid and depressive methods of functioning to more normal mature activity. A group of schizoid individuals is described to illustrate some of the points discussed.

4 ANOREXIA NERVOSA

In November 1977 I was invited by the University of Cape Town to spend six months teaching psychoanalytical psychotherapy to students and to the staff. When I arrived, I took over the supervision of a patient, Miss R, suffering from anorexia nervosa. At the Maudsley Hospital I had had a great deal of experience with regard to the psychotherapy of anorexia nervosa. I had made up my mind that there probably existed one particular psychopathology that can be found in those cases, and I wish to describe it here.

What is especially interesting is that the patient was a highly intelligent young woman, a student in psychology, who wrote up her experiences under her own name in a psychology journal (Rouah, 1980). She was treated in a well-organized unit, using a combination of behaviour therapy, art therapy, growth games, and social therapy. Most important was the work of the nurses, each one having a particular task to foster human relationships. It must be said that there were no psychoanalysts available in Cape Town, but the unit was under the able leadership of Professor E. Nash, who was its life and soul, and most interested in the analytical schools.

Apart from a description of her own experiences in the article in a professional journal, there is also a record of the treatment as Miss R experienced it, which I shall present and discuss in this chapter. It is illustrated as well with drawings and collages. The 'psychotherapist' in charge was a very intelligent nurse who reported to the team responsible for the supervision. I was the supervisor for a period of six months. The unit was located at the Groote Schuur Hospital.

HISTORY

The patient was nineteen years old when she arrived in Groote Schuur Hospital. A second-year psychology student, she came from Durban after an unsuccessful attempt at treatment using behaviour therapy to promote weight gain. She was in a severe cachectic condition, weighing about 32 kg

(72 lb) (she is a tall girl, about 5ft 9in). She was barely able to maintain her assertions that she was perfectly well and not too thin. When Miss R arrived in the unit she was still using the usual anorectic behaviour – vomiting, disposal of food and vigorous exercising. She appeared sufficiently depressed at one time to be treated with an anti-depressant and chlorpromazine, unsuccessfully. Shortly after her arrival there was a crisis where Miss R was near death and required intravenous hydration and tube feeding. She developed a very special reaction to her nasogastric tube, which stayed in for a number of weeks. She was quite prepared, even happy, to accept food given to her through it; however, she persevered with an intense aversion to chewing or swallowing food herself.

Miss R's past history showed that her mother was orphaned at an early age, and later in life was rescued from a camp in Egypt by her husband. Her mother is said to have been very dependent, and to exhibit behaviour more like a child than a mother and a wife. Father was a very strong character, and a dominant personality at home and in business. They came to South Africa via the Belgian Congo after its independence. Miss R had an older and a younger sister. It would appear that she spoke with intense rivalry of the sister, two or three years older than her.

As to the onset of the illness, the patient wrote the following:

Although I denied it initially, I have to accept the painful truth that the changes of pubescence, the increase in size, shape and weight, menstruation and new and disturbing sexual impulses, all presented a dangerous challenge for which I was unprepared and which thwarted what little control I had.

However, things got worse for Miss R at the death of her father, who eight months previously had died of a sudden heart attack that the patient witnessed personally. Mourning her father was very difficult, as her mother insisted that her husband's clothing and other items were left exactly as they had been. The patient felt she was the only one who was coping at all with her father's death, but at the same time she was very resentful that her mother was unable to help her to get through her own grief at her father's death.

The patient talked with a group of people, to whom as time went on she referred as 'her mother'; they included the special nurse, occupational therapist and doctors involved on the unit. She regularly participated in occupational therapy consisting of activities such as growth games, drama and projective art. Her improvement was marked by transition from discussion of sensori-motor relationship to form and 'mother', to symbolic, metaphoric representation of her thinking. The following pages (pp. 49–62) are descriptions of her illness made by the patient herself after she had done drawings which put into symbolic form her state of mind.

GROWTH GAMES

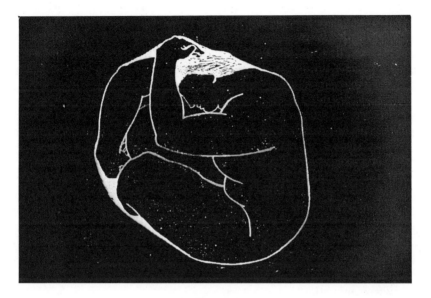

Figure 1

Is this a woman? No . . . a foetus? No . . . a child, then? Wrong again . . . So what is it? Well, there is a long, complicated story attached to her, and the best way to describe her here is that she's a woman in a foetal position.

This sounds very confusing and illogical at first, so let me explain, because this figure is in fact me. I've discovered that there are certain things which are hard to believe until they happen to you, and one of those things is the possibility of growing 'a number of years' in a matter of months. Eleven months ago, I was a foetus, totally helpless, dependent, unaware of myself and of my feelings, in fact, so controlled that I never got round to ever showing what I truly felt or experienced in life. Physically and factually I was put on this earth on 6/11/59, but actually I was 'conceived' about a year ago, and I was 'born' about six days ago. To confuse matters further, I was the foetus and the mother together, so that I have given birth to myself in the form of greater awareness of myself.

I am talking not only of emotional growth, but of physical growth as well, for, when I came into hospital, I had reduced my body to such minute proportions that I was literally helpless and unable to do anything for myself. At that stage, I was the foetus, the tube was the umbilical cord, and the sisters on the ward were my 'mothers'. I was totally dependent on them for being washed, fed, even turned over from side to side every hour on the hour to prevent bedsores. Emotionally, I was doing no work at the time, because I was too weak physically and, more important, I flatly denied my immaturity.

How could anyone accuse me of being an infant if I had been such a support to my family after Dad died? The cheek of it!!! Hadn't I successfully managed to replace Dad in the home? Everyone had told me what a model daughter (or should I say 'husband' and 'father'???) I had proved to be, and here I had the staff and my therapists denying that!!! I was so bloody angry at the time, but I was only a child, a very small, helpless child.

Now I am mature enough to at least recognize my unrealistic aims in the past, and I really respect my 'mothers' for their farsightedness. Sure, I coped on the surface, but I did it at the expense of my health, for I was destroying myself completely. Maybe, I was doing myself a service too, for, by being my Dad, I was escaping womanhood and its responsibilities.

Slowly, very slowly I started to 'grow' and as I became stronger physically, so I began to work on my emotional growth, only to find that that was a far more painful and slower process than putting on weight so as to regain my womanly figure. For the latter purpose, I just had to eat, but there is no food or pills or any such aids to help one grow emotionally. To do that, I had to admit a lot of painful truths, a lot of concealed and crushed anger towards my parents, and, of course, the painful realization and eventual acceptance of my womanhood.

Coupled with that was the increasing antagonism towards food, which, to me, is the thing, the hateful thing that makes one fat, and ugly, and hateful of my body. First, look at how gross, coarse and disgusting the picture is! Just look (if you can bear it?) at those thighs, at that roll of fat around the stomach! No wonder the woman is still sheltering herself from looking at herself and around her! She thinks she's a disgraceful sight, hence her compulsion, at times, to diet again so as to lose all that flab, even though she's been through the mill once already, and suffered a lot in the process.

To get back to me, I think I am a little beyond that stage, in some respects at least. I have been through the birth now, so that I have come to recognize my new role, and therefore my womanly appearance. I do not fully accept it yet, and in this respect, I still occasionally shied my eyes from looking at my disturbing body-image. I almost feel like a 'grown-up', new, fresh and tender, so much so that I am still a foetus or a very young infant in this new role. My wish for increasing independence is both positive and negative: 1) Positive, because I feel it is high time to break away from home and to recognize my individuality, and my rights as such, as well as give myself a chance to live my life as me, instead of going out of my way to always please others and live by their standards. 2) Negative, because I have this urge to extend my independent status to being in sole and total control of my eating habits. It is my body and I have to be happy with both. 'Just one final warning, woman, your mind is still distorted that's all I have to say' . . .

Here she is drawing and describing the stages she went through to reach this:

THE CHICK AND THE SHELL

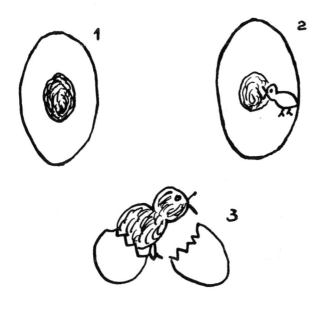

Figure 2

A baby is like a little chick who grows by eating all the reserves in the egg until there is nothing left except the empty dried-out useless shell which it will shatter open, and step out of as a fully grown individual, ungratefully leaving the shell behind, this shell which once fed and protected it.

THE PARASITE AND TREE

The parasite has grown and flourished at the host's expense. It has selfishly sucked up all the goodness out of the tree whose resources are now completely exhausted. It can give so much good and no more, and it is now weak and sick and dying. A dark, heavy, stormy cloud hangs above and before long, the inevitable storm breaks out – it is total devastation, which the tree can't resist.

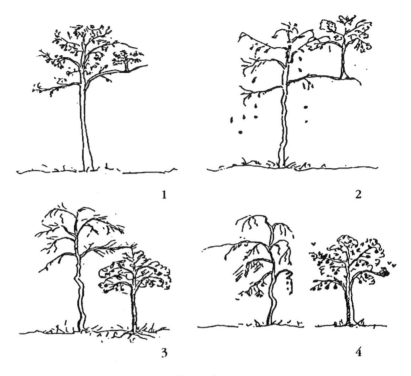

Figure 3

The branch on to which the parasite hangs breaks off and for a while the young tree feels lost, rejected and guilty at having been so gluttonous. It realizes that now it has to stand on its own roots; it is no longer dependent on another for nourishment and growth. If it settles down and anchors itself safely to the ground, it will flourish successfully. If not, it will die. The loneliness is hard to bear at first, and the young tree misses the protection and care that it had enjoyed up 'til now and that it has taken for granted.

It is only when one loses something precious that one realizes its value. As it adjusts itself more and more to its new existence, so the dark clouds clear away, and the sun sends a few warm and welcome rays to shine on to it. The little, helpless parasite has grown considerably since then, so that now, it is a shrub anchored fairly firmly to the ground, putting out roots to meet other plants and creatures around it. It is heading towards adulthood which will mean being productive (hence the fruit) and protective (hence the nests and birds), and it will have to give pleasure to others too by granting shade when it's too hot, and shelter when it's raining. The natural resources on which it depends to grow and survive will always be available. It is up to it to make its needs known and to use those resources adequately.

The parasite flowers and flourishes and the host is bare and totally drained and exhausted. At first it was a healthy tree, until the parasite grew on it and thrived on it at the host's expense. The tree takes in more food from the soil but the parasite is too greedy and increases its intake accordingly.

The parasite continues to blossom, but the tree is not so healthy any more; its leaves are falling and it is becoming diseased. (In pregnancy, the foetus grows regardless of the mother's morning sickness, tiredness, depression or varicose veins.)

A RECURRING PHANTASY

I have, for the past couple of weeks, been attempting to find the link between my fear of obesity and my childhood phantasy that pregnant women swallow their babies.

An individual can be 'obese' for one of two reasons:

1) Overeating,
2) Pregnancy.

In the first case, eating and indulging in food would result in a fat, and to my mind, an ugly and repulsive figure. In the second instance, my phantasy involves that of a foetus being cut up and chewed like food, swallowed, hence landing up in mother's stomach where it would grow and result in the mother's obese appearance. This, the common denominator of the two subparts of my phantasy, is the resulting state of the individual (obesity) which scares me. This had led me to hypothesize the possibility that subconsciously I equate food with a baby being swallowed which to my mind is a barbaric and repulsive act. I feel it is significant that since I have started on this phantasy trip, I have been feeling nauseous very often and have lost my appetite even more.

This little girl (me) seems very aware of her body and the way it is growing. Had growth taken place gradually and at its appropriate time (and here I refer to physical and emotional growth), with my being aware at the time of my body changes, I would have probably been spared all this pain and discomfort and seemingly being a woman but in reality being a young, vulnerable child. But it has not been so. Physically and naturally, I have grown, but emotionally I have remained static hence the resulting discrepancy that I now have to patch up.

IMPRISONMENT

The first picture shows a dark, stormy cloud hanging over the tower in which I am imprisoned. Let the tower symbolize the penis and the cloud the vagina, which contains the egg which, during intercourse, fuses with the sperm

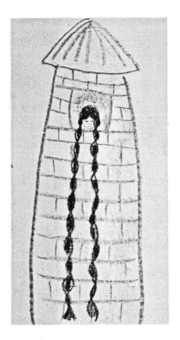

Figure 4a   Rapunzel in the Tower

containing the foetus (see Figure 4b). As the foetus grows, so the shell cracks
and in time, the infant is born. Normal birth stops there, but I have gone
further, for I have given birth to myself. This means that the inner, childish
'me' has had to grow, to meet the apparently mature outer 'me' (my visible
self) in order to lessen the discrepancy between the two. However, contrary
to my expectations, my 'renaissance' hasn't left me with totally 'brand new'
feelings, for I have had to go through a mourning process, mourning for the
loss of the advantages of remaining a child.

But this is not all, because I have got this 'thing' about shedding my outer
body which has something bad about it. The growing 'me' needs a fresh,
new covering, one of which I will not be ashamed. What this entails is for
the inner 'me' to grow just a fraction beyond the outer covering which will
then crack and be shed. I strongly feel that mourning won't be worked
through until I've buried something of myself that I don't like. Crying for the
child I'm losing is just not the issue, because 1) the child will always be there
to fall back on. It will never die and 2) this child is pure, clean, unscathed by
external forces, for it has always been shielded by the outer carcass which
now had to be shed. My point is that the child can't be the object of
mourning, for it is a positive growth. What is frightening and anxiety-

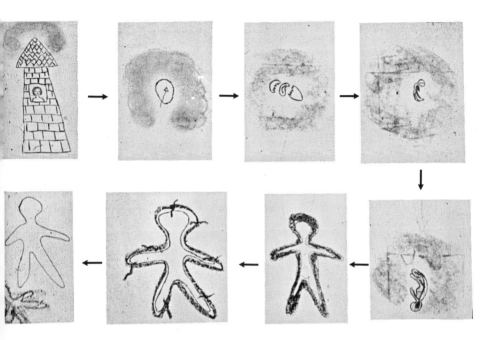

Figure 4b   Growing Child Shedding Carcass

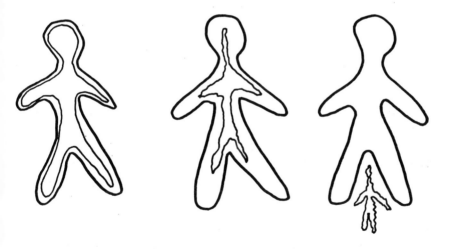

Figure 5   Outer Shell-Excreted Me

provoking is exposing this child to outer forces once the carcass has been shed, for the future is unknown. Will I be able to cope with new demands made upon me? I won't know until I am in that position. It is certainly a risk, but I have to take it, because life is full of risks and decision making. And then, I might find that being an adult can be exciting and rewarding as well . . .

This is the 'me' I've lived with for twenty years: a false, misleading outer shell, protecting a helpless infant that was given no freedom of expression whatsoever, the outer 'mature' me being so much in control. This 'living by double standards' resulted in the discrepancy that has become apparent in the past year, and I realized that I would not be able to keep up my controlled 'mature' pretence for much longer. So, I decided to cut out eating, hence reducing my outer body to match my inner self. This method of solving the problem only led to further complications and proved unsatisfactory, but necessary for my growth process. I reduced myself to a foetus and I've had to grow up from helplessness at that stage to becoming independent and assuming the responsibility of womanhood.

As well as being a child, I've had to be an expectant mother who had to give birth to the child in her, in other words, let that child come out into the open, giving it freedom of expression. It is not mere coincidence, therefore, that in my ninth month of treatment, I was ready to 'give birth'.

This was a difficult experience to cope with and it was difficult:

1) to grasp that I was (and am) a mother and child at once (i.e., adult and child in one, but equally balanced and not the child predominating or the mother having more expression. Each part of me has its say at appropriate times).
2) to grasp that this is a hypothetical pregnancy. There is no baby in me, hence I must not expect to come out of the birth experience as a pin-up.

In the same way that I swallowed the baby bit by bit, it seemed to have come out 'in bits' too, i.e., in a series of bowel actions each one leaving me with an empty feeling inside or feeling that I was losing a part of me that I at once regretted and resented. I regressed into the sheltering and safety of being a child and resented this mass that was making me heavy, sick, uncomfortable and fat. I've thought about the empty feeling further and have concluded the following: this feeling was predominant after every bowel action and it is almost as though, having emptied myself out, the inner 'me' would 'collapse', hence making the gap between it and the outer me very pronounced. Hence I felt a void and a great deal of insecurity and sense of loss. What I seem to have realized and accepted is that the outer 'me' is not the carcass. Rather, the inner 'me' has been excreted and the last step, namely, the excretion of the empty, deflated inner 'me' seems to have taken place. (Figure 5)

And here is the final hurdle of the birth: discharging this empty, useless mass which is only taking up space in me. I think I've gone through it, because although I don't like my body image, I've come to accept

a) that it is mine;
b) that I am responsible for the way it looks. I've built it up from nothing (eleven months ago) to what it is now, through eating.

I feel that in order to start believing that it is a beautiful body, I need others' opinion of it and proof that it is attractive and not as 'fat' as I see it.

Another reason why I feel that the process is more realistic than the first hypothesis is that now, at the end of the process, the mature real me stands purified and it is not the unspoiled child that is exposed. I feel that I've passed that stage now. I'm not saying I'm a fully developed and adjusted adult but what I do say is that I've grown as much as I can for the time being – the rest will come as I get involved in everyday life, in relationships and situations that will enable me to prove my worth.

This is my hypothesized final step of growth: the inner 'me' growing up beyond the outer 'me', causing it to 'crack' and fall away, becoming the childlike 'me' exposed for the first time. (Figure 6) This process, I hoped, would get rid of my distorted body image that I hate so much, but things have turned out differently. With every bowel action I felt I was losing something of myself, something 'bad' that I wanted to get rid of, hence leaving me feeling 'lighter'. I felt the need, the urge to excrete my past with

Figure 6 Inner Child Born

all its bad memories, hence purifying my body and this negates the above
hypothesis, which accounts for growth but not for elimination of my 'bad'
self. Hence, I experienced the following:

ANGER

Figure 7   A Volcano of Anger

How I See It

Anger, to me, is like a hot burning volcano – a fire with the powers to destroy
and to be productive and positive. The destroying powers of a volcano
eruption are obvious, but at the same time, one tends to forget about the
fertility of the lava that bathes the slopes (hence the trees in the picture). The
same applies to anger: I have discovered that bottling it all up as I have done
is destructive in that a massive explosion is bound to result sooner or later
and such a situation is obviously harder to cope with than constant minor
eruptions or rather eruptions at the appropriate time. I consciously try to
show my anger when I feel it and the lesson I've learnt is that a dormant
volcano is potentially more dangerous than a constantly but moderately
active one. Anger expressed appropriately is definitely positive and I am

pleased to have discovered that anger does not inevitably lead to destruction and violence.

How I Cope With It

I believe that having discovered all that I've said above is one big step forward, but it is interesting to note the sequence of behaviour I have come to discover each time I get angry.

Step 1: The feeling of anger and resentment sweeps through me like a wild fire and it often gets so intense that I believe myself capable of actual physical violence. However, knowing that this would not be a constructive way of giving vent to my feelings, I go to the completely opposite extreme.

Step 2: I shut myself off from others completely, hence turning the anger inwards towards myself and punishing myself; that leads to feelings of self-pity and self-torture, and inevitably (although unconsciously at first) it is not too long before someone approaches me and questions my withdrawn state; it angers me even more because the original feeling is now coupled by feelings of possible rejection and unimportance.

Step 3: The position of isolation I impose upon myself soon becomes unbearable so that eventually I have to admit that my feeling of sadness evolved from anger originally. I find this confession therapeutic even at this belated stage and the satisfactory result of acknowledging and accepting that anger is inside me has provided a further incentive for me to try and voice it:

1) as soon after the incident that has sparked off anger in me as possible;
2) directly to the person concerned.

Anger, Loss and Hurt

Anger, loss and hurt have occupied predominant positions in my life so far and I have had to deal with and cope with the emotions involved. I went about doing that in the manner which seemed best at the time, only to find out that in fact, in the long run, I have failed. That has been a painful revelation, particularly since I channelled all my energy into trying to cope successfully, indeed to the extent of neglecting myself. It is very easy now to think of the 'if's' and 'but's' and 'should's', but that is not the point, in fact, there is no substitution for experience. It is precisely because I have dealt with the past in the way I did that new, more adequate ways of coping have come to light. The past is unchangeable but the present and the future is . . .

In all three instances of anger, loss, hurt, I have been thinking that withdrawal into my shell was the best solution, in this way I was not burdening anyone else with my problems. At the same time I was being only too willing to listen to and take on other people's worries as well.

Selfishness has never been my scene, but I have realized that I, like everyone else, have got the right to show and express my feelings and emotions, and that doing this would not be a selfish action, but a healing one. Anyway, up till now I have been ignorant of this fact, so that I have simply bottled up my feelings, letting the tension mount until breaking point, putting up a brave and strong front. Whereas, deep down, my heart has been shattered and overwhelmed by grief, pain and sorrow. Why did I not have the right to mourn my Dad openly like everyone else? True, my mother and my little sister needed a lot of strength and comfort, but didn't I too? Even the toughest piece of elastic snaps when it is overstretched, but my surroundings did not realize that (I don't think I did either). On the contrary, they thought that my pretended 'toughness' was genuine, whereas in reality, I was extremely vulnerable and needed to be anchored and comforted.

As I think about anger I realize that I have often visualized myself as a volcano that has remained dormant in spite of the many instances when eruptions could and should have occurred but were suppressed. I have always been the 'good child' so that any expression of angry frustration has always been very noticeable and frowned upon. BUT it is not because the 'volcano' has not erupted that the 'lava' has been boiling inside. On the contrary, it seems that my anger, compounded by my unexpressed feelings of grief, has been rising steadily over the years, so that instead of being subjected to regular, gentle eruptions, I have had to suffer a titanic explosion in one step, and it has become my task to try and cope with it, and devise ways of solving it. The confusion is overwhelming.

Wow! What a thing to be faced with! How do I start? Where do I turn my attention to first? Is it worth all the effort? It seems like it, because there are still lots of angers, griefs and hurts that I will have to confront in the future and that I will have to cope with in a manner different to the way I have coped with such feelings in the past. Perhaps one consolation is that I have a far greater understanding of myself and I can definitely feel that I have changed in many ways, a very significant change being that I have forced myself to learn to openly express what I feel. I don't find it such a strain doing this in the ward, where the staff actually encourage it; but will my new behaviour be acceptable outside? That question really concerns me and yet I know that I have had to and I still have to change; I could not have carried on in the same path as the one I have chosen up till now. Recognizing the flaws in me and trying to change them has been a very demanding and trying experience and I hope that the people around me will appreciate this and will recognize it as a vital and necessary step I have had to take in order to make me a better and more independent individual . . .

AN OVUM

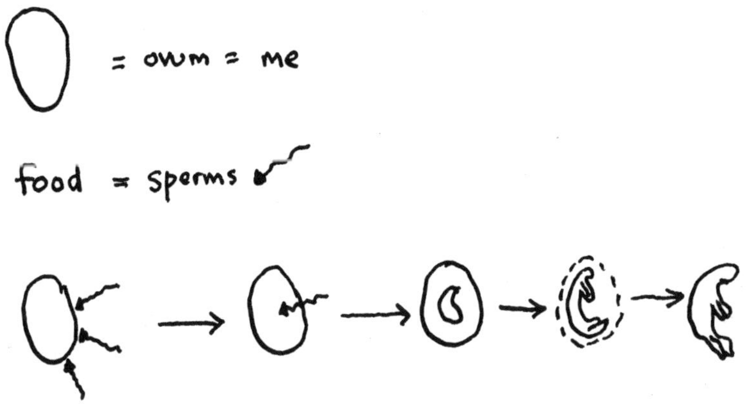

Figure 8   Giving Birth

I am an ovum that has never hatched. If, to me, food equals a plate of sperms, then although I have swallowed a countless number, my shell has been impenetrable, hence I have not allowed myself to be 'fertilized'. But the 'chick' can't remain in its shell all its life and this is the thought that has triggered off my 'renaissance' or rebirth.

Physically, I am growing and in fact I have outgrown my shell which should have hatched long ago. Emotionally and psychologically, I have resisted this because I have felt incompetent in coping with the demands of an adult, mature being. I now seem to have reached the stage where 'fertilization' has taken place even if it's been against my will, this being almost inevitable after swallowing so many sperms and I have ever since had to cope with pregnancy. The time to be born is just around the corner and the way it is happening is not like a normal birth. It is taking place in small steps, each one building up my confidence as an independent, mature woman. The whole process has been accompanied by physical symptoms of pregnancy, so that I do feel the need to 'excrete' the child in me.

I see one trap or pitfall in this whole process, however. Because I am still so obsessed with my image, I only too often take my pregnancy literally so that I tend to think that one day, I'll wake up with a slim and trim figure. But I must realize that this will not happen. The alternation will take place in my mind and in the way I view my body.

SWALLOWING AN EGG

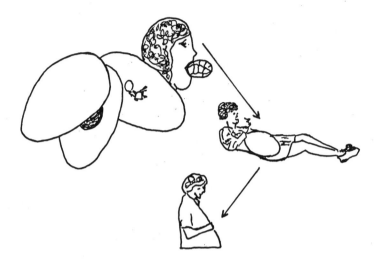

Figure 9 Pregnancy Through Food

An egg, to me, symbolizes potential life, and my phantasy (illogical like all phantasies but real enough to be meaningful and worrying) involves imagining that the egg contains a foetus which will grow in the mother's stomach once the egg is swallowed by her. This phantasy of mine does not repel or nauseate me as much as my first, barbaric phantasy of actually chewing and swallowing a foetus, but the result is still the same regardless: a 'fat', pregnant, mother-to-be with the emphasis on the first two words. I still occasionally resent the idea of my fear of pregnancy, for it goes against my lifelong wish to have a family of my own, to be a model mother and to love my children.

I still tend to think that my difficulty lies with the means of becoming pregnant rather than with pregnancy itself. But then, the 'fatness' principle crops up, and a pregnant woman's figure is not exactly beautiful, but to my mind, being 'fat' as a result of childbearing is excusable and valid, whereas obesity as a result of gluttony makes me ANGRY, RESENTFUL, HATEFUL OF MYSELF AND OF MY BODY. ONE THING I AM CERTAIN OF AND THAT IS, THAT NO ONE WILL EVER CHANGE MY MIND: I HAVE HAD A DECENT FIGURE FOR A LONG TIME NOW, AND LOOKING AROUND ME, THERE ARE MANY MORE PEOPLE WITH THINNER FIGURES THAN ME. WHY IS NO FUSS MADE OF THEM? I AM SICK TO DEATH OF BEING FATTENED UP AND OF BEING BRIBED INTO DOING IT. IT IS MY BODY AND I WILL NOT ACCEPT IT AT THIS UNREASONABLE WEIGHT. I HAVE TO BE HAPPY WITH IT AND OF THIS I WILL MAKE SURE.

DISCUSSION OF THE PATIENT'S MATERIAL
REPORTED IN THE TEXT

In this paper I am describing the observable phenomena present in an anorectic's thinking and behaviour, and showing how psychoanalytical understanding adds meaning to these observable phenomena. I later suggest implications for the treatment of anorexic patients. The focus of my initial remarks is the patient's material just reported.

The patient, Miss R, came to treatment because of refusal to eat. This refusal to eat had most important underlying reasons that we have to consider. It was not just food that mattered to her.

The question that gradually came to the surface was: to what consequences was eating what kind of food leading? By using the word 'food' I mean all sources of food, not only in the sense given to 'food', but as a universal substance that any organism, from the single cell to the most complicated organism, must obtain from another organism to survive and to grow. 'Eat or be eaten' – this is the sense we are giving to food and eating; the universal situation of all things, and not only living organisms, is 'capture or be captured'.

It is now necessary to consider a second aspect of the patient's illness. That is, her problems at the time of the menarche. In her own words she writes:

Although I denied it initially, I have had to accept the painful truth that the changes of puberty, the increase in size, shape and weight, menstruation and new and disturbing impulses, all presented a dangerous challenge for which I was unprepared and which threatened what little control I had. To counteract this fear of losing control, I resorted to rigid dieting and became preoccupied with weight.

Thus at puberty Miss R started controlling food to prevent heterosexual impulses, to prevent womanhood, and to reduce her body to childlike proportions. That is, she tried to prevent all desires and possibilities of becoming pregnant.

The next trauma was the death of her father when she was aged seventeen. She reacted to this event by a kind of manic reaction of being 'in charge' of the situation, and at the same time, in taking the role of husband and father, coping in a manic way with the demands of life. The full anorexic illness developed later, and then she was in a cachectic state, needing tube-feeding to be kept alive.

We must now consider the symptoms Miss R suffered from. First, she hated all forms of fatness. Being fat indicated she had been eating and indulging in food, and the result was an ugly and repulsive figure. Second, she experienced mother's pregnancy as mother eating and chewing the baby ánd then developing a fat stomach, which the patient felt would happen to her if she ate.

All this was connected with an impulse to overeat and get rid of the food, or to not eat and starve. Miss R became more and more preoccupied with her body image, desiring the right one, which she considered to be a child and even a foetus; this was normal size. For her to avoid food and starve meant to, first, remain a foetus, and, second, not to be a mother that chews and swallow babies. Food for the baby foetus is made of the mother herself, and this implies that the foetus has to feed on the mother's body. For the 'devouring' mother, the baby is the food that will make her pregnant.

We see here the clue to the anorectic's difficulties. The problem is a double identification of the foetus-baby with the mother, and the mother with the baby. The foetus-baby imagines that becoming an adult implies in reality eating the mother to grow up, and the reversal of this means that to be pregnant would involve the mother in eating the baby. This creation of the baby-eating mother is clearly a projective identification of the baby into the mother. The problem for the anorectic is how to be a growing foetus without eating the mother to a cachectic state, and, in the identification with the mother, not to eat the baby to become pregnant.

'Feeding' is the universal necessity for all organisms to survive and grow up. But if feeding ultimately means the destruction of the baby and mother, then it becomes the most persecuting experience possible and must be controlled at all costs. The patient, before treatment, was not able to cope with this conflict, resulting in a double disaster only avoided by not eating.

It was necessary for Miss R to solve the problem of the double identification by acting physically and simultaneously the role of the mother and of the foetus. She entered into a pseudo-pregnancy, being hardly able to distinguish between its physical reality and the phantasy. As she said, 'This was a very difficult experience to cope with'; it was difficult for her 'to grasp that this was a hypothetical pregnancy'. She added,

> . . . there is *no* baby in me hence I must not expect to come out of the birth experience as a pin-up. In the same way that I have swallowed the baby bit by bit, it seems to have come out in bits, i.e., in a series of bowel actions, each one leaving me with an empty feeling inside or a feeling that I was losing a part of me that I at once regretted and resented.

The patient needed an actual 'acting out' as near as possible to reality to work through her fundamental conflict.

Something very primitive took place before that. Miss R was near death and having to be fed forcibly to save her life, which was done by a nasogastric tube. She developed a special reaction, a very positive attitude, practically an affectionate reaction, to the tube, which was present for a long time. We can only deduce that by not feeding orally she was avoiding doing the wrong things. *In utero* the foetus is fed via the umbilical cord. Only at a later stage of pregnancy do foetuses learn how to suck their thumb, and even to swallow some meconium, presumably to get ready to suck the maternal breast at birth.

Food in this particular psychopathology is the substance of which everything at first seems to be made. Eating is the way food is obtained. For the 'foetus-baby' and the mother it means eating each other: you either eat or you are eaten. One grows and the other perishes, depending on who wins. But this also means the destruction of the other. Pregnancy through food brings further conflicts of the same order. Even sexual organs are 'made' of food and are the subjects of hate and disgust. Yet the desire for food is enormous due possibly to an innate drive or desire for it after deprivation, or both.

In several chapters in this book I have discussed the primary processes in terms of space and time. I have stressed the importance in early development of 'space-centred' thought – the relative comparison of all processes with their relative, spatial size – and I have given numerous examples. Thus this fundamental basic spatial dimension at first is the 'quantity' of everything. The sizes of instincts, impulses, drives and feelings are in terms of relative sizes. Wishing to be a baby is the reverse of omnipotence in which one feels 'I am bigger/stronger in everything than anybody else.' This kind of necessary wishful thinking based on spatial thinking is one of the main defences at this stage, and may remain so later, for instance in megalomania and mania.

One of the most important common findings about anorexia nervosa is a disorder of the body image. Anorectics maintain that they are of normal size or bigger and fatter than they really are, even when in a cachectic state. This stage of affairs is constantly remarked upon by psychiatrists, possibly as a given genetic characteristic. But another possible condition leading to this belief is not considered. The same kind of remarks apply to food with regard to quantity at first. Food is necessary to grow up, for, as we have seen, taking of food changes relative sizes, creates pregnancy, then a foetus and later a baby. The baby eats the mother, who is the food, and the mother the baby. Therefore, food is prohibited to prevent the baby eating the mother and the mother eating the baby. Greed becomes very important and is the moderator of those processes. Anorexia is the method to compensate for the bulimia. 'Greedy bulimia' must then be compensated for by anorexia – to save mother and baby from being devoured. The feelings for the mother are some primitive form of projective identification of the baby on to the mother; that is, baby-in-mother and mother are given the same impulses and phantasies as those of the foetus-baby.

It is difficult to say at what point the foetus and baby start experiencing the above-described behaviour. I treated an anorexic patient, one of identical twins. Apart from other aspects of anorexia, she also claimed great problems with her sister, which she felt began when her sister occupied the larger portion of the intra-uterine space. Later, as they were living in different countries, they wrote to each other, always claiming they were starving themselves to weigh less and thus occupy less space *in utero* than the other. Being a very good-looking girl, the patient was asked out by young men. She refused their invitations later because as soon as she ate in their presence she developed a pseudo-pregnancy. She was in group therapy, and offered to demonstrate the 'pregnancy' through eating in the presence of the group members.

Great advances have been made in the behaviour of foetuses *in utero*, and the remarkable behaviour of twins towards each other, showing likes and dislikes. Among other observations using the ultrasonic examination method, and reminding us of our patient's behaviour with the nasogastric tube, is the case of the girl with the cord tied around her at birth and many other fascinating observations *in utero*. All such studies are important to extend research on infant observations to prenatal life, and to establish a better knowledge of the possible continuity between prenatal life and life after birth.

Even more important as a precipitating factor is the sexualization of food to bring about pregnancy. The patient, to be described later, has her childhood phantasy of the mother becoming pregnant, that is, having a baby inside her, by chewing and swallowing a baby. She has described in detail the resulting development due to an increase in ugly fatness – the fatness itself being caused by increased eating to feed the baby, as well as the fatness of the mother containing the baby. Those repressed phantasies were reactivated at puberty and given full expression.

TREATMENT

The psychological material revealed by the patient offers some views with regard to treatment.

First of all with regard to food. It is obvious that the anorectic thinks she is doing the right thing in avoiding food: eating food destroys the mother, who provides life. The mother becomes exhausted, cachectic and dies, as illustrated in the pictures above. This brings about the loss of the mother, who is indispensable to the survival of the foetus and later the baby. Because the baby can only assess the desires and needs of the mother through her own feelings, that is by identifying with the mother, the latter does the same thing in reverse to the baby. Therefore, an essential condition is that the baby must not feed on the mother and vice versa. It seems that it is wrong to insist on the anorectic having to eat to save her life (or that of her mother) without the correct interpretations to make the usually very intelligent anorectic understand the difference between 'eating mother as the only food available, or being eaten'. One must insist on the anorectic's wish to do the right thing, that thinking as she does is right, granted she thinks as she does, but that the problem is to start considering other ways than that of eating mother or of oneself being eaten.

Together with this problem comes the question of the disorder of body image. This is the result of the double identification of the anorectic. First, being small means remaining a foetus-baby who shows it is not feeding on mother's body. Second, the claim that they are of a normal size is again through the identification with the mother who does not have to feed on the baby. But it further deals with the problem of the mother entering into pregnancy by chewing a baby and swallowing it, as believed by the patient, the stomach becoming visibly 'fat' and showing what has happened. The disorder of the body image has therefore another explanation, and is not really 'abnormal', granted the phantasies that lead to it; it is those primary phantasies that matter. However, those beliefs and phantasies are so strong that they really belong to some kind of delusion. This is therefore what has to be treated. Now, to do this one must have a metasystem in order to explain the system. There are two metasystems available: first, the formation of symbols and their use; second, the transference situation. I shall deal with the symbolic activity first.

I noticed that my anorectics always began to get better when they started using 'symbols' of one kind or another. I realized that they could not come out of their 'delusional system' without a metasystem into which to project and integrate and transform the material into a higher system than the delusional one. Further, the metasystem and the system must at first have been severely split off from each other. The patient was unable, although intelligent and capable of symbolizing, in one system, to symbolize within the food and size system. Therefore, it was important for Miss R to be actively engaged in the various symbolizing activities such as art, growth games and projective art. For within the delusional field, symbolic displacements and representations were beginning to take place through therapy.

There is then the transference situation to be considered. This must be divided into at least two aspects. First, the transference to the individual psychotherapist. Once the transference has started, the delusional phantasies and beliefs can be compared to the interpretations of the therapist. Positive feelings are then able to develop. It is then more possible to make use of the reparative drive, of the desire to save the mother and the babies or foetuses. Saving life arrives as a possibility in lieu of starving, sometimes to suicide. This starving is at the same time representing destruction and punishment, the law of talion.

However, the transference system would not be easy or even possible if another metasystem was not available. That is the interest in symbolic activities, even if it is to prove how right the anorexic phantasies are. The displacement of delusional beliefs to a higher form of belief makes it possible to add another, more advanced, level of thought to that of the foetus or baby. Transformations then begin to be possible, and we are then beginning to deal with the reversibility of beliefs. For instance, Miss R drew the child inside the mother, then the chick, then the parasite on the tree. These allow a comparison with understandable material as opposed to the very early somatic experience. The work of the therapist and of all the staff of the unit is geared to use this new possibility for symbolization to take place.

One important aspect of the treatment is to keep the patient alive in spite of her delusional beliefs. There can be many cases where it is necessary to use forced feeding, unfortunately against their will, in order to save their life. But we hope that during that time the patient can make some psychological progress.

Another important aspect is the question of control. Who is going to control whom with regard to what? Thus the anorectic will use every possible method to stick to her delusional beliefs and oppose those who want to alter her attitudes. This is part of the strength and size of their beliefs. Even when improving one patient said in the other system, 'I am determined not to change.' This is where the transference towards the therapist and the whole staff is so important. It is through this 'transference love' that the fortress inside the patient begins to yield, and the capacity to make use of the symbols of the metasystem enters into a new model of reality.

This is also where the question of the factor of time comes in. There is a gap between the pathological system and the other ways or systems. Slowly, the two systems or models become nearer, and the metasystems can capture the system and integrate its structures in to a larger system. Food is still necessary to keep alive and to grow, but the 'object food' is a different one from being inevitably the 'foetus-baby-mother-food'. Reality enters more into those early schemas. The baby takes more account of reality.

Another example of the persistence of early sensori-motor schemas is the attachment to and interest in the tube for feeding purposes. It is worthwhile noting here that some studies of babies observed *in utero* and after birth seem to show there is a memory of the umbilical cord which persists after the cord was tied round them. In the case of Miss R the reaction to tube-feeding would indicate that possibly there was at first a satisfactory state *in utero*. Then there is the appearance of the sucking of the thumb *in utero*, to get ready for sucking the breast after birth. Then the appearance of needs, appetite, and then the greed. Subsequently there is the reaction to the breast and sucking. Greed, of course, here is proportional to spatial comparisons. So here we have something that could be, at least partially, a genetic tendency. The identification with the mother would also be partially due to genetic determinants.

The appearance of the full syndrome after adolescence is possibly a reactivation of early patterns due, say, to hormonal factors, and partly to the environment. Due to a very important protein deficiency, hormones at menstruation are now absent. This applies to the understanding of the great anxiety of possible pregnancy, and the problem of the patient facing herself being pregnant with the baby identified with herself, and becoming a mother identified with her mother as explained earlier. It also appears very important that the fixation to space-centred thinking – the fear of growing bigger, fatter, more greedy, and vice versa staying smaller, anorexic, thinner – are extreme measures of thinking based on early spatial dimensions. Only if the factor of time can be allowed to work on the early models can space-centred thought be transformed, as indicated in other chapters in this book. This is again a vital factor of treatment.

Some similar explanation applies to the anger of the patient. An important part of the anger was against the baby, as mentioned in Miss R's accounts. That spatial factors also apply is indicated by the patient comparing the anger to a volcano erupting and its destructive fury – again strength being indicated by size. When looking at the picture of the volcano one is reminded of Betty Joseph's description of a bitten breast being transformed into an active volcano (1989). The same kind of explanations could also be applied to jealousy, which causes father and siblings to separate baby from mother, this need of mother being an ultimate need.

Another extremely important factor was the death of Miss R's father. Circumstances and certain reactions of her environments made the mourning of father difficult. Instead, and in the actual words of the patient, she had to be 'father and husband'. Thus she extended into not only the role of the father, but in her mind became father and husband, and an enormous problem of identity arose. This identification with a male figure was very much promoted by Miss R's slimming and avoiding fatness and a female figure, and, further, a pregnant one. The patient states how difficult it was slowly to recover the female figure and curves. It is also relevant to stress how much the psychological changes were in fact as near as could be to the psychophysical level and sensori-motor level. It is worth noting that this male identification may be related to the extreme physical resistance and amazing activity shown by so many anorectics, together with a marked inhibition in the production of female menstrual hormones. Possibly compensation may also take place via the suprarenals.

THEORETICAL CONSIDERATIONS

I shall consider in this material what appear to be universals for all human beings, and in what way some aspects have gone wrong in the present case. The most fundamental aspects of development after fertilization is uterine growth. I will only consider some factors involved in our case material. The first factor that comes to mind is food. Food is provided by the mother, first via the placenta and then through the breast (leaving out bottle substitutes). Both *in utero* and at the breast this food supply is coming from a part of the part-object, not the whole object, the mother. This is to my mind one of the universal and fundamental factors. Without that splitting of the source of life the destruction of the source cannot be avoided, and in the case of the patient, somewhere that system has gone wrong. As cases of anorexia nervosa are about ten times more common in females than in males, it would seem that the defect is connected with the female sex principally, as the mother is the only source of food. I have also been interested in the situation when anorexia happens in men. Working at one time in a very big mental hospital, I asked my colleagues how often they had seen male patients with the delusion of being pregnant. Their answer was astonishing: 'How many cases do you want?' I was immediately provided with three patients, one of whom had simulated pregnancy by filling his trousers with food. I will not expand further on this except to mention the case of Schreber, who essentially had to be transformed into a woman to give rise to another race of men.

That this need for eating appears *in utero* seems to be indicated by the foetus having to suck his or her thumb in order to 'know' how to suck the breast immediately after birth. Swallowing the meconium could also be an indication of the need for food. After birth, crying for food when hungry (and other needs connected with feeding, such as contact with the mother at the breast and in her arms) is of course a rule. So we can see how important is the confusion of the part-object and the whole-object.

It is interesting to note that the first Greek philosophers were interested in the fundamental matter of the universe, which was water for Thales, air for Anascimenes and a kind of ether, or *apeiron* for Anaximender.

The destruction between part-object and whole-object seems to be fundamental in the experience of being one with, or separated from, mother *in utero*. The conduct observed as judged by new evidence in uterine life and at birth seems to indicate that the process of distinguishing the baby from the mother has started already from the beginning and is a fundamental process.

Obviously the role of father seems to be an important factor in this differentiation. One question is, where is father coming in? Is it a kind of genetic ontogenic process existing from the beginning, or is it only beginning with the advent, say, of the Oedipus complex? This implies considering the phylogenetic inheritance of the combined parents.

Is the coming in of the father a new event, however early it takes place, or is there an equally early process of separation of the phylogenetic combined parents, a genetic constitutional tendency? Some schools of psychoanalysis are now considering a view that would imply a kind of gestalt aspect of the combined parents. An accurate exegesis of Melanie Klein's view seems to imply that she was in favour of leaning towards that hypothesis.

This leads us now to the question of the first appearances of spatial factors and of symbolic activity. Space and time elements are slowly being constructed and structured step by step. It stands to reason that the first steps of this 'mind construction' will depend on what factors are available, and a reciprocal action is inevitable. First, all measures depend on relative spatial dimensions of sensori-motor systems, and then somewhat later on their representation by images and symbols. Small and big, appetite and greed, weak or strong impulses are all dependent on relative spatial dimensions.

Then time is slowly elaborated upon. At first, for instance, a long time is a long distance, until speed comes in and therefore time. The same applies to objects and their domains, the importance of each domain being limited by its size. The passage from sensori-motor schemas takes place through most elementary representation. There are iconic images and then symbols. This very early domination by early spatial factors is beautifully illustrated in our clinical example in which the importance of food is strictly connected with the relative size of the foetus-baby and mother. The size of the hunger and food satisfaction also are similarly connected. Greed is proportional to relative spatial size. Part-objects, for instance, food being not the whole but an acceptable part of mother, are not yet achieved, and we deal here with infinite experiences (Matte-Blanco).

Omnipotence used as a defence of the small against the power of the bigger one depends again on primitive spatial measures. Indeed, at that stage Freud would be great by his physical size, and not by his metaphorical and then intellectual greatness.

It is necessary to return to the question of the combined parents. Using our clinical material we know that the death of Miss R's father played an important part in an exacerbation of her symptoms. It was not possible to introject a dead father and transform him into a good memory, that is, into a good inner object. Instead, a regression to early food and spatial dimensions took place. Having to introject father was equal to eating father and actually becoming him. But that also means that the father's part in separating the combined parents into their individual components could not take place further. This increased the difficulty of the father image becoming a separate unit from the mother. The vicious circle was re-established.

This leads us to the use of splitting by the patient in the early model, which prevented the use of more advanced models for that split-off part. This is the use of a metasystem towards further construction of the system in develop-ments, that is, anorexia nervosa. At first the intensity of the impulses seems to have prevented an extension of the domain of actions of that split-off primitive domain because of the enormous anxiety that paralysed going forward to disaster instead of newer progress; it was split off and suppressed. Further, the role of the male, that is father, is being repressed. To understand that, we must examine the separation of the combined parents and the relative role of the father as well as that of the mother.

The father or the male does not directly help to rear the foetus and baby, he helps with his sperm to allow the ovule to do that. The female develops *in utero* and feeds the baby physically. The male has helped the future human beings (or other animals in nature) to develop by one special stimulus, the sperm. A similar process, I think, applies to the elaboration of the beginning of images and symbols, starting with concrete representations. The penis provides the first model. Its functions are complementary to that of the breast. When the infant, starting from mother, looks for another object, the father, he must create a link between the mother and this new other object – a 'bit' of the first object must be put into the other object (not to lose mother completely) and impart some of its qualities. They are transformed and become part of one of the first important metasystems. The penis thus becomes also a primitive symbol; it represents something else. The processes continue to evolve, until later 'logos' is achieved. The female is the semantic content, and the male the container or indicator or symbol of the contained plus what it adds to it. (See the example of the Tower in our patient's description.) So the penis or phallus becomes what the French and Lacan call '*au nom du père*' ('In the name of the father').

The description of the mechanisms of the illness anorexia nervosa takes us to consider what aspects of those mechanisms also apply to normal development and where they differ from the pathological. I suggest that the early structures we have described apply to everybody; they are the universal, fundamental basic structures followed by the developing foetus and baby. It is the importance of certain abnormalities at certain stages of development that matters in pathology. For instance, the extent of the splitting or the size and strength of the impulses, say of greed. It is an abnormality of those structures that leads to psychopathology. A defect in the domain of symbol-formation may lead perhaps to schizophrenia. A case example is given in this book (see Chapter 8).

What I want to stress is that psychoanalysts have to analyse the very early mechanisms, the very early sensori-motor schemas, especially the space-centred structures, to be able to alter pathology. It would be very difficult to understand how the analysis, say, of the late Oedipus complex could alter behaviour without at least considering what has happened before, as described for instance in this paper. Those are at first the universals and fundamentals of developmental process as well as, of course, the later structures participating.

It is also important here to discuss the role of genetics and environment. In my paper on reparation (see Chapter 13) I have already discussed that subject to some extent. As shown in the present case there can be no doubt about a genetic contribution. Some structures and mechanisms have been affected by genes in the pathological process; they cannot be entirely attributed to environment. The genes are setting a pattern to the form the illness took. Cases of anorexia are alike in many ways.

However, at what levels can genes be interfered with by the environment? The answer is at least at two levels. First by causing abnormalities at the level of the structure of the genes themselves, and second in the development of normal as well as of pathological genes. No normal genetic tendencies can develop without some kind of environment, sometimes favourable and sometimes not. This is not only understandable for the development of normal genetic endowment, but also in the case of a pathological contribution by the genes. We have to consider the treatment of some somatic illnesses where it is possible to make good for the defective genes without a cure for them. The same applies to psychic derangement of the personality, behaviour and underlying phantasies and structures. The prejudice is to declare the postulated impossibility to do so in psychological illness if there is a genetic tendency present. Without Freud's mysterious jump from soma to psychic and vice versa the psychological and psychic world could not exist. It is at that level of representation that psychotherapy takes place, a vital place to influence by environment the future development of the psyche. This is why we must take and give full importance to the phantasies of the patients, to know how they have gone astray. They tell us what to do, how to treat and do reparation.

This point can be illustrated clinically with our present patient. We have seen that Miss R had to go through a pseudo-pregnancy to be able to bring about the separation of mother and baby. She writes:

This was a very difficult experience to cope with and it was very difficult:
1) To grasp that I was (and am) a mother and child at once (i.e. adult and child in one, but equally balanced and not the child predominating or the mother having more expression).
2) To grasp that this is a hypothetical pregnancy. There is no baby in me hence I must not expect to come out of the birth experience as a pin-up. In the same way that I have swallowed the baby bit by bit, it seems to have come out in 'bits' too, i.e., in a series of bowel actions each one leaving me with an empty feeling inside or feeling that I was losing a part of me that I at once regretted and resented.

She had to go through this sensori-motor experience of pregnancy and birth, and as well seems to have used a model or metasystem of a different level, that is, the excretory system.

We have here perhaps the most important of combined figures, that of the mother and the infant which has to be separated to establish the identity of each component and allow the foetus and infant to develop normally separately. This illustrates the point of view of Melanie Klein negating an early distinction of subject and object. It is in the early appearance of an object relationship (of a kind) in the foetus and still more in the baby that the separation of the combined mother-infant structure can take place. The sensori-motor schema and its representation, however primitive, is the necessary place to begin. Somewhere in his writing, René Thom mentions a distinction with regard to evolutionary theories dealing with orthogenesis being the recapitulation of phylogenesis in a linear unfolding and comparing this with a possible more economical model when there are two aspects to satisfy in the same process, say the development of male and female characteristics. In phylogenesis the process starts with the two potentialities, and one and the other in the course of their unfolding separate into the two separate entities.

Perhaps therefore, as was suggested, a mechanism of that kind is at work with regard to the combined mother-child structure, the combined parents, the combined male and female entity, the subject–object structure, the part-object and whole object and so on. I have touched on the mechanisms used to separate those combined structures and tried to describe their action. The continuity of the passage from uterine life to life after birth seems therefore to be of great importance to the anorectic. This has been shown through Miss R's own writings and the psychoanalytic meaning which I have given to them in this paper.

The latest news of this brave and intelligent patient is as follows:

> It seems that she is reasonably well, but still perhaps somewhat food- and weight-conscious. Her greatest source of pride is being the mother of three children, five, three, and one and a half years old. In addition, she is running her own personnel consultancy.

NB: The 'special nurse and therapist' is called Patsy McDougall.

POSTSCRIPT: THE RELATION BETWEEN ANOREXIA AND BULIMIA

Becoming anorexic is a defence against bulimia. In these writings by a bulimic patient we see the difficulties with which he is struggling.

'Opposite of anorexia: continuous craving for food, specifically fattening within very short space of time. I ingest a whole loaf of bread, ½ lb butter, knifefuls of sauce, plates of Weetabix, bran, cornflakes, mixed up together in an indigestible mixture (except that I have a cast-iron digestive system and rarely feel sick or ill). Even when stomach bloated and distended, absolutely satiated with food, still compelled to gorge . . . Compulsive and continuous gluttony.

'Almost as if deliberately making myself ugly with obesity, disfiguring my once good figure with gargantuan meals, covering it with layer upon layer of adipose tissue.

'I eat from morning til night, and during the night as well: my use of language is quite literal – not figurative. However much I eat, I still feel starving and can think of nothing but food, and consuming it as quickly as possible, as much as possible, in the shortest possible time. After huge intakes of food, I then proceed to dream about food and eating, and, upon waking, immediately crave more food. So begins the cycle all over again . . . I constantly have to rise during the night because my desire for food prevents my sleeping.

'I eat anything and everything, frequently too hungry and impatient to eat immediately, to wait for something to be cooked hot which would, in fact, be far more appetizing and satisfying.'

5   A GROUP OF ANOREXIC AND BULIMIC PATIENTS

The purpose of this group for anorexic patients was to try to find out in what way psychotherapy in a group could help these women to voice their problems and enable them to become more conscious of their deep phantasies. The other purpose of the group was to discover if these patients could communicate with each other and enter into a transference relationship not only with the therapist but with each other and the group as an entity. It was hoped that this would be a new experience for them.

These notes on eight sessions of a group of patients, in their twenties and diagnosed as suffering from anorexia nervosa and bulimia nervosa, are reported as written spontaneously after each session. The patients were being treated in the special unit of Groote Schuur Hospital. The members of the group were four adolescents whose fictitious names are Sarah, Jane, Betty and Mary. The group was watched by the staff, that is, doctors and nurses involved in the treatment. The staff found the experience very helpful to them. (The work of this unit has already been described in Chapter 4; it would be helpful if that chapter was read first, and the dynamics of the patients compared.)

As the material that unfolded in these sessions is recorded in more or less full detail already, I will simply comment on what I thought the contributions of those patients meant and the reasons for my interpretations.

FIRST SESSION

Sarah talks about how unhappy she is, cries. Others also are unhappy. Mother does not understand them. Then lots of jealousy appears. Mary says Sarah and Jane should go on their own and she and Betty and I (Dr R) should stay together. They talk about the difficulty in making contact. Betty and Sarah could make contact more easily when in adjacent rooms, they could not see each other and could communicate by tapping on the walls and by writing on bits of paper.

I interpreted how it is safe to communicate when protected by walls of room. They agreed. I then described how they all replaced the wall by a psychological wall by isolating themselves. They agreed and a great deal of talk followed.

An interesting discussion then took place about big and fat being the same. This was felt by the two big girls, Betty and Sarah, while the two small ones, Jane and Mary, do not think big and fat the same.

Also, people – mother, for instance – make them unhappy when saying they look better or have put on weight. They do not want to look well because nobody will realize how unhappy they are.

SECOND SESSION

The young women felt very persecuted by the visits of the staff in their rooms without their knowledge. Finally after a great deal of talk I pointed out that, even if they had been badly treated, we could also consider what others felt the group members did to the others, so that we could also try to understand the feelings of the others. They all talked about what they did to their mothers instead of what their mothers did to them. All the girls are guilty about what they do. They try to control mother by food. Also sibling jealousy begins to appear. As a topic, they all complain more and more about how unhappy, depressed, lonely they are. I repeatedly point out that although food plays a definite role in their troubles, what matters is their sadness, depression, loneliness. No matter what they do with food, it is the reasons for their loneliness that matter. A great deal more of their relationship to mother comes out in the discussion. Many are crying as they speak.

THIRD SESSION

The session is started by Sarah, who gives an account of her terrible marriage with an alcoholic sadist who tortured her, and at times, with a gun, threatened to kill her. She then became pregnant with twins and went back to her mother. It seems food then started to become important to her. I again stress that without knowing how they became depressed, unhappy and lonely they could not be helped. They talk about how immature they are and dependent on mother. It is mentioned by Jane, who says that people say she is hard and composed and has no feelings, and this is the opposite of what she wants to be. Mother is so unhappy Sarah wanted to 'mother' her especially at the time of her mother's divorce. Betty burst into tears – she was so unhappy when she tried to leave home to take up nursing. It was such an ordeal that she returned home and never wanted to leave home again. Mary says how mother never wanted to let her have her own life. Mother always overprotected her. If she went to a party, mother always accompanied her. However, Sarah managed to show that if Mary had wanted to, she could have gone to parties even if mother controlled her. Sarah said Mary herself had chosen not to do things. Mary acknowledged this. Then there were many revelations about terrific sibling jealousy regarding all three of them; it was very marked. Jane felt very guilty that her mother preferred her and lavished love on her and not her two siblings. She was very tearful as she described this.

FOURTH SESSION

Sarah talked about how difficult it was to know what to do when trying to understand her feelings. She made a long recital of difficulties, focusing on deciding which food to eat when there is a choice, and feeling relieved if mother decides. Jane and Mary join in and talk about who takes on responsibility in their lives. Throughout the session Betty refused to join in. (I only learnt afterwards that her therapist was away, and she had been upset by the role-play of a traumatic game of rape.)

I continued interpreting and reinterpreting how food is the index of the impulses, and returned to greed as the motive behind their actions.

Mary says she tried to force her sister and brother to eat while she herself was not eating, even bringing food and sweets for them and waiting for them to finish before she ate, and eating less than them. Immediately Jane tells of her own similar behaviour, and Sarah describes how she forced her children to eat what she wanted even when they did not want to. She added that she said to them, 'Look, I want to please you and you reject my kindness.' Also, making food last was very important. I repeatedly tried to bring Betty in but she refused; she said she did not want to participate in the group. Others said how she had cut them off during the week. Finally, Betty said she felt so fat compared to the others that she did not want to be here.

Repeatedly I point out that fat was an indicator of the greedy impulse. I pointed out that Sarah and Betty both have binges and then vomit, while Jane and Mary are said only to want not to eat, thus not be fat. However, those last two patients have also said that they forced their siblings to overeat (Mary only succeeding with her sister, not with her brother, who was too strong for her). This was acting on displacement of their greed to somebody else, as we saw before, to avoid responsibility.

Then I pointed out that we had talked about people and brothers and sisters and children situated outside them. I added that Sarah had been pregnant, and what about being pregnant and having to know how much to eat for feeding the babies inside? Mary said she would eat enough if she were pregnant, but does not want to be pregnant. Jane said she would eat. Sarah said how much she wanted at the time to be pregnant, and tells all sorts of stories about it. She says how she only had fantasies of eating nonstop, all the time. During her pregnancy there was a good pretext for eating in order to feed the babies inside. There was no thinking about how to get thin afterwards. Then Sarah said she dreams such a lot. She cannot remember everything, but she had a dream of being at breakfast with other patients, especially Jane and Mary (the two thin ones), and dreaming of an enormous jar of marmite. Betty cannot stop laughing at that, but Sarah refuses to say anything else other than to mention the enormous size of the jar. Mary then tells a dream.

I point out that we have mentioned size as a pointer to the size of greed, and even the dream says so. It also appears that marmite was getting low at the breakfast table, adds Mary. But Sarah says she thinks it is because she can eat marmite without guilt instead of jam. I point out that there is the good food, jam, and the bad food, marmite. Sarah says 'Yes. Shall we say the salty jam and the sweet one?'

Jane then takes up the theme of pregnancy and says she dreamed of being pregnant, especially of going into labour. She would quite like having a baby, but her mother kept on saying, 'That is all right, it is very nice, you will enjoy having a baby', and that annoyed her and made her oppose the idea of a delivery. She commented she would really enjoy having a baby.

I in my turn commented on having babies and being born and starting to grow up different from what they were.

They walked out with Betty walking apart from the group. The two 'groups' went in different directions.

FIFTH SESSION

The group was all about control. Sarah talked about how much she had been thinking since the last group about her mind and control. She gave a remarkable account of how she had thought in a thorough way about her controlling impulse from childhood through to adulthood. She had begun to think more deeply about her headaches and the pills she would take for relief. She had headaches until her children were born, then they stopped. Later, when her headaches returned she was given pills. But she gave up the doctor's pills and had only her own pills; she would keep no other pills in her bag. When Sarah looked at her pills she thought, 'Oh, I have not had a headache yet', and then the headache would return. The most important point she wanted to make was the 'totality' of her impulses, thus 'Eat nothing or eat all, binges or nothing, the same with everything'. She gave an example later that she could not pass water at all for a test – all or none – Jane talked about her own controlling being as 'totally' as it could be, but more connected to cleanliness. Later she talked about her brother crying, how difficult he was, and then finally removing herself and playing in her own corner. She was thin and small at birth, and was overfed with porridge and became podgy.

Mary was also pressed to relate her own experiences about controlling. She always refers to her brother on these occasions and now related how he was a mother's boy, not playing but sitting on her lap. It is important to note that Betty refused to talk throughout the session. She did not respond to anything that was said.

At the very beginning of the group Jane had started by saying how worried she had been by the idea of greed. She had never thought of it like that, and realized one could. Later I used this by saying to Betty that the mouth does not only eat but talks, among other functions. Perhaps talking for her is eating, as she said she did not want to be in the group because she does not want to talk about food and others do. She rejected this interpretation. After Sarah and Jane had talked about headaches, Mary said that she too had headaches when tense, adding that with the headaches she had a feeling of some distortion of her face, she also felt that her teeth were moving. She said she knew they were not moving but it felt like that. (She could not be certain whether or not her teeth did move.) On exploring further, she said her teeth were moving up and down and the feeling was mostly in the gums. 'Chewing and biting', said Jane and Sarah.

The other theme was sex and pregnancy. Sarah talked a lot about her past boyfriends and how enjoyable it was. Now she is not interested in sex. Jane said she was interested and would like to experience sex, would like to have children. Mary said she did not know anything about this. In fact, until a fortnight ago she had no idea of sex but then was given books to read. Betty's only contribution was that she had a boyfriend.

They all talked about controlling the boyfriend or husband. The fear of Mary was to be left at home by her husband, who would go to parties and drink. I said I felt that the group, by talking about sex and boyfriends and marriage, was talking also about a baby being born in the group. What was it like in the group to have this birth. When Jane asked for an explanation, I said I meant they were going back to the baby they were, to when they were born, and now this baby was appearing in the group. I wondered what kind of a baby it was – good, bad, greedy, sucking or biting or crying. That was understood at least by Jane and Sarah. What would the baby grow up to be? Then I brought the idea of a break at Christmas. They only talked about Christmas, but not of facing the Christmas break.

SIXTH SESSION

Betty started speaking again by saying she has realized that she is terribly upset by people saying that she should replace her preoccupation with food by interest in people. She cries, saying she feels she can never change, feels desperate. Others agree, saying other people do not stop eating.

In the rest of the group meeting I insisted on the necessity of knowing what state of feelings the food could only temporarily satisfy, but never permanently. Loneliness emerged, terrible loneliness. When I attempted to look with them at the loneliness itself they were all lost, describing only despair. However, slowly, by my helping them to stay with the subject, they were enabled to look at the loneliness. There was the necessity of 'totally being' forever with a satisfying object, but they did not know which was the satisfying object. Mary was very good at expressing how she wanted all the attention, trying to prevent mother from giving attention to her brother. She wanted mother all for herself, and then felt guilty about depriving her brother. Mary then described how mother was so controlling and did not let her grow up.

I introduced 'the baby' and 'the baby' or infantile way of thinking. A part of them is 'baby' and does not know of adult ways, but only infantile ways of satisfaction. We talked more and more of 'the baby', and then I introduced the evidence of wanting to remain small, to have mother all for themselves, which was shown by jealousy of their younger siblings. That went well. Jane said that the only way of having mother forever was to be in mother's womb. But before that Betty had said, 'What you are telling us is that we have been thinking in a wrong way, and we have to give up this way of thinking', to which I agreed.

Then I pointed out how they had last time talked of total control of parts of their body as well as of mother. I suggested that the way to remain a baby and to have a total relationship with mother was to prevent the body from growing: no breasts, no periods, no body fat, nothing that made them be a woman.

Then Sarah burst into uncontrollable tears and finally said this talk of babies upset her terribly. She wanted to shout and tell me to shut up. Then she told about two abortions she had.

During the group I made several references to what they might feel about my confronting them with painful feelings. Was I a hurtful, sadistic person who was putting them into that painful state without believing I could help them to find ways of solving problems? Finally they had gained a certain degree of hope and we stopped. I told the staff afterwards to be alert to the patients on the ward.

SEVENTH SESSION

Betty despairs. She protests that she never will change. The group's attention is centred on her. Her stubborn, fixed attitude goes on, and then they tell her there is no question of making a vow of never eating but she says, 'But that is why I am here'. Then Sarah talks about babies and feeding. She says food and mother are the same, that is, the taking in of the 'mother food'. Then she says she is replacing food by people and enjoying it.

Mary despairs about being able to help Betty (who in fact has created a feeling of paralysis in the whole group). At this point I invite the others to talk about their own feelings and experiences.

Mary says she does not want to see her mother or go home. She feels irritated and rebellious. Later, when Jane had talked about father coming back from abroad I mentioned father and I turned to Mary, who had mentioned her dislike of mother before. Her response was amazing: she said 'Father' with a grimace of dislike, then said how she disliked her father in spite of his attempts to be good to her. Lately she has been thinking she does not want him as a father. She describes how she can't get on with him. He is clumsy, too big, and she can't stand him around her. Then came the crisis with Betty. I pointed out that I could place the others in their families with their likes and dislikes, how they grew up, but not Betty.

Sarah said to Betty, 'I think of you as an orphan.' 'Same with me', said Jane. Then Betty, under pressure, looked down, and began sobbing and sobbing. She talked about hating her mother, of having tried to make father hate her mother, and then how angry she had been with her father for criticizing her mother. She (mother) is good, and she cries about her and her own badness.

I interpreted to her that now we could see the bad part, and her insisting on it, and that it was that which she thought she could not change. I added that this bad part was causing a desert around her. Then I said that unless there was a good part, she would not be feeling guilty and sad about the conduct of her bad part.

EIGHTH SESSION

Jane was absent on holiday with her father.

In this group Betty was again mostly the centre of attention. I used the empty-chair analogy to illustrate an action causing emptiness. Betty talked about her mother, her hatred of mother, how mother beat her and humiliated her when she was a little girl by putting nappies on her, or removing her clothes and leaving her naked. However, all the time she was saying that she could not see the relation to emptiness, the absence of the wanted one. But later she talked about writing to her mother or of explaining her feelings by talking and drawing, 'I am not me', to describe a dark hole of hatred. She also talked about a dream: her mother was dead and that meant God was dead, and thousands or millions of people did not know. She said how powerful mother appeared to her, she was God to her. I pointed out to her what emptiness was. There was not even God left to refer to. She said how religion and going to church had become repulsive to her, she could not stand it.

She cried and cried about the impossibility of ever accepting such a mother as hers. 'Don't want to, don't want to, can't, can't', she said. After she cried for some time, I asked, 'Who helped you most in your life?' She replied, 'Kate – Kate is a friend, a marvellous, kind, love-giving friend.' There was a nice smile on her face about Kate. Throughout the session, I had brought Sarah and Mary, who were communicating well, into the conversation. At this point Sarah burst into tears, saying that there was nobody to help her. At first her father helped, but her mother became jealous of her relationship with her father.

Betty said how marvellous her father was, with a smile on her face. Mary said how much she would like to have a father like the others.

Sarah, still tearful, talked about her father in the past. I asked, 'When did he die?' She said he is not dead, he lives. I pointed out how strange that she had conveyed so powerfully that he was dead. She said, 'Yes, he is dead in my mind.' I pointed out how our phantasies can be so strong as to almost externally make somebody who is alive dead.

Then we talked about Sarah loving her children and her children loving her. I turned to Betty and asked about who helped her young siblings with mother's behaviour. She did not reply to this question. (I had previously learned that she had dreamt three times of helping her siblings and taking them away from mother.) I ended by saying how much food was being replaced by human feelings.

DISCUSSION

In the first session the group members talked about being unhappy. They cried, complained about their mothers, about jealousy, about difficulties in making contact, about food and differences with regard to being fat and big. They spoke of the unbearable experience of being told they are better, which to them meant that no one understood that they are so unhappy.

Talk about these quite conscious feelings, typical of the anorectic and bulimic, was associated with the emergence of much important unconscious material. I was then able to use this material to make connections which they had not so far made. For example, their statements about communicating by tapping on a separate wall allowed me to point out the crucial significance of the metaphorical wall that they had erected between themselves and other people. They agreed that this formulation had important new meaning for them. It is tempting to think of the mother's abdominal wall when in the womb, and the sounds of external noises accompanied by the soothing sounds of the mother's heartbeats.

But this also allowed the therapist to suspect the reasons for the claustrophobia: that external people were dangerous, that the mother was the most dangerous one, that being fat or being big was to be avoided by all possible means, that food therefore was both denied and something dangerous, and that people not understanding that situation were making them unhappy and miserable. The claustrophobia and claustrophobic consequences indicated that they could be referring to the safety and danger of being a small one inside mother's uterus, and food was one of the reasons for the danger. The difficulty was to choose an interpretation that was appropriate and perhaps leave out the other meanings. I chose the psychological wall and difficulties of contact, resulting in a poverty of poor human feelings and depression.

In the second session the theme of the uninvited intrusion of staff members into their individual rooms, and the feelings of persecution that this evoked, allowed an interpretation of the reversal of the situation as well, that is, what they in turn do to the others. The result was very remarkable for they all started talking about how badly they had treated their mothers. This led to talking about controlling the mother by means of food and resenting their siblings' jealousy, this led in turn to their depression and loneliness, horrible loneliness. So I again interpreted that although food was the major vehicle of their thoughts, it was human feelings that led to depression and unhappiness and loneliness.

The interpretations left out a number of important points. For instance, in what way their treatment of the mother and its relation to food were connected. Thus food is dangerous and to be avoided at all costs, yet it is desirable, even greedily desirable. So who eats whom; who eats to grow up? Growing up means not being tiny, therefore becoming stronger and more dangerous. The reasons for being afraid of eating thus became more understandable. The question remains: what to interpret at what moment?

Without going into details of each session, I have now given an indication of the problem of choosing the apparently right interpretations. For example, how does one talk about food? Mother is the source of food, but the baby is, in phantasy, a source of food for the 'devouring' mother, who is made cannibalistic by projective identification. Who then eats whom? Food is the source of growing up and this is bad because one is separated from the mother's womb. But there is also the danger of staying in mother's womb, of eating mother or being eaten, and also, on the other hand, of being deprived of all the pleasures of the external world. Therefore claustrophilic desires bring claustrophobic consequences.

Pregnancy is so dangerous because it recreates the situation of the mother–child relationship which is both desirable and not desirable. Pregnancy equals fatness, equals baby, equals food, equals danger. Father comes in as the one who starts the pregnancy and later separates mother from the baby; thus the complex feelings about the father arise. But it is most interesting to see that in spite of its danger, the greedy desire for food is all the time present. Eating greedily and vomiting, starting to become fat and growing bigger and being pregnant. It was amazing to see the tricks of making siblings eat for them what they were afraid to eat, and the large quantities they tried to force on them. Another remarkable feature was the enormous need for controlling others and the all-or-none quality of their impulses. This also led to the difficulty of passing from the 'totality' of impulses and objects to an appreciation of distinguishing between normal part-objects and whole objects. Yet another important theme was the fundamental inability to distinguish between mother as provider of a part-object – food – and mother in her other functions. One could see how difficult it was to pass from food to people, and to the possibility of enjoying relationships other than that with food.

Despite these defences and disabilities, the underlying depression and loneliness could be approached and was voiced. As has been repeatedly described in other papers depression is the clue to the possibility of change, and was evident in the feelings of the group. But to make use of this depression it was necessary to understand 'the baby' and the original depression of infancy. This could be done by interpreting that pregnancy aroused the associated idea of a baby inside the mother. This led on to the idea that a metaphorical 'baby' might be born in the group and be helped to grow in a different and better way.

I only recorded the eight sessions presented in this paper. I think that the full feelings and impulses of anorectics have been practically presented. I have shown not only the pathology but also something of the treatment through interpretations of their fantasies, impulses, object relationships and the use of depression as the beginning of change. It is important to note the kind of special delusion about food and mother–baby relationship, and its sexualization when one comes to pregnancy.

CONCLUSION

I have shown in these sessions how these anorexic and bulimic patients were able to experience strong feelings in relation to one another and become conscious of the meanings of these feelings both through their own comments and those of the therapist. It is useful to compare their phantasies and problems to those of the individual anorectic described in the previous chapter. Both papers can, I hope, contribute to the understanding and treatment of anorexia nervosa. What was extremely useful to the patients was the emergence of depression, as well as a developing capacity to think and experience mourning and reparation. The group itself began to represent the mother and the birth of a new and more positive baby inside each of them. Although the treatment lasted for only eight weekly sessions with me, it was continued after my departure. At least three of the four patients were able to resume a satisfactory life outside the unit and resumed their studies.

6   MANIC-DEPRESSIVE PSYCHOSIS

Many colleagues have expressed a desire to know more about the actual process of psychotherapy with a patient suffering from manic-depressive psychosis. On the occasion when I spent six months as a visiting professor in a country in the southern hemisphere, I saw an in-patient, aged thirty and by now married, who was viewed by the psychiatric team and discussed after each session. The meetings took place once a week for six months, and subsequently arrangements were made for the treatment to be continued.

A SHORT PREVIOUS HISTORY

The patient – a female of twenty-two years, single – suffered from a manic-depressive psychosis. The illness began at the age of eighteen when the patient learned that her mother was suffering from breast cancer. She became depressed, was crying, tried to lose weight, lost her appetite and all wishes for anything. Following this first depression, the patient showed changes of mood and recovered as time passed on. During the depressive phases she started crying, becoming desperate and having no wishes at all. During the excitation phases the patient was talkative, confident, even exalted, and convinced that she was very erudite, cultured and could face any sort of discussion. These phases were brief and interrupted by moments when the patient was more normal, so the changes in her behaviour did not seem to have attracted the attention of her family.

At the age of twenty when her mother died, the patient became much worse. The depressive and manic phases succeeded each other more frequently, and this made her illness more obvious. She then saw a doctor who looked after her for two years.

There was an earlier history containing signs of manic-depressive illness when the patient was age fourteen. At this time she had a brief period where she felt persecuted and identified with a well-known historical character. This short manic episode did not attract the kind of attention which she wanted, for her friends made fun of her pretensions. When she was about age fifteen until the age of sixteen, she felt somewhat mystical and wanted to enter a religious order but only as a Mother Superior. The rest of her history, that is her birth and her mother's accompanying cancer, her relationship to her mother and father, as well as her relationship to her brother four and a half years younger than her, emerges in the sessions which follow. During these sessions details of her intellectual achievements, her sexuality, and her marriage will also be made clear.

Apart from ordinary childhood ailments, the patient had a left-sided ovarectomy when she was twenty. This event left her afraid of having a hysterectomy and thus mutilated. She also became afraid of not being able to have a child, and was repulsed by men.

The patient attended the psychiatric hospital, receiving drug treatment of haldol and lithium and some psychotherapy until I started the psychotherapy which is reported here. The following are verbatim transcripts of sessions which were recorded and viewed by the psychiatric team; a few have been shortened for reasons of space. A commentary describing aspects of this patient's manic-depressive psychosis will conclude the chapter.

SESSION ONE

P. I'm a courageous woman. (*Crying.*) I accept therapy with you. Yes, I'm courageous, I have a right to live . . . I'm thirty years old . . . (*Tears.*) . . . I've learnt things about myself from others – they say I'm the great lady . . . How can I address you?

Dr. R. We will see all this together.

P. I'm capable of being a comedian, of being honest. I have contradictory desires, like everybody. I want to be happy with my husband, who is very honest. I can still love, I have intelligence, I value the people who have helped me . . . I worry specially about my sex . . . People often disturb me. They seem astonishingly unconscious of this. I have breakfast with my husband. I like to live with him very much. Sometimes I feel absent.

Dr. R. And when you are with me, are you also absent, in another place? Do you run away?

P. At the meals sometimes I'm there, sometimes not there . . . but I approve of you.

Dr. R. You have said 'being happy' – what kind of happiness?

P. I was thinking in a somewhat Machiavellian way. Not only professional thoughts. I love to be in charge, power, therapy and research, I love research . . .

Dr. R. The conditions of your treatment raise certain questions even if you wish to have the treatment. I am going to be here for a short time, about five months, but I think it may be helpful for you. However, you are the one who counts and must decide about the treatment.

P. You please me. I'd like to work with you to understand what is inside, especially on the question of feeling secure. You inspire confidence in me.

Dr. R. I must explain that other people will be present.

P. It's a bit sickening, but perhaps not too traumatic to have the camera. It can help people who are watching. I hope they don't waste their time. After all, it's an art to learn to live more harmoniously.

Dr. R. We are going to look after you, and, as well, you will be of use to other people. You will speak what there is in your head and me in mine, the two of us working together.

P. Right. I'll be here at 9.15. I want to arrive at the right time, not to lose precious time, death, to act, action . . .

Dr. R. Action?

P. Yes – using the mind, to be able to make love with my husband. I'm sensual, not very capable of being sexual . . .

Dr. R. So our session will be fifty minutes – not late like this morning, as you said.

P. To help women, to bring them to my side. There are also men to think of.

Dr. R. We must also talk of the continuation of the treatment after my leaving.

P. I start with you today. I worked with somebody else before, but too quickly. One thing at a time . . . Mrs X will be able to work with me later. Better five months than to lose father and mother.

Dr. R. So you will continue after my departure?

P. Yes. I have faith in these people here.

Dr. R. We must consider the continuity of our sessions. Now let us see a bit, what has taken place this morning. Have you said what you wanted to say?

P. There will be a relation of equal to equal, a therapeutic experience without myself being the therapist, me at thirty years old. I don't know your ways of working – you have knowledge, I don't. You don't know me . . .

Dr. R. (*As patient cries.*) It is a question of growing up, helping you to be different and helping where you need help. There are important people in your head that we will consider . . .

P. There are some people who are very important to me.

Dr. R. And so, shall we start the treatment or not?

P. Let's go ahead.

SESSION TWO

P. My mother died nine years ago.

Dr. R. You are telling me your mother is dead.

P. I wished her death . . . to die. (*Tears.*) Every time at the hospital, oxygen . . . the three last weeks of her life, every time when passing the hospital I said, 'Hello, Mother'. The hospital, a prison, facing a prison. I used to dream, about death. It was important. I was happy to see a friend, then it was terrible. She died in March. I was proud to dream of my father and my mother. Three weeks she was in the hospital. I felt like a failure. Every day, all day, at her bedside. It seems that I've failed.

Dr. R. In your head, your mother has not forgiven you. You condemn yourself to a slow death.

P. Yes, in my head. And the others are also in my head, putting their thoughts in me. But I'm the judge. I've become the mother of my brother, and my father.

Dr. R. We must be precise. What mother? Not a good, kind mother but an unhappy mother, dying [lung cancer]. A very ill mother . . . her body so ill . . .

P. I've also chosen a mother that detested herself. It's her that I've become. But I've specially asked God to send me all my pain and suffering, to relieve her of her sufferings. It had to be in my body, like the cancer she had in her breast. I've had this pain. I've been able to feel it in myself, in my body . . .

Dr. R. Therefore, the mind was able to make you feel your wishes, to suffer in your body.

P. Yes . . . Many things have frightened me. A friend committed suicide. I had a dream in which I saved her life. I listened to the dream. Afterwards I saved her life by going to the apartment. Therefore, this can happen . . . *(Tears.)* . . . but I can't hate someone.

Dr. R. Therefore you cannot think, because if you think someone is dead, you can make it happen. It is important for you to know that I understand, understand what you are experiencing . . . and for the immediate moment, now, we know that you are the dying mother, and wanting her death to end this terrible pain.

P. Yes . . .

Dr. R. Not able or wanting to choose a healthy mother, but rather choosing a dying mother . . .

P. Oh, why not a loving mother!

Dr. R. Let us see what you want to get to – let us verify if we are in agreement about something, because if it is too difficult to understand what I am saying you will continue with your thoughts.

P. But I have great difficulties in following the thoughts of others . . . Yes, it's true . . .

Dr. R. If your mother was now present, would she approve of her daughter thinking of her as vindictive, really believing the law of talion – an eye for an eye, cancer for cancer?

P. It's not that. Others can respond to the Lord in their way. My mother pleaded with her husband, wanted to live her faith, but married someone who was against her faith and its church. My mother was crying. I also wanted to help the sister of my father, help her in helping others to give birth to their babies. Two thousand children! A very strong character, but a little nasty, she helped spread the idea that my mother made love before marriage. That's not my aunt's business. Her speaking like that about my mother, who is so good, so kind, so correct, has upset me terribly . . . Why did my mother prevent me from doing the same? Yes, it's my anger.

Dr. R. Many a mother suffers from this ideal of purity, but it is another thing to impose it on a daughter.

P. But I understand this. How can I know what to do?

Dr. R. In your head, what mother must one believe in? What was your mother like and how did she hope to bring up her daughter? This is in your head. Are you perhaps beginning to understand the confusion?

P. Yes . . . yes . . .

Dr. R. Something else is also very important, that is, to understand the following idea: have you thought that you can do, will do, what the mother in your mind wants you to do?

P. I've thought that my mother was suicidal, my father was also suicidal, but didn't want to do it.

Dr. R. Yes, but what about the power of your thought?

P. (Laughing a little.) If you saw my desk and how it is, I'm blocked, I'm incapable of being alone.

Dr. R. Before the end of this session we must decide about the urgency of the situation, the urgency of what we must do.

P. It's the urgency of starting work . . . My husband, my companion, we must make a start. It's as if life didn't exist. I feel guilty . . .

Dr. R. What has happened between last time and this time?

P. It's a long story . . . A girl who knew my mother had some difficulty with her memory. My mother said would you go and have dinner with them. My husband was there. We've talked together, showed photographs. I wanted to be like a baby with her.

Dr. R. We must find again all these memories. This could help from one session to another.

P. But I can't transform my husband. He's somewhat like that.

Dr. R. We have started . . . It is on the way.

P. Yes, yes. We've started.

Dr. R. So, to next week.

SESSION THREE

P. I don't seem to react. No energy . . .

Dr. R. Not enough life in you?

P. Being able to laugh, being able to give. My husband says I can give a lot in certain circumstances . . . I hope it isn't bad for him to live at his side . . . or for me.

Dr. R. Before going any further, let us first look at the time, the time we said will be 9.20 or 9.15. There is then the question how you work in the treatment. It seems to be me in your head, me knowing what happens to you, knowing you even before you were born, that is, knowing you inside your mother. Then suddenly you think of your husband. You want to give something to your husband?

P. I'm beginning to get better. There's a kind of mutism inside me. Is it better? Or is it something worse?

Dr. R. Let's see what happens to the mourning of your mother, see if it is over. If you live and you are frightened to live, what will happen to you?

P. I'm frightened I don't have the strength.

Dr. R. Let us see what you have to struggle for, and for what purpose.

P. Well, in reality I teach. Occasionally I'm aggressive . . . (*Silence.*) . . . It seems to me that I must be losing control . . . (*Silence.*) . . . Intellectually I can't teach a course . . . I must keep apart from others . . . Not enough confidence in me. I would have more chance of finding myself alone, facing myself . . . (*Silence.*) . . . Can this be forced? What can come out of this mourning? How much energy. Yet I'm certain I really have the energy.

Dr. R. To me it appears quite clear that you have used the mourning of your mother to avoid achievements. You keep inside you manifestations of aggression. For example, you have used the name of your mother saying you must not have more in life than her. You feel you should not be sexual. You have been aggressive and have said that you are aggressive. However, you need to understand other reasons for this mourning, need to avoid using mother as a way of not facing your difficulties. There is a need to learn to use her more helpfully, in other ways.

P. (*Silence.*) My mother, I must take myself in hand, my father, there has been death . . . Yes, to situate yourself.

Dr. R. Your father is dead, your mother is dead. You are alive, but you want to be dead. It is your way of being in the situation at this moment. Instead of seeing and understanding that it is not your mother or myself causing you to behave as you do, but instead being responsible for what you do.

P. I don't think it's my mother . . . It's myself punishing myself . . . What would be the other ways of facing the problem? (*Silence.*) I want to give more but I have nothing. My husband says that I'm giving . . .

Dr. R. You say 'to give' but the sentence is not finished. Give what?

P. (*Silence.*) . . . Love.

Dr. R. Give love or work or do something else, but you say you must be giving something. What?

P. But what makes me behave like that?

Dr. R. I do not know what you think you are not doing.

P. I don't make love with my husband or I don't participate. It's sad, I have only him.

Dr. R. Since always or since when?

P. Since about two months . . . But I was always having periods and I could make love. My sexuality is very repressed . . . (*Silence.*) . . . I'm thinking of caressing my husband . . . I don't speak any more . . . Not myself as a person . . . I don't find in me what to give . . .

Dr. R. I understand that you do not find love to give to your husband. What happened two months ago? Have the feelings for your husband changed?
P. (Silence.) I've been bitter against my husband not wanting to have a child for a time. I can't betray my husband . . .
Dr. R. When this crisis happened was your husband not wanting you to have a child?
P. I went through a crisis in October. I felt reproachful towards my husband.
Dr. R. But about what?
P. I'd like to know.
Dr. R. But we can at least talk about it.
P. I'm thinking of a manic crisis seven years ago. Anger welled up inside me and it wanted to come out . . .
Dr. R. How did it come out with your husband?
P. It troubles me to have forgotten . . . My husband wanted to bring more money home, wait to have children, not sure he wanted children . . .
Dr. R. You were afraid that if you waited too long you would not be able to have children?
P. I think that's played a part. My husband now wants to have children. He's waited two years, but I'm too ill at present and I don't want to.
Dr. R. Since the beginning of this session you have tried with your hand to point to your tummy. But if it is useful to try and be good, but not to have a baby, it does not help very much. What does it mean for you to be a woman, but not to have a child, to become more understanding, but not to have a baby?
P. (Crying.) I must understand myself better to have a child and to continue in life with a child. Without a child one can give to the students, have projects. But I must have a child . . . In the home it's like living death. Life doesn't continue in that way . . .
Dr. R. You have lived a 'living-death' because you did not have a child, and your husband could sense that.
P. It's more complex than that.
Dr. R. I am sure it is.
P. My sexual desires were repressed. Sex was a sort of place in which anger harboured in me, ready to come out, and then I'd lose all control.
Dr. R. To understand and feel an orgasm of love and instead feel anger, what will you do?
P. I don't know what an orgasm is.
Dr. R. You cannot distinguish between love and hate.
P. But surely those two feelings are most important.
Dr. R. Before judging, it is necessary to understand what will happen in circumstances when you could lose control.
P. When we were children, we were always afraid that my father could lose control. He had huge outbursts of anger, he could hit . . . smash the closed

door behind me . . . the control door . . . I'm always afraid of losing control, never learned . . . can one learn such a thing at three years old?

Dr. R. I understand you are meaning the control of very deep feelings.

P. I think one can . . . (*Silence.*) . . . I'm not the only one implicated.

Dr. R. Speak about it?

P. I'm afraid it will demolish me, with questions of morality.

Dr. R. You can see that you are putting in my head the child that your husband has deprived you of, your baby . . . But there is also the love of the child that your mother was deprived of when you did not love her, you remember . . . However, it is not simple. You put ideas in my head, but we have to analyse them to reach the truth. It is such an important event in your marriage, not to have a child.

P. But my husband's career also counts.

Dr. R. Yes, but there is a conflict between what is in your head and in your tummy.

P. At the present moment it's difficult, but I don't want to destroy my marriage. I don't want to bring up this child alone . . .

Dr. R. Your mother comes to mind . . . So full of life . . .

P. But I'm not capable of bringing up a child, of really choosing between my husband or me, of not taking precautions against being pregnant.

Dr. R. You show me your doubts.

P. I'm not accusing my husband.

Dr. R. Have I deprived you of something?

P. No, you're not there to facilitate my life. I must answer my questions myself. I'm afraid . . . (*Tears.*) . . . So lonely, and yet with many people present.

Dr. R. When you have said lonely, it must be a specific situation.

P. I feel I'm alone at work. I don't like work at present . . . empty . . . not professional . . . doing things at the last minute . . . I'm blocked . . . In fact, it's not really bad at all. I'm appreciated at work, but I think about death a lot. My parents are dead . . . My husband's are alive . . . I have difficulty living . . . I remain hidden under the bedspread. This morning I woke at four in the morning. My bed was a live tomb. I don't have the same power over my life. I think that my parents died young. My mother at fifty-two, cancer . . . I'm not going to be like my mother. For ten years she's been dead. In March, when she died. (*Crying.*) . . . I feel depressed like when . . . What a good child, how kind and good she is. I couldn't do otherwise. There was the hospital . . . my brother couldn't look after her, not enough women in the services . . . the collars of death . . . I'm thirty . . . Death . . . I'm afraid of what I must do to live. Her death. Not to always think one is dying.

Dr. R. You have described very well the situation: you are dying and you do not know how to come out of it . . .

P. Yes . . . Yes . . .

Dr. R. You do not know how to come out of being in a state of dying. There is no difference between the dying mother and you. You cannot feel the difference in you. You live the life of your mother, during the last years of her life.

P. I'm very afraid to look at a photograph of my mother. I've had only a few dreams of my mother, but quite often I had dreams of my father after his death. After the death of my mother it was a real desert – clear, horrible, as if I didn't love her. I must work on that.

Dr. R. You are not sure that you have loved your mother.

P. Nearly a saint, too pure, too perfect. In the last years of her life, I wrote to her, instead of talking to her, about my sexual life. I didn't dare speak to her, on untouchable morality. What could she think of sexual relations outside marriage? Thirty years . . . I can see me at forty . . .

Dr. R. At fifty-two when she died – ten years ago – you were twenty, when she died. You have lived a normal life, a 'loving' life, but in your mind it was not so pure, not so pure in your body either. Your living life was not like hers.

P. At a certain moment I was wishing her death. (*Crying.*) Every time that I passed before the hospital, the last three weeks, until the twenty-first of March, I thought she was living there, and every time that I passed the hospital, it was 'Hello, Mother', as if she wasn't dead! Mother was writing a diary for . . . Dreamt important dreams. In my body I have burst out . . . an alarm crisis and then . . .

SESSION FOUR

P. I feel so depressed . . . therapy has calmed me – what could I tell you . . . five months ahead of me.

Dr. R. Today you are more harmonious, more organized but you have said before you are in a state of confusion. Confusion means at least two possibilities and you cannot choose.

P. At this very moment who I am – me – who was I in the manic phase . . . yes, I have spoken a lot . . . I don't know any more where I'm going . . .

Dr. R. Not able to distinguish who you are yourself, who has cancer, whose bed it is, where is the coffin of your mother. But you are not the mother today, not the damaged mother, your body is not the body of mother, so what other body is it, what other thought is yours now . . .

P. My body of thirty years . . . Who wants . . . Who doesn't know if she wants to live . . .

Dr. R. It is not long that we have started . . . you think you are not entitled to have what you want . . . your mother has imposed your sexual life on you. It is she who has the right to decide for you, to settle for you the confusion between your rights and your desires.

P. At this moment I have the impression of not desiring very much . . . I'm afraid you don't have an interesting patient, Dr Rey . . . I'm feeling guilty not having anything to say . . . Same room as that of my mother . . . With my husband in the room of my parents, this is very perplexing. I think about it at night. I'm afraid to relive the depression of the time when my mother was dying.

Dr. R. And the bad also . . .

P. (Smiling.) No, no . . . because I borrowed a hospital bed to sleep in the same room as my mother . . . To hear and listen to her . . . Then my father returned to the room, the room of my dead mother.

Dr. R. How long have you stayed in the room with the dying mother? Have you stayed after she was gone?

P. Yes . . . Now I can't sleep . . . many dreams.

Dr. R. What happened when mother was there?

P. I couldn't sleep . . . When I was in therapy I used to take Anafranil . . . Dr Rey, I'm afraid to evoke those events . . . At this moment I think my husband was right to let that house go to my brother. My brother didn't want to lose the house in which our parents had invested so much . . . He bought our part . . . But my husband wanted to build a house . . . It wasn't healthy to live in that house . . . Yes, it was a part of the cause of my anguish and torment.

Dr. R. It was a powerful link, and the link between the person in a place and the place itself which the person occupies cannot always be distinguished from each other.

P. You're speaking about me.

Dr. R. Yes, of course.

P. (Silence.) . . . Dr Rey, I don't know . . . Should I have taken that path . . . *(Silence.)* . . . of my studies after the death of mother . . . I've dreamt images of my mother. Among other dreams I will or have told one to you . . . I dreamt there were calls on the phone for my brother and me. We were on a voyage, we were having a good time. We were very well, I was joyous in my body . . . I asked my father, 'Are you going to give the news to us?' . . . He doesn't answer . . . I'm reassured . . . But she died suddenly . . . It was her and not her and she didn't answer, as if she was conscious in the message of something not true . . . A somewhat painful aspect for one thirty years old. . . . This summer at my grandmother's house I was lying in the room of grandmother and there were some photographs of her two daughters . . . the photo of my mother in a frame. The frame was changed to white, a doubling of the frame. It was hope for peace and a sexual life for my husband and myself. We were liberated. There were two eyes that were looking and I couldn't tell if it was love or hate . . . I, a young woman, thirty years old . . . During the winter we were camping. I had a dream about my godmother who was calling me to say grandmother had died. She then said, 'No, no, your mother has just died' . . . But this is impossible . . . it's seven years since she's died. Has it been concealed from you?' . . . In the other dream I was crying with relief, as if she were dead. The other part of the dream was about the death of my father . . . I was being ironical towards mother, wearing short skirts, using a little bit of tissue material only . . . The dreams were related to my mother and my father . . . To digest her death . . . and there was confusion in me . . . to die . . . I'm afraid mother was superstitious. I too . . . see special things in everything . . . I'm afraid of that . . . difficulty in having definite points of view if I don't work. I must continue . . . have time to digest her death . . . I must not die . . . a confusion between her and me.

Dr. R. This is the fourth session that we have had. It seems necessary that your mother should be liberated. What is it, in your mind, from which your mother is not free? Even when your mother said, 'I love you', your mother was disapproving of certain things.

P. In the end she wasn't angry with me. It's me who was angry.

Dr. R. It is important that you should put things right with your mother, by being conscious of the care you have given her and by becoming more precise about your confusion, a confusion which is fundamental to understanding the problem of your feelings about your mother.

P. It's so far away . . . I step back . . . Oh, that camera.

Dr. R. At least we can say that this camera disturbs you just at the moment of understanding the situation, the relationship between your mother and you. You therefore miss what situation could develop between you and me in order to accomplish this task.

P. I don't know how to work on that . . . I'm not proud . . . I used to accompany her to the hospital . . . for her treatment . . . The house, the illness, the bed-coffin.

Dr. R. And you live in that house?

P. I was in therapy with Dr X . . . It was only my father I spoke about . . . I was afraid to speak of my mother . . .

Dr. R. Here you have spoken only of your mother, or nearly so.

P. I'm afraid to resemble my mother . . . Generous woman, with a sense of certain qualities.

Dr. R. There is something else to discern about your mother, about her body, her coma, like in the dream, and her sexual relations in between the dream and the awakened state.

P. (Silence.) . . . Dr Rey . . . I should write something . . . I feel blocked . . . Oh, that light.

Dr. R. That light. But there is also the mental light.

P. Yes . . . Of the parts I am afraid of . . . I have a good relationship with my husband . . .

Dr. R. A good relationship with your husband . . . but also afraid of being dependent.

P. Becoming dependent, if it happens . . . But I'm not courageous at this moment . . . I'm easily frightened . . . I'm afraid to plunge into all this. I'd like a normal time for a while.

Dr. R. There is a doubt about wanting to be normal . . . but it would be so good not to be in a state of confusion with the mother. What kind of a person would you then be, were that confusion with mother not there? We must work on that fear of who you are, a condition essential to becoming separated from being mother.

P. (Silence.) Dr Rey . . . I'm not proud . . . I have lost a session with you . . . I don't sleep at night . . .

Dr. R. What is the message that you are being given at night?

P. That you take me, all of me. That you pity me, that you sing a lullaby to me, or cradle me.

Dr. R. So you think that our session is wasted because you feel I should take you in my arms, like a little baby, and do something other than analysis. You have an enormous fear of being separated from your mother, and yet you are a little baby who has been looked after.

P. I'm discovering that I want to be a little baby cradled – protected . . . am I entitled to it?

Dr. R. We must try to understand.

SESSION FIVE

P. You've answered me with my own words.

Dr. R. Where does it come from? From your head? Your tummy? Who is going to look after all these things that are blocked?

P. Is it going to destroy me?

Dr. R. You are very worried about what you are going to bring out. Is it going to destroy you?

P. I can't continue in that way. I must come back to myself. You're kind . . . you try to help me.

Dr. R. Then I must start again with what you have already put into me. We must try to find out what these things are. If you feel you cannot look after those things, then what says that I will be able to? First, as a baby you were in the womb of mother, then the cause of her cancer, of her death [see pp. 126–7]. When you left home you were her ray of sunshine, but everything seems to have gone wrong. You have put all those things into me, and now who knows if I will be able to do what you could not do or cannot do even now.

P. You must look after me . . . It's urgent that I can do something about all this . . . I'm embarrassed.

Dr. R. Towards me. Embarrassed towards me. Somewhat like you have embarrassed your mother in coming out of her vagina.

P. Dr Rey . . . I'd like to work . . . to work with you . . .

Dr. R. Work with me, yes. But we must understand why you try to put everything in me that has made you unhappy.

P. It's not only my mother . . . My mother . . . My father . . . I wish to make use of these moments with you.

Dr. R. Then let us see who else there is besides mother and father.

P. I don't want to accuse anybody, Dr Rey . . . First of all they're dead . . . My father is dead, my mother is dead . . . There is no reason to be in that state.

Dr. R. Yes, maybe. But you are in that state, aren't you?

P. It's very embarrassing to work in these surroundings,

Dr. R. Yes, I understand that you feel there is the camera, the people – all that is preventing you from letting go.

P. I'm very dependent . . . Not understood . . . I hurt those who I love.

Dr. R. And you were good also. You were the ray of sunshine for your parents.

P. To my mother.

Dr. R. You are afraid not to be a wife to your husband and a child to your mother.

P. It's especially at this non-verbal moment . . . difficult to talk . . . in part it's not possible.

Dr. R. What is it that can be communicated without speaking?

P. I don't feel I'm good. I'm not a good candidate for you.

Dr. R. Without speaking then, perhaps bad actions without words, perhaps causing misery to many people.

P. I'm not a bad person.

Dr. R. I understand that, but I do not know all.

P. Listen, Dr Rey. All I can do at this moment is to go to bed . . . It's normal . . . Never able to listen to myself, to work.

Dr. R. Not being a wife to your husband by not being what he desires . . . We could say that you do this with me for you said you could not manage to be the patient that I wanted to have.

P. I need so much to be loved, like everybody, to make a good analysis . . . I'm capable of nothing.

Dr. R. You have concentrated on that which you think you are in the head of all the others. In the head of your mother you are not a good daughter. You have sexual desires that she did not approve of, and then you nearly caused the death of your mother in her womb . . . And you also put things in my head – you think you are not the patient that I wish to have. And you allow your husband to have no part of your body lower than the head. In what place, where, are you at the moment?

P. I would like to discover who I am. Me – who am I? At this moment I feel negative . . . I feel I'm blocked as an individual, not intelligent in anything . . . I'm negative . . . it can't go on like that . . . I have feelings of love for my husband . . . all of me is anaesthetized.

Dr. R. You said you were not able to show love with your head and body.

P. I love him but I can't make love to him.

Dr. R. You show love in your head, but your body does not experience sexual excitement . . . love.

P. It's the name of mother . . . all these feelings I've known.

Dr. R. You speak of you in the body of others. This is how you function, make love and so on.

P. Yes . . . Before that I was living.

Dr. R. You do not say: it is me who does that – it is always the others. You do not bring in your role because of the mental and physical anaesthesia.

P. No hope for me.

Dr. R. You are once more coming back to the others, no hope for you.

P. It would be necessary to demolish myself, start from zero, not to accuse everyone of what I am . . .

Dr. R. Yes, but this is what you are doing. You are responsible towards yourself for what you are. It is imposed by you, maybe for good reasons, but you have done it, but you are conscious that it is you who has decided that you would be non-functional and all the rest.

P. It's me who has imposed this behaviour on myself . . . (*Silence.*) . . . I feel . . . ashamed . . . to have arrived at that stage . . . but not guilty.

Dr. R. But you have punished yourself, therefore you are capable of the law of talion.

P. Yet before this I've taken care of my mother.

Dr. R. Yes, but who declares that you must punish your husband, lose your ovaries? All that is in the head of your mother, who judges you.

P. I wish to come out of that state.

Dr. R. Not deserted by them who want to help, for instance, not by me before we have done the necessary work. There are others who want to look after you, good or bad perhaps, but they try to help you.

P. At this moment I need a rest . . . from analysis.

Dr. R. Yes, but if you do not do the analysis, then you feel yourself guilty, and then punish yourself as you punish your husband.

P. Punish the two of us, but first my husband.

Dr. R. Do you feel that your mother would be pleased that you punish yourself?

P. This is senseless . . .

Dr. R. But it would seem like that in your head.

P. I feel that I'm cutting myself from everything.

Dr. R. Cutting yourself from everybody is also punishing the others.

P. I don't think that I want to punish the others . . . Not until this summer.

Dr. R. Yet it looks fairly clear that this is what you bring to me . . . It appears, as you say, a total fiasco . . . to punish all the others . . .

P. It's necessary that you look after me . . . and after the others.

Dr. R. But if you are destroying yourself you are also destroying the others . . .

P. I'm . . . I'm terrible.

Dr. R. But it is clear that you are not only terrible, as you say.

P. No . . . Quite . . . If other people have loved me, it's because there is good in me . . . good potential, like in everybody else.

Dr. R. To quote an example, we know you have tried to block your sexual potential, is that not true?

P. Dr Rey . . . I have the potential. But I don't know what has happened to my potential.

Dr. R. We must search for what has happened . . . not only for the bad things, but the good ones as well.

P. Yes . . . People are not going to wait indefinitely for me to get better.

Dr. R. Today, together with me, it would seem that you have understood what you are using the anaesthesia for, and now the question is what to do about it.

P. Something to sleep . . . but it would be better if I could dream.

Dr. R. Not only to dream, but to be concerned to live instead of dying.

P. We're going to stay together, Dr Rey.

Dr. R. To search and understand – not only death, but also to understand how to live.

P. (*Silence.*) . . . I don't want to die now. I begin my activities again . . . I've given.

Dr. R. You ask for the permission to live. Should I be the one who decides for you how to live?

P. I feel confused.

Dr. R. Yes, but before you invite the state of confusion, you can decide: to live or not live. Who has decided not to live happily and not to give love?

P. I behaved better when my parents lived.

Dr. R. Yes, and now to next week.

SESSION SIX

P. I've accompanied her . . . (*Silence.*) . . . My God.

Dr. R. Your mother was very ill. You have accompanied her, but not to the end. You did not die with her.

P. The last week . . . To go to the hospital (*Crying.*) . . .

Dr. R. You are not able to live a life other than that of your mother's, the same room, her bed like a coffin, her bed. You do not want to see the difference between your mother ill and you yourself very sick also, in the same state as your mother, feeling yourself responsible for her and 'being her'.

P. I feel guilty, I've been guilty to have survived my mother. I'm very destructive – to destroy, destroy a situation.

Dr. R. And so what about your treatment?

P. What can be done to treat me?

Dr. R. All this is in the name of your mother, illness for illness, destruction for destruction. It is her daughter who caused all that. Is it what you want?

P. And yet I've not caused pain and worries to my mother (*Crying.*). I feel anaesthetized, blocked. I can still hear her . . .

Dr. R. There is a part of you that wanted and tried to put things right, and another part . . .

P. (Interrupting.) It is myself who blocks . . . a fiasco.

Dr. R. You said that you are destroying others, but you have wished and felt that you had to eradicate in your own body an illness exactly like that from which your mother suffered.

P. Self-destruction.

Dr. R. A fear of destroying everything, you and others also – your husband and others too.

P. The others. At the bottom I have good will – I'm suffering, I'm afraid to let out things.

Dr. R. Yes, afraid of the things that could come out here, and you would like me to reassure you about it. You want to destroy me too, like the others. You want me to reassure you that I know your thoughts, yet continue to help you.

P. I'm not as powerful as you imply . . .

Dr. R. It is your suggestion that your thoughts could destroy.

P. Oh, how can I come out of all this? *(Silence.)* How can I make a good analysis . . . It's an analysis that we're doing . . . I've already been able to talk . . . I'm not feeling capable of crying . . . if I could, I would be better.

Dr. R. In your thoughts the punishment is forever, because you feel responsible for your mother . . .

P. When will I not be there any more . . . with her . . . my mother saying, 'Jesus, Mary and Joseph'. Will you assist me in my last agony . . . Ah, my mother, why do you want to die? . . . My mother was saying I don't want to die . . . but I was feeling the wish to die. After last week's session . . . another memory has come to the surface . . . My mother was given a drug for her last minutes. She wasn't recognizing people, and I was powerless, helpless.

Dr. R. We know you felt anaesthetized, unable to revive your mother. You were anaesthetized, and yet here you have revived what happened to your mother.

P. It's unbelievable what I'm doing . . . There was a dream. In the dream I was being told that my mother was dead, but my grandmother said, 'Not at all. Your mother died seven years ago.' That's in my dream. She's in a coma. No, she's dead. I was relieved at last to be able to cry and to speak. How can I be revived, how can I come out of it?

Dr. R. Like the dream, how can you come out of the coma. It is a new feeling, coming out of living what your mother experienced and lived.

P. My father is also dead. How could I function at that time?

Dr. R. At last you are slowly coming out of this dying state of your mother, a state you are imposing on your husband. Is it what your mother wants?

P. No . . . But how can I do it now, free myself . . . I'm speaking of what person I am now? . . .

Dr. R. This is it: render to Caesar what belongs to Caesar . . . to your mother what is hers, and to you what belongs to you.

P. I don't really know who I am.

Dr. R. A new way of living is ahead for you. You are still afraid to discover who you are.

P. To discover who I am . . .

Dr. R. You are not afraid you are still such a little girl worried by the death of your mother. Remember when she said, 'Jesus, Mary and Joseph'. Yes, the death of your mother is in your mind. We have not yet talked about the internal thoughts, thoughts inside your mind.

P. (Silence.) What can we do, Dr Rey?

Dr. R. Do you still feel that I am incapable of looking after the little girl, of her mother's death? Yes, there is a fear that I will not be able to. Perhaps you can begin to think that I can do so now, look after the little girl now.

P. It's important that somebody can look after the little girl inside me . . . I have the feeling that I don't deserve the time when I was the centre of attention. My mother nearly died then, one month at the hospital. My grandmother looked after me.

Dr. R. Your birth has been the cause of your mother having a serious illness?

P. My mother recounted it to me . . . My mother had lost so much blood that I was extricated by forceps. Then my mother remained at the hospital for one month. Grandmother was looking after me . . . the first child.

Dr. R. But what do you feel mother and grandmother wanted to tell you, to make you feel?

P. My awful, dreadful birth . . . I've caused suffering and pain to my mother by being born. My mother said I nearly cost her her life, waiting to speak until I was an adolescent, not to hurt me . . . My life is woven in a drama.

Dr. R. At your birth . . . perhaps even before.

P. It's difficult to appreciate the ambiguous message of my mother, her telling me that I nearly deprived her of her life. Oh, Dr Rey, I'll have such difficulty in catching up with all that!

Dr. R. And yet you are doing it now. I think that in speaking of those fundamental situations and feelings within yourself you are afraid that your mother will reproach you for speaking in such a way about her.

P. (Silence.) I feel uncomfortable if I do reproach my mother. Even at this very moment I'm feeling it.

Dr. R. It may be that you can remember that she accused you of being nearly responsible for her death. That she could have said to you . . .

P. A mother saying that to her child – I can't believe that!

Dr. R. It is a question of what part of you does.

P. It's now seven years that I'm functioning normally . . . You've touched on my mother . . . All the losses when giving birth, but it has to be . . .

Dr. R. Can you think of a good birth, a good death for your mother, that which is good and can be understood? To open up in a birth experience.

P. Such birth can be painful.

Dr. R. I think this is a little exaggerated . . . perhaps I ought to remind you of the forceps to help you speak out.

P. What do you mean by forceps?

Dr. R. I do not yet know, but the pain, her death . . . but there is also a good birth, a normal death . . .

P. When I was a small girl, we arrived in a new town. We weren't on very good terms with my mother-in-law. I was a real ray of sunshine then. It was a honeymoon, but then my brother was born and nearly caused the death of my mother.

Dr. R. But there was also something good. You were a bit of sunshine as you said, a ray of sunshine.

P. I feel that I've given things – been generous.

Dr. R. Good and bad?

P. Yes, there is some good.

Dr. R. We are going to stop here.

SESSION SEVEN

P. It's late and it's cold. I'm afraid that I am wasting your time.

Dr. R. What is making you think so?

P. (*Silence.*)

Dr. R. You have said three things: you were late, it is cold, and you are wasting my time. It is perhaps me who is making you lose your time; it is a kind of reaction, a confusion with your dead mother, dead people cannot talk, or perhaps with the dying mother, or the little girl who wants to punish her mother . . . But it is you that we must help. Have you understood well and grasped what I have said, understood what you have done or not done?

P. Yes.

Dr. R. It is necessary to go on talking, opening up, to explain what you feel incapable of saying or doing. You want something other than therapy, you want to put your head on the breast of mother. Do you remember when you told me that? I am suggesting something else: therapy. You must understand that point.

P. My husband is anxious . . . it prevents him from sleeping.

Dr. R. And what do you do then?

P. I turn and turn in the bed . . .

Dr. R. What are you thinking then – it seems you do not want to do things. One should be busy looking and thinking only of you, a little baby for whom I will do everything. You would like me to show that I have understood all that, that I keep you alive . . . Your husband in the past was so understanding, but now he will no longer know what to do. The same applies to me. You were desperate about your mother. Remember the frock and everything else. It is necessary to understand and then to change, change now, not tomorrow, not in five minutes, but immediately. I would be very anxious if you do not want to live. What is the message you are hoping to tell me?

P. We can't continue in that way.

Dr. R. While you are here today you had thoughts, but you did not tell me about your thoughts.

P. (Silence.) Dr Rey . . . my thoughts . . . to sink, Dr Rey. Who is going to sink . . . my husband, my job, my relations?

Dr. R. It is since we started the treatment that everything is getting worse, I am driving you to sink completely.

P. It's something which is true and which is continuing.

Dr. R. But I should prevent you from sinking, and I am not preventing you.

P. A fiasco . . .

Dr. R. So you would like to turn the treatment into a fiasco, make your husband ill . . .

P. I don't want a fiasco . . .

Dr. R. I understand that you would like me not to ask you to do anything. This reminds me of certain things you, like everybody, must do. It reminds you that your mother is not there to do these things for you.

P. It's nine years that I have waited for the treatment . . . You want me to continue . . .

Dr. R. I have not given any sign that I do not want to . . . you must give an answer to us . . .

P. I want to continue with you . . . I would like to be made to sleep, to be given something. Dr X to give me something . . . to sleep.

Dr. R. Just wait outside and we will look after that.

SESSION EIGHT – A BRIEF SUMMARY

The patient, feeling depressed, describes her childhood fear that bad thoughts lead to severe punishment by God, who could send her to hell. When the analyst describes her fear that if she becomes livelier and more communicative with the analyst she will have destructive and sexual phantasies regarding both men and women, the patient reports a dream of herself 'rolling in the fields' with a man who stopped approaching her sexually 'in the last minute'. Subsequently the patient desires silence, and the analyst interprets the patient's wish to be silent as being linked with the patient using her mourning not to feel, not to be alive. As the session nears the end, the patient returns to describing her despair, suggesting that it is 'too late' to live.

SESSION NINE

P. To be unhappy, this is what awaits me and my husband, like between his mother and his father.

Dr. R. After what you have described in the past, what happens between your husband and his mother is that it is difficult to find love.

P. I'm a divided person . . . a part is compassionate, but I can't give any more to people who are ill . . .I need to look after myself.

Dr. R. It is not easy between your husband and his mother, and you and your mother.

P. This weekend I felt I didn't love my mother.

Dr. R. A part. A part did not . . .

P. (Tears.) How can one not love one's mother?

Dr. R. If you did not have good feelings . . .the regret and sorrow that one part experiences is showing that a part of you loves mother . . .but does not know what to do . . .

P. That's it . . .what to do with this sorrow . . . I've carried a very heavy burden . . . I've started unloading it . . . thus my father with his violent temperament . . . I've been able to tell him that I hated him, and yet at the moment of his death, we were friends . . . But when I was twenty-one, my mother was ill . . . The death of my mother has provoked the death of my father . . . Father died six years after mother. I'd been married for four years, but I'd lived with my husband for six years . . . After the loss of mother, father took his pension. I'd begun a course of painting. I had to live my life . . .My brother told me . . . a lapse . . . My brother for my father . . . Father said, 'I have a niece who looks after her father . . . Why don't you come home with your husband? . . . You are the woman I would have wanted . . . just before dying . . . What is wrong with incest?' . . . He died a few days after. There have been certain aspects that have profoundly troubled me . . . in my own family too many things were said . . . in the family of my husband too many things were not said . . . It isn't good in relations between couples when there is hate underneath, and people die of hate . . .

Dr. R. Let us reconsider the situation. You still, in your head, need your mother . . . to protect you against the emotional threat of father . . . and so I think it is time, although difficult, to do the mourning of mother, for you not to be ill like her, and unhappy. This in a way is the law of talion. With your husband you refused to be physically and mentally his wife. We must understand why you are punishing instead of doing reparation.

P. Yes, I have wanted to die . . . I was a coward.

Dr. R. You still are worried not to be able to forgive your father . . . not to help mother when in need.

P. I loved her . . . We must work on this.

Dr. R. You said you had punished yourself.

P. I have punished myself at first in my body, and my mother had punished herself in her body, her cancer . . . As for me, I had chosen a more rapid death, more striking, more courageous.

Dr R. Yes, breast for breast, metastasis for metastasis. The bed becoming a coffin . . .

P. Also at the level of mental illness . . . It was at the time my mother was ill.
Dr. R. There is also the fact of father, as well as mother, who enters into this. Why leave it to you alone to take care of your mother?
P. They wanted to survive . . . My father continued to work . . . My mother was in hospital in March . . . *(Tears.)* . . . I could not repair mother . . . Never missed going once. The doctor did not understand . . . I've let her drop . . . *(Tears.)*.
Dr. R. It was you staying all the time with mother and you could not help her, for you it meant to 'drop her'. You have to understand that and make your peace with her, not to always think of having dropped mother . . . this is your tragedy.
P. At the moment I'm attending a theatre course, but I'm too much part of the programme.
Dr. R. What you have wanted to do was impossible.
P. Thirty years old . . . yes, I am thirty . . . Grandmother dying . . . in the room of grandmother there were two photos: mother and her sister. I tried to go in to grandmother's room, I tried to look at the photo of mother . . . the frames had become white, a kind of perspective. I didn't want to speak about it. I was thinking of my mother, I was hoping, perhaps . . . A form was approaching me, a form difficult to determine. Her eyes especially. I was looking in her eyes to see if she loved me or not. Me, a woman thirty years old?
Dr. R. For you it is like a punishment. But if your mother is free now, where she is . . . it is right for her . . . But for you it is a punishment.
P. I don't see . . . I feel unblocked at last. I think now I can cry.
Dr. R. At last, reparation.
P. It is curious . . . As an adult I'm strong, an impostor, Dr Rey, who wants a good relationship. There is a part of me that can love but the other part can't. The good and the bad.
Dr. R. We have to deal with reparation for both mother and father. For your mother it is better understood, but for father you are feeling perhaps guilty, and also there is incest.
P. I have a feeling that there is a lot of him in me . . . We must go slowly . . . To drive myself into reaching . . . A woman raped, an archetype of woman . . . But with my father I was nearly husband and wife . . . I went away . . . He was crying for his wife and also another woman . . . My mother had said, don't stay at home . . . your father is here . . . and with my brother, the fear of falling again into painful things. I was afraid to be in the manic phase . . . I thought I was . . . not in accord with such things . . . afraid that in those situations the adult was becoming guilty.
Dr. R. The two parts split off, one against the other.
P. I'm judging, I'm afraid.
Dr. R. A part feeling angry thinks of the other part. One part opposes and

contradicts the other . . . And so which is the correct part? . . . At times the good is felt as the impostor . . . it occupies more room.

P. There isn't enough room for both parts . . . What am I to do? . . . I have to destroy things in me.

Dr. R. Why destroy . . .? Why not reconstruct . . . Give the right place to mother.

P. I think of the dream about death . . . the dream that announced the death of mother.

Dr. R. A mother now in peace.

P. I hope that she knows and understands more today. I accept this more and more, but I'm not yet settled on this.

Dr. R. Not yet successful, perhaps, in accepting that the good part is still called the impostor.

P. I'm afraid to be a monster . . . I think that one part refuses the reality of evil . . . I wanted to change the world, wanted everybody to return to the church, I was distributing pamphlets everywhere, even at the football matches.

Dr. R. So in the manic phase you were excited, feeling almighty. You wanted to repair the others, for instance, in the building yard.

P. Not the yard . . . After the manic phase, the need was to share the house, to contribute to the well-being of my brother.

Dr. R. Reparation . . . to construct and reconstruct . . . but become omnipotent as well.

P. I wanted to be the mother of all . . . But in the building yard the work of a man . . . Man or woman? A part yes, a part not. The man-part was taking more and more room . . . but I was good in looking after mother.

Dr. R. But others did not approve always.

P. All the time I tried to look after mother, but not enough. I can't feel.

Dr. R. We stop here.

SESSION TEN

P. I feel depressed . . . Don't eat enough . . . The functional animal doesn't function . . . I sleep badly . . . Still not menstruating . . . I have to have the test done . . . I don't think I'm pregnant . . . I have had beautiful dreams . . . I'm still bad with my husband, but I think our contact is changing . . . I'm feeling . . . tired . . . not enough sleep . . . I need to recuperate . . . but I can't do it.

Dr. R. What do you think of when you are not sleeping?

P. Thoughts that jump from one thing to another . . . Regrets . . . The me of today . . . and I can't believe it to see . . . Too much life . . . shining around . . . I'm so afraid to make a start.

Dr. R. Listen to me. If you repetitively speak of returning to life it means that you have desires and dreams, and other desires if you return to life . . . You are afraid . . . it means if you come back to life we must know what fears, what anxieties it gives you . . . all the demands and wishes you have, and so on.

P. I desire perfection . . . too high . . . for that which I can't reach . . . in life one must struggle, especially these days . . . I don't feel the strength.

Dr. R. Perfection for what? It must be stated. Perfection for what goals?

P. I feel capable of teaching better . . . To look better after my husband and other things. My husband wishes to make a career, change his job, to travel. He wants a larger house. We are poor people. I feel the need to live a complicated life . . . with certain people . . . my values are not very well expressed . . . There's a fear to lose myself if I wish . . . I want to stay with my husband . . . At this moment I'm dependent on him. What causes me anxiety is that I hide my needs, and that, perhaps, these needs are not there.

Dr. R. You have clearly said that the needs of your husband and yours are not the same.

P. At this moment I don't know my desires . . . Perhaps they're not compatible with the life I want to live.

Dr. R. Not compatible, but they may exist?

P. My husband is a solitaire – he can do what he wants. Me, I'm at a turning point of life . . . He has found in him the required energy. A man alone . . . receptive . . . Glad for him.

Dr. R. You say you are close to him, but he is a solitaire. His career is more important than you are. A part of you says you cannot live in the same way as your husband.

P. It's quite complex . . . A part of him is interested in me.

Dr. R. It is difficult if your husband has to fulfil your desires. For instance, who feeds you, looks after the kitchen, washes you, dresses you.

P. Not different to that extent . . . I ask of my husband other things . . . My husband and I have a relationship . . . Not like people with violent reactions . . . who shout all the time . . . I have been a companion for my husband and a strong mother too . . . but sexuality is not achieved . . . (*Silence and then tears.*).

Dr. R. There are good tears. We are going to understand more.

P. I feel the desire to be loved . . . like a woman.

Dr. R. Before being able to be loved like a woman, there is also the need to be loved as a child by one's mother. By the mother and the father, but first of all by the mother, and also to love the mother.

P. Can I change my relationship, Dr Rey, not only towards my husband, but also towards my mother, so as not to let my mother die? It's possible to look for reparation between mother and daughter. How can I change this relation? I want to learn from you how to live . . . therefore, to have the taste to live, perhaps with you, for five or six years.

Dr. R. Tell your husband . . . the dream that you have told me with man and woman, the man who was mother, with affection and love.

P. (Nodding in agreement.) It seems that I need to . . . I am thirty years old . . . And yet it's important, it will erase what I have done, even succeed in giving . . . *(Crying heavily.)*.

Dr. R. You are asking how to repair. We must understand together what you have received from mother and father, from your husband, all that you have received.

P. Yes, I've received things . . . things which were mixed, received love. I'm convinced that to come out of the illness that I've been through there are messages that conveyed that I was vulnerable, hints from my father, always vulnerable, also from my mother, like all the children . . . Messages which I received from them . . . I must find them again, from the beginning. His mother is still alive . . . I feel that he's still very attached to her. I like his mother.

Dr. R. His mother?

P. At the beginning I had no compassion . . . I couldn't feel pity and compassion for her . . . rather like a monster . . . It's important to understand me. I don't feel for her, I don't feel capable of this . . . Just neuter . . . What counts most is the relation with my husband, it's not a relation of man to woman, but like a child, a substitute mother and child . . .

Dr. R. Not the only relation. Perhaps you were asking too much of mother. *(Patient agrees.)* What were your relations to her? Listening to your efforts to have mother be grateful for what you have given, to sleep next to her, looking after her in all ways . . . There is the experience of having received, and then the feeling 'I have received and therefore I can give.'

P. Many things were taken for granted . . . Mother was preparing our lunch, our meals, until I was nineteen years old. I have felt it a lot, lots of other tasks, it wasn't a joke at all for her.

Dr. R. Yes . . . You have also said that father and brother did not thank mother.

P. On the one hand, yes, but on the other hand, I didn't write about them in my diary after I was fourteen. It was egoistic and mother ought not to have listened. There was the sharing of tasks . . . which I've done . . . With my husband I've shared tasks.

Dr. R. When you were ill and identifying with mother's illness. Your husband was continuing to do what he could . . . There was also at the time a conflict between your mother and your father . . . and you said at the time that you joined with brother and father against mother.

P. At the time there were many conflicts between father and mother. I was caught between the two . . . I tried to help mother . . . Lying next to her . . . horrifying for a child . . . I was upset and angry and had said to father, 'Go to the brothel.' Horrifying to say that to one's father. I was torn between my father and my mother, between my brother and my husband . . . Lapses now in naming my brother in the place of father . . . My brother lived at home when his house was being built. I was being his mother and also the spouse of my mother, and also being the mother of my father. At that time I was out of my mind; the adult-in-me being my husband and my father – out of my mind that autumn, taking charge of everything . . . I was busy feeding all the people . . . I was all the time on the building-site being important, using the hammer and the nails, making love without affection to all the people who were there, as if the market was shared.

Dr. R. Sorrow caused by the father and brother who did not give to the mother.

P. It is me, Dr Rey.

Dr. R. So everything was shared . . . for instance, using the axe and hammer . . . But if mother had died thinking that her husband and her son did not love her . . . A daughter who had to be all to everyone . . . be the mother of your mother, and also her daughter, and then mother of your brother, mother of everyone.

P. I'm a lot of people, Dr Rey . . . a little girl who wanted to be everything for everyone. It seems to me that there was a part of me that was masculine as well as female . . . I had to be everyone . . . No menstruation, therefore not a woman, too difficult to be a woman.

Dr. R. Too difficult to be a woman . . . a woman who is everything to everybody else.

P. There was the mother of my mother who was very ill. Dying at eighty-nine, but she could talk. It was she who looked after me during the first days of my life . . . in some ways she was my mother . . . I don't think I have loved my husband solely as my mother.

Dr. R. You have wanted to do reparation for mother, brother, father and others . . . therefore you have had to take the place of others, to take on the task of reparation. Render to Caesar what belongs to Caesar . . .

SESSION ELEVEN

P. I have . . . discovered that I wasn't feeling . . . Had to help nature, tried to take prunes and other things . . . I'm afraid I'm going to burst . . . I've taken magnesia. I feel sick. I'm not strong.

Dr. R. You feel full of bad things.

P. Everybody around me says that I'm full of good things.

Dr. R. But you do not say that you are full of good things . . . it seems that you are centred on bad things.

P. It is . . . (*Silence.*) It's hard at this moment to become aware that I'm not giving but receiving things, hard to find out what I'm learning from others . . . But I know I have given . . .

Dr. R. The other part of you says your body is full of excrements . . . It is understandable . . . that you say you have nothing good . . . a need to get rid of the bad stuff, here particularly . . .

P. It seems very hard for me to reject somebody, to have ill-will towards

somebody. I've always wanted to be on good terms with everybody . . . If I
hear people shouting, it disturbs me. I give all my heart to my students . . .
to my colleagues.

Dr. R. Some time before you mentioned that you could also hate . . . There
seem to be two aspects – a part filled with excrements . . . so, for instance,
when hating you could attack me with all this badness inside.

P. But why attack you?

Dr. R. Not that you are necessarily going to do it, but you are afraid that you
might do it; that part is worrying you, obviously . . .

P. Another part would like to work more successfully with you. Yes, you
have asked me that, but I only come here once a week. That's the situation.
Yes, yes.

Dr. R. But what is making you anxious is the capacity to do evil. I mean, that
is the capacity you fear.

P. Yes, capable of creating good and evil, to be honest, to tell lies. An inverted
potential, Dr Rey. I'm sick, afraid it's going to come out of me. No, it won't
come out . . . I can control myself – I won't attack you.

Dr. R. Yes, but there is the fear you could do it.

P. The fear of being an evil one.

Dr. R. Then you have to try to have a good breast, good heart, good thoughts,
what we need is to do therapy together successfully.

P. I must try to continue to get all the thoughts out of my head.

Dr. R. Yes. There is more progress from the last interview, more in contact
with the little girl.

P. To be angry.

Dr. R. Yes. To make more contact with the little girl – the one who you are
in your head.

P. It's a person that doesn't want to share love . . . I'm afraid to work without
giving . . . to work without love, with my colleagues, my students . . . I'm
afraid that this capacity to love won't come back . . . I'm a teacher who comes
and goes, out of the clan . . . I don't have the strength at the moment . . .
There are many adolescents who need to be looked after. I need to look after
those who have suicidal tendencies, negative feelings. I need to face things,
to understand what goes on in the head. To face death. There are several
tendencies at different levels . . . To contribute to society or to vegetate like
a vegetable. To renew oneself, like I've done until now, to do better.

Dr. R. I think you are afraid not to be able to help the little baby inside you,
and you branch out to the adult one.

P. I'm running away, am I?

Dr. R. The little girl needs help. If I want to help the little girl, I cannot
abandon her.

P. You're right, Dr Rey, you're right . . . It's difficult to remember the
thoughts and desires of the little girl. A month ago I hid something from you –
I started to wet the bed. I managed to stop without too much damage . . .

Getting angry like a child . . . I've never done that. It's amused me . . . I've
stayed in bed instead of getting up. What was I looking for under the blanket?
I'm not sure of death.

Dr. R. The bed of the baby.

P. Yes, of the baby – or better, of the uterus.

Dr. R. It is possible.

P. Hidden under the blanket, I feel good. I know that at my birth, the first
child, born in the house, a difficult birth, my father let out a horrifying shout.
My aunt said she'd never heard such a thing. A doctor was also there. It must
be terrible for a child who comes out of her mother – a shout of death. Think
of all my own complexities, and having to understand father, mother. I have
the right to be angry. Yes, I understand myself. It's such a long time since all
that.

Dr. R. The little girl is here, in this room . . .

P. Not anger!

Dr. R. No. I did not say that we were speaking of anger. We are saying it is
the fear that the good side has of being displaced.

P. Yes. Exactly . . . It's not normal. I want it to change. Can one rationally
speak of anger?

Dr. R. We were saying about anger that if you are angry with me, I will have
to understand it.

P. You would be struggling with this anger.

Dr. R. That is with myself.

P. I saw my god-daughter again. She came to see me with her friend. Her
daughter is two and a half years old, an adorable child, and I've realized that
a young child knows good and evil. I've had ambiguous feelings towards my
god-daughter. My feelings weren't questioned, of course, and yet a lot were
actually questioned. I can't really question my feelings towards somebody I
love. I didn't feel that I could give much to the little girl – I even felt 'me' in
her.

Dr. R. You inside the little girl, and what then did the good and the bad parts
think of you?

P. I've sometimes thought that I was detested by my parents.

Dr. R. You've thought of that?

P. No . . . I excuse myself for not having thought of that . . . I hope it's not
too late to come back to the feelings of the little girl. I lack unity in my
personality.

Dr. R. Yes. The question is what the little girl was doing to her parents, and
what you were doing in the role of the godmother, and also in relationship
to me.

P. Yes, I've thought of that . . . In my diary I haven't related why I got a
spanking . . . from a mother of so many children. It will help me to be a
mother later on . . . I've understood that two years ago – it's been a few
years that I've been thinking of children. I've stopped taking precautions

preventing me from having children . . . I'm afraid at this moment. I don't want children. Not romantic. Won't fill the pages of a novel. Very difficult.

Dr. R. In your head, it is the angry little girl, full of excrements, that is with the bad part who could be your child. You are not thinking that you could be the good mother and help the child. You are not sure it is possible to help your god-daughter. You are afraid she seems irreparable if her mother does not help her.

P. What must I do to help the little girl?

Dr. R. This is what we are trying to do.

P. Why do I feel pain? Why, why, try to develop oneself? People don't care for human beings two and a half years old. At that age the family was coming to town. At the village everybody spoke to each other, everybody said hello. We visited. A lot of all this – and then nothing.

Dr. R. The little girl you are talking about was born when?

P. Two years now.

Dr. R. Even before your birth, the little girl didn't feel loved.

P. I did feel I was loved . . . but there was a great sorrow in my mother. A great anger also. My aunt, the nurse, didn't get on with her. I was having to cope with too many things, too many words from the others.

Dr. R. I have to say to you what I think. You seem to be saying, 'What am I doing for the sadness, the tears of my mother?' You seem despairing about helping your mother. Yes, your mother, in her sadness, and perhaps also your father. Above all, you are despairing of not being able to do reparation to mother when she fell ill.

P. My mother was engaged to someone else before she met my father. They separated and then my father came. I've asked myself if she loved him. They've quarrelled a lot. I must understand who I am.

Dr. R. You have helped, and in a way are helping mother not to be unhappy. But for you there is also my help. Can you feel I can help you?

P. Listen. I see many photographs when I'm laughing. I'm happy and laughing with mother.

Dr. R. The little ray of sunshine.

P. But yes, of course . . . But why am I telling all that story? . . . I must tell all this publicly. They don't know who I am . . . (*Tears.*) . . . Dr Rey . . . I want to work with you. I am working . . .

SESSION TWELVE

P. Seduction is a thing I hate. Seduction is horrifying. I'm a woman, but not really. No periods, no menstruation, no real sexual activity . . . At the same time, I profoundly feel that I'm a woman. When is the therapy ending?

Dr. R. I am going to leave at the end of May.

P. It's a time which for me is very intense . . . I also have a very intensive course to give. We're already at the fifteenth or sixteenth of March. I'm progressing very slowly.

Dr. R. You have said in the past that I was not going fast enough in my thoughts. You or me?

P. I'm not able to go fast . . . I'm very slow.

Dr. R. I think that for you being slow or fast also has a meaning.

P. My mother was slow . . . my father alive and quick. I caused many difficulties, terrifying difficulties. And me, I was between the two of them . . . Why was I deeply dissatisfied? Or was it somewhat afterwards . . . I couldn't say . . . I've never been so blocked . . . I feel I resemble my mother a great deal.

Dr. R. For you, what was stopping your mother was the fear of seduction, and now there is, I think, this same fear of seduction with me . . .

P. I'm already a woman . . .

Dr. R. Would you say a whole woman?

P. In my diary I saw only kindness in you. I have confidence in you. It means more to me, that I'm not trusting . . . (*Silence.*) . . . Dr Rey . . . I don't follow your thought . . .

Dr. R. Let us see. When you discovered incestuous wishes in your father, what did you do?

P. I went away . . . He wasn't a harassing father . . . He was sick . . . I went away, but not against him . . . It was horrifying . . . He was my father . . . It was repulsive . . . Seduction . . . Seduction . . . Like everybody, I found that disgusting . . . Seduction . . . To have charm is one thing . . . I love that. But seduction is impossible. There is ambiguity between the parties . . . It's a situation of life . . . You're the therapist for a time. I've considered you as sexless, and I, too, for a time, as sexless . . . I can see very well that you're a man . . . and that I'm a woman . . . How can I become different? I'm not mad. In the phase that I've gone through, I was confused, not clear in my statements. How can I take the role of a woman? I've hidden myself. I'm afraid still. There is also the man I love . . .

Dr. R. In the dream you were a woman or a professor. A man had taken our place, therefore, in your place with me, as my patient, there is confusion.

P. This summer I was with my brother. I was saying brother or father . . . and I was feeling sexually for my brother, not anxious . . . The last step . . . a link with the family.

Dr. R. Your father?

P. I have difficulty separating sensuality and sexuality . . . I was feeling my mouth as a mortal sin. My mouth, the purity of an ideal, not for me, not worthy, and yet all the fear was in my head . . . (*Silence.*) . . . My companion was not upset by purity – it didn't prevent him from masturbating . . . Too naive.

Dr. R. This question of purity touches on the dying mother, who comes again to the surface.

P. Yes, me and my mother.

Dr. R. And you in a bed-coffin, not really alive.

P. In my little head, sexual life was my father and mother . . . When father made suggestions to me I wasn't a child.

Dr. R. For you, all sexuality is impure.

P. To have my sexuality, being conscious of all I'm doing, is to have a repressed sexuality that is coming out. I haven't been afraid of making love with other men . . .

Dr. R. First of all, there is the relation with your husband. Then, as you said, for you I was too kind a person to think of me in that way.

P. You are intelligent, for sure. You question me in that way to help me, but I can't, I don't want to define you sexually.

Dr. R. Is there a fear somewhere?

P. This has happened to me at work. What is it that happens to me then? Do I love my husband? As for him, it doesn't prevent him from functioning, and loving me.

Dr. R. Being unfaithful to somebody else? Is that it?

P. When my father was ill, I was guilty. I went away, left my parents . . . dropped them.

Dr. R. And what about me? In May are you going to just drop me?

P. No.

Dr. R. So it was hard to drop father.

P. When I was a child, they dropped me. I don't let people down. At this moment now I let people down. I want to find the way again. Surely I'm afraid to drop you, let you down.

Dr. R. We have to understand if this separation means to drop me . . .or something else?

P. In the eyes of others I'm too often too fragile . . . I'm afraid that often people will let me down, at the same time you're going to leave. I want to find again the path of life.

Dr. R. I am thinking of the difficulties between your parents, the liveliness of your father and the lack of liveliness of your mother. Thus it is father who had life, or is it?

P. To change I must also change to a new model of woman.

Dr. R. So who has life? The penis? To escape death, women must have what?

P. The penis is embarrassing me . . . Women want and desire the penis . . .

Dr. R. And who has said that?

P. It's in the books. It's life.

Dr. R. Then a source of life, not of death.

P. A spring of life in me. I have had orgasms . . . Not often, but I've felt it. I don't know my body well. My companion at this moment is the source of life. He's found out at last who he was. And me, his companion – I've found that we are together . . .

Dr. R. With life?

P. With life.

Dr. R. And how did you discover life, with a dying mother, a father more alive, more a source of life?

P. Dr Rey, I can hardly believe it . . . I have difficulty in functioning, emotionally, intellectually, with everybody at the moment . . . Listening. . . . to what you say . . . (*Silence.*) . . . Father was the source of life . . . and my brother . . . In a couple, I had the impression for a certain time that I was the stronger one, but now I don't know. I'm at a turning point. What am I going to do with me? I feel my compassion is stronger. It's good for me, good for him . . . Oh! Women are good sources of life.

Dr. R. But in the past there were sources of death as well.

P. There was pain, sorrow and pain, because mother was putting breaks on me. I was sixteen years old. Yet I've tried to love that woman at the same time. She was the model . . . my brother managed to escape. It's all right for him, he functions well. For me it's very difficult . . . In the last phase, I was troubled by her body, embarrassed, even sexually. Then afterwards, I worked. I functioned normally. Now I'm still tired. It's terrible at thirty. I want to come out of my depression and stagnation.

Dr. R. It is, of course the treatment that is necessary . . .You say 'my mother in that state', 'I loved her' – but there are also so many other things. You felt it was peaceful to die, to render life to your mother, 'to my mother', and we know who was the source of life.

P. My mother who is inside me . . . my mother, Dr Rey . . . My mother is dead, and I'm beginning to accept that. Yes, the twenty-first of March is over. It's moving forward. My mother is dead and I'm alive. I have difficulties, but I feel that I'm going to come out of it.

Dr. R. Yes, there are other ways of being the source of life.

P. We know who was the source of life. For my father, when I was manic, I was the source of life. It's important for me to become a person, to feel I'm a normal woman. I'm afraid of madness.

Dr. R. You may be thinking that it is me who thinks that you are 'mad'.

P. It is I who must save myself.

Dr. R. If we follow you, we know there was a very tired mother, and a father who was a source of life.

P. I must make peace with my mother . . . I feel that now my mother should surface . . . Source of life . . . I have a source of life . . . I have been a source of life . . . I'm searching ahead . . .

SESSION THIRTEEN

P. My feelings of dependence . . . to be protected . . . Not many things in a day, few things. I feel that I'm not changing, that I'm the only one doing nothing. I'm not even working in the college.

Dr. R. How long do you think it is going to last? In the two last sessions you had begun recapturing many respective identities. Thus, to be the wife of your father, after the incestuous suggestion, and, we hope, to try and recapture the dream. Then there is the asking too much from your husband. The problem of being a man and a woman is not different – in the dream it is a man who replaces you.

P. In a certain way I've lost my status, man or woman. In several professions there is equality for man and woman.

Dr. R. Yes, but it is your husband who is involved. It is not only in the professions. After all, he is your husband.

P. I'm conscious that there is a problem in our marriage. A friend lent me a book which says that even in the eyes of science it's healthy to fight a bit. Where one takes a stand in life there is a greater understanding.

Dr. R. To argue perhaps, or not always to have the same opinion, then the marriage becomes difficult, as it can fulfil all the roles . . . But you are in yourself all the roles. What is your identity in the marriage? Thus, for instance, are you too much the man, not enough a woman to receive the penis, become a mother, have a child? What is the identity of your husband in the marriage, and what is yours?

P. What is my identity?

Dr. R. And the identity of your body?

P. It's very serious, what you are saying.

Dr. R. Yes, serious, but nevertheless it is the problem to work on.

P. It's . . . (*Silence.*) . . . I'm a woman and something else, a teacher. You yourself are a man and a professor.

Dr. R. In the dream there is too much lack of equality of the sexes, not enough of the spouse and of the body of a mother.

P. My mother was suffering . . . she wasn't happy in her role.

Dr. R. And you?

P. At this moment, I'm not happy. I've lived and had five years of happiness with my husband. I still have it, but probably not as an adult.

Dr. R. Not adult, not the body of a woman. It was not the idea of the body of a woman that you had.

P. Dr Rey . . . I nevertheless don't have a heart of stone . . . I am neither a woman nor a man.

Dr. R. We agree you are searching, a kind of non-conformist, something that suggests not becoming attached to the norm, but rather going further.

P. If we understand clearly, we can make a big step ahead, not only from the point of view of civilization . . .

Dr. R. You have to be a woman who can enjoy the penis and can have a child.

P. In all honesty, what should I do? Leave my husband, live alone . . . undo everything?

Dr. R. But surely this is not what we are doing together, the two of us together in the treatment, not what you say.

P. To work . . . Then my husband should accept me. It seems he must also

have a problem of identity. He was the first one to remark on how to
change . . . At this moment I don't want to take any identity. I'm afraid of
you.

Dr. R. That is, afraid of where I am leading you to?

P. But to become what woman? What is the woman of today?

Dr. R. There is the problem for the child, that is, to become a woman like
your mother with all her problems, or to be an incestuous daughter . . . Is
that what it is to become a woman?

P. When my mother died, she wanted to leave the house. She didn't want to
stay with my father and brother. The sisters of my grandfather weren't
married and they looked after their father and their mother . . . I was in
therapy, where I met my husband. He had an ascendancy over me that you
didn't have. A part of me didn't love him. How can I change? By looking at
my mother . . . or looking only at a face . . . You should realize that a normal
woman realizes herself in her work . . . My husband wants a woman who
works and who shares everything.

Dr. R. You have said, 'and shares everything'.

P. It's love . . . sexual relations . . . At the beginning it didn't work well . . .

Dr. R. You have said you rarely have had an orgasm. You had to avoid being
a woman, ill with cancer, and then soon afterwards you were asked to
become an incestuous daughter . . . It was difficult to become a functional
woman.

P. The first time that I made love with a man, at twenty-one, I said to my
father, I'm not a virgin any more, but the product of consummation. This
isn't the right way to look after a woman. He was a friend who I didn't love.
The gynaecologist thought that I was pregnant, when in fact I had done
nothing . . . It's not easy to be a woman . . .

Dr. R. For you, at this moment, the first time the sexual experience was not
pleasant. You said to your father, 'I am not even a saleable product.'

P. There are moments when I've found it good, very difficult to define,
sometimes good, not always bad.

Dr. R. Yes, but it was felt often as destructive, making you unsaleable.

P. Yes . . . Destructive . . . Thirty years . . . How to change . . . A lack of
energy, of confidence, of willpower.

Dr. R. To become a daughter, a woman, a success, but apparently not what
your father and mother wanted . . . And me, what do you think I am thinking,
as did your parents?

P. To do things for myself first of all, although also to please you . . . You are
not a judge, but you say things that I feel are judging me . . . What is a woman,
a man, in your head? Your own head. How long has it been so, Dr Rey?

Dr. R. You feel that you have to escape from the woman that you are in the
head of your parents and also that you are in my head . . .

P. At the moment I need a lot of love. Not a sexual love, real love . . . Nobody understands me, that I'm depressed . . . All of a sudden something has been building up . . . It's very upsetting.

Dr. R. In our last session, the part that did not love mother seemed to be coming out, and the desire to escape from the father, like in the dream that was not a dream, the frame and the eyes of mother, a struggle between the parts.

Dr. R. Perhaps a professor with a task to do for this week. So I am a professor, and you are both, as we know, a professor and a pupil.

P. It's me, the professor, the husband, the pupil . . . always in the role of student and professor . . . I'm now the pupil having great difficulty in making decisions. Together with my husband. For instance, what are we going to eat? Difficulty in deciding, fear of ending in a crash, lower still, Dr Rey.

Dr. R. So, to what level do you come down to restart anew. There is a danger, and we must understand all that.

P. I feel that I'm in a certain danger. I must understand more. When are you leaving in May?

SESSION FOURTEEN – A BRIEF SUMMARY

There are a few sessions left when the patient describes her profound desire to be taken in the arms of her mother and of her father, to feel loved and to love them. This wish to be with both parents together with each other was accompanied by both intrusive wishes to see and hear the couple's sexual intimacy, and memories from the past of sounds from the parental bedroom.

A sense of being abandoned by the analyst as he departs leads the patient increasingly to desire to be recognized as a gifted genius having a lively intelligence. As the sessions are about to end, there seems to be an underlying anxiety regarding leaving the therapy and feeling abandoned. At the same time, the patient becomes interested in reviewing a diary of her dreams which she had compiled over eight years. She described the following dreams from the diary:

I've dreamt there was a blue van without brakes. There were two groves and I saw a girl in front of me. I was afraid to hurt her fatally. I shouted, 'Be careful', but I had gone through the girl, and the girl disappeared. She was myself to some extent. Then there was a beautiful villa. I didn't get to the villa, and even by the next day I hadn't entered the villa.

This was a dream of my birth in the room of a maiden. It was an unclean pregnancy. I was a month old when I was born. Things went too fast. The baby was born. She was normal. We were looking at each other. The atmosphere around at the birth was very serious, very solemn, not joyous. No one knew what our relationship would be.

I was in my mother's uterus. I had a feeling of well-being, but decided to get out.

The analyst described how during the course of the therapy the patient has brought the little girl excluded from the sexual relationship of the parents, then her own sexual relationship with her husband, and then her own life endangered in the sexual act.

The patient talks about her own difficulty in comprehending what is a good sexual intercourse producing a baby and what is a bad sexuality, filled with impurity. First she talks about how, prior to getting married, her mother had had a miscarriage, followed by her brother being born. The patient states that she often has had the phantasy of an intercourse in which the husband batters the wife, who then responds with latent aggressiveness. This phantasy often accompanied her when she was passive in her own sexual relationship with her husband.

SESSION FIFTEEN

P. I don't know now if you understand, it needs a lot of courage and the right philosophy and the church. Going to the church alone, there are no miracle remedies. There are Catholics who gain an immediate pardon and make no effort to be transformed. I was at a concert the other evening with a friend. It was a requiem by Fauré. After the death of my mother I heard this music with my father. This time I wasn't touched in the same way. There's another part which is anaesthetized, not related or linked to the therapy. Now I don't touch the flute and musical instruments. They're not related to the therapy . . . It has remained as it was, well regulated. There are people who say to me that I'm changed – sweeter and more peaceful, but the sweetness could be fear if I don't know what it's about. I'm no longer the same person . . . There are destructive elements, like something that belongs to Satan. When I'm reading a book it has one sense, but the writings have no sense. I'm not yet well adjusted. I'm subjected to my emotions. What are the others expecting of me? I don't know. I'm alone, abandoned in the middle of the crowd. Nature is kind. I have things to do. As far as acting goes, I'm blocked. It remains the untouched sheet of paper.
Dr. R. What is it that has happened since last week? It is important that I can keep a memory of you, to remember a capable person, intelligent with all your capacities, adjusted to life. But we have to understand that you will continue the treatment with another person. You will not stay blocked, at a standstill.
P. This is true, very true. Like when my mother died with a statue-like picture in her head of a certain person.
Dr. R. At the end there will be a continuation of the treatment with somebody else.
P. I've definitely decided to continue with a particular person. What I have to say . . . is important it won't only be with the team.
Dr. R. Perhaps there is a little touch of rebellion there . . . about who decides.

This experiment is needed by someone. The group will take certain decisions. Your line of conduct will be imposed by somebody else.

P. My father is there . . . It is me with father, me with mother, but my father was frightening me when he asked for something. I felt very revolted at the sound of my father's voice. It's difficult to think of being repulsed, rather fear than revolt. Sexuality was imposed, wasn't allowed to be felt; therefore I was directed by frigidity. By whom was the organism imposed?

Dr. R. Once more caught between father and mother, caught by the two of them. It has perhaps been created by you in your head.

P. It's me . . . But I'm by force excluded . . . (*Silence.*) . . . Keeping sides that way . . . I'm responsible for myself . . . not a victim of my past, but at the same time there are too many memories crowded in my head . . . I'm going to tell you something important which troubles me . . . The medical gynaecologist . . . I asked him about my genitals. He said the hymen has a tear after my first sexual experience and that I have an ovarian cyst. Then, after the first gynaecological examination, he spoke to me about my clitoris. I was confused. I didn't understand. I had amenorrhoea for three months. I'm confused. It's difficult. I'm certain that I never had a sexual relation. The hymen was broken, all by itself. It was after that first sexual experience. It's touched something in me. It was before the amenorrhoea. The first time he hadn't been able to penetrate me. Later, I made a mild attempt with somebody, to graduate to the experience slowly . . . I had enough affection and enough confidence within myself to explore and become aware . . . When I was a little girl my mother took me to the doctor and he gave me a cream that stained my pants . . . I didn't know what it was . . . I have to verify certain things with my parents . . .

Dr. R. Yes, but now the parents are not there any more.

P. Yes, and they could be mistaken.

Dr. R. Do you think you have had sexual relations without being able to remember?

P. Yes. Yes, I can remember I was living near my father's family, and my father's brother, who was under psychiatrists, touched me. I was afraid to go back home. My mother said he hadn't touched the sex, but the fear was there. My uncle was violent. My father shouted at him and told him off. They were twelve children. Imagine a woman with twelve children. Sexuality expressed in a dirty way. I've often been disgusted by it . . .

Dr. R. A part of you is afraid of that dirty past . . .

P. Many men speak of the cloaca. (*Tears.*) No dignity . . .

Dr. R. Nevertheless, you have taken your courage, to try to make something different from a cloaca.

P. There is a desire in me to be strong. Having been unable to love mother, there have been other women who have been victims as well . . . I've tried to be a man . . .

Dr. R. But we know you have tried to be a man. A man does not have a vagina.

But maybe it is possible to remain a woman with a vagina rather than a penis . . . It is a consequence of thinking that the vagina is a good part of the body.

P. I've seldom heard, apart from my companion, of the goodness of the vagina. At the beginning my husband had difficulty putting his hand near my vagina. Yet other men have tried to separate sexual love from tender love, to include intelligence, everything, the whole being.

Dr. R. We have heard what so many people have said about this vagina – a cloaca. I want to try to bring you from what the others have said to what you have thought yourself about it. It is very propitious ground to examine and understand.

P. Yes, there are the school memories. They laughed at my naivety. The small ones used to go and say to the teacher that I couldn't touch myself under the bedspread. That I thought that my grandmother, mother, my aunt, all of them were going to see me and know . . . I was very small. It disturbed me a lot, when alone. But even when alone I was thinking or feeling that my actions were being watched and examined.

Dr. R. So it was even necessary to destroy your thoughts, and not only the outside world.

P. Yes . . . After all, what was left to me? If only I had permitted myself to think . . . I'm feeling sick . . . to look and see. It's unbelievable! If only I was permitted to think, to think what was important.

Dr. R. Those thoughts were in the name of whom? They came from somewhere.

P. I've placed and classified all those thoughts in the head of the others.

Dr. R. It is not that they have not said it, but that it had an ascendancy over you.

P. There was a lack of courage, of taking risks. The little boys and girls, I was afraid of being seen by them. In the manic phase I fumbled things, thinking about what I'd done and not done. My companion buys books and says to me 'Don't hide yourself.' He has a soul. Yes, the soul is important for me.

Dr. R. The soul that demands perfection. Fine for the others, fine also for Dr Rey.

P. I imprison myself because of the soul.

SESSION SIXTEEN – A BRIEF SUMMARY

Following the fourteenth session, in which the patient talked about her wishes to intrude into the couple's bedroom, she had difficulty seeing and hearing, as well as having a tic and a urinary infection. She also joyously experienced the return of her periods. Alongside this was the news that her cyst was dissolving spontaneously in her body. She hoped that going out of her body alongside the cyst would be her anger. The analyst describes the patient's difficulty seeing and understanding what she thinks is still bad in her body, and he comments on her difficulty seeing what she fears would be bad in the little baby. After the patient mentions her blocks in speaking of her mother, her father, her family, she highlights her particular block when talking of her mother. The analyst then points out the patient's inhibitions of closing of the eye, the closing of the vagina with no menstrual cycle, and the constipation.

In this session, the patient also attributes different states of mind to different parts of her body. For example, she describes a difficulty on the right side of her body, and notes the good parts in her body. As the analyst accepts all the 'bad things' that the patient puts into his head, the patient describes her wish to bring him a bouquet of flowers, something really beautiful to show her affection to the analyst and to be loved.

Gradually the patient acknowledges her increasing consciousness about that which she is giving and doing. She is aware of her own pretending that things are going well and questions, 'How can I move on to a role which is honest – how can I have the heart-naked?'

The later part of the session is filled with the patient acknowledging her difficulties regarding being successful. She compares herself to others more intelligent than her, and shows how her own learning is impeded by self-doubts. The analyst describes the patient's battle between the loving part and the part that wants to do the wrong and dirty things, which is afraid of being seen.

The patient responds by saying that she feels there is something of great beauty in her, but she is afraid that her good part is not safe within her. She also acknowledges the need to deal with her negative part, and expresses a wish to stop neglecting her husband.

SESSION SEVENTEEN

P. We are meeting for the last time. (*Crying.*) I'm feeling deprived, deprived of a constant relationship, and I haven't been able to appreciate this chance, during all this period of time. At the same time, disillusion for me was touching the ground level? I'm not very strong at this moment. I've started working. I started yesterday, six hours a day. I'm extremely proud, and I fear that everybody knows what has happened to me. No, it's not that. I'm the professor, an ordinary professor, who does her job. I'm not strong. I could do more. At least I have the assurance of having given some lectures. A student criticized me a little. The lecture was unstructured. I love grammar, and I love to structure what I'm talking about . . .

Dr. R. How did you answer her? Have you been confident enough to do that?

P. I commented spontaneously that it depends on what choice you make. There was a barrier between her and me. I could have pretended that I wasn't in the best mood, not bouncing up to the ceiling . . .

Dr. R. At the beginning of this interview it is very hard to say, 'It is finished', that sentence in itself is 'finished, ended'. But there is also a part which is already finished, the other side which does continue. For instance, your mother is dead but something else goes ahead. Thus I physically am going, I leave you, that is to say, you the external person. I am leaving because I cannot stay. But the mother, the internal mother, is not going, that is what makes 'nothing remains' not true.

P. I'm thinking of my relations with my father . . . my mother . . . my brother . . . my husband . . . I've approached many things. I've started discussing them with you . . . I want to live . . . (*Crying.*).

Dr. R. You are teaching the English language. If you go away, is there no more English language?

P. It depends on whom I'm teaching . . . But working with you, Dr Rey, was possible.

Dr. R. We have decided together on the continuation of the treatment, and you must be thinking also of the person who is going to take my place.

P. I can't compare two different persons. You are Henri Rey, she is Mrs X. I didn't see her during my therapy with you. I'd like to know if it's possible for me to continue to work in therapy as I've done with you.

Dr. R. I think we must find out why you asked that?

P. For me it's clear that I haven't come out of the woods . . . It's a question only of doing the mourning externally, but . . .

Dr. R. The idea is that you will be helped to be able to go on mourning and come out of the mourning.

P. I was in therapy with Dr Y. I was taking lithium, I was a depressive. But I was feeling like I was in a desert . . . Depression means to cry and never stop crying . . .

Dr. R. You have nevertheless succeeded in having another attitude. Not to cry all the time, not to sleep on the couch of death, and not to have to speak to mother when passing in front of the hospital.

P. She is really *dead* now.

Dr. R. Yes, her body, but not all of her . . . Perhaps there is a fear of not being able to accept that I am going . . . A fear of how to have the therapy with another person. It is not only missing me, but it is also necessary to accept having done the treatment and the fact that it is successful, that it has worked well and that another person is now needed.

P. Anger and resentment . . . This is difficult to accept . . . Yes, anger . . . I feel pain . . .

Dr. R. This is quite possible, and normal pain can be good.

P. I'm jealous of my brother who, when I was four and a half years old, came and utterly changed my universe, preventing the family from helping me . . . (*Tears.*) . . . To be loved . . . I'd like everybody to love me. Never mind me then . . . I'm a responsible person. If in my head I was better, more real, looking at myself in the face, with a more individual aspect to me, maybe you would have stayed longer.

Dr. R. It would not be worthwhile to stay because what you said was a real rejection of me, of the treatment.

P. Yes . . . there is a part of that . . . (*Tears.*).

Dr. R. You must start facing the problems that you will have to look at in the future. You think that you are being rejected because you were not a worthy candidate for me, so Dr Rey prefers other patients – you are not worthwhile for him.

P. That's it, that's it. Not important enough in the head of the one who is leaving . . .

Dr. R. You feel the others do not appreciate what you really are. You deserve to be appreciated, but people do not understand that. There is a kind of injustice somewhere in that people do not recognize your qualities.

P. Yes . . .Yes . . .

Dr. R. Perhaps it is a question of who is being envious, who devalues what you are doing at the school . . . You are doing always more and more and not feeling appreciated.

P. To go to my mother. With my father I didn't care a damn. He thought I was reading all the time. He thought this wasn't normal: I did love reading, a love coming from my mother. I wanted to please her. I was playing tennis, music, piano, the flute. My father was a lover of music. He appreciated classical music – a workman who appreciated music! He wasn't a religious person, but we had religious music as a source of pleasure.

Dr. R. It sounds like hypertrophy of the sense of appreciation in you?

P. I was told that my mother loved me as much as my brother, but in my perverse head, why didn't she say that to me? Why, when I was four and a half and my brother was born, why did my mother say to me, 'Don't cut off his penis, he could die if you do.' She must have felt that I was jealous . . . In the kitchen, when he was having his bath, I thought if I cut this organ he could die. My parents loved us the same. Her statement increased my doubts. She was so frightened of sins, hell, religion. Somewhat obsessional. There are mothers who prefer their sons. I'd like both.

Dr. R. And you, when you think your mother prefers your brother, then there is, for you, no means of changing.

P. It's beginning to get through, all that time was needed to reassure me.

Dr. R. Everything was devalued because of that.

P. Yes . . . Yes . . . I'm so afraid to say 'never' . . .

Dr. R. 'Never'. One must try to make you realize the power of 'never'.

P. Yes, exactly. And know I can't love everybody. (*Tears.*).

Dr. R. No, it is not correct. It is not like that. We have to do a bit of analysis here.

P. I have good friends, all quite intellectual. I'm blocked. I've stopped. I must accept that my brother has taken half the table space. It was because of his penis that my brother was preferred to me.

Dr. R. The goal, the aim that has driven you to achieve things . . . the goal that we must get right. For instance, could music be for the sake of music and not for another reason? It seemed necessary to make yourself not just loved but be loved more than your brother . . . You must find again the correct aim. Let us take the treatment. What is the correct aim of this treatment? We must see that what has been done together does not disappear with my leaving.

P. At the very beginning, when Dr X and Mrs Y told me about having a treatment, they suggested it could last three years . . . It lasted seven years, then there was a relapse. Then Dr X and Mrs Y said, 'Do you want to work with Dr Rey?' I was flattered. (*Laughing.*) The first meeting when I saw you, I was already less self-conscious. (I think it was September.) I felt myself to be an artist with no fear of life, a little manic . . .

Dr. R. What is this manic phase for you?

P. I mean, at last, I'll be able to live with sexuality in a mad way, happy, letting go. I'll meet people, not be abandoned, feel omnipotent, unconventional. But the people didn't reject me. 'You are analysing yourself, you are going to change, you will not be in psychotherapy all your life.' That's what I thought . . . Everything is related . . .

Dr. R. At last with regard to mother you have accepted that she can die peacefully. She has become replaced inside you by her memory, no need for an excess of words, no need for an excess of life, because there is no excess of death. If all goes well with Mrs X maybe there is no need for an excess of life.

P. Now that my mother is dead, gone really, there is something that remains . . . Very important.

Dr. R. I wish the best success to you. You must continue . . .

P. Best of luck to you also.

COMMENTARY ON THE TREATMENT OF MANIC-DEPRESSIVE PSYCHOSIS

EARLY HISTORY

The patient was twenty years old when she first became severely depressed. This depression occurred when her mother died of a mastectomy, breast cancer. The patient said that as her mother was dying she did not want to leave her. She followed her mother to hospital, and during the dying period, which lasted for three weeks, she slept in a hospital bed which was put in the room with her mother. She described this cot near her mother's bed as 'a live tomb'. Subsequently the patient thought that she herself had cancer, like her mother. In the analysis she then returned to phantasies of beginning her own life *in utero*. When her mother was pregnant she had had a haemorrhage. The patient had blamed herself for this haemorrhage as well as her very difficult birth, feeling she on two occasions had nearly caused her mother's death; the patient's family confirmed the fact that she had nearly caused her mother's death 'by being born'. After the mother's death had occurred, the patient had passed the hospital for a long time, saying, 'Hello, Mother.' She seemed unable to acknowledge her mother's death.

PATHOLOGICAL SPLITTING

Various splitting of feelings for her mother, as well as splits of feelings between mother and father and splits within her own personality, were prominent. For her, mother was a 'saint', 'so nice', 'so kind to people', 'a model for all women'. The patient felt 'how awful it was to have caused so much illness', and even the death of her mother. She said, 'I love my mother so much'; 'I was a ray of sunshine to mother'. At the same time the patient was severely critical of her mother, saying 'I did not love her'; 'I wished her dead'; 'she imposed her sexuality on me'; 'she was obsessional'; 'she was obsessed by moral sins and by sins of her own inferiority'.

The degree of splitting of the patient's own personality was severe. Almost simultaneously two parts of her personality appeared opposite to each other: 'I love my mother', 'I don't love mother'; 'I looked after her'. 'I wished her dead; 'I took on her illness', 'I did not take over her illness'.

An examination of the splitting mechanisms indicates that each part of her personality became completely identified with different split-off aspects of the object, for instance, mother. The patient was not in an ambivalent state, but rather in a pre-ambivalent split. These identifications with part-objects extended not only to psychic parts of her personality, but also to her body; for example, she was intensely identified with the physical illness of her mother. The patient could not distinguish the split-off parts of herself and her mother; the identities of mother and the patient were confused.

So powerful was her identification with mother that it was necessary for me to give the patient interpretations which were addressed to the physical part of her. This was an important technique of treatment in which I said, 'In your head you . . .', rather than saying, 'In your mind you think like this and that.' This interpretation was designed to help the patient think of her own body and separate it from the body of her mother.

PROJECTIVE IDENTIFICATION

There was a complex process of projective identification in this woman. She always talked about what others thought of her, describing how they liked her or did not like certain aspects of her. This process of projective identification started by the patient putting her own thoughts or actions into the mind or head of others. Subsequently, her projections, which trans-formed the thoughts of others into a kind of delusion and hallucination, were re-introjected by her in her own mind/head. The problem was that the other part of her desperately opposed these re-introjected thoughts, as if the other 'person' or part of a person created by her had to be denied. As a matter of fact, one had to analyse two people, but within the same person, the patient.

The use of projective identification just described interfered with her introjective identification with her mother. For example, the patient constantly projected her own thoughts and body into her mother. This process also interfered with the major process of projective identification which needed to occur for development to take place. Because the patient had projected bad parts of herself into the mother, there was no possibility of establishing good internal objects which form the core of development of a stable personality.

As I began recapturing the little girl, and even the-baby-*in-utero*, and helping the patient with the possibility of establishing a relationship with a good mother, the possibility of establishing a good inner mother and other good internal objects occurred.

QUESTIONS OF LIFE AND DEATH OF THE OBJECT AND OF HERSELF

The dreams of this patient and continued thoughts were so concrete when they were discussed that they appeared at times to be borderline delusions and hallucinations. This could be seen remarkably well in several of the patient's dreams, which were both dreams and belonged to reality; the patient could not distinguish between the two. For example, there was a dream in which she saw her mother in a picture frame. The picture frame became white and then split into two frames, with one frame containing a picture which was a double of the other. In looking at the dream, the patient thought, 'If only I could see mother.'

In another dream there was a telephone message from father who was going to tell her brother and her of the death of mother. But the patient was told in the dream that she had been kept unaware of the fact that her mother had been in a coma for seven years. This attempt to make the transition between the dream and internal and external reality reminds one of the transitional state of Winnicott: it is partly physical and somatic and partly representational. The reader of the text can see the interplay between internal and external reality. The dream of mother as being dead related both to the patient's external mother and to growing insights regarding damage to her internal mother.

Also present in the session was the patient's relationship with her husband, whom she always called 'my companion'. In her split personality the patient stated, 'I love him', and 'I don't love him'. Her anger, as was analysed, took the place of orgasms, which she was unable to experience with her husband. Apart from her frigidity there was also the problem regarding having a child. She was deeply ambivalent about becoming pregnant, which had a double origin. At first she, or rather part of her, had wanted to become pregnant. Her husband, however, wanted to wait until they had more money, a house, and were more settled in their life as a couple. She, on the other hand, felt she was being deprived of a child and also of orgasm, for she did not treat him as a husband but rather as a 'companion'. This was perhaps part of the patient's vengeance against him for not allowing her to have a child at the time she chose.

Another problem was her deep identification with this child to whom she was to give birth. Projected into the child to be born was her own child-self, who had brought every possible misery and illness to her own mother. In thinking of being a mother the patient identified with her own ill mother, who had been depressed and unable to be a real good mother. In other words, there was a double identification: the patient identified with her mother, but was also identified with the little girl that was still in her mind as a possibility.

The method of interpretation was to make the patient conscious of this 'little-girl-in-her-head' and 'in-her-body'; to make her aware of the conflicts, guilt; the identification with mother and the attempted identification at times with father. The purpose of this analysis was to help 'the little-girl-in-her' to grow up. During this growing up she also became the mother of everybody – of her mother, her father, her brother, her husband and other members of the family.

The projective identification and the identity problems were made still more complicated by her belief in another part of her that she was omnipotent. The patient explained how if she had bad or sexual thoughts or if she masturbated under the blanket, God and everyone at school would know. In fact, she felt the world would know everything about what she was doing. This is a kind of obsessional thinking which went deeper because the patient thought that her thoughts could also influence other people in their mind and body, as well as transforming her body. For instance, she feared that her thoughts would cause both cancer and other bodily illnesses. As a punishment due to intense guilt she maintained she inflicted various illnesses on her body in order to be like her mother. Of course, because she felt her thoughts could destroy her body, she felt she must destroy her own thoughts. In the treatment she complained not only of not being 'alive', but of being 'anaesthetized' and of not being able to do anything, not even to 'think'. This necessity or compulsion to destroy her own thoughts may have led her to consider suicide in order to destroy the unwanted thoughts.

It was possible for the therapist to address the other part of her and help that 'alive' part to remain alive. The patient's task was to try and do some more mourning for her mother, which implied abandoning the law of talion and achieving forgiveness instead of vengeance. The other task was to transform the 'transitional', 'post-traumatic part-representation' of mother into a mother that was becoming more realistically dead, while helping the patient to establish a good inner object.

IDENTIFICATION WITH A MALE FIGURE

As the pathological attachment and identification to mother slowly altered, the patient's feelings became far greater in importance. In her attempt to undo this pathological attachment and identification with mother, she naturally turned to father as a new object of love and as an object with whom she could identify.

In normal infancy the child projects mother and feelings about mother into father for a while so as not to lose mother completely. This takes place at a primitive level by the projection of the breast into the penis. This part-object level is very important. For the patient, the projected part of mother-in-father imposed a certain identity on father in her phantasy, making him different from what he was in reality. The child and this patient then relate to the combination of both mother and father. The same, of course, applies to boys as well as girls.

The patient had a split image of mother. On the one hand there was the depressed, ill mother, a repressive mother, and on the other hand an equally non-acceptable idealized mother. The patient's father was likewise experienced with very ambivalent feelings. There were a number of hateful remarks about him, including how violent he was, how bad he was to mother, and the awful relationship between father and mother. At the same time the patient said, 'I hated him', she would think, 'I loved him', or she would say, 'There is him in me'.

At other times the patient made comments about her sexual feelings about her father. She manically mentioned thoughts about sleeping with her husband to evade important interpretations regarding this. It became apparent in the period after her mother's death that father wanted the patient to come with her husband and live with him because he felt 'you are the woman I have always wanted to have'. The patient was appalled by her father's sexual overtones to such an extent that she left the house and did not talk to her father again. A few days later her father died without her having seen him. This theme of the incestuous father incited her to remember earlier feelings regarding the possibility of an incestuous father–daughter relationship. These themes became very important in psychotherapy.

The patient's mother expressed concern not only about the patient's relation to her father, but also to her brother. The brother, four and a half years younger than her, was a source of morbid jealousy. She said, 'I lost half my face' when he was born. She also told a story of how the mother told her not to cut off the brother's penis because he could die. The patient wanted to cut off her brother's penis, a thought that came into her mind when she saw her brother being bathed and dressed. She would think, 'He could die!' Much later, the patient worked on a building-site at her brother's house, working very hard, 'like a man'. As well as her jealousy of her brother and her wish to castrate him, there was also a sign of reparation to compensate for her phantasy of castrating him. At the same time, some of the extreme jealousy towards her brother must have contributed to her masculine identification, which recaptured some of what she had lost after his birth.

The patient had been in a manic phase in the past. Her doctor described this, saying:

> . . . the patient refused to attend her doctor, refused to continue medication, became more and more agitated in her behaviour, she was hyper-excitable, moving about, gesticulating, with her reflections she was interrupting all discussions around her and trying to bring herself to the attention of everybody by all sorts of antics. She was convinced that she was very erudite and cultured and could face any sort of discussion.

The first attack happened at the age of fourteen when she was persecuted and identified with a famous historical character, a woman who played a very masculine role in history. At other times the patient wanted to enter a convent as a Mother Superior. Whenever there was a possibility of participating in any activity, she tried her best to be leader. Even when only part of her was hypermanic, she thought of being very successful in her teaching, a great lady, appreciated by everybody, and had phantasies of how she could do 'everything'. For instance, because of her wish to compete with father, who was a music lover, she felt she could play musical instruments. She also had the phase of manly activities, such as working on the building-site.

Manic patients boast about being bigger, more capable, more successful, more intelligent than anyone. They know everything, they identify with more figures, and in other terms they experience themselves both bigger physically and mentally. This manic phase coincides with a period of failed 'growth', which, when it comes to an end, leads to depression. It was in such periods of mania that the patient attempted identification with father. This was a repetition of a failed earlier infantile attempt at moving from mother to father.

There are at least two ways of becoming 'greater': one is to become convinced one is 'bigger' than the others; the other is by belittling others with terrible contempt and thus feeling 'taller' and more important, a 'super person'. It is the part-object representation of the male, the penis, with which the manic patient identifies. This identification with the penis leads to the grandiose aspects of the manic state.

ATTEMPTED REPARATION

The normal phase of turning from mother to father was never successfully completed by this patient. First, there was a very deep split in her personality so that the two parts could not act together towards one aim; there was, for example, the depressed mother and also the idealized mother. Second, the attachment to mother, based on guilt, could not be resolved sufficiently by the introjection of a good internal mother. Third, the temporary identification with father which occurred before beginning to look at him as an object was impossible, not only because of the split depressed and idealized mother which she projected into him, but also because of the ambivalence towards him which was linked with his ill-treatment of mother. This also prevented using him to do reparation to mother. She could only attempt the pendulum action in which at one moment she was depressed, and the other moment she was manic. This oscillation made it impossible for the integration of the two parts of her to take place.

The patient who is manic has difficulty in making reparation. This patient's inability to achieve the mourning of mother and develop a good internalization of her stimulated an omnipotent belief that mother was not dead but rather waiting to be repaired. If the patient could not repair mother, then she was waiting for somebody else to do it for her. When the patient in a manic state attempted to repair mother, she identified as well with her very depressed mother who was dying. The mother could not be repaired by the manic daughter who, as a little girl, in a sudden jump ahead, could not mature into a normal grown-up. This attempt to jump into maturity through identification with her father was totally incomplete as he was no good to mother. The girl's sexuality, therefore, was of no use as a method of reparation.

It is worth mentioning one aspect of the damaged mother which this patient was attempting to repair. The mother died of breast cancer. The breast/mother is the most important part–object representing the mother. It is most probable that the cancer stood for the little girl's destruction of the breast. The breast had to be repaired and the penis was an essential necessity for this task of reparation. The attempted reparation was by identifying the breast with the penis and by projective identification, hoping the breast would acquire the 'goodness of the penis', if the penis was good. Reparation could occur at a higher level of sophistication by giving a good baby to the mother, who would fill her breasts again with good milk and the pleasure to be whole and complete. All this the patient could not achieve by herself.

Another attempt at reparation by the patient was psychotherapy. Although the therapy consisted of only seventeen sessions on a once-weekly basis, the patient was able to make some progress. The little girl, whom the patient projected into the mind of everybody, was now reintrojected in herself. There was a diminution of the use of splitting and of projective identification, with a lessening of the splitting distance between the parts of herself as the parts came together. Progress was practicably visible as the patient ceased jumping from one subject to another and using unfinished sentences, developing a more sensible and much clearer discourse. There was a beginning of an integration of the personality and of the possibility of the internalization of the good object represented by the therapist.

The context in which all this was taking place was the transference. At first the patient pretended to respect my knowledge and my status saying,

'You know, I don't.' Later, my role as a good mother was established. At times I became a father in the transference, which was a complicated one. The patient made protests in the transference about my sexual feelings and hers. She said I was a professional, and wondered how I could suggest that certain feelings of hers might be sexual when there was such a difference of age between us. She described how I was experienced by her more as a respected father-figure, and mostly as a kind and good mother-figure. As a therapist I provided models needed for her to use appropriate object relationships and a proper introjective identification, leading to sublimations and transformations. As a psychoanalytic psychotherapist, I give great importance to the feelings of reparation and the repeated efforts to help the patient to achieve reparation, especially of the mother and the little girl that she was, as well as reparation of the relationship to father. However, the primary task of these sessions was for the patient to introject and internalize a good mother.

COMPARISON OF ANOREXIC AND MANIC-DEPRESSIVE PATIENTS

There is a continuity between my descriptions of the anorexic patient (see Chapter 4) and the manic-depressive woman in this chapter. In the case of the anorexic patient, the conflict was with the mother and the foetus-infant, who was devouring or being devoured. This conflict was reactivated at puberty, when the original problem of double identification with the baby/mother returned. In the case of the anorexic patient, this had to be relived in a physical role, that is, by getting pregnant.

In the case of the manic-depressive patient, the *in utero* situation was hierarchically one stage more advanced. The patient felt she had endangered the life of mother by the difficulty mother encountered in the pregnancy and then at birth. The patient's identification with mother was again present as she was feeling not only depressed, but physically ill like her mother. She experienced internally the law of talion – eye for eye, tooth for tooth, breast cancer for breast cancer – the cot being the deathbed or the 'live tomb'. Pregnancy was so dangerous for the manic-depressive's mother that the patient, so identified with her mother, was afraid to have her own baby.

The way in which both the anorexic and manic-depressive patient experienced death was different. In the anorectic death was through starvation, while for the manic-depressive patient death was through not being alive when actually alive. Both identified with the father. The anorexic patient attempted to act father's role with regard to mother and the whole family. This was followed by a period of regression in which the patient went back to a special sort of delusion of being *in utero* in the first months of life. This regression to being *in utero* had to be physically acted out by the anorectic. The manic-depressive patient also regressed but there was more of a psychic identification involved. In other words, the manic-depressive level of regression remained at one hierarchical level higher than that of the anorectic; the manic-depressive patient did not have physically to act out the regression.

The splitting processes occurred in the manic-depressive patient in different emotional depths from the anorexic patient, who became ill in one part of the split-off self, while the other part of her functioned fairly well, enabling her to think rationally in many ways. The manic patient, in contrast, experienced the split-off parts in less separate ways, and pathology was obvious in both parts of herself. Both patients, however, had been able to enter university.

The role of father and identification with father was somewhat different in each of the two patients. The actual death of the anorectic's father precipitated a depression. The patient went through a phase of identification with father, behaving as a man, and she attempted to act his role with regard to mother and the whole family. This heralded the period of regression which followed. In contrast, the manic-depressive patient made a vigorous attempt at male identification with father. The failure of identification with father occurred when the manic-depressive patient made drastic attempts to be a man and repair mother in order to move away from her depression. When the manic identification with the male – penis – failed as it has to, there is a return to depression and identification with the damaged mother. At this point the regression previously described occurred in the manic-depressive patient.

I am presenting this patient as a means of demonstrating a therapeutic approach to the complicated structures of a manic-depressive patient. The patient continued treatment with an able psychiatric worker, and later gave birth to a boy and managed to keep her job. She is a brave woman who tried very hard to succeed, and in many ways she did.

COMMENTARY ON THE PHYSICAL FACTORS IN MANIC-DEPRESSION

I would like to add a few words with regard to the somatic or drug treatment, but above all to the genetic factor in the causation of this illness or of any other mental illnesses.

The patient had received and was receiving drug treatment. No doubt this was helping her and may well have prevented shifts from one mood to another. When I saw her, aged thirty, although there was less fluctuation in her moods, her problems were enormous and had not markedly changed with the drugs.

But what must be done is to decide what is the part played by the 'genes' in the manifestations of the disease. When more is known about genetics we may understand better their specific roles. We can accept that the splitting processes, the projective identification, the excitation, the mood of depression and many other manifestations might have a genetic background. However, to take an example of a child learning to speak: it is not genetics that decide if he or she speaks English, French, Chinese, Arabic or anything else. The genes make it possible to learn to speak, though its mechanisms are inherited, but the role of the environment remains crucial.

This then applies to every other aspect of our mental behaviour. That which is deficient, not there, abnormally present, can be compensated by an adequate environment that helps to achieve, at least in part, what the genes could not do. Furthermore, without a correct environment the genes cannot develop, for reasons such as lack of proteins at a moment of maturation. For example, the development of certain aspects of sight is grossly interfered with if the brain cells do not receive light stimuli. Furthermore, a certain specific moment or period for development necessary for growth to take place, which is genetically determined, may not happen because of interference by the environment in one way or another. A small, insignificant event may later on so enormously increase in significance in the patient's mind that it is impossible to predict what the result of this factor will be.

Therefore, to treat a patient only with drugs, even if they are helpful, is very wrong because the part played by genes and other physiological factors cannot be assessed to the full extent. My early work on the complex relationship between hormonal activity and schizophrenic mental states has left me in no doubt that genetic, biochemical and psychodynamic factors must all be considered in the assessment and treatment of psychotic patients. Current research supports my notion that a combination of drug treatment and psychotherapy is more effective than either of the two treatments on their own. For this reason the question remains: why deprive a patient of a treatment that could become helpful?

7 PSYCHOLINGUISTICS, OBJECT RELATIONS THEORY AND THE THERAPEUTIC PROCESS

Psychoanalysts and analytic psychotherapists use words to treat their patients. How can the use and manipulation of words bring about a change in the structures underlying behaviour, phantasy life, thoughts and object relationships?

This paper examines certain statements of patients, including their behaviour and non-verbal activity, and relates them to what is known about the stages of formation of language as selected for this specific purpose. An extensive use has been made of examples of schizoid thought processes. These examples suggest that there is a stage in the development of language when the manipulation of objects and the manipulation of words is so intricately combined that the subject can hardly distinguish the action and concrete content from its verbal representation. Investigating the persistence of those early stages in adult thinking and adult relations to reality, side by side with more advanced stages of symbolic activity, suggests to the psychotherapist the level at which he or she has to operate to bring about a change through words.

A summary will be given of those psycholinguistic structures present in the therapeutic attempt to help the patient reach the stages of structuration of behaviour and thought where such structures can be undone or destructured in order to be restructured in a different way. This will imply a different kind of object relationship and a different understanding of the use of words. The therapeutic process through language involves various aspects which I shall summarize.

Language is not ready-made; it results from a process of construction that starts very early in life. Both Piaget and Klein have stressed that the infant's views of external reality are influenced by the projection of his own phantasies. This structured object is then reintrojected and reprojected a number of times leading to a personal construct by the subject. These are the objects of the inner world which are in intrapsychic relationship between themselves and also in confrontation with the actual objects of the external world. The two worlds only correspond up to a point, and in severe pathological states may differ considerably. This Kleinian view may be compared with the well-known mechanisms of Piagetian cognitive psychology, namely assimilation and accommodation, with equilibrium between the two processes or predominance of one or the other. What is apparent is the complementarity rather than resemblance between inner and outer worlds.

Every time someone uses language to formulate a thought or to communicate it to others he engages in a process of construction. He constructs with words joined together using bits of experience formed into words; he constructs thoughts in all sorts of patterns just as he has done with objects other than words. A process of non-verbal construction goes on simultaneously along with verbal activity. When verbal activity develops and becomes more and more complex, the constructional activity does not close – it continues to take place. A reciprocal influence goes on between non-verbal and verbal constructions.

Through this process of construction one becomes conscious of the experience and information he is integrating by means of words arranged into grammatical structures. This process of reification of experience and 'ontogenic recapitulation' is necessary to generate ideas and communicate them.

In order to understand a message, the recipient has to analyse the message into bits or units of information, and to reconstruct the message for himself. It is not certain that the reconstruction will be the same as the sender intended. Words are sounds that are just bundles of vibrations to which both personal and shared meanings are assigned. However, during this process of analysis-synthesis, the receiver becomes somewhat aware, through the participation of both his own constructions as well as the speaker's.

In therapy, reconstruction of faulty constructions takes place through insight into bits of constructions, and their relationships, followed by putting these 'bits' meaningfully together again. During therapy the therapist has received the message of the patient, and, rather than being passive, has had to analyse and synthesize the message. The analysis of these bits and their re-synthesis generate insight in the mind of the therapist. When he makes an interpretation, the patient will have to proceed in the same way as the therapist and become aware of the new construction proposed by the therapist. Insight by the therapist into linguistic modes of functioning becomes a very relevant aspect of therapy.

The processes of organizing information during the paranoid-schizoid and depressive phases of development play a vital primary role in this analysis-synthesis or dissolution-reconstruction activity. A satisfactory working through of the passage from the paranoid-schizoid to the depressive positions will result in acquiring mental processes necessary later to negotiate higher levels of constructive activity such as language. One of the vital functions of dream activity is to facilitate the working through of the paranoid-schizoid and depressive phases in relationship to problems arising in life in general or in psychoanalysis.

Let me clarify the Kleinian concepts of the paranoid-schizoid and depressive positions. In the paranoid-schizoid phase, object relations occur through introjective and projective activity which includes identifactory phenomena. Projective identification is an important concept. There are two types of part-objects in this phase. In relation to future whole objects such as breast and mother, at the beginning normal part-objects play a part in relationship to the more advanced concept of mother. Another type of part-object results from splitting activity. Because of the aggressive sadistic impulses in the form of greed, envy and jealousy, objects – in order to be protected – are split into good and bad. Those split-off objects, as well as split-off parts of the self responsible for the impulses, are projected into outside objects. This is followed by omnipotent denial of the process. Thus good and bad objects are created. Some objects are over-idealized to preserve them or to preserve the self from persecutory activity. The objects containing bad bits become persecutors and are projected. A particular kind of part-function psychology is thus created. For instance, objects are classified according to one quality; edible or inedible, hard or soft, bigger and smaller than the mouth, and on the basis of sharing one quality they are treated alike.

At a very primitive level this depends largely on projective identification. But confrontation with external reality constantly corrects distortions due to projective identification. Destroying the bad parts would destroy the good. Feelings of 'compassion' in the most primitive form begin to appear; reparation has to be made. At first this is a concrete procedure, that is, restoring the object to what it was before the attack. Then more sophisticated procedures are used, especially in the healing of internal objects, a mourning process which must occur if the infant is to move forward to a more sophisticated mental life.

The mechanisms of transformation elaborated during those two phases become available for further transformations and passage from one kind of object to another – from a lower to a higher level of functioning in later life. As levels of representation become more sophisticated and abstract, the schizoid and depressive processes also acquire a higher quality of semiotic complexity. As well as a longitudinal process, there is also a vertical hierarchical organization, as in Piagetian psychology (see Figure 10). By vertical hierarchical organization we mean that as more objects are discovered and more structures are constructed, there emerge more sophisticated levels of functioning. Thus the imitation of an action by an action later becomes performed in thought, symbols and signs – that is, at higher levels of functioning. The accompanying diagrams illustrate some of the possible methods of structuring experience. Figure 10 borrows from the Piagetian idea of a horizontal and vertical hierarchical organization of

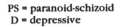

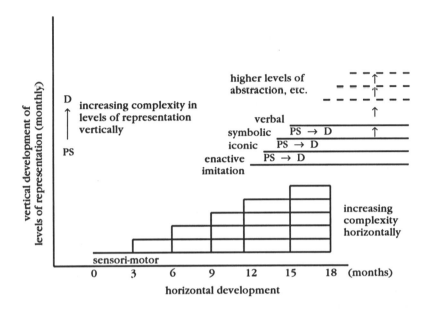

Figure 10

thought in combination with a Kleinian approach. Figure 11 represents three of the many channels of structuring experience.

Let us imagine that the tetrahedron A (Figure 11) represents the three-dimensional space in the subject where various activities take place and his experiences are constructively organized. Among the many factors participating in this organizing and transforming activity, three are particularly important for therapeutic understanding.

First, personality structures. At apex P we have the line of development as evaluated from the psychoanalytic point of view. The infant structures his world through object relationships under the sway of love and hate impulses, and of the epistemophilic tendency, K as Bion calls it, for knowledge. The infant constructs increasingly complex hierarchically organized personality structures by stages. Thus he passes through the well-known phases of personality development; oral, anal, urethral, phallic and genital and auto-erotic to narcissistic, allo-erotic, and so on. This transformation activity involves the paranoid-schizoid and depressive processes of transformation specific to each particular level of organization, sophistication and abstraction.

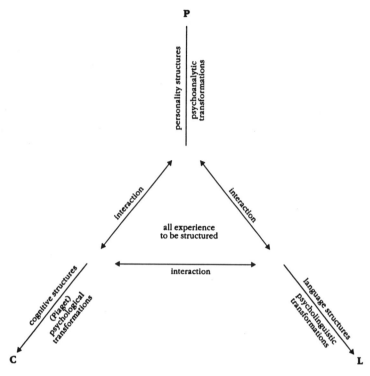

Figure 11

Second, cognitive structures. Apex C is the line of development more closely concerned with the construction of cognitive structures following the Piagetian model. These structures are constructed from experience and, in the course of the maturation of the nervous system, develop into more complex patterns permitting more complex mental operations involving the external world. These structures are organized in hierarchical strata as new levels of representation emerge: sensori-motor, enactive, iconic, symbolic, verbal. There is progress from sensori-motor to semiotic activity and within the semiotic function are the various levels of semiotic organization (see Figure 10). I will use extensively the Piagetian notion that whatever is learned and organized at one level of activity has to be gone through again at the next higher level. There is a sort of mental ontogenesis by analogy with evolutionary ontogenesis. Again we can apply the Kleinian contribution as to what mechanisms are used when passing from one cognitive structure to another, more complex, hierarchical organization. That is to say, the passage from a simpler to a more advanced cognitive structure also involves the use of paranoid-schizoid and depressive processes of transformation specific to that stage.

Third, psycholinguistics. The same applies to psycholinguistics represented at L, the third apex of the triangle. A Kleinian theory can illuminate the 'psycho-' part of psycholinguistics. When babies begin to speak, they are already well equipped with what Moerck (1977) has called the antecedents to language development. At the sensori-motor level they are capable of non-verbal exchange. They are capable of acting on objects, precursors of a grammatical structuration into a subject, verb, object relationship. The infant and child go through very specific stages in producing and learning new words, new parts of speech and new structures linking them together. These become the grammatical structures of language in all psycholinguistic theories. Thus they can bring two objects together, act on an object and be acted upon by an object. These and other activities are antecedents to the well-known linguistic structures needed for building up sentence constituents, and for forming embedded clauses. In order to communicate, infants first use non-verbal gestures and sign language, such as pointing to objects they want or giving them to somebody else. Facial expressions are extremely important in sign language, but they also use sounds in their own way to express themselves. This is a very important process for later when they will learn to use sounds that are imposed by language. Thus infants will modify their personal language; labials, dentals, occlusives.

The rest of the paper will deal with the contrast between non-verbal and verbal personal languages and socially constructed language.

First, let us see from an object relations perspective how infants give meaning to sounds. By nine to twelve months infants begin to use the sounds or phonemes of their native language – sounds which they have picked up from their environment, especially repetitive human noises or those from inanimate sources. From object relations theory, the infants discover their own insides, which are structured by incorporative and introjective processes, especially introjective identifications. By projective identification the infants also structure their objects. The mother is the first object, but all objects will acquire an inside and an outside. These two mechanisms of introjective and projective identification give 'meaning' content or semantic content to objects. Any container has a content to be the 'container', or sign. Meaning is what that content conveys to various people. For example, to some the content is a woman, but to others it is a mother, or even a mother doing a specific task. I have used the word 'semantic' to refer to one of two aspects of linguistics, that is, syntax and semantic. It does not matter whether an object has really got an inside, for inevitably it is given one in phantasy. Thus one patient would not lie on the couch because he was afraid he would sink into it and be enclosed by it, with only his feet protruding. He later associated in his own schizophrenic way that the divan was his mother; the divan with no inside was structured as the mother with an inside.

At an early age sounds are treated as objects because of the perceptual quality of sound. This sound-object can also be structured, given an internal and an external space or domain and a content by means of a piece of experience projected into it. This construction can be manipulated like other objects. The mechanisms of relating to that sound-object, the mechanisms of defence against the dangers of that object, the mechanisms of connecting those sound-objects with others, can only be the mental structures that are available at any particular phase of development. During the first years of life, they are the paranoid-schizoid and depressive processes. Here are a few examples:

One young man would immediately feel anxiety and marked depersonalization symptoms when the noise of his motor bike stopped. If the noise existed, he existed. When the noise stopped, he lost the part of himself that was projected into it. His self only existed if contained in an object sound. Another illustration is the situation of an intelligent woman who felt enveloped by the sound of music. She experienced being inside the sound like a foetus might be in the womb. Further therapy indicated the sound probably meant parental intercourse. Sounds acquire meaning through their content. In this case, sound contained a foetus that was herself, the music the container or womb, and this foetus (herself) which developed in the musical womb was experiencing something about the intercourse of the parents. Thus the music was transformed into a container containing the foetus; but it is obvious that the very primitive *in utero* experience was later given a much more sophisticated meaning.

Those structured sound-objects can also be orally introjected. Thus a woman who had difficulty talking in therapy managed to tell her therapist that she could not speak because she felt that the words were mouldy, poisonous, dangerous objects inside her. She said they would attack the therapist and hurt him if she spoke because she would expel them on to him. She was so convinced of this that she later simulated suicide on several occasions in order to have a gastric lavage to get rid of the dangerous word-objects.

I saw a little boy who wanted to become a girl and had started dressing like one. He used an idioglossia, which drove people crazy. I recorded a few expressions: 'chopbolder' meant 'leave me alone, I'm angry'; 'thombombur' meant 'you are very horrible'; 'cappoottee', 'you are too nasty'. They apparently represented the babbling of a little sister of whom he was desperately jealous. He wanted to take her place, and, identifying with her, he constructed a sound language with his sister's own sounds.

There are many examples of children refusing to give up their privately constructed language; sometimes they learn language and understand what is said to them but refuse to express themselves in a conventional language. Jakobson (1968) cites several cases. In one amusing example, a child insisted on using her own jargon for certain words, but when her mother used her jargon, the girl angrily said, 'Please, Mother, will you use French properly.' Such examples show the processes of the paranoid-schizoid stage at work, with splitting of the self and the use of projective identification resulting in the creation of normal sound-objects, but sometimes in abnormal combinations of abnormal 'phonemes' into abnormal words.

None of my patients had worked through the depressive phase. However, because of splitting, and/or regression a partial working through of the depressive position is possible. Thus a schizoid or borderline person may split off a part from the rest of the personality that still functions in a schizoid way while another part can proceed further. Such a schizoid person has not acquired the capacity to stop pathological splitting, to be able to join parts together and to mourn in order to part from an object, a situation, or a level of representation that has become inadequate in order to pass to another, more suitable, one. One remarkable example was a man who suffered from the worst claustro-agoraphobic syndrome I have ever come across. He complained of hypochondriacal sensations in his body, and although very intelligent was amazingly devoid of phantasies. On a very rare occasion, he remembered one dream of himself with a sort of bubble coming out of his mouth. It was like the bubbles in children's comics that contain the words that people in the drawings are speaking. However, the bubble was empty; there were no words in it.

One of the most fundamental ideas of Freud is his concept of the primary processes and methods of representation in the unconscious. Becoming conscious implies the decoding of the message using the knowledge psychoanalysis has given us of primary processes and primitive methods of representation, which Freud called thing-representation. To become conscious it is necessary to know non-verbal symbols as well, and to link both non-verbal symbols and thing-representation to word-representation. In psycholinguistic terms this implies that the analyst has to analyse the global message into parts. According to his own abstract capacities, the analyst must try to rectify the experiences of his analysand's message, and become aware of the concrete meaning or content of the word-objects and their relationship in the mind of the analysand. He cannot apply the ready-made syntactic structures of language he or she uses as an automaton, but must relive the experiences of the analysand as experienced by the latter at the levels they are expressed. The analysand can then share with the analyst a new reconstruction which is less pathological and allows a move to a better level of functioning. For this to occur, both analyst and analysand need to share in this process of analysis-synthesis. In this process they become conscious of what they are doing because they are manipulating objects again.

It is indeed interesting to compare these views with those of Piaget, for whom the phenomenon of insight, or becoming conscious, is linked also with reconstruction. In Piaget's views the common sense approach of comparing 'becoming conscious' with a ray of light making visible an obscure spot is insufficient or even erroneous. Using the Piagetian model of the mind, becoming conscious means that certain elements belonging to an inferior unconscious level move to a superior, conscious one. It is not a simple displacement, because a fundamental aspect of this displacement implies a reconstruction into a new organization at the higher level of what was already organized at the lower level. For Piaget this activity has both a functional utility and implies the use of certain structural processes.

The structural processes involve the use of the mechanisms elaborated during the passage from the paranoid-schizoid to the depressive position; for the mental processes acquired when negotiating the depressive position are of a much higher level of consciousness than are those of the paranoid-schizoid position. The functional utility of this is that there develops a capacity to relate to the object in a very different way, in a much more mature and satisfying manner, and with a greater degree of freedom of choice in dealing with life situations.

Here is a clinical example demonstrating the passage from non-verbal language structures to acquired language. The processes will be described in terms of the paranoid-schizoid–depressive mechanisms.

The patient was a single man aged twenty-one. When I saw him he was having his third attack of schizophrenia. He talked a great deal, and at first I had very little to do apart from making an occasional remark in order to be with him and show my understanding, or ask clarifying questions.

He was confused about practically everything. He was unsure whether he was male or female, homosexual or heterosexual. He complained that his left side was split into a right and left side, which had different sexual identities. He complained, saying that his parents had never taught him real human relationships. What he knew he had learned in books. He was very angry with his parents. Then he said that speech had no more value to him, saying, 'I can but do not speak.' What emerged was that although he still used language, it was meaningless to him. Instead, he was preoccupied with a very complex non-verbal language entirely created by him. This consisted in the giving of meanings to bodily movements and appearance as well as to the relationships between various colours.

Left and right in his body had different identities. The left side was split vertically; the split was experienced as a tension in the mid-line of the leg from the knee downwards; the knee felt damaged and full of tension. His left hand was also split between the three digits and the ring finger and little finger, which became in a state of tension if he moved them apart, and that puzzled him a lot. His head felt as though it had a right and a left side; the left side also was split and the split experienced in the form of tension. If he thought of his left leg or his knee, or moved the left two fingers mentioned, he experienced a tension at the site of the cleavage, similar to that experienced in the left side of the head.

Associated with the right and left side were the colours blue and brown, respectively. Brown was derived from the colour of his mother's eyes and blue his father's. He had brown eyes. This, he complained, caused him extreme confusion: brown was female and blue was male – yet he had brown eyes.

The sides of his body were also linked with colours in the following way. There were at home three 'generations' of beds which had been used in succession by his parents, then by the children. In all three 'generations' of beds his father always slept on the right side and his mother on the left side. He repeatedly said it had always been so, that is, right sides of beds were always blue and male, and left sides always brown and female. He was absolutely positive he had always slept on the left side of the bed. Further, he had shared a bed with a brother who slept on the right side and he on the left side. One traumatic experience was when he once had slept with his father in the same bed, father on the right and him on the left. His most vivid memory was of his father's blue eyes looking at him.

To add further to the confusion it turned out that the experiences in his left side were derived from an identification with his father's left side. His father had many traumas on his left side – he was bitten by a dog, then a pig, and then paralysed by a cerebral haemorrhage. The patient had also experienced a feeling of lifelessness in his left side. Further, at home his mother was dominant, that is, the female over the male. He felt so confused that he decided he would ask for a transsexual operation but did not do so because he broke down and came to the hospital.

Apart from brown and blue, other colours had meanings of their own, some he understood, some he did not. White, red, green, yellow, grey and black were meaningful if he or others dressed in one or if he saw signs coloured in grey or saw the flags of Canada or Quebec. Green and yellow seemed to be associated with apples, apples with the farm, and the farm with animals, and animals with him.

In other aspects of his thinking there was a whole series of similar symbolism and sign language. He thought he had a female metabolism because he helped his mother at home by working in the kitchen and washing dishes. He was always influenced by the moon and he would rub his tummy when making that statement. He was interested in learning and he considered his mother the more educated parent, although he had utmost contempt for his parents' lack of education.

Anything hard, such as a steel plate or a cement pillar, gave him a feeling of being crushed and evoked the splitting of the body I have described. He said friends had tried to arrange for him to have sexual intercourse with a girl. He was terrified and absolutely refused when he saw butter being cut with a knife; he was convinced this indicated the danger of sexual intercourse. He also described a situation with an aunt which in his mind was equivalent to having sexual intercourse. He liked this aunt and thought she liked him and was pleased to talk to him. Also she liked cats which indicated something sexual. On one occasion there was an exchange of eye-blinking between him and his aunt, which indicated that sexual intercourse had taken place between them. Further, he had developed a blinding tic which consisted of screwing his eyebrows and blinking, but not closing, his eyes. He would turn his eyes away and not look. He constantly complained of his inability to look, of his great fear 'to look'. Proof of sexual intercourse having taken place was also afforded by the fact that after the incident with his aunt he had developed a toothache – on the left side.

If we consider that this man had regressed to non-verbal language it becomes interesting to consider levels of organization in the non-verbal mode of representation. First, there is a body image or body ego level of organization. A vertical series of splitting processes separated the right and left sides of the body. The splits had been caused by hard objects. The left side was female and the right male. But the left was further split into a female part and a male part which was damaged. The two parts of the left side had acquired sexual meaning by being transformed into penis and vagina. The two parts were linked in destructive intercourse, and the model for this was provided by the aggressive relationship of the mouth and breast. This came about by a series of processes. A horizontal split and a displacement upwards brought his abdomen and its contents, anus and genitals in contact with eyes, nose, mouth, ears and with the inside of the head. By projective identification each part was transformed into the other. Thus the activity of any organ was given a special meaning, and it was that meaning which he thought was conveyed by him to others and by others to him. This was at the sensori-motor level of organization.

A second level of organization was provided by the meaning attributed to perceptual qualities; colours were provided with special meaning. The mechanisms used were clear: being the same colour meant that objects were alike, and thus would have the same content projected into them which would replace any other quality they possessed. What was projected was both very primitively structured and quite complex. These pathological constructs were derived from a series of splitting processes, displacement by projection of one into the other, and a sort of confrontation process resulting in giving certain aspects of the one to the other. For instance, grey was the colour of steel, steel was hard and hard was dangerous because teeth are hard and bite and tear dangerously. So grey came to mean all this. Blue had a male quality because of father's eyes and brown because of mother's. But his own were brown and so brown in man meant a female man. This did not only lead to homosexuality, but also to being able even to become pregnant. Red was terribly complex. It struck him as vitally important in the flag of Canada, combined with white. He thought of it as blood, warmth, then of red eyes. Eyes had clearly been penises before that. Red cars with white inside appeared at the same time as well as red carrots as penises. Carrots were food. This led to the mouth, which is red with white teeth. But white is milk, is breast, is butter, so there was a biting mouth and damaged breast. This is the mouth-breast relationship that was the model for the combined parents in the primal scene of not 'make love' but 'make war'.

With sounds, words were sound-objects structured as described in the first part of the paper. They stood for milk, breasts, faeces, sperm and even babies coming out through his head. It was only when the affects, methods of relating to objects and mechanisms of defence against them had been sufficiently analysed to allow depressive mechanisms to be used that he began to analyse the symbolic meaning of words as a preliminary phase to accepting the mother tongue.

This is the moment to introduce the dream function in relation to the working through of the paranoid-schizoid to the depressive position. It was remarkable that the working through was done in a series of dreams which dealt with every step and transformation in minute details. This allowed the undoing of the pathological structures I have described – of rendering to Caesar what belongs to Caesar, a mouth is a mouth, a vagina a vagina, a breast a breast, a penis a penis, and a sound is a sound and a word a word. More realistic relationships between objects were then made possible permitting a new 'syntax of behaviour', to use Lennenberg's expression. This of course led to returning to using social, non-personal language.

Mother as well as father and family were split-off and suppressed. The patient had been born and brought up on a farm, including the slaughtering of various kinds of animals. But it was decided together with his parents that he should go to town to study and, if possible, acquire a university degree. He wanted to become a real 'Français', but in order to survive in town he had to become a different person, and so he split off and denied his life on the farm. Returning to the farm for visits made him lose his city part, while in the city there was none of the farmer's personality left. All this had become part and parcel of the schizophrenic process.

In treatment, all the farm life – all the split-off part of him which had been denied –reappeared in his dreams. It seemed that he could not yet begin to integrate that part, and so he attempted to do so by projecting bits into dream-life. This assimilation was done in part by dream-work itself and in part by bringing it to the therapist to assimilate and transform so that the patient could then introject this new produce and assimilate it. The reintegration of language was achieved as part of this process. From the start the patient had a very intense transference towards me; I constantly analysed good and bad aspects of the transference.

The first indications of the patient approaching the depressive phase came very early in treatment. In his third session he had a dream in which there was ice and all sorts of channels, perhaps like blood vessels, which were frozen but were melting. A day or two later he had another dream where there were ice-creams, creamy cakes and things of that sort. The two dreams had occurred in the interval between two weekly sessions. In these associations he said he was feeling changed. There was less tension in the left side of his body, more life – it was unfreezing, he said. When talking about the ice-cream dream, he said he had felt more internal warmth, that ice-cream and creamy cakes were good things. He felt 'things' were proceeding, were getting on.

One of the essential aspects of the schizoid defences is the freezing, hardening, of that which is soft, warm and loving because of the vulnerability of the soft parts. At this concrete level of thinking, good, warm, and compassionate feelings are experienced as soft and vulnerable parts of the subject's body and of objects. Soft parts are protected by being identified with hard objects through projective identification. The result is disastrous, for the price for armoured security is the loss of human feelings.

Only when the aggressive impulses diminish in intensity does splitting of the soft parts and their projection into hard objects diminish also in intensity. Slowly and very cautiously, the reverse of a vicious circle takes place. In Quebec, of course, ice and snow often enter into phantasy life.

Following this there were dreams about funerals, about a hearse, about cemeteries and graves. He consciously felt the woman part in him had to die. Before that he had said he had killed the man in him. At this point the dreams were repetitively full of sexual themes, naked people, people going together into a room, cars and farm tractors as well as farm animals, which began to appear as if there was a resurrection of life everywhere. Then there was an important dream: he was digging into the earth and found huge potatoes and long carrots; further digging brought out guns and revolvers. Klein had described how genitals, breasts and babies are looked for in the mummy's tummy, the Mother Earth. Important here is the splitting into food genitals and hard steel or teeth genitals.

In another important dream, a car was red outside, white inside. In the front seat there was a naked man. The patient said to him 'felicio'. In this association he said 'felicio' meant to him felicity, happiness. I asked about fellatio. He got the point and said, 'Pleased at having the penis sucked by a woman'. I said, 'Or of him sucking a penis', and linked it later with sucking the breast. He had more associations, but what mattered was the emergence of the sucking, as opposed to the biting, mouth. Further, a word had emerged and the method of giving meaning to it had been brought to investigation. The good, sucking, pleasurable mouth allowing a good vagina emerged in another dream. His penis was inside a vagina. He could feel the 'suction' (his word) of the vagina, and his pelvis and the woman's were moving at the same rhythm as the suction.

At last a mouth emerged that could speak. A most remarkable series of dreams followed where the first words to appear were proper names of people which also had a vocabulary meaning. Thus, my name appeared in the form of 'Uncle Henri', also the name of a real uncle. Then the name of the doctor who looks after him outside the psychotherapy appeared. His name in French means 'warm bread'. The patient likes him: he said, with his eyes lightening, 'Warm bread, warm, warmth.' He dreamt of a real man called Richard Labonte 'rich in kindness'. The patient was delighted.

He was very preoccupied with the French language. He thought I was French. He used to be mixed up in his mind about French Quebecois and French men. He said in one session that his friends had teased him about his French pretensions. He had told them a lie, that he had studied French at university. He said, '*Maudit Français*' ('damned French'). In the next session we returned to this and I said there was a double meaning, '*maudit Français*' meant me being the damned Frenchman, while the other meaning was the damned French language.

All this was in the context of talking more and more about warmth and love, that he had turned into ice and steel and that he was now unfreezing. He became very pensive and slowly said, 'That explains why I refused to talk any more, as a child. I gave up spoken language and turned to all those other peculiar symbolic languages. It has been a long freeze.' Then he said, 'I feel warmth coming into me.' Then his eyes became wet and he said, 'I admire you.' After a silence he added, 'I love you,' tears falling from his eyes. After a further silence he said, 'I wish I were at home with my parents. Just to think of all the nasty things I have done to them, it's terrible.'

His mother was a teacher '*maudit Français*', that is, of the mother tongue. Somehow it seems that at the same time as terrifying relationships and objects were abolished, words also had to be abolished. They reappeared as proper names, their meaning being made explicit by bringing into dreams a person with that name and who was doing a certain specific action or sometimes only by means of a name with a double meaning. This was linked with reparation as well. Thus Dr 'Warm bread' was saved from drowning in cold water in the previous example I reported. In one of the many dreams about the farm and the animals there, the patient was haymaking, which resulted in one haystack and one heap of manure. It was good work he was doing. We see here not only the split into good and bad objects but something else: manure is necessary to growth, to new life, and thus it was good faeces used for reparative processes. Then there was a very telling dream: there was a mother bird; she was nursing a little birdie. The patient then wanted to play his part with its mother in helping the birdie by placing it near a protective wall to increase its feeling of security. This represented the emergence of pity and compassion.

The return of warmth as a source of love, of affection and of compassion is an essential aspect of an effective and satisfactory working through of the depressive phase. It emerges when defensive mechanisms of the paranoid-schizoid phase lessen in intensity. I have described them in detail.

Now I want to give one example of the attempt to work through the depressive position in a dream. It is from a schizophrenic woman age thirty-five treated in an analytic group. She dreamt that there was a man with a knife. She was with a woman and some children. Somehow she had to protect them, but then she could not distinguish clearly in the dream whether the man had the knife or she had the knife or both had a knife. In a sort of confused fight between the two of them, two things happened: one knife went soft and bent and she saw that the man had horizontal marks or wounds on his chest. Then the man walked towards the woman and children menacingly. He had a steel plate on his chest. She became very frightened. The menace then disappeared and the man became compassionate.

In her associations, she thought the woman and the children might have been her mother and some of her siblings. In this dream we see all the mechanisms described previously, but in the same dream. This relationship could be seen as aggressive and sexual probably, with danger due to aggressive hardness. It is doubtful who is aggressive, as shown by the confusion about who has a knife and who is wounded. Then the knife becomes soft instead of hard. What will the man do about his wounds: revenge or forgive? At first he hardens himself with a steel plate, he 'steels' himself to hurt and be protected. But then compassion and forgiveness appear in the place of aggressive impulses.

A few months later the patient was reminded of this dream in the group and she repeated it but with some modifications. On this second occasion she talked very vividly about the dream. This time she had a knife that was soft and it was the man who was going to attack. She was much more positive it was her mother and some of the mother's other children. Again the man was all cut up and bleeding. When he advanced towards her he appeared to be all dressed in black; that was very vivid. But when he approached he was soft. At first it did not seem that black was soft, but her association was that he was soft when he approached. She had to be reminded by the group that the first time it was not black but metallic. She then remembered the metallic aspect. The patient said that she had had the soft knife. Metal was replaced by black cloth, which we can take to indicate mourning. Thus the man had to mourn, to become soft without being afraid. But the 'mourning' of the man is a projection of her own development of the capacity to mourn. The mechanism is even clearer: first metal, then black for mourning, then softness, compassion and forgiving – love, hate and reparation.

8   CHRONIC SCHIZOPHRENIA: A GROUP ILLUSTRATION

In one of my six-months' visits to Montreal, I participated in a hospital at a weekly meeting of a very large group of twenty-five or more schizophrenics. The idea was to give them a chance to talk to the psychiatrists and to be free to express themselves. The patients were all long-term in- and out-patients in the hospital.

After a while, I thought it would be interesting to limit this large group to smaller ones of about seven patients who were diagnosed as chronic schizophrenics and chosen partly as being fairly intelligent. The idea was to investigate if those patients were able to participate in a weekly therapeutic group, enter into a transference situation, talk about their problems, and, above all, to analyse their symptoms, delusions and hallucinations.

The patients who were selected were known to the psychiatrists who had looked after them and treated them. It is worth mentioning that I interviewed each one of these patients to find out if they accepted the idea. I saw them individually in a room with a one-way mirror. The interview was watched by the remaining patients and the psychiatrist in a watching-room, and the interviews of each patient were discussed by all. The general comments were extraordinarily interesting. As for the symptoms and reasons for the diagnosis, this will appear fairly clear in the actual text of the sessions.

A co-therapist attended the group in order to carry on with the patients after my departure. The group initially consisted of seven patients. Two patients stopped attending. The patients' respective names were: Mary, Susan, Michele, Eva, James, William and Peter. In this paper, five group meetings are described.

SESSION ONE

In the earlier group, James produced the most amazing statements about his brother. He wanted to talk, but when he tried he said it was too difficult to find the words. I said it was understandable that he had had an experience and felt the words would not make us feel the experience as he did. He agreed. However, he proceeded then to explain that he could not bear it any more, because his brother would never leave him alone for a second. People asked him how that could happen and he explained this experience was in his thoughts. James said he was obsessed with his brother, who never stopped implanting himself in his (James's) thoughts. He was adamant that it was his brother who did it. The brother was annoying him, irritating him, never leaving him alone; he was a constant source of aggravation. Mary insisted on understanding whether or not James had explained this to his brother. James said yes. She asked if James spoke to his brother. James said no, he had told his brother in thought. Eva suggested he should talk to him. James was pensive and seemed to be considering this possibility. He was also angry with his father who did nothing to stop his brother from intruding. James also spoke of himself, saying he was a good chap and not aggressive, as was his brother.

I asked about the position of the brother in the family. James said the brother was one year younger. I then, in a number of interventions, tried to attract the attention of James and the group to the fact that at one time James existed with no brother, and then the brother came. What did that do to James? What went on in his thoughts? The brother's appearance in the family did force his existence into James's thoughts. What kind of thinking went on in the thoughts of James? I proceeded to hint that it was possibly James in his thoughts who was preoccupied with his brother because of the forcible physical intrusion of the newly arrived brother in his life. It was obvious James did not want to or could not see the process of the transfer from the concrete and physical to the metaphorical and mental.

Michele said James was jealous. She said she had a twin brother who was very trying at times. She had quarrelled with him and had been jealous. Some members, especially William and Peter, laughed heartily at this and made a remark about the 'little prince'. Peter corrected the quotation reference, saying it was from Montherlant. Mary described her own jealousy or preoccupation about her sister, whom she nevertheless did love. James would not accept jealousy in himself at first: he was not jealous, not aggressive; he was a very soft person, this could not apply to him. During this discussion, Susan repeatedly said that babies were little angels.

However, James now proceeded to say that when he was three he went into his brother's room and proceeded to beat him. Later he said it was not a direct memory but he was told so by his mother. Susan repeated that little babies were little angels. I pointed out that she refused to accept what the others had said, and insisted that little children could only be good.

William turned to James and said, 'You have teeth missing like me.' James agreed. I stressed what William had said. Again Susan said babies are angels. William explained what I had been trying to describe to the group that babies wee'd and that little children were not solely angels.

During that time, Eva had been analysing in a most subtle way what was going on between mother and brother. However, she could not get to the point that James may have played a part in resenting his brother. She made many attempts to explain that the mother for some reason had given her love to James's brother. However, Eva's reasons were definitely to absolve James from any responsibility in the relationship with his brother.

They also discussed forgiving and indifference, as well as good and bad forgiving, saying that forgiving with comprehension and understanding was the only good forgiving. Mary played a great part in this.

SESSION TWO

The group started, and the more cooperative members spoke very easily and there was a good exchange between them. At present, being hospitalized, Mary was hearing voices that were criticizing her. James and Susan had come to the meeting to say that they would not come any more to the group. After the last group, with more focus on 'neurotic' experiences, there was a discussion of 'psychotic processes'. William aptly described his stay at home at Christmas, which was filled with happiness. Peter joined William to say how happy he was too. Then William said more about his experiences at home in his family. He explained that he had understood from what Michele had said earlier that his own family in reality needed help, and more than ever he must help them. He had to obtain large sums of money ($80,000) from the rich man in his village.

Now they started talking about 'voices'. All members said they have heard voices. Michele spoke very easily about this experience. I asked Mary if she could tell us what the voices were saying. It turned out that her voices were always women who criticized her. This led to a discussion of Michele's mother and sisters who criticize her sexual life. She said she was now thirty-six years old and she wanted a child. She felt it was a good thing to have such a desire, but Michele had a friend who said she was too keen to make love. Since that day Michele no longer had sexual desires and the wish for a child. However, Michele could not understand the move from the family reproaches to hearing the voices, or, rather, she had doubts about my interpretation to this effect. After all she *had* heard the voices. Michele explained that the voices told her what to do. She believed she was an air pilot and played with planes. Her twin, Michael, also played with planes. She had even been to the aerodrome to more fully experience being a pilot. She recognized her jealousy towards her brother: she wanted to be a boy. She then seemed to understand a little the passage from her desires to the delusions of being a boy, a pilot.

Eva then spoke about the voices from inside and outside herself. She made a distinction between the two. William spoke of Michael (a brother of

Michele) and of another person called Michael who also played with planes and collected two hundred planes.

Later I spoke to William, reminding him that last time he mentioned that he was small and weak. William said that he had well understood when looking at his family that they needed help more than ever before and that he must be strong, not only strong but also understandable. Towards the end of the group Peter said that it was evident that he was a poor little child, very weak, and he did what he could to try to surmount his weakness.

Eva told a very long dream in which she figured. It is very dirty, it needs order. There seems to be a mattress full of dust. All sorts of things happen, but most importantly she is going to be operated upon and she is very frightened. In a previous dream somebody had tried to operate on her and remove her mind. In this dream, just when everything was 'clear', something or another created distress and this saved her from being operated upon. It was no longer possible to operate ('*opérer*' = O + *père* = Rey, the group father). The purpose of operations in the dream was to transfer her mind (through the brain) to another person. She would then be just nothing and would have nothing. The other person to whom the mind would be transferred is a woman, a woman who is 'first class and very remarkable because of her good sexual balance'.

In analysing the dream, I suggested to her that someone is taking her mind to put it in some other head, and the question is, who will take the characteristics of the other? Curiously, Eva remarked that her mind had very good qualities, especially clarity. The other mind has profited from this superior clarity. I noted that the other person was very well balanced and had a good sexuality. Eva seemed to think that that also could profit somebody. I then suggested that Eva often said that her mother always gorged herself on her daughter's mind. Then I suggested that perhaps the woman in the dream was her mother. She smiled frankly and said, 'Very probably, for the woman was my sister and maybe also my mother.'

I then interpreted that Eva frequently said that it was her mother that gorged on her. Eva had never spoken about her desire to gorge herself on the mind of her mother, to take in the mind of mother, but this is what happened to her own mind in the dream. Once more she had a frank smile and said, 'I am greedy.' She accepted spontaneously my remark that one must find out in what way and for what reasons she always said she wanted to change in her mother's mind, in order that she, Eva, could change. I then related how a patient of mine who had changed a lot for the good, nevertheless used to say that she was still bad in her mother's mind, and her progress did not serve any purpose. The group members all understood and gave signals of approbation, meaning that this was true but not reasonable.

At that point Eva asked if the problem in the group is homosexuality. I commented that I did not know what was meant by the word 'homosexuality', and we had to understand through their experiences what it meant. Eva replied 'To rub your sex on the sex of another woman.' Then she said that she had had homosexual experiences . . . in dreams . . . it consisted in rubbing the sexes together and also rubbing against the breasts.

A discussion about sexuality took place in which I said that the vagina is also like a mouth that receives the nipple. Eva said 'And that sucks and we must not forget that.' I reminded the group that William in the past has spoken about teeth to James; there was sucking but also biting. I added, let us not forget that Mary has had difficulties with her vagina, and reminded them of what Mary had previously said about voices of women always criticizing her.

Michele said that she had not had sexual difficulties before. She said homosexuality could well have happened to her for there were lots of girls of her age at the convent, but physical exercise saved her.

What seemed important was the analysis of how they all thought of being criticized by the parents, or educators in the case of Michele, and all have heard voices. Michele had spoken of inner voices, as well as Eva. As for William, he thought that the voices ceased to be his own thoughts, for when one was too small, too weak, one could not understand any more. When one is unable to understand any more in that feeble and weak state, the voices become external.

James and Susan, the two who had announced they were leaving the group, were discussed in the group and their attitude commented upon. Susan was said to be too infantile, too frightened of everything, and it felt very difficult to help her. James did not want to move from his fixed idea about his brother interfering in his mind. Someone said this happened to him when he was the small, little one when his brother was born. William remarked on the fixity of thoughts, including James's thoughts, and said that when James drank he became quite fixed on that same idea.

I thought the idea of small, weak, infantile and needing protection had entered the group.

SESSION THREE

In the group Peter had made a remark about Trudeau, who was at the time Canadian prime minister. William said that he had had some painful experiences the previous night before falling asleep. In the dream, while being homosexual, William met an old friend who was also a homosexual. This old friend was now lobotomized. In the dream William felt guilty because he thought that it was the homosexual relationship that had led to the lobotomy of his friend. He said, 'They have cut his brain.' From there he had thought about what Trudeau had said about cutting the price of petrol, and the subsequent consequences of cutting things which were important for the country. Then he said that he had been at home and had 'cut off' from his father. On the contrary, previously he had made it up with his father. Then

William told the story of a little black boy adopted by a family. The child was not recognized by the father, who had something to do with cutting off the relationship with the little black boy. William described himself, saying he had cut himself away from his father. Now he experienced great difficulties before falling asleep and had a painful time.

I reminded them of what William had related, and then pointed out that Peter had 'cut' himself away from his own history to live in philosophy and politics, and that Michele always said 'I have nothing to say' and had cut herself off from her past. I then turned to Eva and asked her to look at herself sitting with her head down, closing her eyes, occupying her hands by rolling cigarettes or folding her hands. I suggested this indicated she had cut herself off from the external world. William immediately connected to the subject of being cut off, remarking on how painful it was to be in that situation.

The comments suggested that Michele agreed and so did Mary and Peter. But Eva reacted very vigorously. She said that she closed her eyes to abolish the light. Light was part of the external world, which has caused her so much suffering. For this reason she turned herself inwards and towards obscurity. She thinks there are two difficult situations. She replaces the external world with her phantasies, and then regrets that she has abandoned her religious morality, which is the inner light.

SESSION FOUR

In the following group Mary was not there and there were four present. In a very lively situation they addressed each other individually with feelings and curiosity. There was a little conflict between Michele and Eva, but it was Michele who spoke, made important remarks and showed a sense of humour.

Eva questioned, 'Dr Rey, is latent homosexuality the cause of our problems?' Then she explained, in a masterful analysis, what led to homosexuality: it was the lack of an intimate relationship with another human being. I remarked that the word 'intimate' implied the notion of the body, but not necessarily its sexual aspects. It is the rapport of mother and child, the caresses, the touching, the kisses, which influence the valorization of the body. When this intimacy with mother is missing, there is no way of avoiding the affective emptiness, the sentimental deprivation, the lack of development of the personality. One searches for and tries to fill up this deprivation and from this emerges the homosexual relationship.

Peter added some very relevant remarks before departing into philosophizing. Peter's sentences and structures of his thought are initially presented in reasonable order, but then he shifts towards his defences, towards the social and the philosophical thoughts: 'I am a little philosopher.' Then follows disintegration. One can see not only the disintegration in the defences but also the breaking up of the sentences as well as the disintegration of defences and thoughts.

I stop Peter and say that we must come back to the body theme that Eva had told us about. She spoke of the body language which if missing makes it impossible to develop a good personality and good relations with the others. I notice their posture, arms folded, hands covered, their fear of using the body. At that point William stretched his arms, his hands, rubbed his arms and his hands, while speaking about how he must start playing the piano again, must exercise his hands.

The group went on with the discussion. However, as William carried on moving his hands, Michele said, 'But what are you doing with your hands, you don't seem to stop.' William started to talk about his love sorrows. He said that he had experienced great conflicts between the spirit and the flesh. The group members encouraged him to talk. William then spoke of Peter's previous discussion about his philosophy masters. He said Peter has had bad teachers, while he, William, has had religious teachers. There is a little altercation between Peter and William.

I then remarked to William that while Peter used his philosophy in order not to speak of his conflicts, he, William, had conflicts connected with the spirit and the flesh. I said that the spirit for him was the religious spirit and his teachers were religious. William then talked about a love affair he had with the daughter of a millionaire who was a very important gentleman of the village. For William the importance of the daughter was connected with her father's importance. William was madly in love with the girl, who had been in a terrible hysterical crisis in a car with him. The relationship of William with this girl is discussed with interest. It is not clear whether or not he had had sexual relations with the girl. Afterwards William talked about a previous relationship he had with Marie, the daughter of a judge. Then he takes from his pocket a letter that he wrote to Marie. It is a very well-written, matter-of-fact letter. He tells his love for Marie and his desire to find her again. In his description he confuses his former girlfriend with the Virgin Mary. Eva applauds his beautiful literary style when he has finished. Later, Michele says to William that he always chooses the daughter of an important person. This remark is discussed by the group. They asked William, do you want the daughter or the father? He said that the two go together, the daughter and the money of the father. William was still trying to find a way of getting to the money of the millionaire. His ostensible reason was to help his family, which was in financial difficulty.

Towards the end of the session I made an interpretation about the father. Peter would like to be a father, and if he did not get a son he would like to adopt one, not deficient but handicapped; he would also accept a girl. William speaks all the time of 'the' father; Michele constantly talked about her father. I then said I am the age of a father, with my baldness and the remaining hair being white! A genuine hilarity followed.

SESSION FIVE

Peter started by saying, but when did the group start? Other members tried to remember the date, but what was astonishing was witnessing them trying to understand their actual loss of memory, their attempts to recover the exact date on which the group began. Perhaps this was linked with an attempt to find a lost object, for Freud said an object found is always an object re-found.

I could see Peter unconsciously, and William more or less consciously, try to recover the mechanisms of his memory. I understood that by recovering an exact date and a souvenir (or memory) they at the same time recovered a part of themselves that had ceased to function. Thus Peter, who previously did not want to be able to remember, and poor William, who had complained that the loss of the capacity of his 'head' to put order in his ideas, in his life, to classify all was to be cut off, joined in a struggle to remember. As William said, 'it was still very difficult but it was improving'. Mary explained that she had forgotten to wake up in time for the last session she missed and regretted missing the group. It was possible to speak about their 'memory' and their fear that in retrieving their lost function they would fall ill again. Throughout this time the group was animated, with a lot of exchanges.

A bit later Eva embarked on a remarkable analysis of her relationship to her mother and to other people. She always discussed the same subject – of not being able to receive from her mother what she was missing. At first it was mainly that the giving part of mother was giving nothing good, which was causing a kind of emptiness inside her that was characterized by something negative. The others joined in with Mary and Michele saying there had been some good from the mother, and William also, saying there had been a good side to mother and nothing bad or very little that was bad. Eva continued her analysis of her mother, saying she was not her real mother. It was really her way of explaining her mother's incapacity to show love to her daughter, and have good things to give. At once Michele said that everyone goes through a phase of imagining similar things; her sister did the same. She added that even though she was brought up by other people, she had imagined that her parents were not her parents.

Michele now talked much more, speaking more of her childhood, especially around the age of fifteen. Since five she had had suicidal thoughts, and then at fifteen, disgusted by her controlling parents, she sent everything to hell by going out – especially with her parents' disapproval – on a motorcycle with a young man. She pursued this pattern of going out, dancing, drinking a little, making love. All the time she was suicidal and trying to end her sorrows and unhappiness. However, at seventeen, disgusted with this dangerous life, she became ill and she decided to stop this bad life. I do not know what happened at that time, but Michele stopped being suicidal only a few months before when a doctor had shown her that suicide was a mutilation. For instance, when I asked if she wanted to cut herself any more, she replied no, for life was good.

Somewhere during this exchange Eva had said that her mother was not all bad, she had her good sides, especially patience; she had some good and some bad parts. Nevertheless she, Eva, could not use her insight; her solution to the problem was her belief that her mother is not her real mother. At some opportune point I made a summarizing interpretation, reminding them that last time they had talked about fathers. I gave examples, reminding them that we had talked about the absent father, and also of the one who is present, and I had spoken of myself like a father, bald and white-haired! Then I said that during the week I had had a thought that the group was a mother, a mummy, a real mummy. We had seen that they were afraid to recover the memory of their illness and of their past; to speak about it would be to fall ill again. I thought that they were trying to see if the group was a good-enough mother, a good-enough mummy. And if they became real little babies and the group a good mother – not like the bad part of mother that they were afraid of – they would not be afraid of her any more. It was as if they had to be born or reborn in the group, and then to grow up in a different way, a better way.

The response of the group was extremely favourable. Everybody approved. Peter was enthusiastic, laughing and repeating 'the group a good mummy, yes, yes', and they all talked about this thought for a while. Dr Jones, a second therapist, preparing to take over after my departure, commented on the memory of being held tightly by the muscles during birth by mother and being held by mother. This made them think how real they experienced their birth in the group as being.

I again discussed the group members' preoccupations with children: Eva and the child and her mother; William who is afraid of having a child like him; Mary and her child, and Peter who wants a wife of his age and wants to look after a little handicapped boy. And what about Michele, I asked? Had she thought of having a child? Yes, but she did not tell of her fantasy of having had a pseudo-pregnancy. They spoke of father again and how the group was both a father and a mother. I then said perhaps the father is a bit of a mother also. Is that possible? There was great enthusiasm expressed for this idea, especially from Peter, who said yes, of course, but a daddy can also be a mummy.

COMMENTS

These five sessions of a group of chronic schizophrenics show that schizophrenics are capable of functioning in group psychotherapy, and are able to interact individually in a group, develop group cohesion, analyse their schizophrenic symptoms, and participate in the transference situation. A clear picture of the progress taking place emerged in those five sessions, lasting over a period of about one month.

I shall mention some of the striking phenomena of how change took place as patients revealed their phantasies, beliefs and symptoms. The first event to mention is the schizophrenic interference in the mind of the patient by somebody else. One patient, James, accused his brother of endlessly interfering with him in a most concrete way. When he was questioned, he said he had complained to his brother through his thoughts. He had not considered actually talking to his brother. He was angry against his father for not stopping his brother. He experienced his brother as physically interfering with him in his mind, but he talked to his brother in thought. In both experiences, then, action and thought were confused and were felt as being the same experience.

There are two explanations which could be applied to this. The first is that there has been a regression to the period of maturation when sensori-motor schemas are forming representations, and the distinction between sensori-motor activity and representation is not well defined. But, second, there is the possibility of the use of the situation relating to the brother for defensive purposes: that is, James was not admitting that *he* was the one who wanted to hurt his brother and he was using the psychotic process to achieve this defensive purpose. This is interesting because it raises the problem of the psychotic remaining psychotic in order to avoid reality. This defensive use of psychosis is of great importance in treatment, for if it is not understood and analysed, the patient will persist in using it. This is what happened to this patient James, for, in the next session, before anything could be done, he came solely to announce that he would not come to the group any more. I have met several such instances when the psychosis was much more preferable to the patient than reality.

There is also the hearing of voices. They all accepted that they had heard voices, however, it was clear that these voices came to them particularly in the form of parental criticisms; they all complained of being criticized by people who turned out to be in the parental role. Thoughts about sexual behaviour were particularly a source of criticism by the voices. Becoming aware of the problem of 'voices' appeared in a dream of Eva's, who dreamt of a woman who always criticized her, who turned out to be a sister and then a mother of whom she was very envious. Eva felt her mother was always gorging on her. Then there was another explanation when one patient explained that when one was still young and weak the voices could not yet be felt as one's own thoughts. They thought that a person could not understand things any more because of being in that weak and feeble state. At this point William said, then the voices become external and are mixed up with the voices of the others. The group's awareness of the difference between inner and external voices was also remarkable. When at one point I interpreted their actual behaviour and postures at the body level, Eva made the distinction between 'inner light', which she recognized as a metaphor, and having to close her eyes to avoid external light, which interfered with the illuminating inner light. The group could describe their relation to voices and the interference with their thoughts. I understand that projective identification played a major part in their experiences.

The regression to sensori-motor schemas in these symptoms was obvious in the images of the woman who was an air pilot because she played with aeroplanes and went to the aerodrome to feel she was a real pilot; the hearing of the voices going back from silent thought to concrete voices; the gorging on mother's mind linked with being greedy for food; the transfer of the mind by an actual physical operation involving transferring the brain itself; the actual transfer of meaning from metaphor to actual 'cutting'; and the thinking of playing the piano accompanied by movements of the hands and fingers. There was also the instance of the fixity of the delusion about brother interfering physically in the patient's mind. The disintegration of language, for instance from metaphor to concrete schema, was exemplified by one patient, William, who showed disintegration both in talking and in action simultaneously.

The explanation given by Eva about homosexuality seems to me to show the depth of thinking of these patients. I am referring to the lack of a mother to give good things, the emptiness that follows, the horrid emptiness, and the necessity of creating a better physical experience by actual contact with the body, including caresses, kissing, which were not necessarily sexual, but rather 'motherly'. This probably implies that there is present in the group a psychological experience of entering the depressive position and having thoughts of reparation.

It would be possible to elucidate many other points, but the primary importance of presenting this group is to illustrate how these psychotic patients were reflecting on their thoughts and actions, not merely encountering their symptoms. They immediately made use of their own remarks, commenting on each others' ideas as well as paying attention to my interpretations and comments. There was evidence both of the working through of the group transference individually and as a group, towards each other and towards the therapist.

There were interpretations about individual moments and also those that helped the group to develop. It was obvious that the group was gradually talking about father, mother and the child, and it was important to relate this to the transference. For this reason I spoke about myself as the father, bald and white-haired. Then on another occasion I said that I had thought about the group while I was outside the group and it occurred to me I might also be a mother for the group. A later theme was the child inside them being born inside them. In this way the relationship of child, mother and father was becoming a reality. The group members were remarkably understanding and accepting of all this. These five sessions illustrate how psychotics understand more quickly than neurotics their deep phantasies and pathology.

In conclusion, the question of the use of groups to maintain and support schizophrenic patients seems worth considering. These patients when left alone frequently, if not always, do deteriorate. Being 'kept alive' through long-term group meetings, especially for the more intelligent ones, could be a useful solution. These schizophrenic patients seem to need an active external metasystem, because it is difficult for them to internalize 'helping figures', and drugs often provide insufficient support for them.

9 BASIC SCHIZOID STRUCTURES AND SPACE–TIME FACTORS

It is an undeniable characteristic of the human mind that it wants to know more and more profoundly and in more and more detail how the universe is structured and how the human mind itself works. The psychoanalyst is of course no exception, but he or she has another important incentive. In order to treat patients, he or she must profoundly know in detail how the mind is constituted. It has become very clear to the world of science that the understanding of the universe and of the structure of matter is synonymous with the understanding of how space–time is structured, from the smallest particle to the largest bodies in the universe.

It has taken a long time for psychology to investigate this space–time structure of thought in a systematic way. Indeed, it is a very interesting fact that Freud did not make more use of one aspect of his greatest discovery, that is, of the spatial mechanisms of the dream-work, such as condensation, displacement, absence of time sequence, absence of negation, concrete representation and action. Instead, analysts have not investigated in a systematic way the relationship between their psychoanalytical observation on thought behaviour and the notion of a developmental structuration of space and time. Instead, they have extracted mental structures or so-called psychoanalytical mechanisms from their analysands' phantasies, and through introspection they have formed such constructs as introjection and projection, splitting, denial, repression and symbol-formation. It is only latterly that a few systematic attempts have been made to investigate the relationship of these mechanisms to the developmental aspects of cognitive structures. Psychoanalysts could not work without the concept of introjection and projection. However, it is unlikely that there exists any piece of work relating the qualitative differences in those mechanisms, as the child passes from one stage of development to the other, thus showing the dependence of those processes on the cognitive stages of development.

Interest in the analysis of children, psychotics and borderline patients has made it imperative to enter into this realm of the human mind. Now many psychoanalytical studies are appearing, such as the work of Wilfred Bion on transformations; of Benjamin D. Rubinstein on the classificatory activities of the mind; of Marshall Edelson on language and dream structures and of Matte-Blanco on symbolic logic and the unconscious. But perhaps it is the flourishing trade with Piaget which is the most active of those attempts.

In this paper I want to indicate the kind of processes involved in the active construction of the object and the self by the infant and growing child in terms of the structuration of space and the development of the notion of time. I want then to consider some aspects of the schizoid organization of personality and schizoid mental processes. I shall try to understand them not only from the affective point of view, but also within space–time limitations and in the context of certain cognitive stages of development. My choice of schizoid mechanisms and structures is linked with their dependence on a varied spectrum of primitive stages of development, side by side with normal adult capacities. This will serve the double purpose of presenting both clinical material and theoretical considerations at the early stages of space–time structuration.

Before proceeding I shall describe space–time structuration and the spatial construction of objects with reference to objects in the psychoanalytical sense. Usually, when people think philosophically of space, they think of vast spaces, empty spaces, interstellar space, space on the surface of the earth. But there is another kind of space more familiar and belonging to everyday language – it is the space immediately around us, the space occupied by familiar objects, or between objects, the quantity of space for this or that, and the space defined by certain activities, such as the tennis court and the car park.

This second concept of space is defined by specific actions on specific objects. An example of this is the psychoanalytical psychotherapy group. The group space is structured by chairs organized in a circle and people sitting on those chairs. Remove the people and instead of a circle of people there is a circle of chairs. Remove the chairs as well and there is only an abstract concept left in the mind, together perhaps with some visual image evoked by the concept of circle. But this concept has a great many properties from inside the group and outside the group. Instead of an unstructured crowd, we have a structured group forming a boundary separating inside and outside. The position occupied by each person is different up to a point because of the different neighbours on either side. Communication between members is affected by their relative positioning.

The same consideration applies to the third dimension of space, that is the vertical disposition of objects. The chair is supported by the floor, which supports the person, itself supporting the brain, which supports brain electricity, which supports thought but is not thought. Thought itself will have a hierarchical structuration into increasingly elaborate structures and levels of representation during developmental stages, as described in the developmental psychologies of Freud and Piaget.

This kind of topographical way of looking at space is easily lost sight of because of the use of metric measurement of space, involving lengths, areas, volumes. Yet for psychological purposes this topographical concept is a much more important area of thought than a quantitative approach.

Similarly, the everyday concept of time is also based on measurement by means of clocks and watches, and for this reason one can have insight into the stages which the infant and the child go through before he or she acquires the notion of mathematical time. As Piaget has so beautifully shown, a well-defined series of stages must be gone through by the child for him or her gradually to develop the adult notion of time, involving primitive or sensori-motor time, practical time, perceptual time, intuitive time, and operational time. The notion of the body image or body ego and the notion of the object also results from the interiorization of sensori-motor schemes of a more complicated nature, organized in a hierarchical way into increasingly complicated and abstract structures. Just a few words about schemas and structures to clarify to what I am referring. Piaget says the child co-ordinates 'the actions among themselves in the form of practical schemas, a sort of sensori-motor preconcept, characterized by the possibility of repeating the same action in the presence of the same objects or generalizing it in the presence of analogous others' (Battro, 1973). Thus the infant who brings his thumb to his mouth to suck it discovers he can bring other things to his mouth. This may be extended to another schema of, say, using a rod to retrieve an object out of reach and put it to the mouth.

But this new schema is not an association of isolated elements – rather the new schema is a

> . . . definite and closed system of movements and perceptions. The schema presents, in effect, the double characteristics of being structured, thus structuring of itself the field of perception or of understanding, and of constituting itself beforehand as totality without resulting from an association or a synthesis between the previously isolated elements. (Battro, 1973)

Therefore the 'sensori-motor schemas are not simply what we sometimes call "patterns", for they have further power to generalize and to assimilate'. As to schemas relative to persons, Piaget says, 'they are cognitive and affective simultaneously. The affective element is perhaps more important in the domain of persons and the cognitive element in the domain of things, but it is only a question of degree'. An 'affective schema' means simply the affective aspect of schemas which are otherwise intellectual.

There is a definite sequence of stages in the process of complex structuration. As given by Battro, stages are '*découpages*' in the genetic evolution, which fulfil the following conditions:

1) It is necessary that the order of diverse acquisitions should be constant (thus the notion of volume is always posterior to the notion of weight).

2) Each stage is characterized by a structure and not by a simple juxtaposition of properties.

3) The structures constructed at a certain age become a part of the structures of the next age. There is an integration of inferior structures in the superior ones.

4) In each stage one distinguishes a moment of preparation and one of accomplishment.

5) It is necessary to distinguish the processes of genesis from the final forms of equilibrium which are always relative.

Each structure is to be conceived as a particular form of equilibrium more or less stable in its restricted field, and becoming unstable at the frontiers of the latter.

Unless I am quite wrong in my assessment of psychoanalytical literature, it would seem that the idea of structures has not played a fundamental role in psychoanalytical theory except to describe such structures as the id, ego and super-ego. The structuralism of Lacan is also something quite apart. However, in the very first chapter of *The Interpretation of Dreams*, Freud writes: ' . . . every dream reveals itself as a physical *structure* which has meaning . . . ' The importance of this sentence has been stressed by Edelson in his paper on 'Language and Dreams' (1973). Freud, in the Rat Man for instance (1909), makes constant references to structures. In Part II, entitled 'Some General Characteristics of Obsessional Structures', Freud points out that ' . . . obsessional structures can correspond to every sort of physical act'. He gives a very good description of endopsychic structure when he writes:

In this disorder, obsessional neurosis, repression is effected not by means of amnesia but by a severance of causal connections brought about by a withdrawal of affect. These repressed connections appear to persist in some kind of shadow form and they are thus transferred, by a process of projection, into an external world where they bear witness to what has been effaced from consciousness.

He also describes projective identification, not only projection, when he states that the projection of the repressed connections in the external world so affects the external world that they 'bear witness to what has been effaced from consciousness'.

Before examining schizoid behaviour in terms of space–time structures, I would like to remind you that Freud also postulated an order of development of the individual. He described how the infant goes through an auto-erotic phase where parts, or structures, or schemas in Piagetian terms, are separate and unintegrated and there is no reference to a unified body image. Laplanche and Pontalis (1973) point out that this complex notion is clarified greatly by considering the next stage postulated by Freud, that of narcissism. They write that the ego is the object of narcissistic libido, while auto-eroticism by way of contrast is defined as the anarchic stage preceding this convergence of the component instincts upon a common object. But for our purpose it is also important that Freud maintained the view that apart from being considered as a stage of development, auto-erotic activity can manifest itself at all stages of development.

Object relations theory as it has evolved within analysis is a valuable development for those interested in the role of space–time in the structuration of the mind. We start with the internal space of the mother into which the foetus first begins moving his limbs, using his mouth in sucking his thumb, using his thumb as an oral object at the level of reflex organization. He responds to sounds, and presumably there is some primitive reflective awareness of touch or of being surrounded closely. Already *in utero* differences in awareness exist, for the foetus also shows sleep cycles which are in some way connected with the sleep cycles of the mother and the foetus towards the end of pregnancy. Within the mother, the foetus moves with mother in space.

After birth, a drastic change takes place in the activities of the infant in the 'external womb' or marsupial space, provided by the mother's care. Then the infant also 'creates' a new space for himself other than the one in the womb. A first stage in this phase corresponds to the time he cannot walk and displace his whole body but only his limbs, and a second phase which corresponds to the time he can start crawling and then walking. Finally he rapidly increases his personal space, which merges into general space. But we must not forget that during that time, just as his mother had an internal space which corresponded in part to the space of the foetus inside mother, the infant, by taking in and putting out 'objects' from his body, has also created an internal space inside himself bounded by his body surface. The other boundary is the boundary between his personal space and the universal space created by the displacement of himself and of his objects. As we have seen at the beginning there will be the possibility for many boundaries corresponding to the areas of certain specific activities.

As a corollary it will have become obvious that not only will the subject carry with him or her an internalized personal space or domain, but in reality, according to circumstances, this domain will not always be the same in importance. Both the external spaces and their internalized representation will be different in different activities such as eating, or sleeping, or making love or lecturing. It is obvious that as an object among objects, his internal objects will also have their own internal space and their own domain of activity. (I use this notion of domain of objects and apply it to the domain of words in Chapter 10; there I describe the importance of the domain of objects in the psychoanalytical process of understanding, meaning and change.)

I have spoken of boundaries or frontiers between domains. Of vital importance is the crossing from one domain to the other. To illustrate this process I will take the two ultimate frontiers. When the foetus is born and becomes an infant, he crosses an amazingly complicated frontier. Suddenly he becomes 'aware' of gravity, of the necessity of breathing, of the capacity for making sounds, of the impact of light and of objects not enclosing him. All this occurs at the level of his genetically endowed reflexes. But also his brain is already a very complex structure capable of quickly structuring the sensori-motor inputs both external and internal. There are frontiers between all domains, more or less difficult to cross or alter, more or less different in equilibrium, more or less capable of re-establishing equilibrium when disturbed, as exemplified by the foetus at birth.

The other drastic frontier, of course, is death, or crossing over 'to the undiscovered country from whose bourn no traveller returns'. This other domain belongs to the world of imagination, of philosophy, of mysticism. Nevertheless, it illustrates the anxiety, perplexity and hopes involved in that passing from one domain to the other in the more mundane situations of everyday life with which I am here concerned, for example, going to school for the first time, or going to an unknown place and taking a new job. We have moments of integration in the maturation process that although done in bits more or less suddenly produce a new organization of the personality. This process is seen in the passage from auto-eroticism to narcissistic integration, and from narcissism to object relationship, or in the Kleinian model from the paranoid-schizoid to the depressive position. There is also the reverse of this in the phases of regression and disintegration which involve so many domains that a great chunk of the personality is involved; schizophrenic disintegration is such a process.

I shall now describe the schizoid patient as he or she presents to the clinician. This picture is of course a composite picture of the main features found in different degrees of intensity and importance in different people, but nevertheless fundamental to the state we call schizoid or borderline. Frequently such patients are in their early twenties. They complain of an inability to make contact with others, and find it impossible to maintain any warm and steady relationship. If they actually manage to enter into a relationship it rapidly becomes intensely dependent and results in disorders of identity. They quickly and transiently form identifications with their objects, and as a result experience a loss of their sense of identity with accompanying intense anxiety, fear of fragmentation or dissolution of the self. This relation by identification is very characteristic. They have seldom firmly established a sexual identity, vacillating in their experience of maleness and femaleness. They are not homosexuals but have fears that they may be, and their choice of love objects or attempts at choice of love object are just as vacillating.

They are demanding, controlling, manipulating, threatening and devaluing towards others. They accuse society and others for their ills and are easily persecuted. This may be associated with grandiose ideas about themselves. In fact, their feelings are dominated by feeling small and unprotected, and when feeling in danger they may defend themselves by uncontrollable rages and various forms of impulsive behaviour. Another characteristic aspect of their abnormal affectivity is reflected in the sense of futility about which they complain. This is reflected as well in the special kind of depression afflicting them which is really a form of depersonalized depression. It involves boredom, uselessness and lack of interest, but it is noticeable that the pain sometimes present in depression has been deadened. Together with this deadness there is a search for stimulants and a production of sensory experiences by means of alcohol, drugs, hashish, cutting themselves, masturbation, perversions and promiscuity. They often complain of various abnormal sensations, body-image disturbances of various kinds, as well as noting depersonalization and derealization experiences. Their body ego is no more structured and stable than their personality, ego or self. Their underlying state of perplexity and confusion is frequently apparent.

Their work performance varies a great deal. Often when they come to treatment they have given up their studies or their work, or they are doing some form of manual or low-level occupation although they may have achieved university standards. However, it would seem that their working capacity may be preserved if they work in a structured situation. There is one difference, in my personal experience, in the way the two sexes present themselves. It would seem that we see many more men answering to the description I have given than women. In the case of women, hysterical manifestation, that is to say hysteria-mechanisms of defence, mask the underlying personality structures; in contrast to men, the women show more histrionic behaviour, acting out, hysterical fits, cutting behaviour, and more overt claustro-agoraphobia experiences.

However, the claustro-agoraphobic syndrome is always basic to both sexes in a latent and distorted way. The schizoid person is a prisoner. He is in prison. He is craving for love but is prevented from loving because he is afraid of the destructive forces of his love. This inhibition is similar to that of the wolf who loves the lamb: he dares not love for fear he will destroy. He finds himself enclosed in a dilemma, enclosed in a limited space, with limited objects and limited relationships.

Thus the borderline patient is on the border of psychosis at one end of the spectrum and of neurosis at the other end. He is on the border of schizophrenia sometimes and of depression at others; on the border between maleness and femaleness; homo- and heterosexuality; childhood and adulthood; small and big; hate and love; in and out; fullness and emptiness. He is neither here nor there.

John Steiner (personal communication) has grouped all those manifestations I have described in what he considers to be four main categories. He says:

> There are first the symptoms of schizoid withdrawal, second the attempts to counter the consequent deadness and isolation by a search for stimulation, third some of the special features of borderline relationships and fourth the consequences of the balanced borderline state which tends to develop.

Here are examples of various mental states of patients in psychoanalysis or psychoanalytic psychotherapy:

> A young man refuses to stay in the room with the therapist unless he stands by the door or a window even though there is no possible escape through that barred window. He does not say why. He refuses to lie on the couch because he says he will sink into it and be enclosed in it.

> A young man is afraid to go out of his room, and he communicates with others by using his telephone or by looking at people outside through his window.

> A very seriously disturbed man dreams that he has produced an immensely long stool several hundred feet long which is not detached from his anus. At the moment of leaving the room he enters into a state of terror and says, 'Help me, help me. If I go out I shall be turned into a mass of liquefied shit.'

> A woman is afraid to go out into the street or shopping or to travel in buses. She says she does not know what it is which makes her frightened. When I enquire she replies, 'I do not know why.' I insist. She says, 'I'll do something mad, I'll shout in the street.' I say, 'A shout is something coming out of you. What else could?' She becomes extremely anxious and fidgety and says, 'May I leave the room?' I say, 'If you want to but if you say what is on your mind you may save yourself months of treatment.' She calms down a little and says, 'Faeces and urine.'

In analysing these patients, we find that in the first case the patient is afraid of being unable to escape from the room where he is situated with a frightening object, the therapist. The room is actually a three-dimensional space. In the second example an object without internal space is transformed into an object with an internal space in which the patient would be engulfed. The object has been structured by the patient according to his projected phantasies. In the third case, the patient is in a protecting space, his room. He cannot cross the border from inside to outside, and he communicates from the safety of his domain. This is the reverse of the other two instances. In the case of the man with the dream, he is the one who is a space containing an object, his faeces. But just like the faeces coming out of him, if he goes out of the room he will be transformed into faeces. He is identifying the room with his body and himself with the faeces. In the case of the woman, she was afraid of what would come out of her, from her inner space into the outer space. But that outer space was itself a very limited space, the therapist's room, and she wanted to take herself out of that space.

These examples are all linked with the descriptions of internal space, personal space and general space described earlier. They involve the displacement across frontiers, with the presence of threatening objects in certain domains. In seeing a wide variety of patients with the same kind of phenomena at a level of symbolic representation, not only entering in and out of a physical space, but in and out of a situation such as a job, marriage, or some kind of commitment, I realized the fundamental nature underlying all these experiences, that is, the structuration of space and objects. I realized that schizophrenic patients were the worst claustro-agoraphobic persons of all, and this was missed in the descriptions of classical textbooks because it is only in long-term psychodynamic treatment that it all emerges. As a consequence I decided that the model of the foetus inside a mother as his domain, the infant in his personal space, the adult in general space but preserving ghosts of earlier basic domains, was a primary aspect of the basic structure of the personality. It also became clear to me that I had not pushed the consequences of the use of the object relations theory in psychoanalysis to its extreme implications. I did, however, subscribe to the notion that all activities of the subject with his objects resulted always in a structuration of space and an unfolding of action in a sequence that is time. The resulting psychodynamic spatiotemporal structures provided supporting domains for further structuration, stored as virtual structures capable of unfolding activity in the mind. If there is an interference in this process, new experiences in life do not help to create new structures. Instead these experiences are forced by projection into inadequate structures that distort them; the result is abnormal mental processes and behaviour. This is a crucial insight for psychoanalytical therapy.

A more detailed example will illustrate the whole process. It is the case of a little boy of nine years, probably a case of infantile autism or infantile schizophrenia. When I first started his treatment he did not want to talk except with a jargon of his own or by writing meaningless sentences on sheets of paper. On the other hand, he used to belch, salivate, fart, take hold of his penis and pull on his prepuce, try to pee on me or my raincoat, run the tap water to cause overflow, and the like. He also used to make special kinds of noises and produce some athetoid kind of movements with his body and hands. He was capable of producing noises in his stomach and guts at will. He made me listen with my ears against his tummy and then got very excited, exhibiting all the movements I have mentioned, reaching a crescendo of excitement before he stopped and wanted to start again.

Then we had to play a game in which the curtains were pulled. I had to sit in total silence, without making any noise or movement. He imitated a train going from London to Brighton, passing through all the intermediate stations one by one. He knew all the names of the stations subsequently. The train had to return from Brighton to London through every station. He indicated that his parents were in the train, but should not know that there was anybody who knew they were there. He imitated the train by making noises and movements of his body that left no doubt about their sexual nature. When the game was finished, he broke into the same excitement and demonstration that followed my listening to the noise located in his tummy. If I made the slightest noise or movement the game was stopped, the curtains opened up, and the whole procedure started all over again, while he made great reproaches to me. The worst reproach was when we had nearly reached the return destination, after an interminable journey through every station. Because something was not perfect in the journey, it had to be started all over again.

From this session I understand that he was making me listen to a parental intercourse inside himself, as it was the same climax of excitement as the parents' intercourse in the train. This internal space-action schema was projected on to a train. The train was chosen as an external object with the real parents inside at night. Then the train was made to produce sexual movements and noises. Thus an external object was structured by projective identification as his internal space and the space corresponding to the primal scene at a certain time, which was night. There is still a very primitive beginning of symbol-formation at the stage of perceptual and concrete displacement, with action giving the meaning. The train, its noise and movement were the signifier, and parental intercourse the signified.

There was also my role for the boy and the transference situation. He had formed a great attachment to me. Not only me but my room could be used to act out in a reified way his very primitive phantasies, both the sexual ones and also the oral, anal, urethral, phallic, sadistic and affectionate impulses. In other words, he had structured me and my space or domain according to his compulsive need to re-enact his unsolved needs in a permissive environment. So much of what is described by Mrs Klein is demonstrated here, including the role of the transference situation.

Perhaps this is the right place and moment to pass on to the unfolding of action in an ordered sequence so as to introduce the dimension of time. In the same way that a genesis of space and of the distinction between stages of space organization before metric space is reached, certain stages must develop before the notion of metric time is possible. The child must become capable of a number of operations which consist in de-centring time from space by actions that are displacements of the object, that is, 'movements' or actions of the subject displacing objects. Space becomes seriated into units, and then into a sequence of groupings. The relative speed with which objects will be displaced in these series will lead to the notion that an object travelling faster, thus overcoming another one, will not have covered the same distance as the slower one if they are stopped simultaneously. Thus the notion of duration and time will emerge. It depends on the ability of the children to master simultaneously two variables: space travelled and speed. This enables the child to move away from the notion that a long distance is a long time. Time will depend on speed of travelling; that is to say, the notion of time will be added to its precursors, space and movement or speed.

The case of the little boy shows clearly the seriation of distance into units, as in the distance between stations. He has built a strict succession or grouping of those units into a certain order. According to him, it is not possible to bypass any unit. Reversibility is still tied up with space in his mind because he cannot return from Brighton to London unless he undoes what he did in the one direction in exactly the same way in the opposite direction. In his mind time is still linked with space, which was also shown by the fact that he could not tolerate my inability to see him at the same time of the day for each of his sessions: he would simply take my watch and set it to the time he wanted. Mental processes are involved in the unfolding of action, the order of events, their location in space passing from one to the other and the speed of the displacements. I am referring to those processes not only in the external world but to the internal representation of those processes. The experience of time and of duration will therefore depend on the particular stage of the development of the time constructs that a subject will be using when experiencing the world.

In catatonia, movements are suspended as completely as possible in order not to disturb the relative position occupied by both external and internal objects. The movements and positions of the objects are experienced very concretely. In depression, speed of movements and of displacement of objects is greatly reduced and there are gross alterations in the sense of time and duration. In mania the reverse takes place. I leave it to you to imagine what is ultimate immobility and ultimate movement. However, in all these conditions – mania, depression and catatonia – the unfolding of displacements in the mind is interfered with and all mental processes are thus affected. Also the speed of both external and internal action plays a very important role in the stability of mental structures. For some people changing the order of things too quickly brings about disintegration of personality structures, while for others the personality is felt to be kept together by the speed of action. A woman revealed to her therapist that she could not leave the hospital immediately after her session. She felt she would be torn apart and parts of her would be left in the places she had to leave. She would sit in the hall and then wander slowly in the hospital grounds, and then leave very slowly and gradually catch the bus. The thought of leaving quickly, disappearing quickly with the bus was intolerable. Similarly, for many people movements bring about separation and loss, and if separation comes fast there is a catastrophe.

Rigidity, frigidity and impotence are all defences against such possibility. The French seventeenth-century chronicler Tallemant des Réaux tells us of a certain duchess who was terrified to sit on a lavatory seat because she thought her bottom was made of fragile glass and she would break up in pieces. She therefore had to do it very slowly and very carefully.

The concept of part-object is an extremely important aspect of object relations theory which has been given a great impetus by the work of Melanie Klein and her followers. Let us consider the breast. In the adult way of thinking it is obviously a part of the whole woman. However, for the infant who has not yet constructed a complete body schema of the mother, the breast during feeding represents the whole of the mother. Similarly, we can say that the mouth represents the whole of the infant. Further, the mouth-nipple-breast combination, although it is only a partial situation, may represent the whole of the world at the time – nothing else exists. Meltzer (1967), for instance, writes of the omniscience of primal objects, so that especially the mother's breast may be experienced 'as having the meaning of containing all possible knowledge'.

I will not consider here what is so important when an adult unconsciously uses the part for the whole, resulting in the possibility of a catastrophic situation. Instead I want to illustrate the actual passage from the adult understanding that a part is a part, to that state of mind when the part becomes the whole. In anorexia nervosa one can come across patients who are afraid that the food will become a baby, that the baby will grow inside, gradually not only filling the uterine cavity, but also the whole of the mother's internal space; the sensation is that the womb becomes enlarged and distended like a balloon. The baby is felt to leave it after expulsion as a large, empty, depleted bag. Similarly, anorectics may become very afraid that they themselves will grow up to an enormous size that will fill the room in which they are, especially if it is a small room, and they will be unable to escape.

I had worked for quite some time with one of my patients on his compulsion of making the part equal to the whole with no success as he rejected my interpretations as not being correct. However, one day he said he thought I was right because he had remembered recurrent dreams of childhood. They were about a tiny little sphere, the smallest that could be imagined. The sphere became bigger and bigger, making the highest mountains look like nothing. 'Piflin' was his word for describing them. The sphere filled everything, and he was petrified with awe. He had recurrent dreams, and after a while his fear gave way to a puzzled sense of interest. Some days later he told me that he remembered that at school he had become fascinated by the infinite (I had never used the word), and he made a sign with his fingers, of 'OC'. He said he knew nothing about this, but was there not a curve that comes nearer and nearer to a line and never meets it? His imagination was thrilled by this thought. He himself imagined triangles whose sides would be made longer and longer at the vertex without ever meeting, although coming nearer and nearer. He thought that this was the process by which his obsessions invaded his mind but he could do nothing about it. This process was the structure that governed his relationship in any situation. At any moment this structure became the whole of his life. Thus he had enormous rages and would leave the room in a terrible state. I began to realize that he was afraid the rage would fill the room and nothing of him or me would be left. This process was repeated with a vast number of objects and situations.

In a remarkable book Matte-Blanco (1975) has dealt with unconscious processes on the basis of properties of infinite sets; it is a fascinating piece of work. Gradually I found that there were many bits of behaviour in my patients that I had been unable to analyse because I had failed to reduce the phantasy to the spatial level of development that it represented. Here is an example of the role of relative size. In schizophrenia it is very common to find ideas of grandeur, phantasies in which there is often an identification with such figures as Christ. In the case of the previously mentioned patient, his diagnosis was uncertain between schizophrenia and borderline. He was neither hallucinated nor deluded, but his capacity for work had deteriorated and his social relationships had collapsed. He could not stand authority, and he had refused a commission in the army where he had to do military service. At one stage he had put a crown of barbed-wire on his head and crosses on his forehead. Analysis of his fear and hatred of authority, of the ambivalence of his attitude to father, of his fears of omnipotence, guilt and punishment had not brought about much change in his phantasies.

It was then interpreted that being identified with Christ made him an omnipotent son of God. In this way he acquired power to deal with God the father, but nevertheless he was only the son, inferior to his father. Although the patient was interested in this interpretation, he did not noticeably change.

But then it was possible to say to him that the size of his feelings was proportional to the relative physical size of his father and himself. His notion of space and size were evolved when he was little and his father was big, when no other possibility of measuring his feelings existed. When he heard this an amazing change took place. Insight appeared and a flood of psychical material burst into the open. Dramatic, positive changes took place. It was necessary to proceed beyond metonymy, that is to say, back to a hierarchical level from which metaphor and metonymy proceeded. Similar considerations also apply to interpretations relating to the manic state and the manic defence, as well as to the castration fears.

10 THE PSYCHODYNAMICS OF PSYCHOANALYTIC AND PSYCHOLINGUISTIC STRUCTURES

It is necessary to state the aspects of language and psychoanalysis I intend to deal with. The relationships of one to the other are so numerous that it is necessary to make a choice. I have no doubt that they both can contribute to each other because they study human behaviour from both the point of view of semantic constructions and language structures. However, I think it is fair to say that the psycholinguist's main preoccupation is not to restructure human behaviour through language, for this is the main task of the psychoanalyst. It is also fair to say that Freud never considered psychoanalysis to be merely a method of treatment, but primarily a method of investigating the workings of the human mind, and in this method semiotics plays an important part indeed.

The analysand utters a message in words to the analyst. His message can also be non-verbal. The analyst does something with this message: he analyses it. This means that he has to first get the message registered at the level of its actual face value – one could call it at the level of a syntactic structure. The next move is to look for all possible semantic messages contained in the utterance, and in doing so the analyst uses the psychoanalytic model, a model that he has acquired through his training. The variations of models which are found among analysts are most definitely developmental and ontogenetic. The analyst takes the utterance in the light of the complicated phantasy system that he is supposed to be acquainted with. This implies that there is a system of levels of meanings, and, according to his previous knowledge of the patient and of the context in which the utterance was made, he chooses the meaning from which he believes the analysand would derive most insight.

At this point the analyst is to the patient a metasystem which provides this particular metasystem or point of view needed by the patient to understand the system. The patient may possess this metasystem, but for emotional reasons he cannot do the necessary displacements and transformations within his own system of systems: the degree of freedom is restricted.

You may compare this to Gödel's Theorem, which states that a system cannot explain itself, and that you have to have a metasystem to explain the system or metasystem. It must be clear that a similar process takes place in the mind of the analysand when he has to analyse a verbal interpretation of the analyst, or for that matter a silence or a non-verbal message. The only difference, but a very important one, is that because of emotional blockages he is not likely to have the same degree of freedom as the analyst to analyse the message into its semantic components.

You can therefore see the importance for the analyst to have at least tried to diminish his own blockages while undergoing the process of analysis. It is true that as he does not have exactly the same blockages as the analysand he may see more clearly what the latter cannot, but at the same time he may be blocked to certain messages of the analysand. The long training of analysis, not only through the analysis itself but through the supervision of patients in analysis with the trainee, submits the latter to an increasing chance of becoming aware of his own blockages by a system of differential blockages. That is to say, the trainee analyst and his supervisors are unlikely all to have the same systems of blockages.

From time to time, psychoanalysts have attempted to contribute to the understanding of both psychoanalysis and psycholinguistics. Until a few years ago the list of contributors has been very small indeed. Marshall Edelson (1973), in his masterly comparison of Freud and Chomsky, has listed the main contributions up to 1972. However, since then the subject has aroused a sudden interest and many papers are comparing every aspect of psycholinguistic theory, taking into account the most famous to the most obscure work on the subject.

Since it is not possible to state the general views I have formed, I want to concentrate on one point alone: among psycholinguistic theories, I want to take the point of view of those who consider the role that general cognitive and affective structures play in coded speech areas – grammatical rules, syntax and lexicon.

In Chapter 9, I attempted to describe the therapeutic process as being dependent on a process of dissolution-reconstruction, which is a part of the process of analysis-synthesis of structures which have developmentally evolved in the course of object relationship activities in space and time. Those structures are hierarchically organized, that is, in an increasing degree of complexity and they subtend various types of mental behaviour expressed in phantasy systems or scenarios in the mind of the analysand. The phantasies are conveyed to the analyst in verbal and non-verbal communications, mostly verbal. The messages are re-analysed by the analyst, who tries to allocate them to the structural level of organization of the mind of the analysand to which they belong. Thus, with the help of the analyst the patient can become conscious that he is applying inappropriate methods to events and experiences in his life, at certain moments.

It must also be stated that analysts have fully realized that in order to create permanent changes they have to go deeper to reach the levels at which dissolution-reconstruction or analysis-synthesis must be effected. In doing so, especially with children, borderlines and psychotics, they have unearthed the genesis of some of the very early basic processes of the mind. They can contribute to psycholinguistic theory, at least by attracting attention to those phenomena they have witnessed. I will therefore choose a few examples of psycholinguistic statements chosen entirely to illustrate my point.

At times language can be considered in certain statements to represent a recapitulation in space and time, although the utterance is instantaneous and global, of a developmental process from which semantic, grammatical and syntactic rules have emerged innately and experientially. This includes word coding or lexicon. Both the analysand and the analyst can look at the level of the developmental hierarchy at which thought is functioning in the context of the session. It is obvious that the decoding involves all the various aspects of semiotics from the elements with which language is constructed. An abstraction can be reified, and with reification the attitude of the subject to the object and vice versa can be understood. In this way a greater degree of freedom of choice becomes available.

Analysis cannot remain only at the levels of symbolic interpretation of metaphor and metonymy. Metaphor implies having to go back to the exact level of cognitive system of classes and subclasses as Rubinstein (1972) has described; metonymy must lead to the most primitive aspects of part-object psychology.

The point of view I am adopting about psycholinguistics is that semantic structures are derived from maturational processes of both brain and environment. The coding in words depends in part on those general semantic principles and in part on special functions of the speech areas of the brain. This view fits in with the basic maturational and developmental views of cognitive structures in psychoanalysis and cognitive ones in Piagetian psychology. It also is in accord with the psycholinguistic formation of the concept of strong, weak and erratic universals. As far as semantic structures go, the strong universals are the universal cognitive capacities as in the Piagetian model, and according to the work of De Swart (1972), the weak element is the innate system of word coding. As for syntax, although the semantic contributions must affect word order, lexicon and the innate capacities of the speech areas are strong contributors. In psychiatry a remnant of this non-verbal system is clearly seen and can be studied in hysterical methods of communication, as well as in the mechanisms involved in the failure of linking systems with word-representation. This knowledge can be deepened by the study of schizoid personality structures and of the primary dream processes.

I will now proceed to give a few examples from psycholinguistic studies which are relevant for the hypothesis of dissolution-reconstruction which is the basis of psychoanalytic practice. Bronowski and Bellugi (1970) analysed the importance of word order and its relationship to the workings of the human mind. They emphasized five important steps. The fifth one is described as

> ... the structural activity of reconstitution, which consists of two linked procedures namely a procedure of analysis, by which messages are not treated as inviolate wholes but are broken down into smaller parts, and a procedure of synthesis, by which these parts are rearranged to form other messages.

Reconstitution is the means by which mind replicates nature. It allows man to construct events displaced in time, and is the superstructure of abstract thought. The child gradually sifts language through increasingly precise categories and distinctions; he demonstrates the 'logic that binds the development of language to the evolution of the human faculties as a whole'. Small children whose cognitive processes are limited in many respects show a remarkable ability to reconstruct the language they hear, just as they reconstruct (give structure to) the experience of their physical environment. 'This model of language', says Bronowski and Bellugi, 'expresses in miniature a deeper human capacity for analysing and manipulating the environment in the mind by subdividing it into units that persist when they are moved from one mental context to another' (p. 699).

This human capacity to reconstitute the environment symbolically through language and in fact through technology rests on another ability to reify experience: 'an analysis into part of the objects, properties and actions of life which, as concepts, can be manipulated as if they were objects' (p. 699). Bronowski and Bellugi give a clear example of how even for a simple sentence such as 'The chain broke' the child must carry on a complicated series of analysis into parts and by co-synthesis, of which processes they give full details. Hewes (1974, p. 63), an authority on the origins of languages, considering the evidence for the possibility that there is a relationship between a person's ability to put together both actions in a series and words in sentences, brings our attention to the fact that damage to certain parts of the brain can affect both activities. Again, it is the dissolution-reconstruction I want to stress. Hewes writes:

> Neither tool-using actions or words, whether gestural or vocal, normally appear as isolated bits of behaviour. Instead they are more complex programmes of actions. Such programmes can be disorganized or destroyed in cases of damage to the brain, and the disturbances of language are remarkably similar to those in motor skills. Some forms of aphasia are syntactical – the patient can still produce words, or recognize them, but cannot combine them in meaningful sentences, just as some forms of apraxia exhibit a deficit in programming sequences of

meaningful action, rather than in isolated motor acts such as reading or holding. The condition known as ideomotor apraxia . . . suggests a disturbance in an underlying deep structure very similar to that which makes propositional language possible. Both motor-skill sequences and sentence construction are adversely affected by the same lesion in many instances. It could be that this fundamental capacity to acquire and utilize complex patterned sequences, expressible in tool-manipulation, in gesture-language, and later in speech, is the 'deep structure' Chomsky really should have been writing about. In the long course of humanization it is the evolutionary growth of this kind of syntactic capacity that has been so important, and not its separate manifestations in technology and language. (p. 63)

This is very similar to the Piagetian view about interiorized action schemes organized into more and more complex abstract structures underlying thinking and language. My choice of quotation is more to illustrate the process of dissolution-reconstruction and to relate this to object relations theory in psychoanalysis.

I wish to consider the findings of Sokolov and the Russian School and their research on inner speech in the well-established tradition, starting with Sechenov as far back as the 1870s, through Vygotsky to the present.

When external speech is internalized, do we think with or without words, and is there such a thing as concrete non-verbal thinking? Sokolov and his co-workers, through ingenious experiments interfering with the speech musculature and with the central analysers, have investigated what happens when subjects are asked to perform verbal tasks and concrete visual tasks such as the Raven's Progressive Matrix under such interfering conditions. Here are some of the results:

The data cited permit us to characterize concrete thinking as verbal concrete, or mixed thinking, where the verbal component is represented as verbal with the weak (non-contrasting) components of the complex being perceived; the strong (contrasting) components were for the most part singled out visually, without verbalization. This permits one to distinguish perception as an act of immediate reflection of real objects and phenomena from concrete thinking. The latter always presupposes the presence of the situation perceived of a finite task (to find something or to determine or do something in a given situation) whose accomplishment is only possible through a more or less prolonged analysis of the situation; and in a person with a mastery of speech this is always related not only to visual (or graphic-pictorial in general), but also to verbal processes. (Sokolov, 1972, p. 238)

Hence it may be concluded that the verbal was always involved whether or not associated with language,

... although at individual moments or phases of this process verbal actions may be absent or inhibited. We have no grounds whatever, however, to separate one phase of thought from another and to infer the existence of thought with language. Such an interference would be a completely unjustified assumption since the thought process as a whole cannot be replaced by one of its phases. For the same reason thought should not be identified with speech, for thinking contains not only a verbal but also a non-verbal (concrete object operational) phase of action, usually accompanied by a certain inhibition of speech processes. (p. 238)

Thus according to this work, not concerned with infantile non-verbal thinking or with dreaming, there is always in thinking not only a verbal activity but also an object operational activity.

René Thom (1973), inspired by work by Greenberg (1970) on the typology and classification of languages based on order of words and other considerations, seeks to explain certain theoretical considerations of Greenberg which are of great importance to us:

Consider C, the signified content of a phrase P, to be addressed by the speaker to the listener. Semantically speaking, C up to a point has a unique existence, a global form conceived by the mind. To be transmitted to the listener, this series of words or elementary vibratory elements, is perceived by the listener who has to resynthesize by resonance in his mind the global content C. Therefore any linguistic communication is the result of two types of processes: an analysis into coded parts for transmission and a synthesis or reconstitution of the message C in the listener's mind. (Thom, 1973)

According to Thom, the optimum order of words for the two tasks is not the same for the two processes. There are two fundamental processes: an order or typology of emission, and a typology or order of reception, being in principle the reverse of each other. Professor Thom gives a chemical analogy to explain this. When a chemist wants to dissociate a substance into its constituents, he may heat that substance. On the whole, the more volatile parts will evaporate first, and in that order of decreasing volatility, the more stable substance will be left last. Comparing this with words, he suggests that there is a concept of semantic density. This involves the notion that the greater the possibility of there being a more permanent trace or image left in the mind, the signification of the word/missing sentence will leave in the mind a more permanent trace or image. Therefore, it would appear that concrete concepts are more 'dense' than abstract ones. Once liberated by analysis, the 'elements' or 'words' are in a much freer state than in their bound state, and the content C can be reconstituted by the listener putting the elements together using a different order for dealing with elements suitable for reception instead of emission. Although this is done rapidly and easily, there may be faulty reconstructions for a number of reasons, giving rise to partial significations incompatible with the total signification C. Thus, ambiguous sentences may be constructed. On the whole, the order of reception is the inverse of the order of emission, that is, of volatility and density. However, this is by no means the only order compatible with the reconstitution of the meaning of C. Factors other than volatility and density are also operative.

The question is how to evaluate the relative semantic density of traditional grammatical categories such as substantive, adjective and verb. Professor Thom's semantic theory assumes there is a certain isomorphism between the stability of a concept Q (our interior schema) and the actual physical and material mechanisms that ensure the stability of the real object K represented by Q. (In our model, the concept of the actual object is the construct resulting from the real actions that have been interiorized.)

In the external world, what are the activities that are the most virtually 'dense' for the individual, so that the word representing that object or activity will itself have become endowed with semantic density? The palm is won by the animated beings, and probably man. An animal has to survive before anything else, must perform periodically a number of activities such as eating, sleeping, movement. To those fundamental activities for man we must add mental activities nearly as important for the maintenance of that which is human: speaking, thinking, believing, which constitute a form of regulation which is superimposed on and presupposes the more primitive system. Thom then proceeds to analyse the semantic density of all parts of speech and the way they relate to each other. Here is an illustration of his ideas: consider a simple sentence of the subject-verb-object type, for example, 'The cat eats the mouse'. How are we to order its elements in increasing semantic depths? Thom has shown that the verb is more 'volatile' than the substantive (I cannot describe here the procedure).

But how do we choose between the two substantives, subjects and objects? Thom shows that in a transitive sentence, the object is more volatile, less semantically dense than the subject. He points out it is often possible that in the actual process described by the sentence the object perishes entirely in the action, such as in a sentence 'Eve eats the apple'. On the other hand, it is practically impossible to find an example in a transitive sentence in which the subject perishes in the action and the object survives. So in our sentence, 'The cat eats the mouse', with the word order subject-verb-object (SVO), the emission in terms of volatility of semantic density will be verb first, object second and subject last (VOS). He then goes into the complexities of the process, the various permutations and combinations not only for emission but for reception of messages and compares his results with the language typologies of word order in Greenberg's article.

Thom (1975) stresses a fundamental point, which is that the investment that the speaker has in being understood by the listener always exceeds the interest that the listener has in understanding the speaker. It would thus ensure that the main work of connecting the typology of emission with that of reception will be the burden of the speaker. Therefore, derived from this principle of dominance is the fact that there is always a dominance of the typology of reception over the typology of emission.

Thom has also described in detail how words act as chreods, that is, forming a kind of nuclei for the 'domain' they command, their so-called 'basin of attraction' or 'obligatory path', and the dynamics regulating relationships between basins of attraction. This last remark will become more meaningful when I remind you that the organization of structured underlying mental processes involves each object knowing its own personal domain or personal space and also an inner space. It is as if all objects had a container as well. This is specially so in the early phases of construction of the world by the infant and young child when thought is perceptually space-centred. The ways in which schemes relate to each other and become more complexly space-structured hierarchically as well as extensively organized have been mentioned.

I will now consider words as objects structured like any other objects, with their domain or basin of attraction. I will then use the dream to illustrate the dynamics of the process of dissolution from words to semantic content, and then the reconstruction from semantic organization to syntax and communication with words.

With regard to the problem of meaning, I would like to consider the possibility of explaining this in terms of the hierarchical organization of structures in a vertical and horizontal plane. Thus, in a vertical system of structures A, B, C, D, and so on, seen as levels, structure B comprehends structure A, and structure C comprehends B, A. However, the domain of A, B or C, and so on, can be extended horizontally when A's domain of structuration extends to more objects but performs similar activity. In the hierarchical organization, when B comprehends or captures structure A, structure B becomes conscious of A and apprehends the meaning of A. This is a curious use of the concept of consciousness and meaning. But just as we have the concept of part-objects as precursors of the full object, I am considering the possibility of part-consciousness and part-meaning as precursors of a more comprehensive phase. In Kleinian terms, a more comprehensive phase will correspond to the passage from paranoid-schizoid to the depressive position. Thus, in the depressive position the not-yet-united parts of the self and the object constructs come together to form a much more integrated self and object simultaneously. The subject becomes aware of the object at a much higher level of consciousness than the phase of part-consciousness and part-meaning. In this model it is obvious that consciousness and meaning are explained in terms of object relationships.

As a prototype let me remind you of a patient who would not lie on the couch for fear he would find himself enclosed inside the couch. It appears that he identified the couch with his mother and feared that his father would believe that he was inside his mother and would cut off his protruding feet.

Here we see a structuration of the couch by projective identification. But instead of such an object as the couch, we can have instead a sound as an object. Thus a woman, who was not psychotic, would not talk because she said that words were mouldy, poisonous, dangerous objects inside her stomach, and if she talked they would hit the therapist and do him great harm. She simulated suicide on many occasions in order to have a stomach washout. Another patient felt that any question put to him by the therapist was, in fact, an act of biting something out of him if he answered in words. We can see more precisely that sound can be structured as a container by projective identification in the case of the young man who felt alive when the noise of his motorbike was on, but became depersonalized when the noise stopped. An intelligent woman felt enveloped by the sound of music; this was equivalent to thinking of an infant in the womb, but at the same time there were good reasons to believe that the sound meant the sexual intercourse of the parents.

The word has been considered as a perceptual sound-object and I propose that we do the same for the sound-object concept. Like every other object it organizes its space, and this domain or basin of attraction of the sound-object develops also in space and time as maturation of the infant proceeds. In other terms, words have a life of their own. But the sound-word – the sound becoming a word as it acquires domain (meaning) – is at the same time acquiring an inside space, like we have seen for other objects. This inside of words, or words as containers, is brought to our attention through a great number of expressions in the language, such as empty words, words that are hollow, the content of words, words full of meaning, unctuous words, sweet words and hard words. Phenomena of displacement and condensation, achieved by projective and introjective identifications, structure objects. Words are similarly structured. Experiences are projected into sounds, making them words by projective identification. Thus when words are used, they evoke the experiences they contain.

This implies that some sort of phenomenon of becoming conscious of the experiences evoked must take place. This is why words are connected with making the unconscious conscious. This is also one of the meanings of meaning: finding meaning is to become conscious of an experience or of oneself, or someone else potentially carrying on an object-directed action or a virtual action which has motivation and purpose.

Consider the expression 'self-conscious'. Everyone is supposed to understand what it means. In fact this is not true, as a brief analysis can show. If we say, 'I am conscious of myself', the expression becomes a bit more meaningful, although the word 'self' is not defined. If we say, 'I am conscious of myself doing or thinking something', then the self is defined and more or less full meaning is achieved. To return to the consciousness of words, and keeping in mind the levels of development of affective and cognitive structures, it stands to reason that there cannot be a theory of meaning, but of meanings.

When the perceptual level of development has not been passed yet, then meaning will be at the perceptual level. Only when a metasystem, a more advanced affective and cognitive level, is reached will there be a different meaning attached to the word. It is difficult to say whether this line of development is a continuous or discontinuous one; it is probably discontinuous. A word can only attain universality at a very abstract level of reference. Therefore, meaning is not only multiple because of levels, but it is always both personal as well as universal for language.

What I have said for words obviously applies to combinations of words in a sentence. For this reason, the permutation and combination of meanings is infinite, and the construction of meaningful sentences is also infinite. However, the syntactic order of words for a language is not.

I shall now describe how words are used for the interiorization of experiences or structures, and the fixation of these experiences in memory. Sounds are structured into words by means of projective identification. It is necessary also to understand what happens. It will be easier to consider a stage of development where the perceptual combination is still strong. Then the word will be treated as an object which is assimilated by introjective identification and by processes of transformation becomes part of memory of self. Words can also be expelled as unwanted objects, or they may remain inside without being assimilated. Innumerable expressions in the language are testimonies to those stages of word formation when words were not yet quite separate from the perceptual and other primitive stages of their formation. Because of their connection with their oral origin they were treated as oral objects undergoing the same fate as those objects. As for primitive stages of object formation, they were located in space at the site where they originated or were displaced. We talk about making people eat their own words, or swallow what they have said, or of word indigestion, diarrhoea, words stuck in the mouth or in the throat.

In this model we have given meaning to sound by projective identification in order to face a number of problems. There must be a shift at a certain stage in the infant's life where his choice of sounds differs from sounds produced by himself. For example, babbling, and sounds of all kinds can be used to project his meaning into a phrase where he has to use arbitrary sounds belonging to the language of his environment. These sounds have an arbitrarily appointed meaning. This passage from one system to the other is of great interest for psychoanalysis.

To understand it one must consider the mechanism by which a particular place or space possesses the same meaning as the object located in it. If the particular object is displaced, the replacement object acquires the characteristics of the displaced object by now being located in its place. I have observed a little boy extremely jealous of his younger sibling, who was constantly displacing his brother wherever he was. If his brother sat on a chair, he sat on the edge and displaced the brother until he sat in his place. He would not sleep in his own bed or play in his room, but would lie on his brother's bed or play in his brother's room with his brother's toys. He was always trying to be in the place of his brother. One day the little boy did something and accused his younger brother, who was not there, of having done it. His father said, 'But your brother was not here, he was away at the time. You did it.' 'Ah,' said the boy, 'once I was first, then he came and took my place.' So there he revealed the mechanism of the place occupied having the characteristics of the occupying object, and identification resulting from the occupation of that place or space.

There can also be a wish to go back to the womb itself, as in the case of a little Chinese boy who had been adopted by a white family. His adoptive mother loved him very much. She also had other children of her own. At the age of four he used to say to his mother, 'I want to go right back into you and come out just like my brother and sister and then I will really be yours.' In this example, the location of action is at the site at which the experiences are perceived or where the action has taken place. Thus a girl started having hallucinations where she felt two voices were located in her ears and were quarrelling. Her parents actually quarrelled over sexual matters and parted. At that time the girl had located her parents in her ears where she had perceived them. One schizophrenic patient described how he had witnessed his sister having intercourse. In precisely the next sentence he said, 'There is one thing about which I want to be certain. My eyes should be given for grafting after I die.' One could multiply examples, but this has been summarized beautifully by Piaget (1972) as a normal process in the following quotation:

> For the child to think is to manipulate words. Three confusions are implied in this belief, and three dualisms will emerge because of the elimination of these confusions. There is firstly the confusion of the sign and the thing itself: thought is considered to be tied to the object. There is confusion between internal and external: thought is considered to be situated simultaneously in the air and in the mouth. Finally there is the confusion of matter and of thought: thought is regarded as material body, a voice, a breath.

There must be a continual process of abandoning egocentric or personal construction of sound-meaning and adapting or accommodating to externally constructed sound-meaning. Nevertheless, words, aside from their universal meaning within a language, will always keep some of their personal meaning. In some extreme cases of idioglossias perseverating in later life, we can have a distorted and exaggerated picture of the process. A little boy I saw who wanted to be a girl and dressed as a girl had an idioglossia which drove his parents crazy. I managed to get a few expressions from him such as 'chopbolder' meaning, 'leave me alone, I'm angry'; 'thombombur', 'you are very horrible'; 'cappoottee', 'you are too nasty'. In fact, this represented a regression to using the babbling of his little sister, who provoked his jealousy. He constructed a sound language of his own that he used when feeling rejected and angry.

During the transference situation, sometimes the analysand abandons the superimposed meaning of his cultural environment and the level of cognitive development he has reached. He attempts to restructure the analyst as the original object that he had constructed before the passage from egocentric constructs to later more abstract and external reality-centred objects. Then the words are used in their original personal sense and make conscious to the analysand the original schemes constructed by his object-directed actions, both affective and usually perceptually centred. The analyst must be extremely sensitive to this change and be ready to put a new meaning on the utterances of the analysand. This is not very easy and sometimes so difficult that the analysis fails.

As an example, I had a patient whom I failed to understand for a long time. When she said something and I had given an interpretation, she inevitably answered, 'I did not say that'. So I would say, 'This is what you have said,' and repeat what she had said, and she would agree. I would say 'Have I repeated it correctly?' 'Yes.' Then I would say, 'I will now tell you what I believe that means.' I would repeat my interpretation, but she behaved in the same way. You may say, 'Why not take what she was saying at face value instead of putting an interpretation as to the meaning?', and you would be wrong. What I discovered after a very long time was that her most irresistible wish was to be one with me, fused with me. If I said something different from her, however right it was, then her wish was refused because a different meaning meant two people and not the fusion of one thought, one wish, one person, one bliss.

Following this transfer from one stage of thinking to another, personal words will evoke personal action schemes, which will then be reified in the here and now and thus be brought to consciousness. Then the working through process can take place because the past is now the living present and action can be modified.

I will now examine the contribution of dream study to this subject. In order to dream, a number of conditions must be fulfilled. Changes in the physiological state of the brain must take place, we must be mostly cut off from external stimuli and there also must be a special kind of paralysis of the locomotor systems for some activity in the limb extremities and in the muscles of the eyes. Psychologically, dreaming is a unique form of thought. R.M. Jones (1970) writes:

A dream can be characterized as a form of thought which is experienced as action. It thus occupies a unique place in the spectrum of symbolic functioning in that it seems to be what it is not, i.e., action, and is what it does not seem to be, that is, thought.

There can be no doubt that dreams are virtual actions, experienced as actual action through visual imagery of a hallucinatory character. The relationship to Piagetian interiorized action schemes is obvious. To allow this activity, nature has realized a remarkable set of experimental laboratory conditions. The partial or complete elimination of speech and word-representation in the process of dreaming, and the re-establishment of the speech process on waking up, produce for us every night a great deal of what the Russian workers I mentioned earlier have attempted to do. However, although they blocked speech musculature and interfered with the cortical analyser of speech, they did not manage to do as well as nature.

I shall use a dream of a patient cited in another chapter for a different purpose. The dream is as follows:

> I am dining with friends and get up from the table. I am thirsty and I start to drink. I realize that the bottle in my mouth has a neck shaped like a feeding bottle; there is no teat, but I think that I can feel the flange which normally holds the teat in place. While I think of this I begin to see the bottle more clearly. I hold it in front of my face and see that it has the shape of a feeding bottle. In the bottle I see water. The level of the water falls and bubbles of air mount through the liquid, and because of this I am aware that some of the water has become part of me. I am anxious because I can neither understand nor feel the water passing from a state separate from me to become an intimate part of me. While I am thinking thus, the bottle becomes bigger. I see at that moment that on the inside of the bottle facing me words are engraved on the surface in raised letters which give instructions on how to wean an infant.

The dream allows us to analyse: thought as interiorized action; the hierarchy in developmental terms of the space or domain of action; thought as visual imagery and non-verbal symbols; the process of introjection; and the emergence of speech and how it is linked to thought. I will concentrate here on processes of dissolution and reconstruction shown in the dream.

Having dissolved external reality as it is in sleeping, the dreamer proceeds to use it as he wishes; that is, to proceed to further analysis or breaking up of the hierarchical organization of the feeding process. At first he is an adult having dinner with friends; this is domain one. Then he passes to a more primitive stage, feeding with a baby's bottle, domain two. We can see the transformations necessary for this: from food to liquid and from adult bottle to infant bottle. But he cannot pass to the ultimate domain and fulfil the wish: it is a bottle and not a breast; it is water and not milk; it is a glass ridge and not a teat – it is not mother, it is he feeding himself.

This results in a defective object relationship and a defect of introjection. It is true the water is a part of him, but the breast-mother is not. There is no understanding of the process of transformation since there is no nipple in the mouth. So there will be interference with transformation and representational processes so important for processing further experiences. In fact, this patient was never able to form a satisfactory relationship with women. Although he endeared himself to them and was an extremely nice person, all relationships ended with a feeling of absence, of nostalgia and a kind of deadened depression.

One can see how the process of reconstruction takes place in the dream. After he fails to fulfil a wish for a good feeding experience, a higher cognitive level, logical capacity, returns. This is shown by his reasoning that if the level of water falls and bubbles of air rise, then the water has left the bottle. The water must be in him since he was drinking from the bottle.

On the verbal level, the words are written in three dimensions – that is, spatially – on how to wean a child. Notice the infinite subtlety of everything in this dream. The words are inside the bottle. Instead of milk, a nipple, a mother, there are words. Those words are also instructions. Into them is projected the experience of weaning, the anger and sadness about words and instructions which are mother. Syntax has replaced semantics and syntax has become the super-ego: you will obey.

This is so important for the treatment. The very vehicle of communication is perverted. This patient in his life had substituted other objects for mother, and had devoted great interest to being able to write properly himself, in literature and in the fashioning of language.

When dissolved by falling asleep, the link between experience and thought, between semantic and verbal structures, persists as ghost structures, which are reconstructed at the various stages of the return of consciousness. Freud spoke of 'connections that appear to persist in some sort of shadow form', and Piaget said, 'structures do not exist as distinct notions in the consciousness of the subject but they simply constitute the instruments of his behaviour'. After all, before the infant could use words he was capable of some form of non-verbal thinking.

11 THE PSYCHODYNAMICS OF DEPRESSION

The assessment that a human being experiences a state of depression is made on psychological grounds. Whatever bodily manifestations may accompany the psychological state, such as a loss of appetite, loss of weight, loss of sleep, loss of energy and other such manifestations, they are clearly possible consequences of an emotional state. The underlying causes of these bodily manifestations could as well be physical. However, it is a remarkable fact that a large number of psychiatrists not only assume that depression is primarily an organic condition and that the content of depressive thoughts is irrelevant, but consider that the onus of proof that it is not so is entirely a matter for the psychologically minded. In fact, it is the reverse which is true. The diagnosis of depression is made on psychological grounds and the organicists postulate a causal underlying physical substrate. The psychodynamically minded in no way deny this physical substrate. They observe the psychological picture, they follow its evolution, and they investigate the possibility of psychological methods of influencing the typical, repetitive, prototypical mental processes always present in depression.

Before dealing with the description of this picture and the mental structures or mental substrate involved in the state of depression, I will briefly examine a particular aspect of the role of the brain in a depressive experience. I shall examine only one aspect, namely, the brain as support.

Consider the room in which you are at the moment. Without its floor, for instance, there would not be the chairs, without the chairs there would not be the possibility of being seated, and your body would not be in the position you occupy. These states are not causally related yet they are not unrelated. We could say that a certain electrical activity is one factor that distinguishes other cells of the body from brain cells. We could imagine the brain cells as the support of this electricity, and we could postulate brain electricity as the support of thought. However, it is not thought *per se*. As a result of studying manifestations of brain damage to the frontal and temporal lobes, it has been suggested that during the growing stages, damage to the frontal lobes resulted in certain functional disorders of the temporal lobes. However, once certain functions were acquired by the temporal lobes, damage to the frontal lobes did not matter any more. I call this an example of a supportive function during a certain phase of growth, and structuration of the neuronal structures. I wish to consider the concept of the supportive function in more detail; in other words, to examine how a disorder of the supportive function may affect the psychological state.

If we postulate a disorder of support, we know that we have to explain the differences in the psychological picture of, say, schizophrenia and depression. Either the difference lies in the organic disorder of support being different in both conditions, or the psychological organization is different and the same disorder of support results in a different clinical picture. Finally, both support and psychology may be contributors.

The meeting place of both aspects of the problem may be profitably looked at in the phenomena of sleeping and of dreaming. Leaving out gradations of one kind or another, there are three main states in which we can exist: alertness, sleep proper and dreaming. Ordinary thinking processes are abolished in sleep proper; thinking in the state of maximum alertness is as distant as possible from brain support in the model defined above; thought and bodily functions are more closely related to the dreaming state. It is during the dreaming activity of the paradoxical phase, as opposed to dreaming in the other phases of sleep, that the closest connections between psyche and soma exist. To understand this statement, something must be said about the phylogenetic and ontogenetic development of the paradoxical phase of sleep. There is an increase in the importance of the paradoxical phase from birds to man, which seems to be proportional to the increase in the complexity of higher nervous functions.

Ontogenetically speaking, towards the end of pregnancy, in the foetus there is an increase of the REM phase of up to 40% of the sleep cycle, which diminishes to 20–30% at about ten months.

The paradoxical phase is accompanied by a number of well-studied somatic activities which are not present at other times, especially processes dependent on the autonomic nervous system. The important point is that these somatic activities exist even before and independently of a proved psychic content. However, as soon as the infant can talk, a content can be traced. The behaviour of infants during the paradoxical phase and on waking up also seems to indicate that dreaming could be taking place before language. It is through the mental content that meaning is given to the increasingly rich psychosensory phenomena of the REM phase. Freud himself pointed out differences between children's dreams and adults'. He pointed out that often with children the dream was very simple and did not appear very different from external reality, dream-work and symbolism being hardly necessary. His ideas on the day residues and experiences being incorporated in the dream-work indicate that the psychological mechanisms of the dream become increasingly more controlled by the meaning of the dreamer's experience. That is, there is a closer integration of somatic and psychic phenomena, the latter gradually playing a more important role.

I have gone through this development in some detail in order to describe the emergence of psychic meaning and its controlling function. We thus have not only biochemical or molecular structure, but also thought structure to take into account. It is the study of those thought structures which should be called the study of the psychodynamics of depression. According to the circumstances, the depression may or may not have an independent depressive activity of its own within its own psychic domain. It is repeatedly said that the depression should first be treated by drugs and then, if necessary, psychotherapy can be provided as a sort of extra. It is less known that in cases when anti-depressant drugs have failed they may become efficient after psychotherapy has altered the depressive psychological structures but where the organic element does not respond to the psychic changes. That is because the state of depression is over-determined psychologically in those cases.

In the same way as there is a hierarchy of supporting processes in the organic field there is a hierarchical organization in the psychological supportive system. The understanding of this hierarchical organization is absolutely vital in understanding the dynamic of depression. Depression is a mood, a sensation-feeling related to the experience of loss. But it is not only a loss; the statement must be completed. What is lost must be defined, for it is the hierarchical organization of the relationship within the psyche of the object lost which is of vital importance. In reactive depression some loss is apparent, for example, a loved one, a job, an ideal, self-esteem or money. In the so-called endogenous depression the loss may not be apparent and more bodily involvement is noted. Manic excitement comes into the picture as well.

I wish to consider the problem from the angle of: first the hierarchical organization of the personality, and then the hierarchical organization of the object relationships.

In order to convey what I mean by the hierarchy of object loss, I will start with an example from *The Soul of the Ape* (1969) by Eugène Marais, the South African author of the better-known book *The Soul of the White Ant* (1973). Marais describes how a mare that lost her foal by drowning in a river kept going back to the site where the foal disappeared. No matter what efforts were made to show her the recovered body of the foal, she ignored it and returned to the place of its disappearance. Marais contrasts this with the behaviour of an ape who had lost her baby. She showed signs of sorrow, stopped her restlessness, touched the body, made sounds of endearment, put her face and lips close to the dead infant, uttered a succession of cries, and then sat in a corner. Later she returned to her normal interest in the environment. The loss of the object in each case was experienced differently.

Compare this with Piaget's experiments with small infants with regard to disappearing objects. If an object is covered with a cloth at a certain age, the infant looks for it at the place of disappearance. Even if the object is moved after its disappearance under the cloth at site A to site B in the presence of the infant, he still will look for it at A where it originally disappeared. However, as an object becomes more and more meaningful and its mental representation in its absence becomes more permanent, the infant reacts differently to the absence of the emotionally meaningful object. Thus, we know through the work of Spitz that infants deprived of their mother between the ages of seven and nine months may show various kinds of separation anxiety, including a most severe state of despair called anaclitic depression. This reaction does not occur at an earlier date.

We have a hierarchy of physical processes supporting other physical processes and more closely connected with mental processes. We have seen how in the paradoxical phase of sleep, physical states and mental representation or meaning are more closely linked in a psychosomatic union than in deep sleep or in the state of maximum alertness. Now we are seeing the possibility of a series of hierarchies within the psychological series itself and in its own rights. We have to find where in the hierarchy the system 'reaction to object loss' is situated to produce the well-known clinical picture of depression.

Once more we must point out the error of a Linnaean classification in rigid categories as applied to mental illness and substitute a Darwinian approach. There can be no doubt at all that we see patients who at times show a schizophrenic picture and depression at other times. We know of mixed states, of schizoaffective disorders and of recurrent cyclical states where schizophrenic and depressive manifestations alternate. Even Kraepelin has described intermediate states. Assessed in the light of the hierarchical psychophysical organization of the personality, it has been suggested that a schizophrenic breakdown proceeds from a schizoid stage of development, and depression from a depressive organization. These are not just words but refer to the behaviour of the infant during the sensori-motor preverbal stage of development. What matters to us is the nature of object relationships during this phase. They are of primary importance in determining whether a loss in later years will result in one case in a breakdown of the self, and in the other case in a breakdown of object relationships characterized by the syndrome of depression.

In the uterus, the death of the mother brings about the death of the foetus: self cannot survive the absence of the mother. During the first few months of life the mother or substitute mother, reconstituting an external womb by her care, mainly exists so that the baby can preserve its existence. Only slowly does she acquire psychological meaning. After six or seven months the situation is different: the mother, biological or substitute, becomes emotionally meaningful and her loss produces severe separation anxiety known as anaclitic depression, as previously mentioned, although the infant could survive biologically through a substitute.

This is the second birth, the birth of what is human in terms of a meaningful emotional attachment, however primitive it may be. Unfortunately, the term 'depressive position' used by Melanie Klein has been the source of misunderstanding among psychiatrists, research workers and even psychoanalysts. It does not mean that the child goes through a depressive illness. It means that at about the time of the organization of the self and of object relationships the infant can react with moods of either sadness or depression to the loss of the object. The distinction will depend not on external circumstances alone but on what goes on in the internal or psychic reality of the infant, as opposed to what happens in the external situation or external reality.

It is essential to stress here the difference between internal or psychic reality and external reality. The situation in the mind of the infant must be understood. One factor of immense importance is the degree of anger that the infant feels when frustrated. It is important to note whether or not the anger is accompanied by phantasies or infantile attacks and revenge towards the mother. When the aggressive frustration arising from either within or without is strong enough, a primitive sense of responsibility or primitive link between anger and loss brings about the mood or syndrome of depression, as opposed to sadness.

A vital mistake is made in studies attempting to relate early deprivation to later incidence of depressive illness. All infants do not react in the same way to situations. The rhetorical question is what kind of an infant met deprivation, real or phantasized, and was the deprivation in external reality or was it an experience in internal or psychic reality and constructed by the infant?

It is now necessary to relate the state of affairs to the model of hierarchical supports. If this particular storey in the building – not quite the basement, which is reserved to schizophrenia, but shall we say the ground floor – is sufficiently pathologically organized, all other floors relating to object relationships will suffer structural distortions. Later in life any loss of any kind as described previously will be structurally and symbolically linked to the earlier experiences through a series of pathologically structured storeys.

A large number of psychiatrists and therapists of all sorts and denominations believe that they are treating depressive patients by therapy when chatting with their patients. In fact they are treating nothing at all. They have no regard for the specific, and do not give consideration to the fact that, under its manifold facets and varied symbolic expressions, the state of depression in proper treatment unfolds itself in a very specific way. Although in many cases the state evolves spontaneously to some sort of recovery, helped perhaps by an object relationship of a kind in the transference situation, this has nothing to do with the know-how based on the dynamics of the depressive state, especially in cases that do not respond to drugs or kindness.

It is obvious that the state of depression can be started from either end of the hierarchical system. If it is started from the psychical end it may remain situated within the domain of psychic or inner reality, or it may spread to the physical hierarchies. If it starts from the physical side it is only when the psychical domain will be involved that the state of depression will be experienced because a depressive meaning will be provoked. I am convinced that there exist physical states which, although the same as in overt depression, are not accompanied by depression, for instance in certain biocyclical states. This is because the depressive psychic organization is missing. Without it the physical process cannot produce the psychological picture known as depression.

No physical changes in the neurones can bring about the experience of depression. Only when the depressive organization pre-exists can a change starting either in the neuronal domain or physical hierarchy at one end, or in the psychological domain or hierarchy result in depression. Otherwise the stereotyped mental structures of depression, only symbolically different in their expression, would not be inevitably found and depression diagnosed. It is possible to proceed to a precise description of the psychic hierarchy and the psychodynamics of depression.

I shall now consider some of the symptoms of depression in terms of meaning as revealed during the analysis of innumerable states of depression all over the world, irrespective of culture. The impact of early infancy later leading to depression has been described. If we take the fate of the bodily functions, for instance, the picture is impressive. In the infant both the love and hate feelings have a normal strong oral character which fits well later in the depressive as shown by the disturbances of eating, lack of appetite and resulting loss of weight; or vice versa, by the bulimia and increase in weight observed in the course of a depressive illness. This is connected with the aggressive or angry rejection of the love object or the fear of cannibalistic attacks on the breast-mother. The bulimia is an attempt to replace the mother by food, as is well known, in a greedy, envious way. The mouth is also used to attack by means of words or angry noises. The analysis of depressive phantasies has also revealed the aggressive and destructive nature of excretory functions resulting in constipation or sometimes diarrhoea.

In an attempt to control the destructive processes, depriving the patient of his or her internal objects projected in the external object, the process of retardation sets in: the patient becomes less and less active, slower, and sometimes reaches complete immobility and stupor. This abolition of activity as revealed by phantasies expressed in treatment or often spontaneously, if one cares to listen and observe, is carried on in order to try to control the destructive activities of the body as part of a psychodynamic regression to early methods of thinking and behaviour.

Movements are stopped in order to do no harm; the same applies to the mouth both for eating or for speech activities, which are experienced as aggressive, and constipation sets in to stop the outpouring of destructive faeces, and so on. The sexual impulse undergoes the same fate: libidinal impulses are dangerous as they bring the subject in contact with his loved object with possible dangerous consequences due to the destructive impulse, and also because of the need for a hurtful rejection. Regression may extend to biochemical processes such as interference with gonadal activity and many others. Thus sleep is disturbed. There is less sleep, more drowsiness or restlessness, a diminished phase IV, and a diminished REM phase and therefore less dreaming. It is tempting to suggest that what is not expressed in the dream may be lived vividly in awakeness.

It is clear that the method used in this process is a psychobiological attempt at abolition of function. This process is pathological and in a way is part of the destructive process itself. However, after a while it seems that the process of control comes to a stop and life begins to return in some cases but not in others. The blocking can be located in either the physical or the psychical hierarchies or both.

Freud clearly saw those processes of dissolution and reconstruction, for in *The Ego and the Id* (1923) he compared them to processes of metabolism and anabolism. It is also clear that for him it was more than an analogy. In 'Mourning and Melancholia' (1917), Freud gave the first and most important clue to the beginning of the understanding of the psychodynamics of depression. In melancholia the object attacked and damaged is introjected and the subject identified with his object. The self becomes damaged and mood is depressed. However, Freud saw more than this. He realized that the self-reproaches of the melancholic were not to be taken at their face value. They at least have a twofold meaning: by this process of identification of the self with the object, the self-reproaches are still directed towards the object as well as to the subject. Thus, the attacks are not given up and recovery is impossible. Guilt and despair predominate. In mourning, the attacks on the object and the sense of responsibility and guilt for the damage to and the loss of the object are missing. We now know a great deal more regarding this process. That is, we know about the defences used in depression, the reasons for their failure, and we know more about the processes of recovery and of reparation. Melanie Klein and her followers have contributed a great deal to this knowledge.

Having substituted or identified himself or herself with his or her object does not mean that the attacks on the object and sufferings caused to the actual environment by the behaviour of the depressive cease to exist. Another manoeuvre is to split the object into a good and bad part in an attempt to save and preserve a good object. This often results in an inability to relate to good objects for fear of destroying them. Yet here we see an important germ of the reparative process, that is, the beginning of a caring feeling although selfishness may still be at work.

The subject often develops a sense of persecution by the bad object which negates the aim of the splitting defensive process. The more schizoid the subject, the more splitting will be resorted to and a vicious circle results. The underlying process is obvious: the subject cannot give up his aggressive impulses and his revengeful attitudes; he is governed by the law of talion: an eye for an eye, a tooth for a tooth. There is no reparation but guilt and punishment. Despair dominates the picture because not only do the attacks fail to cease but the damaged object has to be repaired in a concrete way, as in the example of the mare looking for its foal as it was before death, while only God can bring Lazarus back to life.

Therefore, if omnipotence has to take over as it does when reality has to be denied, a manic state sets in. In this state, a falsely repaired object replaces the damaged object. Instead of sadness, emptiness, guilt and despair, which are the appropriate moods in response to the state of the terribly damaged object, a mood of denial of psychic reality takes over, characterized by the falseness of everything, a mood of false activity, or elation, and the pretence of corresponding to the omnipotently created false replacing object. This state is very difficult to treat. In the manic state the replacing object is a manufactured grandiose phallus as opposed to the breast-mother in depression. The mood and behaviour in each instance correspond to the state of the internal object to which the subject is relating.

The depressive must be treated in the state of depression and not during recovery or manic elation, when everything is more difficult. By recovery I mean recovery without profound changes in the psychic organization of the self.

It must be made clear that the statement of the patient that he or she is not good, has caused damage, has brought about misery, must not be contradicted. In his or her own psychic reality everything the patient feels and experiences consciously or unconsciously is true for him or her. Reassurance that this is not so is wrong and can only increase the patient's despair of being understood. Instead he must be helped to understand this painful mood, and feelings of guilt are quite appropriate granted that his belief and experience are that he has acted and acts badly, causing misery to others. When this is understood the situation changes. Without this sorrow and regret there is no hope of giving up the destructive process in order to make reparation.

However, despair still predominates. The patient does not know how to stop the aggressive impulses and to repair the damaged object. This is because he does not trust his love impulses and because his sense of reparation is concrete and directed towards the external object, which could in fact be irreparable. The patient must then first be helped to see that the sense of regret and despair could not exist without a good, loving and sensitive aspect of self being active, and that this part must be trusted and used more constructively than savagely to punish him or herself, which is of no use to the object. Second, since the damage can be either entirely in the inner world of phantasy or in the external world, it is the inner object that must be repaired first. The sense of compassion and caring for the object helps to diminish the aggressive impulses. The necessity for splitting into good and bad diminishes. The patient can then gradually see that the same object may at times be good and bad; he then realizes that the same applies to himself. Compassion and forgiveness replace the law of talion and revenge through the conscious emergence of his previously unrecognized aspect of the self. A new relationship emerges between the subject and his internal objects. This new attitude is then directed towards the external objects. The original distorted primal object relationship is no longer projected into and on to the external world and throughout the inner world of hierarchical organization of object relationships. A new world of object relationships may then be achieved through an internal psychic change.

It remains to mention the so-called masked depressions and depressive equivalents. They really are of two kinds. The more schizoid the patient, the more he or she will rely on the splitting, projection and denial of the depressed part of the ego. This results in a deadened sort of attitude, sometimes accompanied by depersonalization and derealization as a result of the loss of a feeling part of the self. The other defensive process is either physical or hypochondriacal somatization. Just as there are biochemical structures there are psychic structures that can also be strictly described, and whole properties must be understood in order to understand the dynamics of depression. The dynamic explanation, a great progress in itself, will also have to find its metasystem. But it is certain that this metasystem will have to take the dynamic metasystem into account, for according to the order of things it can never bypass it.

12 REVERSIBILITY, DEPRESSION AND THE THERAPEUTIC PROCESS

I wish to consider the nature of the therapeutic process from a psycho-biological point of view, and in so doing first of all examine the conditions that regulate equilibrium and reversibility in a psychobiological system. This is because only on the basis of the existence of a reversible state can therapy be possible. Then I would like to consider the role of depression as one of the very important factors associated with the reversible state.

The scheme evolved by Kubie (1958) to describe the elements that constitute a drive, or, as I will call it, a unit of behaviour, appears to me to fulfil many of our needs. In his views, an instinct or drive consists of a biochemical substrate, a neuronal net and a psychological superstructure. At one end of the spectrum the biochemical process is all-important and the psychological plays a very small role, while for other drives the reverse is true. If this point of view is accepted, it follows that when attempting to alter behaviour all three systems are involved to varying degrees: conditions governing equilibrium and reversibility of physico-chemical systems as defined, for instance, in Le Chatelier's principle, but also other complicated processes connected with the emergence of cellular organization and governed by the laws of homoeostasis.

The situation becomes still more complex in a psychobiological system when the conditions that regulate the equilibrium and reversibility of psychological systems must also be taken into consideration. Metabolic processes, for instance, depend on a complicated equilibrium between anabolic and metabolic processes, and this equilibrium depends on the reversibility of the reactions involved. Added to this, organisms grow and decay and irreversible reactions make their appearance. An example is that as the result of research on embryonic life it is now known that the embryo can only develop properly if the anlage – the embryonic tissues in develop-ment – is acted upon by specific organisms at a particular time and not before or after (Jost, 1953).

If, as there are reasons to believe, a somewhat analogous situation exists with regard to physical and psychological stimuli acting upon the growing infant from inside and outside, these findings are of great significance with regard to the problem of reversibility. The increasing complexity of the organization of instinctual life with increasing mental representation, that is, with increasing symbolic activity, is well known to us through the psychodynamic schools. Primary and secondary processes, to use psychoanalytical terminology, enter into amazing numbers of permutations and combinations, developing into systems of thought related to behaviour. During the developmental stages each level influences the next level of organization. Certain patterns become irreversibly fixated while others are more flexible. It is through this complex organization that the therapist and patient must work their way. The degree of freedom of an individual to adapt to a given situation must therefore be determined by the number of processes at his or her disposal to deal with that situation. At the physical level this can be limited by inheritance, and by biochemical and neuronal factors. At the emotional and representative level this can happen in at least two ways: first, in so far as emotions have promoted or restricted mental development, especially factors affecting symbol-formation and object relations. Second, by interfering with the proper use of existing mental endowment.

I have referred to the equilibrium and reversibility of psychological systems, and I must now attempt to enlarge more upon this subject. Psychoanalysis is essentially concerned with the understanding of the forces contributing to the state of mental equilibrium; with displacement and distribution of libidinal and aggressive cathexes; with symbol-formation; with interchanges between the inner and external worlds; with psychological fixations, regression and progressions; with introjections and projections. Normal mental functioning depends on the relative reversibility of these mental structures, and this is clearly implied in psychoanalytical thinking. However, it cannot be said that psychoanalysis has been concerned with a systematic exposition of the phenomena governing reversibility. To put it concisely, in psychoanalysis we have the two principles of mental functioning – the pleasure–pain principle and the reality principle – but there is no reversibility principle.

In some obscure way the reversibility principle may be the reverse of the repetition-compulsion drive. For a systematic study of the principle of psychological reversibility it is necessary to turn to Piaget (1950). Unfortunately, reversibility as seen by him is a vast subject that he has covered in a very large number of publications, and the subject cannot be summarized succinctly. A brief reference to it is given here in order to introduce the notion of reversibility in psychology. Take three objects: A, B, C. Given that A = B and B = C, operational logic tells us that A = C, B = A and C = B, that is, there is equilibrium and equality based on complete reversibility. But how has this knowledge developed? As Piaget has demonstrated, in stages. He recognizes a sensori-motor stage with little representative thinking, a preconceptual and intuitive stage and a final stage of operational logic (Piaget,

1947). First the child can only compare A and B perceptually and by using motor displacement, and may conclude that A is like B but not yet B like A unless the comparison is repeated in the other direction: B is compared with A. This must be repeated with B and C. Only at another stage will he or she be able to compare relationships, that is, the relation A = B is compared with the relation B = C as entities. Further stages lead to the complete operation at the level of operational logic.

What is most important for us is what characterizes the passage from the sensori-motor level and type of operation, to the intuitive and preconceptual activity. Through processes of accommodation, that is, a modification of internal schemata to adapt to external objects or situations, and processes of assimilation (the modification of external objects or situations to adapt the internal schemata), there is, first, an increasing degree of representation and symbolization; second, a diminishing dependence on the external objects as 'significant' in symbol-formation and an increasing importance of internal schemata; third, a loss of individuality of each object, accompanied by becoming increasingly considered as a member of a series, a class, a group, allowing generalization and abstraction to take place.

At the egocentric stage, with primacy of assimilation over accommodation, there results symbolic play and creative imagination, while with primacy of accommodation over assimilation there is reproductive imagination and representative imitation. With equilibrium and reversibility between assimilation and accommodation there is the formation of preconcepts and intuitive thinking, leading finally to the level of operational activity (Piaget, 1945). Thus conceptual equilibrium and reversibility is achieved by a gradual process of decentration or lessening of egocentric activity through the gradual elimination of ordinates of space and time. These ordinates make an object or event or relationship a specific one at a particular place and at a particular time, giving it the quality of uniqueness.

It could well be that this decentration and lessening of the egocentric activity corresponds to a lessening of the use of projective identification. This explains why in therapy we have to deal with mental mechanisms in a concrete and specific way, and with the specific and not with the conceptual. It goes without saying that there are plenty of situations and problems in life that can be solved at the conceptual level of operational logic, but there are some that belong to earlier systems and cannot be solved by the use of logical structures. The earlier systems must be recreated, experienced with their appropriate emotions by making them again individual in time and space and in affective states. Thus love for women becomes love for a number of specific women and then for one specific woman at a certain time of life. There is then the mother or mother-substitute. It is because of the existence of an inner psychic world of representation, symbolization and memories that we can reach the situation to be altered.

One aspect of the role of the therapist in individual treatment or of the therapist and patients in group therapy is to bring about the reaction of specificity, that is, to reinstate the ordinates of space and time. The patient is angry with the therapist or a specific member of the group about something specific and wishes to act in a specific aggressive way towards that specific person. That is transference. The redistribution of affective forces may be enough to bring about a readjustment. This is non-specific psychotherapy. When the relationship with the therapist is ended, the patient's psychological schemata may remain altered for better or for worse because of experiences having occurred non-specifically during the time of the transference relationship, or may revert to their previous structure. In the latter case a more specific approach is needed. That is to say, specific interpretations are given with regard to the specific systems evoked at various times during treatment in order to alter their structure. This is psychodynamic psychotherapy. Experience has shown that the evoked affective state plays a very important role in promoting the conditions necessary for the reversal of a behavioural structure. The affective state may be fear, anxiety, anger, pleasure, pain, greed, envy, sexual feelings, love or aggression.

I want to suggest that depression is an affect which has a very special meaning in relation to reversibility. Clinically, lasting depression is looked upon as an illness often limited in time and showing spontaneous reversibility into recovery. There is even a type of recurrent depression in which there is a more or less recurrent sequence of depression and recovery. But this reversibility of depression is of a special character: it has the character of a pendulum action and is not a state of equilibrium based on an instantaneous readjustment in the system of one change by another in order to maintain a steady state. In the spontaneous recovery from depression one state or system replaces another, but no structural change takes place. Depression itself has been considered by doctors and psychiatrists as an illness, as something bad to be got rid of by every possible means. No thought has been given to its biological role, for instance as has been done for inflammation or Selye's stress reaction, which postulates that part of the disease process is due to the reaction of the body to eliminate the stressor or compensate for its disruptive effects.

The point I want to make is that the emergence of depression in an illness of any sort corresponds to the organism entering into a state of possible reversibility, which, if used properly, can allow structural changes to take place. This can occur if the role of depression and its mechanisms is properly understood. Let me just remind you of the remarkable fact that in severe obsessional states, obsession and compulsions may disappear when deep enough depression appears; or that in schizoaffective disorders the schizoid aspects may disappear when depression dominates the picture. It is therefore essential to examine the state of mind of a depressed patient in the course of any illness whatsoever.

Depression is characterized by a feeling of loss, sadness and guilt, by the uselessness of everything, by despair reaching even to the extreme of wanting to die; depression may also end in suicide. Why is it that so many people who often have not even lost something apparently in the external world behave as if they had? Psychoanalysis has illuminated from the subjective side the meaning of the mental and behavioural happenings.

The emotional organization leading to depression has its roots in infancy. At that time, when the child experiences feelings of both love and hate towards the mother or mother-substitute, a predominance of feelings of aggression leads to the psychological destruction of the loved object. Because of feelings of love and dependence, this psychological destruction is experienced as a tremendous loss and, because of having brought about the destruction, an equally tremendous feeling of responsibility and later of guilt is experienced. This state of mind brings about an intense desire for restoration of the loved object and of reparation towards it. This is the essential aspect of depression, from the point of view of reversibility. Without the sense of loss, regret, responsibility and guilt, there can be no urge to repair, to restore – that is, to reverse the dreadful situation. To get rid of the depression by the various means currently employed in psychiatry, or to assess a patient as being worse when depressed and better when not depressed, without taking into account the different reasons that bring about the change, is one of the most serious mistakes of psychiatry. This mistake leads to approaching the illness only at the biochemical substrate, and/or at the neuronal net, while ignoring the psychological superstructure.

I want to enlarge a little on this picture and to consider some of the symptoms of depression in more detail. A common one is retardation – the patient does increasingly few things and does them increasingly slowly, sometimes reaching immobility. His speech also is slowed, as well as his eating processes; his bowel action becomes sluggish; his sleep is disturbed; he makes less contact with the outside world. There are many other aspects, but these will suffice to illustrate our point of view. If we investigate the meaning of this process to the patient as revealed to us through the understanding of the inner world of psychic reality, the whole process makes sense. Two main factors predominate and they illustrate what I call false reparation, or the wrong way of reversing the pathological processes, though showing that the desire for reversal is strong.

First, because of self-inflicted punishment the patient becomes more and more like the damaged or dead loved objects, that is, less and less alive. There is, in fact, introjection and identification with the loved object (Freud, 1917). At this point the patient is giving up all his substitutes for the original loved object because of an increasing preconscious awareness that they were used practically solely to deny the real underlying situation. Second, each bodily function is more controlled because of its aggressive and destructive components, directed against both external and internal or introjected objects, that is, cathected internal schemata, the components of which include with varying degrees of importance a biochemical, a neuronal and a psychological component, forming a unit linked in certain instances to organs of the body by neurovascular connections. Hypochondriacal pains viewed at the level of the psychological component indicate the damaged or suffering state of the introjects. Movements are stopped in order to do no harm, similarly with mouth activities, and the patient becomes taciturn and anorexic. Constipation sets in to stop the outpouring of destructive faeces, and so on. The sexual impulse is also interfered with: libidinal attraction is dangerous because it brings the subject in contact with the desired object, thus creating a dangerous situation because of the co-existing destructive impulses, and thus loss of libido ensues.

Regression can also take place at the physical level. Thus by studying gonadal activity in women daily over periods of months by the vaginal smear technique, it was possible to demonstrate that if the emotional process goes deep enough gonadal activity may become impaired or completely arrested. From a biological point of view it can be hypothesized that in this way the physical component of the libidinal and aggressive drives is thus diminished or abolished in an attempt to stop forces contributing to the development of the dangerous situation. The loss of function that ensues causes more depression, guilt and despair and a vicious circle sets in. What causes despair to the depressive is that he or she has no more hope of stopping the destructive processes and of restoring the lost loved object.

There are two main aspects to deal with in order to make use of depression in therapy. First, it is to help the patient to understand that to feel sorrow and regret in response to what he feels is a bad action in his own inner world, far from being something to be afraid of or to reject, however painful it may be, is a tremendous asset because it is a most important aspect of his or her humanity, that which distinguishes him or her from the unrepentant criminal. Without sorrow, regret and a sense of responsibility there is no wish and no urgency to repair. It is amazing to observe the change in the patient who has grasped this fact: he is still depressed, but he understands that in the depression itself lies his humanity, his dignity and his cure. But he still despairs because of the failure of his reparative methods in spite of good intentions.

The failure is due to the fact that false reparation is entirely based on control mechanisms, as previously described, and on the law of the talion, something like, 'If your hands do harm, cut off your hands.' But then there are no hands to help the victim. The understanding that his despair is due to the fact that he does not know how to put things right, but that other, more effective ways exist has another remarkable effect. At last hope can take the place of despair, though for a time the patient may become very dependent on the therapist in order to experience the new way. When instead of the rigid application on to himself of the law of the talion he understands more fully the meaning of compassion, care and forgiveness, the situation begins to reverse. In other words, when he can use internally and externally more constructive methods of reparation as time goes on, a new life becomes open to him. He becomes increasingly able then to distinguish between his internal schemata and the undistorted aspects of the external world. As the confusion diminishes the external world becomes less destroyed, more friendly, more hopeful.

Thus we come to postulate what would appear to be a paradoxical situation: the appearance of depression in the course of dynamic psychotherapy is not necessarily a bad sign, and could even be a very hopeful sign. In fact, in some instances we might have to know very carefully how to foster depression so that we can reach a state of reversibility, at which time we can effect structural changes in the self.

CLINICAL EXAMPLE

Working in a teaching hospital, I have been struck by the fact that doctors in training also become more hopeful when they have acquired understanding of what depression means and how to approach it. Here is a clinical example to illustrate the treatment of a patient with depression by a doctor in training, after ECT, occupational therapy, rehabilitation – all had failed.

The patient, an unmarried woman of twenty-two, had been treated twice with electric shock therapy apparently with great success. However, each time on the very day of her discharge she relapsed and she was then referred to the psychotherapy department. She was depressed, and spoke hesitantly in a voice that was hardly audible. She wanted to go home because she wanted to help her mother. A young female doctor undertook her treatment with my help and supervision.

It soon emerged that the patient was very preoccupied with the idea that her parents were very unhappy, especially her mother. Much of her trouble was attributed to her grandmother, who was very difficult and part of mother's life, for she lived at home with the patient's parents. The grandmother showed no open aggression, but found nothing right at home. By contrast, the parents of her fiancé were marvellous – such a contrast! She was helped to become aware of this strict separation of good and bad, all the badness being at home.

At times the patient would break into attacks of urticaria, and for the first time in her life had an attack of asthma. The attacks of urticaria always occurred when she visited her fiancé. This was interpreted to her, and feelings of aggression then started to appear, at first mostly directed towards grandmother, then against mother. She became extremely guilty, and linked the feelings of depression and guilt with those attacks. At that point the whole situation changed. The patient realized that it was normal, human and appropriate to regret hurting the loved ones. She started reparation by going to work to earn more money for the household, and looked after grandmother to help mother with that task. She also worked through her aggressive and sexual anxieties, which had been displaced on to her fiancé. The most dramatic moment was her realization of the meaning of her depressed feelings. She was able then to repair in a more effective way, and to internalize a good inner mother.

SUMMARY

In this paper I have attempted to introduce the idea of reversibility of psychophysical systems, upon which all our efforts in psychotherapy depend. I could only give a very succinct idea of the concept of reversibility of structures. Since I did not know of the consideration given to those ideas in psychoanalysis, I felt at the time I had to use Piaget's ideas on the subject. However, this led us to consider, in a psychodynamic system involving impulses, emotions, feelings as well as structures, the degree of reversibility and irreversibility of the system and of its metasystems. It would seem obvious that, for instance, schizophrenia and borderline cases are more irreversible than depression. Further, within depression we can assess differences between psychotic depression and neurotic depression and their degree of reversibility. The factors leading to reversibility have been considered, and it appears that new developments in the maturation phases of depression lead to greater advances in the possible use in treatment of the concept of reversibility. On the one hand, phases of the progress of reversibility are more conceptual, while on the other hand the dynamic status of the patient involves the realization of the sense of 'being', in a way not achieved before the working through of depression.

One could say that depression is a metasystem to schizoid mechanisms, which itself is a metasystem to sensori-motor schemas. Reversibility increases from the more primitive to the more complex systems.

13 REPARATION

[handwritten margin note: Loss/rejection causes ego to deny int/ext i.e. attack while in P.S (death instinct) Halluc/delus = psychotic reparation. When ego can stop attacks i.e. When realises what is happening, reparation can begin. This involves accepting loss + replacing it with something different (the symbol) The Melancholic is still attacking. The obsessional isn't but can't repair so repeats. The Mourner can, but the manic is still too spacial + the reparation is concrete +.: false Larger than life.]

The subject of this paper is the psychoanalytic approach to reparation.

Reparation is a process so widely active in nature that it is necessary to situate our theme within some kind of boundary. We are familiar with the renewal of life when spring repairs the winter destruction and life reappears vigorously, creating new life everywhere. It is not only in the plant world that this happens. In the animal world new life is created to replace the dead. Not only does new life replace dead organisms, but repair takes place within organisms themselves – thus the salamander repairs and produces a new tail to replace the damaged one. And it is not only at the macroscopic level that this process takes place. Tissue repair takes place at all levels, macroscopically and microscopically. Processes of life and death are based on anabolic and catabolic processes and their metabolic balance, or one dominating the other.

Coming nearer to our subject, that is to say, the psychological side of reparation, no one can miss the role it plays in mythology, religion and folklore (though not, to my knowledge, in so-called scientific psychology). The famous Egyptian *Book of the Dead* is full of such striking examples, even in minute details, that can be compared with the processes of patients revealed by analysis. Unfortunately, I know of no studies relating to a real exegesis of the concept of reparation within that area of thought. However, sacrifice, punishment and penance are themes that have attracted innumerable studies.

Medicine, traditionally known as the art of healing, is therefore essentially linked to reparation. The enormous progress made in the organic aspects of illness, anatomical, physiological, biological, genetic, and so on, has shifted the balance towards a better understanding of concrete, biological repair. A comparable progress as to the understanding of psychological structures and mechanisms can only be traced to the great contribution of Freud and of his followers. Without this new psychoanalytic approach there would still be little more to do than apply the 'bedside manner' type of psychotherapy.

Only a better understanding of the mechanisms of the mind can help to achieve for psychological medicine what has taken place in organic medicine, for the understanding of the mind.

In spite of progress, the simplicity of attempting organic repair as opposed to the complexity of psychodynamic reparation is overwhelmingly tempting. Hardly any analyst nowadays sees patients where biological repair for mental problems has not been and is not being attempted.

It seems necessary here to clarify the level of functioning of the mind to which this paper will be referring. It will be dealing with psychological reparation from its earliest appearance in the infant and across developmental stages, focusing on both theory and clinical experience. In Part I an effort will be made to trace some of the ideas of Freud relevant to the concept of reparation, and to follow the evolution of the concept in Melanie Klein's writings. In Part II, I present my own observations and interpretations of the concept of reparation.

PART I

Freud used the word 'reparation' three times, and I shall return to those occasions later. Much has been written about what he thought the therapeutic process was; here, I am interested only in his ideas or preoccupations that can be considered precursors to Melanie Klein's concept of reparation. I will only attempt to present some brief considerations on a subject which demands a most complex study.

At first and for a long time psychoanalytic theory was concerned with the *instincts and their vicissitudes*. Freud never wrote an equivalent paper on the vicissitudes of the object. The importance of the object and object relations has grown with time. Instincts were treated as energy undergoing transformational changes varying in distribution and quantity. Repression is the cornerstone of psychopathology. What is repressed is libidinal energy. The concept of reparation emerging at such a phase of psychoanalytic development would meet with great difficulties. Energy cannot be damaged; objects can.

With better understanding of the role of the object, the relation between narcissism and object relations was clarified, especially in connection with the differences between neurosis and psychosis. When interest shifted from hysteria, repression and symptoms connected with the return of the repressed to the understanding of obsessional neurosis, the importance of the concern with the state of the object (and the subject as an object among objects) becomes clearer in the doing and undoing aspects of rituals, as well as the damaging role of aggression. The compulsion to repeat can be understood because reparation cannot take place. Reparation involves stopping the attacks and repairing the object by methods to be described.

Further, punishment is not reparation; neither sacrifice nor punishment nor penance is of help to the victim, which belong to the law of talion.

With psychosis the problem is more approachable. In one of his most amazing insights, Freud saw and described the process of restitution in the psychotic processes of hallucination and delusion. As he pointed out, in psychosis a piece of external reality – the object – is suppressed. He saw restitution as the attempt by the patient to restore the suppressed piece of external reality, substituting in its place a phantasized construction of his own of a pathological nature, such as a delusion or hallucination, or some distorted view of reality. It also raises the question of reconstruction at the perceptual level and the whole problem of vertical hierarchical levels of representation in patients' attempts at reparation. This is a vital difference between the paranoid-schizoid and the depressive positions.

It is Freud's momentous contribution to the understanding of the dynamics of depression in 'Mourning and Melancholia' (1917) that has made possible further progress on the fate of the ego and of the object in depression. He described the loss of the object due to the attacks by the subject and the melancholic's despair about restoring the object to its previous state. Although the concept of internal object is not there, Freud saw the self-reproaches of the melancholic as a continuation of the attacks on the love-object through identification of the subject with the object. His detailed description of the process of mourning is basic for the understanding of working through, and, with Klein, of reparation. Of great import is Freud's extension of the concept of loss of the object, which includes damage done to the object. Thus,

> In melancholia, the occasions which give rise to the illness extend for the most part beyond the clear case of a loss by death, and include all those situations of being slighted, neglected or disappointed, which can import opposed feelings of love and hate into the relationship or reinforce an already existing ambivalence.(p. 251)

Further, in the same paper Freud attempts to relate mania to melancholia. The dynamics of mania seemed to have been a difficult subject to unravel for Freud. However, his description of the liberated libido increasing the subject's narcissism, leading to an ego equal or superior to the super-ego, is an extremely valuable contribution to a very vital problem. Through the mechanism of being able to feel superior to the menacing and punishing object the subject tries to feel safe. If this is experienced at the phase of development when, to use a well-known Piagetian concept, mental processes are space-centred, or, for Freud, there is thing-representation instead of word-representation, a special kind of problem is created. To say Freud is a great man simply means Freud is a big or tall man, and the subject must become bigger and more powerful to overcome the menacing object. This is done by: being bigger than the object; by making the object smaller. As this experience is at the concrete level of thought-representation, it can only be achieved by resorting to omnipotent thinking and getting further and further away from reality. Reversibility of this process then becomes increasingly difficult. I have dealt with the problem of space-centred thought extensively in this book.

Freud first used the word 'reparation' in 'Some Character-types met with in Psycho-analytic work' (1916a), where he spoke about Richard III: 'We all think we have reason to reproach nature and our destiny for congenital and infantile disadvantages; we all demand reparation for early wounds to our narcissism, our self-love' (p. 315). But the important reference is 'Loss of Reality in Neurosis and Psychosis' (1924):

> And, in fact, some analogy of the sort [with neurosis] can be observed in a psychosis. Here, too, there are two steps, the second of which has the character of reparation. . . . Neurosis and psychosis differ from each other far more in their first, introductory, reaction than in the attempt at reparation which follows it. (p. 184)

A relevant turn in Freud's thinking for the present subject was the emergence of the concept of the death instinct in 1920. Since the aim of one of the two instincts was to destroy both internally and externally, to return to the original state from which life emerged (this being apparently desirable), the organism or human being could survive only because of a repairing and creating life instinct. It was also at that time that Melanie Klein started her work. At the beginning of this paper I mentioned how processes of life and death are based on anabolic and catabolic processes and their metabolic balance. In *The Ego and the Id* (1923), Freud writes:

> On this view, a special physiological process (of anabolism or catabolism) would be associated with each of the two classes of instincts; both kinds of instinct would be active in every particle of living substance, though in unequal proportions, so that some one substance might be the principal representative of Eros. (p. 41)

It suffices to point out that Eros can also be considered as the representative of, say, the anabolic processes, and Thanatos of the catabolic processes in a close metabolic interchange. The concept of psychic representation of metabolic processes offers no difficulty, and plenty of serious work exists on the subject experimentally as well as theoretically. The psychoanalyst Lawrence Kubie (1958) has attempted to define as precisely as possible the structure of a drive. Briefly, he considers a drive to be the resultant of a complex structure consisting of a biochemical substrate, a neuronal net and psychological superstructure seeking an appropriate object. For certain bits of behaviour one end of the continuum is more important, and vice versa for others. Using the model, reparation can take place at all three levels. I am

aware that many analysts reject the two biological substrates, and that even
Freud is reproached from time to time for not having sufficiently freed
himself of the biological approach. Those who want to bury their head in
the sand so as not to hear and not to see are free to do so. On the contrary,
insight into this problem allows the analyst not to be in conflict about levels
at which the patient operates. It is also my opinion that Freud's ideas on the
struggle of the two great instincts – their fusion and defusion, their arising
from inside, and their diversion or deflection externally, seeking external
objects, their creative and preserving functions – can all be derived from this
metabolic model of instincts.

Reparation is a Kleinian concept. Indeed, Joan Rivière (1937) wrote, 'The
value attributed to reparation phantasies is perhaps the most essential aspect
of the work of Melanie Klein.' This concept has a history. It is useful to trace
its evolution before it takes its more or less final form with her ideas on the
depressive position. Not only is *reparation* used; she interchanges words
such as 'restitution', 'restoration', 'reinstatement', 'repair', 'construction',
'reconstruction', 'creation' and perhaps others, which contribute to various
aspects of the concept of reparation proper.

What is it that has to be repaired? How was it damaged? How is the damage
to be repaired? These are three simple questions which lead to extraordinarily complex answers. It must be remembered that Klein started with the idea
of an early object relationship, with an intellectually damaged little patient,
Fritz, and with Freud's new turn of thought – the life and death instincts of
1920. It is not possible in this paper to follow step by step the evolution of
her ideas, which J.M. Pétot (1979a, b) has done masterfully.

It seems possible somewhat to systematize an answer to the first question.
As concepts gradually arise of an incorporated object, an introjected object,
and finally an internal object – as well as of the good and bad objects both
internal and external – then out of chaos order emerges. These are the
concrete external objects of external reality, the phantasized external objects
and the phantasized internal objects. All these objects are constructions of
the subject. The concrete external objects are not only constructions of
phantasy, that is, having emotional meaning; they are also the result of
sensori-motor laws following a strict developmental sequence. The resulting
structures can go wrong at any stage. This may pervert large areas, or all of
the thought processes, including the phantasy life of the child and later of
the adult. It is not sufficient to consider the constructs of external reality only
from what is given to us by psychoanalysis, but also to include a recognition
of how external reality is constructed. As an example, the developmental
views of Jean Piaget are fundamental in understanding how the infant
constructs his or her perceptual and intellectual world in a strict sequential
order. This can go wrong for many reasons, especially through emotional
distortions. Thus I have tried to show in other papers that in the paranoid-
schizoid organization thought is still space-centred, and that this method of

functioning throws light on schizophrenic and schizoid mental processes and psychosis in general. Remnants of such thinking persist also in neurosis and in normal people in varying degrees. An excessive pathological fixation of space-centred thought makes psychic reparation impossible, as will be seen later with examples.

Obviously the other object damaged is the subject him- or herself. Freud made a point in 'Mourning and Melancholia' about the state of the ego of the melancholic in identification with the damaged object. He made a great advance when he understood that 'the shadow of the object fell on the ego', and that when the melancholic indulges in constant criticism about himself he is also continuing his attacks on the object with which the ego is now identified. This process is in part responsible for the difference between mourning and melancholia, as the guilt of the continued attack prevents any working through and coming to terms with the loss. Klein underlined this process in 'Early Stages of the Oedipus Conflict' (1928). After describing the fear of the girl with regard to the attacked and damaged mother's retribution against her, she writes:

> Here we have also one root of the constant concern of women (often so excessive) for their personal beauty, for they dread that this too will be destroyed by the mother. At the bottom of the impulse to deck and beautify themselves there is always the motive of *restoring* comeliness, and this has its origin in anxiety and sense of guilt.

The word 'reparation' is not yet in use. Further, it does not seem apparent to me that the distinction between object lost and object damaged has been made sufficiently up to now by analysts when it comes either to reinstating the object or to repairing it. Following 'Mourning and Melancholia', psychoanalysis has turned more to the loss of the object, but not, as Klein did, to the damaged object as well. Along with clearly defining the classes of objects that have to be repaired and making the distinction between object lost and object damaged, it is necessary to consider the methods of doing damage before being able to describe the mechanisms of reparation.

Klein considered that the life and death instincts are active from the beginning of life or very early, and that they have an object. Her use of the term sadism has been severely criticized. However, if one accepts the early control of the death instinct not only by deflection outward but also by the moderating influence (fusion) of the life instinct, or the libido as Freud postulated, then the term becomes less objectionable and certainly at least understandable. Klein also considered that sadism reaches a crescendo at a certain stage in the life of the infant and then seems to go on diminishing. After a number of vacillations about the exact stage for this peak of sadism, she wrote,

... the phase of development in which sadism reaches its maximum height begins, in my opinion, with the emergence of the oral-sadistic instincts and ends with the decline of the earlier anal stage. (1931)

What is the nature of the sadistic attack? It comprises oral tearing, biting, spitting, faecal and urinary attacks – everything conceivable through any part of the body. Repeatedly Klein came back to the fact that the infant attacks with all the means his or her sadism can muster.

What are the reasons for the decline in the intensity of the attacks on the object and the resultant change? Two factors seem to have preoccupied Klein: one is the intense anxiety generated by the fear of talion, the other the emerging sense of guilt. As the infant becomes more and more aware of his or her objects – that is, as aspects of the object come together and the object becomes more complex and acquires a status of its own, even though it may be via projective identification – the infant becomes more aware of the feelings of the object and thus more aware of what his or her treatment of the object means to the object. A purely narcissistic extreme anxiety is slowly transformed by a consideration for the object's experiences and a sense of responsibility, so to speak, for the anguish caused to the object. Thus,

> But such a manifestation of primitive tendencies (sadistic attacks) is invariably followed by anxiety, and by performances which show how the child now tries to make good and to atone for that which he had done. Sometimes he tries to mend the very same men, trains and so on he has just broken. Sometimes drawing, building and so on express the same reactive tendencies. (1927)

In 1929, two years later, Melanie Klein added two more dimensions to the concept in one of her most remarkable papers 'Infantile Anxiety-situations Reflected in a Work of Art and in the Creative Impulse' (1929). In a Ravel ballet it is pity, compassion and the desire to alleviate suffering that help to alter the damage done; in a painting of Ruth Kjar an object created by the *patient* replaces the object loss, i.e., the importance of a sublimated creative impulse becomes an important factor in reparation.

I also see here a difference between the object damaged and the object lost. There is, as well, the restoration of an inner stage, that is, the emptiness inside Ruth caused by the loss of an external object is restored through an external object, but not the same object. It is not omnipotent replacement but sublimation. This is a precursor of the role of the internal object in reparation, the most important of all the considerations involved. Without the possibility of repairing the internal object, in the presence or absence of the external object, psychic reparation is not possible. This will be finally settled with the concept of the depressive position, but a number of factors must be dealt with first. In the Ravel ballet example, the sense of pity plays an important role. What is this role? Klein quotes Freud as saying that pity is the opposite of cruelty. In 1915 Freud wrote:

> For the sake of completeness I may add that feelings of pity cannot be described as a result of a transformation of instinct occurring in sadism, but necessitate the notion of a *reaction-formation* against that instinct. (1915a, p. 129)

And,

> Reaction-formations against certain instincts take the deceptive form of a change in their content, as though egoism had changed into altruism, or cruelty into pity. (1915b, p. 281)

In 'From the History of an Infantile Neurosis' (1918) Freud wrote:

> Then suddenly, in connection with a dream, the analysis plunged back into the prehistoric period, and led him to assert that during the copulation in the primal scene he had observed the penis disappear, that he had felt compassion for his father on that account, and had rejoiced at the reappearance of what he thought had been lost. So here was a fresh emotional impulse, starting once again from the primal scene. Moreover, the narcissistic origin of compassion (which is confirmed by word itself) [German *Mitleid*, literally 'suffering with'] is here quite unmistakably revealed. (p. 88)

In this amazing passage Freud relates the primal scene, that is, genital impulses and the epistemophilic impulse, pity and compassion, and the reappearance or restoration of the lost object. It also raises for us the question of the working through in dreams, of reparation, of loss, and of depressive feeling.

To return to Klein and to the sequence of her ideas, there are now a number of factors to explain how the infant is led to diminish the intensity of his sadistic attacks. First, there is powerful anxiety about object retaliation, then guilt feelings, then love, pity and compassion towards and for the object. All this is also linked with depression and emptiness inside, as in the case of Ruth Kjar. Before going further with depression, it is necessary to point out that if it is vital to stop damaging the object so that reparation can take place, then new functions or qualities must appear to allow reparations, which cannot take place at a certain level in the hierarchy of a system, to become operant at another hierarchical level or metasystem.

Freud called pity and compassion a reaction-formation and was concerned to make a clear distinction between reaction-formation and sublimation. For Klein it is certain that right from the beginning, in her papers of 1921 and 1923, she is concerned with growth and sublimation and, somewhat later, symbol-formation. I think it is permissible to postulate that the necessity to

[handwritten margin notes: "Reparation Sublim"; "genital impulses"; "Oedipus"]

repair the intellectual deficits and the late development of Fritz played a decisive part in her early thoughts and later in the new systems needed to accomplish reparation. Those two early papers give clues to the development of her later thoughts.

In 'The Importance of Symbol-formation in the Development of the Ego' (1930) Klein states clearly the importance of symbol-formation for progress and describes the constructive role of moderate aggression or sadism in prompting the interest in new objects, new cathexes and new symbols. In the case of Ruth Kjar, Klein had aligned sublimation with the work of recovery in depression. Although near to 1935 and the enunciation of the depressive position hypothesis, the two other factors first to be considered are the role of the genital impulses in reparation, and also the Oedipus complex.

Since for Klein sadism diminishes between the first and second anal stage, it follows that this allows the genital impulses to become stronger, less dangerous and more loving in quality. It must be remembered that for her, from the fourth or sixth month, with more complete objects appearing, the archaic Oedipus and therefore also genital impulses come to be more active. This explains how genital impulses are to play such an important part in reparation. What is destroyed has to be recreated, and thus arises the importance of creation, babies inside mother, birth, breasts full of milk, and preoccupations with growth, how limbs grow, how they are linked together, how size increases and – very important – the role of the penis in all this. This creative drive belongs at first to the biological, concrete level of thought, then appears at other levels of thought with the increasing powers of representation and substraction permitting more symbol-formation and more sublimations, which in turn can be used for further progress.

In 1935, having all the ingredients in hand, so to speak, Klein enunciates the concept of the depressive position, and in 1946 that of the paranoid-schizoid mode of being, which she had hypothesized before while recognizing her debt to Fairbairn.

Some writers call her work before 1935 the proto-Kleinian system and after 1935 the Kleinian system proper (Pétot, 1979a). Reparation proper belongs to the depressive position. In fact, it is impossible to separate one concept from the other, and Klein's ideas on reparation have, it would seem, led her to regroup her findings and appreciate how different the psychic functioning of the infant was at that period of its maturation. Reparation proper belongs to the depressive position and its mechanisms of functioning, but there are also pre-depressive-position *attempts* at reparation, the failure of which leads to mechanisms of defence characteristic of the paranoid-schizoid position. This failure stimulates the infant to use new possibilities that arise out of biological maturation as its substrate and emotional drives as the structuring force, or, vice versa, it blocks progress.

PART II

What follows is my own point of view, whether it corresponds to Kleinian thought or not.

In the paranoid-schizoid position we deal with part-object psychodynamics. Objects that are felt to be complete, such as breast, penis, faeces, urine, milk, mouth, teeth and anything one may think of, are only part of a later whole. Because of the intense splitting taking place due to anxiety there is another kind of part-object. Any one of the previous class of part-objects may be split into good or bad parts, which themselves may be split again. The mechanisms of relating to those part-objects are specific and obey the laws of primitive introjective and projective identification. Those mechanisms serve either construction, growth and progress, or pathological defences that stop growth or progress. The role of libidinal and destructive impulses has been mentioned. Driving forces are closely linked to, and motivated by, need, desire, greed and envy. To understand the precursors of the process of reparation it is necessary to understand how objects are made or felt as good, and, vice versa, as bad. Klein writes, in 'A Contribution to the Theory of Intellectual Inhibition' (1931):

> To return to the point: I think that the child's compulsive, almost greedy, collection and accumulation of things (including knowledge as substance) is based, among other factors which need not be mentioned here, upon its ever-renewed attempt (a) to get hold of *good* substances and objects (ultimately *good* milk, *good* faeces, a *good* penis and *good* children) and with their help to paralyse the action of the *bad* objects and substances inside its body; and (b) to amass sufficient reserves inside itself to be able to resist attacks made upon it by external objects, and if necessary to restore to its mother's body, or rather, to its objects, what it has stolen from them. Since its endeavours to do this by means of obsessional actions are continually being disturbed by onsets of anxiety from many counter-sources (for instance, its doubt whether what it has cast out was really the *bad* part of its inside; or its fear that in putting more material into itself it has once more been guilty of robbing its mother's body) we can understand why it is under a constant obligation to repeat its attempts and how that obligation is in part responsible for the compulsive character of its behaviour. (1931, p. 265)

This is as clear an answer to a difficult question as one can expect. However, it is easier to imagine how *bad* things in *good* things can make them *bad* rather than the reverse. Klein is aware of the problem, for in a footnote she writes:

> In a discussion on this subject Miss Searle pointed out that the child's impulse to restore things is also hindered by its early experience of the

fact that it is easy to break things but exceedingly difficult to put them together again. Factual evidence of this kind must, I think, contribute to increase its doubts about its creative powers. (1932, p. 240n)

It is not possible to insist too much on this need to reverse the bad situation that has been created by the bad impulses. It is an essential aspect of what I will call paranoid-schizoid reparation. Thought is concrete. It belongs to the sensori-motor level, and representation is of the enactive sensori-motor imitation type in the hierarchy of representations. It lacks symbol-formation, sublimation and higher levels of abstraction. Further, it can be said that the result is that not only is reparation concrete and belonging to *thing*-representation and action, but, being the inverse of talion, the object must be a) repaired exactly as it was before the damage, or b) the situation must be restored by denial that the damage has happened and that things are as they were before. Omnipotence must be preserved in both cases and seriously paralyses progress, which demands the gradual giving up of omnipotence and acceptance of reality.

Among the class of *good* and *bad* part-objects the penis must be distinguished from its role as part of a complete, or more complete, object. As part of a whole object its role is easier to comprehend. It puts either good or bad new life inside the mother, life not only in the form of babies, but repairs the body, for instance, the breasts with milk. It can also damage, be it, for instance, by putting destructive babies inside mother or because it contains projections of destructive bad objects, for example, tearing mouth, bad faeces and urine.

But during the stage of dominant part-object psychodynamics, the penis is treated as a whole object, the part being equal to the whole (cf., Matte-Blanco, 1975). The reparative aspects of the penis are linked to its being an object with unique physical characteristics. The thumb has no life characteristics of its own: it has a fixed form, is not a source of sensations in itself, is not erectile and extensile, it is a poor substitute for the nipple, which possesses all the above qualities. When the hand, as an extension of the mouth, discovers the penis (or presumably the clitoris), it rediscovers the nipple. The penis then becomes the universal reparative object – that is, its main function, its life, is borrowed from it by combining with it to give new life to other objects that have been damaged and deprived of it. This process is the source, I believe, of all bisexual symbols, the precursor of the combined parents, and most probably a main source of libidinal cathexis. Some thirty-three years ago a schizophrenic patient, aged nineteen, told me of having phantasies of inflating a flabby and empty breast by pushing through it a penis that would just protrude, presumably the glans taking the place of the nipple. He also had phantasies of an empty space like a pocket inside his chest at the site that appeared near to the external breast, where he could put all the bad things. Apparently the penis he used was not bad and was used to repair. What is the link between the empty breasts, empty mouth, empty vagina, and the empty inside of mother? The penis itself is frequently used as a container and has an inside space for projections of all kinds of objects.

A little boy of four told me he had a bad dream. He dreamed his mother had fallen into a horse trap. I asked him to draw his dream. Without hesitation he drew an unmistakable penis, with glans and meatus. I asked him, where was mother? He immediately drew his mother inside the penis. Combined symbols are indeed very frequent. But it is the reparative function of the penis which not only replaces the damaged object by the penis, but gives to the damaged object its life-characteristics through identification of the damaged object with the penis. This process takes place very early in life, and I have been struck by the fact that the penis may well be the first, or among the first, universal representation of objects at the concrete level of the hierarchy of representations and a necessary stage. This is why, as Klein has pointed out, too early sexualization as a defence may lead to fixations and defective development. Certainly a fixation of that kind leads to a combined parental figure that cannot be separated into its constituents. This leads to an inability to proceed with differentiation of sexual identity, in my judgement a universal state of affairs in schizophrenics, schizoid personalities, borderline patients and homosexuals, and so on.

In the paranoid-schizoid position, failure of proper defences may lead to a failure to negotiate the passage to the next metasystem, that is, the depressive position and its mechanisms of relating, of defence and of reparation. I will consider two such failures: first, destruction of the *state* that cannot be repaired without seeking new methods; and second, the manic defence and manic reparation.

Attempts at reparation by the young schizophrenic with the penis-breasts produced the following behaviour while in treatment with me. I went to fetch him from a side room in one of the wards of the hospital. Not being sufficiently experienced, I asked him to come with me for his treatment but walked ahead of him. Next thing I heard a cry of terror and turned to see that he had hit on the head an old man who looked very decrepit and ill. Fortunately, he did not damage the old man severely. For some time I had noticed that my patient had been very suspicious during the sessions with me, staying by the door or by the window and watching me carefully. We had been analysing his feelings about his father, whom he considered to be a no-good, an alcoholic who did not work and was entirely dependent on his wife and a nuisance to her. He also had in the course of the treatment formed a very intense transference towards me and was very fond of me. What I thought I discovered was as follows. While dealing with his father it was becoming more and more difficult for him in his psychosis to distinguish between his father and me. Because he despaired of his father being restored to a good and satisfactory stage, the only thing to do was to remove him completely from the scene. But because of a psychotic transference and identification of father with me, he was afraid that fate would be mine, and so hitting the man was a way of warning me to take care and for him to sacrifice the old man to save me.

Failure to conceive of proper reparation, followed by loss of hope and then despair, led to a typical schizoid elimination of the bad object, a piece of excising surgery. It would be possible to give any number of such examples, some of the most subtle being the killing of people to prevent them suffering a phantasied bad fate, such as a schizophrenic who killed his brother and sister for such a reason; or another schizophrenic who cut off his genitals to facilitate the possibility of his sister identifying with him. The reason was a typical piece of concrete reparation, for he revealed to me the phantasy behind it. When still very young, he watched his younger sister being fed and he wished then to bite off his mother's nipple, swallow it and keep it inside him so that nobody could come and take it away from him (his own words). His idea of making reparation was for his sister to identify with him to regain that which he had deprived her of. The equivalence between the nipple-breast and penis-nipple-breast is obvious. The reversal of his own wish to identify with his sister is also obvious in his phantasy of her identification with him. Finally, the wish to identify with his mother to possess the breast-nipple, and his punishment (according to the law of the talion of the paranoid-schizoid way of being) by identification with the nipple-breast castrated mother is also obvious. This patient also illustrates the difficulties arising from the actual destruction of a physical object that cannot be repaired, but where only some kind of reparation at the psycho-analytical level can be attempted. After the terrible total self-castration, the patient's mother urged him to wear a bundle of some kind or another to simulate a penis. Not satisfied with what he had done, the patient also wanted to tear out his eyes.

Manic defence and manic reparation does not belong only to the depressive position or to manic-depressive illnesses. It is also operative in the paranoid-schizoid phase. The breast being the original neonatal first object that replaces in part the enveloping womb-mother after birth, it is not difficult to see that the object lost or damaged in the paranoid-schizoid and depressive positions is the breast, and the infant can either return to the inside of mother, or replace the breast by another object in order to avoid the intolerable loss of the good breast. In depression, for instance, the subject is relating to a damaged and/or lost breast, not properly mourned and projected in new situations during growth.

The question that arises is: in mania, what is the object that the subject relates to, and is identified with? The answer is the penis, and in mania proper a penis in erection and even of a gigantic erection. The more the object of either the paranoid-schizoid or of the depressive positions is damaged, the more omnipotent – not potent – the penis must be, and because of the space-centred level of thought, omnipotence is expressed in hugeness of erection and size. The resultant clinical picture depends on what degree of concreteness of thought the subject is in. Thus at body-level identifications the body itself feels it is getting bigger and smaller as the penis is felt to be in erection or losing its erection. In paranoid patients the picture is one of megalomania, and in depression of mania. The defence is the same: to deny the damaged or lost object by means of the megalomanic or manic penis, either by becoming the penis itself by identification with it or, at the less primitive levels, by possessing such a penis. To accentuate the tallness and the triumph over the feared persecutor of the talion the latter has to be made smaller either physically or by contempt. The content of the anxiety is, of course, different in paranoid defences from that in depressive anxieties.

As I have given numerous examples of the great size of the manic penis and of the manic reparative penis in another paper (Chapters 2, 9), I will quote from Klein (1945) instead. Of many possible quotations about the reparative powers of the penis, here is one:

> Again, both boy and girl, though in different ways, feel that the penis which damaged and destroyed the mother in their sadistic phantasies becomes the means of restoring and curing her in phantasies of reparation. The desire to give and receive libidinal gratification is thus enhanced by the drive for reparation. For the infant feels that in this way the injured object can be restored, and also that the power of his aggressive impulses is diminished, that his impulses of love are given rein, and guilt is assuaged.

As to the importance of the relative size of the infant and of the external world both real and in phantasy, there are also innumerable examples in Klein's writings. I can only quote one or two relating to the penis and omnipotence and manic defence. Even in 1921 one finds such statements as,

> He often describes how he has put out the eyes, or cut off the tongue of the devil or the enemy officer or the king, and he even possesses a gun that can bite like a water animal. He gets stronger and more powerful all the time, he cannot be killed in any way, he says repeatedly that his cannon is so big that it reaches to the skies.

Even dreams can have a *size* relating to a huge penis. Thus,

> He accounted for the impossibility of telling it [the dream] by saying it was such a long one, he would need the whole day to tell it. I replied that then he would just tell me part of it. 'But it was just the length that was horrid', was his reply. That this *horrid length* was the *wiwi* of the giant about whom the dream was concerned soon dawned on him.

No wonder that the penis needed in the manic defence and manic reparation (and schizoid reparation) should be even bigger, in fact the biggest possible, to be able to act as a counter-agent.

The role of the penis in reparation (difficult sometimes to distinguish from its role in defence), perhaps therefore of the male and of the father, has been described. What about that of the mother? The role of the breast in alleviating pain and frustration, in restoring emptiness to fullness, absence by presence, and so many other functions, is too well known to be elaborated upon. But the inside space of the mother is a more complex problem. To Klein it is the universe of the child which contains good and bad objects. But what is the function of that space in concrete reparation or repair, in reconstruction, regeneration, transformation and rebirth? An example will illustrate this point better than a long explanation.

A female patient had the following experience. After the birth of a Down's syndrome child, she had adopted a little Chinese boy. She also had other children. The little Chinese boy adored his adoptive mother, who well returned this love. When still very young, he said to his mother, 'I wish I could go into you and come out like the other children, then I will really be your little boy.' That story is disturbingly touching. The fact that objects and situations are projected into mother for transformations that the infant or child cannot achieve by themselves is a well-known process, but it must be linked with reparation, as in this case. Further, here the concrete thinking preventing reparation is obvious: the wish of the child can never be fulfilled.

It is strange that so many analysts, be my judgement right or wrong, have accepted as a truism that the return to the womb is all a state of bliss; there is plenty of evidence that it is more often than not associated with intense anxiety. As a matter of fact, I have suggested that it is at the origin of the claustro-agoraphobic dilemma, basic to psychosis and severe personality disorders (see Chapter 2). Thus a very schizoid patient dreamt he was quite happy inside mother but he wanted to know what it was like outside. So he went out and had a good time doing sexual things and aggressive things. Then he felt insecure and anxious as he realized he was not protected outside from the objects he could have frustrated and annoyed. So he decided to go back into mother. But he became extremely anxious because he realized he could do the same inside mother and thus destroy her and his security, and also be deprived of all the life outside the womb. He was caught; there was nowhere for him to go.

It seems to me that when the foetus starts to move inside the womb, towards the fourth to sixth month of foetal life, it must experience some discomfort. It kicks about to separate itself from the uterine wall and create a space for itself, and it experiences extreme discomfort when coming out of mother, although this may be a relief. I wish to distinguish what goes on inside the womb, or mother's internal space, from birth. What is usually left out in interpretations of return-to-the-womb phantasies is that the foetus grows, comes to life, starts movements of limbs, sucking of thumb, hearing sounds and, the latest discovery, opens its eyes and produces eye movements, including eye movements during the paradoxical phase of sleep. Growth – parts being put together, getting bigger, and the onset of movement – are the essential ingredients of life, the opposite of destruction and death. For a long time this remains an essential aspect of concrete reparation, and may never be given up. Its origin takes place in the internal space of the mother. Already in 1921 Klein writes about it:

> After he (Fritz) had put the question, 'Where was I before I was born?', it cropped up again in the form of 'How is a person made?' He was told about growth in the maternal body. Then later the next day he asked me, 'How do people grow?' When I took a little child of his acquaintance as an example, and as further examples for different stages of growth, himself, his brother and his papa, he said, 'I know all that, but how does one grow at all?' (1921, p. 3)

And on another occasion, 'When she tried once more to explain how the little head and limbs, etc. grew, he said, "Please, mama, but how – where do the little head and the little tummy and all the rest come from?" (1921d). Thus, in the inside of mother important objects are assembled and grow. When they are damaged, that is where they have to go back to be put together again and be assembled. Then they can be born again. But the act of birth itself is another quite different matter.

In another phase, it is, of course, the penis that puts the damaged and dismembered parts together again. Thus a very intelligent schizophrenic patient who complained that the various parts of his body were badly adjusted together had the following experience. He was watching the evolution of fishes in a bowl. He was struck by the harmony with which they were moving. Suddenly, he had a huge erection, the biggest he ever had in his life, and he felt all the parts of his body coming together harmoniously and functioning in a coordinated way. Of course, in schizophrenia the structure of the body ego or body image is of tremendous importance. Various limbs, organs, parts of the body are frequently identified with objects, often dying but not dead objects, and relate between themselves as those objects relate to each other. The body ego only functions harmoniously when the objects and the situations between the objects undergo reparation.

The borrowing of life from the sexual organs in masturbation is an important function of masturbation, and not only discharge of tension, and so on. By bringing about sensations in the sexual organs, those sensations (that is, experiencing life) are projected in phantasy into objects that need to be brought to life. As to movement, as mentioned above, it is the very mark of life. I was shown a little boy six years old. Since the age of three he had suffered from a tumour of the frontal lobes. At the time it was considered that he would not survive. He was said to be a hyperactive child. It was discovered that the father could not face the idea of the death of his son and whenever the child was quiet he excited himself into action, presumably to deny the absence of movement that would be equal to death. The little boy was himself aware of his possible death, and perhaps of his father's anxiety. For completion of this example, it may be mentioned that the mother, unable to face the loss, had produced another baby. Two examples, therefore, not only of defences and denials, but of false concrete attempts at reparation.

Melanie Klein has written beautiful descriptions of death and absence of movement and libidinal investment. As she has also described how parental coitus is phantasied to take place inside the mother or the child, that is, in internal spaces, the role of the mother in concrete reparation becomes more evident and complete. Perhaps – at least to me – it becomes clearer how the internalization of the good mother, more complete than the breast-mother of the paranoid-schizoid organization (that is to say, the mother who has negotiated the depressive position), corresponds to the phantasy of having inside oneself an object capable of all these activities.

It was mentioned earlier that the role of the internal object is the key to reparation proper. It stands to reason that making reparation only to the external object, real of phantasied, would make analysis impossible. Somebody having to make reparation to a dead mother could never do so. Even if the mother is alive but does not respond to the reparative efforts, only despair would result. It is the internal object that must respond to the reparative efforts. An internal mother must emerge in inner reality, in this example, capable of responding. Then efforts may be made towards the external object, which may or may not respond. To take an extreme example, one can consider the case of those who have actually committed murder, so that the object is not only destroyed in phantasy life, but in external reality as well. How does the psychoanalyst approach this problem, if not through the concept of the internal object? In my limited experience with the subject, I wish to say that the patient's despair of being able to restore the object as it was before does lead to a psychotic or a severely disturbed patient remaining ill. It raises the question of secondary gains in psychosis, for instance; but it is a secondary gain within the process itself.

External reality will remain psychotically distorted until the wrong omnipotent efforts at concrete reparation are interpreted, and other possibilities are offered, leading to diminution of psychotic omnipotence and despair. The achievement of forgiveness through the internal object seems to be a vital aspect of reparation proper. An absent external object cannot participate actively in the subject's act of reparation. This raises the question of what ordinary good characteristics the internal object must achieve in order to consider that a good working-through of the depressive position has been achieved. This would mean that both mourning and tolerance and the capacity for maintenance and care have replaced intolerance and depression.

It would be a serious omission not to mention the role of the unconscious in reparation and in the working through from the paranoid-schizoid to the depressive positions. For this, it is necessary to consider the contribution made by dream-life, which I have done in considerable detail in another paper (see Chapter 7). However, mention has been made, in a previous quotation from Freud about the Wolfman (see p. 214), of the contribution of one of the patient's dreams to the emergence of a new feeling of pity and compassion for the victim when an important object was restored. I do not know whether there are in Freud other similar examples. It is clear in the work of Klein that she has interpreted dreams in terms of both functions (paranoid-schizoid to depressive and reparation) but I cannot be sure that one can say that she has explicitly thought and stated that it was part of dream function to contribute directly, to make a direct attempt in the dream, as part of the dream's task to contribute to the working through from the paranoid-schizoid to the depressive position, and/or to do the same for the working through of reparation.

In 'A Contribution to the Psychogenesis of Manic-depressive States' (1935) Melanie Klein wrote:

> However, the paranoid position, which had been very strong in the patient at the beginning of his analysis, but was then greatly diminished, did not appear much in his dreams.
>
> What dominates the dreams are the distressed feelings which are connected with anxiety for his loved objects and as I have pointed out before, are characteristic for the depressive position. In the dreams the patient deals with the depressive position in different ways. He uses the sadistic manic control over his parents by keeping them separate from each other and then stopping them in pleasurable as well as in dangerous intercourse. At the same time, the way he takes care of them is indicative of obsessional mechanisms. But his main way of overcoming the depressive position is reparation . . .

Thus, in this passage, Klein sees the manifestation in dreams of mechanisms and mental content of the paranoid and depressive positions, of the manic defence as well as obsessional ones. She had not yet fully described the paranoid-schizoid position, which she did in 1946.

In 'Mourning and its Relation to Manic-depressive States' (1940), Klein clearly uses the dreams of Mrs A, a mother who had lost her son, to follow the working-through processes of the manic defence and of depression through achieving mourning:

> The associations showed that in the dream she had decided that she would not die with her son, but would survive. It appeared that even *in the dream* [my italics] she felt that it was good to be alive and bad to be dead. In this dream the unconscious knowledge of her loss is much more

accepted than in the one of two days earlier. Sorrow and guilt had drawn closer. The feeling of triumph had apparently gone, but it became clearer that it had only diminished.

I would like to consider another dream related by Klein which I would have interpreted differently on the basis of the role of the manic penis in manic defences and manic reparation or pseudo-reparation. In 'Notes on Some Schizoid Mechanisms' (1946) she gives the dream of a patient who wanted to leave analysis and her interpretation:

> . . . there was a blind man who was very worried about being blind; but he seemed to comfort himself by touching the patient's dress and finding out how it was fastened. The dress in the dream reminded her of one of her frocks which was buttoned high up to the throat. The patient gave two further associations to this dream. She said, with some resistance, that the blind man was herself; and when referring to the dress fastened up to the throat, she remarked that she had again gone into her *hide*.

Mrs Klein interpreted the transference situation, but the patient interrupted the analysis, which was resumed later.

I am not suggesting how the dream should or should not be interpreted, but it says to me that the manic defence has failed in the following way. The dress buttoned high up to the throat is the denial of the breasts and therefore of the depression. The blind man with whom she is identified is castrated (blind). Attempting to replace the breasts by the penis has failed. She leaves the analysis because she is not consciously aware of the failure not only of the defence but of reparation by means of her own phantasied penis, and therefore not aware of other ways to do reparation proper. She was apparently a typical manic-depressive with suicidal attempts. In my experience, manic-depressives characteristically show this oscillation between identification with the depressed breast-mother and identification with a father possessing a phantasied manic penis. Reparation proper fails until not only the manic defences but the doomed reparative attempts are understood and analysed.

In her clear and concise book on Klein's work, Hanna Segal (1973) in the chapter on reparation uses a dream to illustrate reparation, but does not state that it is a possible normal function of dreams to attempt the working through. Later, in an unpublished paper 'Ego Functions in Dreams', she enlarges on possible ego functions in dreams but does not deal with the present problem.

If one keeps in mind the hierarchical organization of the personality and levels of primitiveness and complexity, it seems to me that at the early and primitive levels of experience and representation, the unconscious is more in touch with the mechanisms to be used for working through. It knows, so to speak, how to bring difficulties in the language of dreams to the analyst, who can use a higher metasystem to help solve the problems. In my paper mentioned previously, this is exactly what my patient did.

There are a number of other very important feelings that are at work in working through reparation. There are, among many, hope and despair, revenge and forgiveness, and envy and gratitude. I believe too little has been made of them in analysis except for envy and gratitude. Despair must be about the commonest feeling found in mental illness, in neurosis and psychosis. It is most evident, of course, in depression. It means there is nothing to be expected any more. In hope it is the reverse – there is still desire for something to happen, something is expected to happen. I think despair is closely linked with failed attempts at reparation. I found two quotations in Klein linking reparation and despair:

> The attempts to save the loved object, to repair and restore it, attempts which in the state of depression are coupled with *despair* [my italics], since the ego doubts its capacity to achieve this restoration, are determining factors for all sublimations and the whole of the ego development. (1935)

Later she writes:

> Another disturbance of the capacity for reparation and consequently for sublimations arises if, owing to a failure in overcoming the depressive position, the hope of making reparation is impeded or, to put it otherwise, if there is despair about the destruction wrought on loved objects. (1952, p. 225)

This confirms the importance during analysis of searching for the hidden efforts of the patient to do reparation, and their failure, a point I have repeatedly made in this paper. Too often there is a confusion between failed reparation attempts and defences of one kind or the other.

As for forgiveness, which I believe to be an important feeling in the overcoming of the depressive position, I could not trace a reference to it in Klein. Interestingly enough, it is a feeling which seems to have been a preoccupation in Freud's mind, as well as its connection with revenge and guilt. (I can only refer the reader to his many scattered references to the subject, among others: 1913, p. 37; 1914, p. 232; 1916b, p. 226; 1930, pp. 110, 120.) Repeated attempts with my patients have led me to consider that forgiveness is a key concept, for nobody who has not forgiven can be expected to feel forgiven. Lack of forgiveness means the desire for revenge on the object remains active, and therefore the feeling that the object still seeks revenge and has not forgiven. 'Forgive us our trespasses as we forgive those who have trespassed against us.' Freud quotes Heine, 'One must, it is

forgiveness implies less than perfection [handwritten annotation]

true, forgive one's enemies – but not before they have been hanged' (1930, p.110n).

Only when the super-ego becomes less cruel, less demanding of perfection, is the ego capable of accepting an internal object which is not perfectly repaired, can accept compromise, forgive and be forgiven, and experience hope and gratitude. Perhaps it is then that love has won the day and a good working through of the depressive position has been achieved.

Reference should be made to *Envy and Gratitude* (1957). This is said to be Melanie Klein's last major theoretical work. Only a mention can be made as that paper deals with every aspect of mental functioning. I wanted to deal with the differences in reparative techniques when dealing with greed, envy and jealousy, respectively, and also the role of gratitude in reparation. For obvious reasons this ambition cannot be fulfilled here.

CONCLUSION

Reparation is a process widely spread in nature. A model has been proposed to situate its various levels of operation and then deal only with psychic reparation. A short survey of some of Freud's contributions to the future concept of reparation is made. Reparation proper is a Kleinian concept, which permeates through all the work of Melanie Klein.

An attempt is made to trace some of the developmental stages of the concept. Reparation proper belongs to the depressive position. In this position, sadistic attacks, for reasons studied, decline while loving impulses are more able to oppose the hating ones. Also in the reparative style the law of talion diminishes considerably in intensity. The cruelty of the primitive super-ego, and guilt feelings thus diminish considerably in intensity so that guilt feelings thus become more appropriate.

Derivatives of love appear and may take over certain functions. There appear the first traces of forgiveness instead of revenge, of hope instead of despair, of gratitude instead of envy. The establishment of a good inner object capable of all these activities, including maintenance and care, contributes to make reparation possible. Damage is no longer repaired inversely to talion, that is, the object has not got to be restored to the exact condition in which it was before the damage, which when impossible, as it so often is in reality, needs the persistence of the use of denial and omnipotence. Reparation begins to take place within the limits of reality.

Stress has been put on the pre-depressive position precursors of the mechanisms of reparation proper. They mostly belong to the stage when the child's thought is centred on concrete and spatial preoperative factors. The importance of considering that thought (representation, symbol-formation, levels of abstraction, and so on) is hierarchically organized is pointed out. At each new level a different organization emerges which includes new capacities to be used, and the mechanisms of reparation differ and are modified or undergo transformations at each new level.

There are many more levels than just the primary and secondary processes. The same applies to the mechanisms of the paranoid-schizoid and depressive positions. A term should be found for the pre-depressive mechanisms of reparation proper. The part played by dream mechanisms in the working through from paranoid-schizoid to depressive and the establishment of reparation proper was considered. It is important to distinguish between failed attempts at reparation and defences. Certain defences are seen to be resorted to because of, or even to emerge from, failed reparative attempts. Later, those defences may be used to oppose the use of new capacities belonging to new levels of functioning, and a vicious circle is created.

14 THAT WHICH PATIENTS BRING TO ANALYSIS

It is a truism that what patients think they are coming to treatment for and that which emerges in the course of treatment could be very different. It may be useful to mention what are the main aims of this paper, and thus possibly facilitate keeping up with the unfolding argument.

The main theme is how very frequently, if not always, help is asked with regard to improving oneself, while the real request is how to bring about the reparation without which the subject's self cannot function normally and happily. The patient does not know how to do it, cannot do it; he or she seeks help with regard to those objects without a conscious realization of what he or she is looking for. A central aspect of the problem is that threatened and dying objects have to be kept alive for this purpose by the use of mental manoeuvres of a very complex nature. An attempt to describe the mechanisms used will be made. The contrast between concrete repair and psychic reparation proper appears to be fundamental in the failed efforts to repair, and the resulting difficulties.

I believe that in very ill patients, borderline and psychotics, the detection of such psychic behaviour is relatively easily achieved. However, the same processes expressed at different levels go on in psychosomatic, hypochondriacal, neurotic and less ill patients. Therefore, I will give examples of various kinds of patients functioning at various levels of pathology, including patients treated in a group.

Finally, I believe that the discovery by the patient of his or her real aim is a dramatic event leading to dramatic changes in the treatment. The real aim has to become conscious to the patient and the therapist to allow work to proceed with success.

EXAMPLES IN A GROUP

I will start with material that emerged in a psychotherapeutic group that I was conducting. It consisted of three women and three men. The three men were in their forties and married. One woman was married and in her

mid-thirties, one unmarried woman in her early forties, and another unmarried woman in her late twenties. They had all been ill for a long time and had
had supportive treatment. They were all intelligent, never missed the group
sessions, and felt they were in need of help. I will only discuss the material
strictly relevant to my theme.

Miss R, the older unmarried woman, seemed to be nearer to a psychotic
state. She had been diagnosed as a manic-depressive, and at times as a
schizophrenic or a borderline, as well as a chronic neurotic. She started the
first group by saying, 'I want to kill my mother.' In fact, her mother had died
some time earlier. The material that emerged in the course of the treatment
is as follows. Miss R's mother was psychotic, said to be a chronic schizophrenic, highly obsessional and repetitive, talking endlessly and full of
reproach towards the children, whom she made feel very guilty. The patient
had led a most miserable life, unable to cope with her mother and yet unable
to separate from her. What she meant when she said 'I want to kill my mother'
was how much she had wanted to kill her mother in order to be free of her,
but that death had not freed the patient because she had not killed her
mother. Perhaps it meant that 'Although dead, my mother is not really dead.'
Gradually, as the treatment proceeded it became evident that Miss R had
intensely identified with the illest aspects of her mother, had taken on her
mother's illness, had given up working (she was a trained librarian) and had
led a kind of psychotic life like her mother, chronically attending various
hospitals.

One day she came to the group and said, 'Here we are, I have hallucinated,
I have heard voices.' She explained that this was the voice of her mother,
but the voice was not saying anything specific. A complicated process
gradually unfolded. She had felt very guilty and very unhappy not to have
been able to help her mother. Her identification with mother had a complex
origin. The important point was that it was not a straightforward identification through guilt. She had identified with her very ill mother in order to keep
her mother alive – mother and daughter being one, she being alive, mother
is alive – and then sought treatment. Having failed to help mother herself,
she wished that others might be able to do so. So her hallucination was a
psychotic proof of sharing the same identity with mother.

The regret at not having killed mother was connected with her impotence
at reparation, of making mother well, but of course never doing it because
of the great drive to keep mother alive and find those who would be able to
do it for her. A fundamental motivation to repair mother was the immense
desire to have a good mother, to know what it was to love a mother and be
loved by her. Freeing herself from mother by killing her would deprive her
of a good mother for ever. I was able, in due course, to interpret this material,
and it was a moment full of deep emotion for the group (and for me) when
the patient said, in a most touching way, 'I want my Mummy.' And so,
through a whole lifetime this patient, unable to repair her mother, had kept

her alive by lending her her own 'being alive', and going from therapist to therapist to have this internal mother cured.

The other unmarried female patient, Miss B, was a very disturbed girl. She had taken a very active part in bringing to the group material and dreams indicating an extremely disturbed personality bordering on psychotic phant-asies in the psychoanalytic sense. Once more I will select material from her huge pathological production that is strictly relevant to the theme being discussed.

When she was a little girl Miss B's mother had died of Hodgkin's disease after several years of illness. One memory stood uppermost in her mind: she was constantly told that she must always be quiet, make no noise and play quietly, because an excess of activity could bring about the death of her mother. She was still frightened of expressing herself in any way, was phobic, inhibited and markedly obsessional. She was very attention-seeking and quite intelligent.

Apart from this relationship to mother, there was another fixed idea about her: she said, in an unequivocal way, that her mother had been a prostitute. She thought the maternal grandmother, too, had been a 'bad woman'. The excuse was that they were poor immigrants and had been under stress. Miss B was convinced she could have caused the death of mother by not being quiet enough, and also was very afraid that she herself would become a prostitute like mother and grandmother. Having suffered from certain physical illnesses, she had thought she might die, like her mother. She thought that a sister of hers was a bad girl who had had a sexual relationship with father, who at the time was a background figure, and, in fact, she was jealous of her sister.

Miss B's pattern of progress in the group was to make spectacular progress with true insight, and then come back with deeper and deeper and more profoundly pathological material and regressions, and then proceed ahead again. Gradually, she started having doubts whether her mother had been a prostitute at all, or a 'bad girl', and finally she puzzled the group by announcing that, through an aunt, she had been most definitely told that her mother had never in any way been a 'bad girl'. She started realizing that she had been creating a very special mother, partly as a result of her mother's illness and partly because of her own guilty murderous feelings and sexual feelings.

In the session when Miss R had announced having heard a voice, Miss B had also not actually heard voices, but her thoughts had been so intense that it was as if people were talking to her, and she also brought terrifying dreams. She had kept her mother alive not only through guilt, but also by being herself alive and identified with that inner mother. She could not repair mother, but had brought her to treatment to have others do what she could not do. Mother could not be allowed to die until she, the patient, had repaired mother; for instance, it was necessary for mother not to be physically ill but cured and not a prostitute any more. Many other aspects of mother also had to be put right. Miss B became conscious more and more of who was really the one she had brought to treatment.

But before expanding more on this patient I wish to consider the case of Mr K, one of the three married men. He complained that he suffered from terrible panic attacks that paralysed him. He repeatedly emphasized that despite the fact that he was a man sufficiently well regarded to have been given charge of more than forty subordinates, he would become intolerably panicky when he had to talk to them. He also experienced panicky sensations. In the treatment the panicky sensation was in the head (often experienced at the hairdressers), then in the stomach, and clearly in the penis. His attitude in the group was characterized by denying constantly that he knew anything about the causes of his panic, and constantly insisting that the therapist should tell him what it was.

Mr K revealed information about himself very slowly, and bit by bit. He had been married twice. His first wife had left him. He had two young children from his second marriage. Then he remembered that his first panic was connected with the occasion when his wife and children had gone on holiday and he had been left alone. He also talked frequently about his father being a no-gooder, an alcoholic, and a weak character. The main point he insisted upon was how father was weak, and he felt himself to be a much stronger character. The next thing was that Mr K started admitting that he was jealous of the attention his wife was giving to the children. For instance, when coming home he was not paid enough attention, while the children got all the attention. The theme of being afraid of being left alone by his family became more important, and he admitted he was like a child left alone by mother and too weak to cope.

Then one day Mr K astonished the group when talking about his mother and how father ill-treated her by saying with great anxiety, 'After all, I sent father to hospital for six months.' Asked to explain by the group, he related how one day, in trying to defend his mother from father's aggression, he had somehow broken his father's leg. Some complication or other had caused father to stay for six months in hospital before he could return home. Then it became clear that Mr K was feeling like a little boy who was terrified of father castrating him, and was defending himself by pretending to be big (although he was in fact a big, strong man) and by needing mother's protection, and this explained his panic when his wife was away. But he did not know how to put father right.

Actually, Mr K worked in a town quite distant from his parents, who were still alive. He did not visit them, and when offered job advancement in his parents' town, refused it. He had brought his father to the group to be repaired because he could not do it. He lived in fear of castration, identified with the father he had castrated not only because of guilt but, unless father was repaired by the group, mostly by the therapist, from whom he demanded total and exclusive attention. He had to remain identified with father, who was the one being treated through the identification, and he would have no more problems if father was cured, and would not need his mother-wife's protection. The subsequent development of the therapy seemed to show that, not until putting his father right was taken over by the group, could Mr K proceed with his obvious problems with his mother and his wife.

Dr D's problems were very complex. He was intelligent, highly neurotic, married, had children. The relationship with his wife could not be worse. His mother had committed suicide and the family had broken ties with father, whom they accused of being responsible for his wife's suicide because of the way he treated her. However, by the time Dr D had come to treatment he had written to his father to say he was not holding him responsible any more. Also, the patient kept his marriage going because he was a practising Roman Catholic and did not think he could contemplate divorce. Once more, I will deal briefly with this example.

Dr D suffered from a marked inferiority complex, especially at work, and felt extremely dependent. But it was revealed in the treatment that he compensated for this by a secret belief in his omnipotent 'indestructibility' (his own word), which showed itself when he had drunk too much (he was only a social drinker), and then became very violent and totally unafraid.

During the session when Miss R revealed her hallucinatory experience, he reminded the group that he had told them that he thought he was predestined to some special mission, and that driving home after the previous session he had decided to have a direct conversation with God himself, and he had done so during the whole drive home. As the other patients had been bringing their damaged objects for reparation, he became more and more preoccupied with his mother, but was still unable to show any feelings for her. However, during that time the relationship with his wife took a dramatic turn. He became more and more ambivalent towards her. She also was a very ill woman. He felt the beginning of some pity for her, and also tried to resume sexual relations with her. However, he also challenged her all the time, wanting to prove his indestructibility.

It came to a climax when she threatened him with a knife and he did not defend himself, challenging her to attack him, because he knew he was indestructible. However, when he realized more fully how the other patients had brought their damaged ones to treatment, he suddenly arranged for his wife to have treatment. Everything else in the treatment had indicated how this patient had identified his wife with his mother and repeated with his wife the relationship with his mother. When Dr D sent his wife to treatment he had her partly as a substitute for his mother, since he had not yet brought his mother to the group, but his wife instead. However, the realization that it was mother he really wanted to bring to treatment began to dawn on him. It seems also that his need for believing in his 'indestructibility' was connected with making the inner mother 'indestructible' until help had become available.

Mrs M, a married woman in her mid-thirties, had also had previous treatment. She complained that she was tied up at home and could not go out. She did not hide the fact that one reason she wanted to feel free to go out was to meet a lover, as she had done in the past. She was still living with her husband and had two children. Mrs M was difficult in the group. She repeatedly said that nothing was wrong with her except not being able to go out, and all she wanted from treatment was to be able to do so. However, she gradually described to the group how she hated her mother. Her mother was so egotistical, and could only talk about herself; she was jealous of her daughter (the patient) who was very fond of her father, who was very different from mother. The patient was very jealous of a younger sister.

Then Mrs M said that, in fact, she had married to get away from her mother. After a time, the enormous obsession with her mother became obvious in the group. She then said she had had a lover for ten years and how marvellous it was. But then she revealed that throughout the ten years her lover had always been impotent. Leaving out various details, the next revelation was that her husband was so much like her mother, amazingly similar. This was most perplexing, to say the least, to the group, as Mrs M's previous constant description of him was that he was so perfect, it was not possible to be so good; if only he had some things wrong about him. Mrs M was vehement in her complaint. She was confronted in the group with all these contradictions – that she was complaining about her husband and wanting to leave him, and that, in fact, she had not married a man but, in her own words, her mother. Further, she had chosen a lover who was not a real man as he was impotent, and had remained with him for ten years. In order not to be able to leave the mother-husband, she had become claustrophobic.

It was slowly becoming clear that Mrs M had left mother by marrying, but had compensated for the lost mother by having a mother-husband and a mother-lover. In her mind she had terribly damaged her mother (her Oedipus anxieties were obvious as well), and her attempt to create good or idealistic mother–substitutes had failed in her main need, which was to repair mother and then feel free to live her own life. Her attempts at reparation were clearly remarkably concrete and omnipotent, and doomed to failure. She wanted a good mother for herself; she attempted to create such a good mother, obviously failed, but could not tackle the real problem of putting right the inner mother and her relationship to her, followed by a possibly better relationship to the external mother.

Mr Z, the last patient to be described, was a man in his mid-forties suffering from panic attacks and claustrophobia. He was very reserved, but always participated in the group in a very measured way. His technique was to use some contribution from another patient and compare this with his own experience on the subject. We learned that before becoming a businessman he had been in the army and in a regiment famous for its strict discipline. One could detect the control that he always exercised on himself. He never criticized others. He always talked about his father and mother as being perfect. His wife had had a car accident, with a serious trauma to the vertebral column, some years before. She had been in constant pain, but apparently was somewhat better.

The first complaint appeared very gradually, about the attitude of his wife to the children and having to protect them. Then he started relating how, from childhood onwards, he had been brought up on the basis that children never cry. Whenever the children (he had brothers and sisters) showed pain or began to cry, this was stopped by the parents. No expression of emotion was allowed; yet he went on saying to the amazed group how good and perfect his parents were. He found it difficult to see the contradiction; however, the frozen, bad side of the parents was coming nearer to the surface.

In one session Mr Z announced that he had had an extraordinary experience. He had been to a garden party and people had started dancing. His wife joined in, and at one point asked him to dance with her. He simply could not. Even before she asked him he had felt completely tied, riveted to his seat by not only the thought, but by feeling acutely the actual presence of his parents forbidding him to dance. And yet, as he himself pointed out, they lived in another country 15,000 miles away (he had emigrated) – yet they were present there, paralysing him.

Soon afterwards he learned that his father had died, and he went home for the funeral and to deal with family affairs. He returned as soon as he could, as he missed the group and wanted to talk about his experiences. What mattered most was that the whole family, while showing their reaction to the death of their father, had all complained of the strict, inhuman way they had been brought up. They never stopped talking about it. It was only then that he was able to talk freely about what he had suffered, about the dreadful life his wife was imposing on him and his fear for the children that they would suffer as he did. Going back to his experience of the vivid presence of his parents at the party, he now could see a bit better how he had kept them mummified within himself, and had himself behaved in a paralysed way from fear not only of what they could do to him, but what he could do to them. His denial of anything wrong with them was connected with not knowing how to change and repair them. No doubt unconsciously he felt responsible for the way they were. Further, this not knowing how to repair his inner objects had been projected on to his wife, who herself was in need of treatment, which now he was beginning to realize.

This group showed very clearly that each member did not bring only themselves to treatment, but that they were primarily concerned, at a borderline conscious–unconscious level, with damaged inner objects where successful treatment was vital to their welfare. They could not do it without help but had kept these inner objects going in the hope that help would come one day. Every patient in the group had been seeking treatment for years previously. When those inner objects become alive in a session the therapist is confronted with a very strange feeling. Who is really there? Who are the real patients forming the group? To whom is one talking?

In another paper (see Chapter 8) I described a somewhat similar situation. I quote a short reference to this:

> I, as therapist, had an extraordinary experience that we were not six people in the room, but a whole crowd of people of all ages, sexes and statures, speaking and acting in all sorts of ways. It was a real encounter with a very concrete projection of the autonomous primitive groups (of inner objects) into a Tower of Babel, a crowd made up of an assembly of subgroups of unrelated part-objects.

DEATH AND DYING IN THE UNCONSCIOUS

Freud made an important distinction between the representation or experience of the death of oneself in the unconscious and the death of others. In his paper 'Thoughts for the Times on War and Death', Part 2, 'Our Attitude to Death' (1915b), he writes:

> To sum up: our unconscious is just as inaccessible to the idea of our own death, just as murderously inclined towards strangers, just as divided (that is, ambivalent) towards those we love, as was primeval man. But how far we have removed from this primal state in our conventional and cultural attitude towards death! (p. 299)

However, the whole of Part 2 must be read to get a clear idea of Freud's complex thought on the subject. Also, what he thought after the new directions he took with the concept of the death instinct, I am not sure. After all, he suggested that a part of the death impulse remains inside, although bound with narcissistic libido, and is not directed outside. That portion left behind was responsible for primary masochism. In 'Mourning and Melancholia' (1917) he made the great discovery of the identification of the lost external object with the ego of the subject, and the continuation of the attacks on the object by the melancholic by attacking himself with self-recriminations. I suggest that the object was thus kept alive by this identification for reasons other than guilt alone, that is, for the sake of being able to carry on reparation as well, a notion unknown to Freud, or not developed beyond the concept of restitution.

In Kleinian metapsychology a great deal has been written about all the manoeuvres to keep the good object safe against attacks and destruction by the bad part of the self and/or the bad objects. Those human beings who have sufficiently worked through the depressive position and reached a true capacity for reparation are in a very different situation from those who have not reached that stage, as with neurotics and depressives but most markedly with schizoid, borderline and psychotic patients. The latters' task is to manage to keep their damaged good objects alive in the hope of putting them right. In previous papers I have extensively described the efforts of those patients to do concrete repair, that is, reconstruct the object as it was before damage, and at the level of space-centred thought characteristic of this level, as well as their attempts at pseudo-reparation (like manic reparation), and the defences that are used after failure to achieve reparation.

Defences must not be confused with the real problem, which is not knowing how to repair (see Chapter 13). The concept of imagos is a very abstract one and difficult to make use of for describing reparative processes, although maybe not impossible. The idea of a layer of the mind whose representations are felt as concrete and thus experienced as real objects, although obviously not so, is very useful for understanding the material I have described. After all, dream objects, however, fantastic, are felt to be real.

EXAMPLES IN INDIVIDUALS WITH DIFFERENT PSYCHOPATHOLOGIES

It may be helpful to make some remarks about hierarchies in the organization of personality structures and corresponding object structures at various stages of maturation. Since structure of self and structure of object are inseparable for various levels of maturation in the Kleinian model, the use of the paranoid-schizoid and depressive positions is a very useful one. A young schizophrenic girl who had lost her father dealt with his death through denial by keeping him alive inside her. She showed some manic manifestations in her way of talking when she explained that she had a nice little house inside her where her father lived. She tried to keep him happy, and ate good things that he liked in order to feed him. Asked what colour the house was she said, without hesitation, 'Blue of course; his eyes are blue.' She spontaneously proceeded to explain why she had to keep her father happy in the nice little house: it was in order to keep her mother well looked after and happy, and thus keep herself happy. Father was the only one who could provide for mother and keep mother alive and happy to look after the patient.

According to the level of the paranoid-schizoid position, reparation meant denying death, providing a concrete inner space for him so that he had only changed his abode, and making him happy by feeding him concretely with good things. But the reason, as we saw, was she could not have a happy life unless mother was kept alive and well. Once more, objects had to be kept alive and repaired for maintenance and care. Her capacity for symbol-formation and the higher levels of representations was deficient; she had not reached and worked through the depressive position to achieve mourning and keep in touch with external reality and create new symbols. She lived in a concrete, schizophrenic world.

Another schizophrenic girl I treated who had lost her father had introjected, or rather incorporated, him alive. As she was afraid he was very weak and could easily be hurt, she had developed very complicated rituals to avoid movements that could hurt him inside her, including the taking of catatonic postures, but not in a fixed way. Her relationship to that internal live father was highly sexualized, and, although avoiding hurting him was part of a fear of retaliation, the fact was that unless father was repaired, there was no hope for her. So he had to be kept alive.

We can compare this with a woman who before the death of her father had been very normal for all practical purposes, and a nice person. She was in her thirties and she had gone on holiday, somewhat worried because her father was not too well. Her father became very ill, and a radio station transmitted a message for her, which she was lucky to hear. She drove back as fast as she could and arrived just in time 'for his last breath'. She had consulted later for attacks of asthma, was not responding to medical treatment, and the story was elicited. The attacks of asthma were occurring most frequently at three in the morning, the actual time when her father had died just after she arrived. It was now months since the event.

She also revealed spontaneously that sometimes she felt her father was inside her, and sometimes outside her and next to her. It was striking how real her experience was, and she talked about it in a very natural way. And so, again, this non-psychotic woman was keeping her father alive so that he could be saved and so that she could be forgiven and herself cured. She had done so at two distinct levels – one by identification with the dying father at his last breath and developing asthma and not letting the last breath be the last; the other was by keeping father alive, both externally and internally, that is, feeling him concretely inside her and alternatively next to her outside in a most concrete manner. In this case the efforts to keep her father alive and seek help had led to a denial of his death through guilt feelings. When she came to treatment, although she had developed symptoms of a psychosomatic illness, the link was still existing sufficiently clearly between her father's death and her disturbance of breathing. However, the concreteness with which she had experienced the presence of father inside her, or immediately outside her, according to constitution and personality structure, could have led to hypochondria by identifying father with some part or another of her body, or frankly to a psychotic state. The relationship to hypochondria of failed reparative efforts to inner objects is so important that an example should be given.

A married woman in her late twenties, and mother of two little girls, came to treatment because of severe recurring depression and a neurotic personality. In spite of her severe difficulties she proved to be a good patient who worked very hard at her treatment. After several years of analysis she had made good progress. One of her main preoccupations had been with the bad state of the inside of her body. At the time of the events to be related she had moved to a beautiful new house, about which she was very excited. She had a series of dreams where each room of the house was being relocated, and the last one was the dining room. Pleased with her progress, her husband gave her a much-desired new fur coat. She then became extremely pre-occupied with the necessity to become as well as possible to fit in with the beautiful fur coat. However, at that time she was most preoccupied with some vague and very minor kidney trouble, following a pregnancy. She insisted on having herself investigated incessantly and was obsessed with attempts at curing the trouble. It must be stated here that the patient had in external reality a very difficult mother and their relationship was very bad. What emerged in the analysis was that her kidney had taken the place of mother by identification. It was a very complex process. She had identified with her own baby in pregnancy, who had hurt her as she had hurt her mother. The kidney stood for a condensation of herself as a baby, her baby and her mother. This had to be undone so that her baby should not be confused with her, leaving her relationship to the internal mother available for treatment and reparation of mother, and not of her kidney.

The next example will serve to illustrate the transfer of life so as to keep important objects alive to make their treatment possible. I quote from an interview with a patient, a single woman, of twenty.

> Her history showed what seemed to be a necrophilic tendency – she described career ambitions as including being a 'mortuary attendant' and has expressed fascination for laying out dead bodies. (This seems to be quite genuine, rather than an attempt to shock.) When I thought of her 'suicide' attempt (which seems to have been very serious medically) I thought it was connected with her apparent necrophilia and thanatophi-lia. I explored her fascination with corpses, and she said that her life is of no use of her; what she really wanted to do was to put her life into the dead body so that the dead body would be able to live [her words]. I suggested that for her to 'commit suicide' or 'to die' really meant to become a dead body, who could then have the experience of being penetrated by some life, out of which could come a reborn self who could start again and have a better life. She responded at once by saying that she believes totally in reincarnation, that after death you go to some place where your sins are evaluated, and according to that you are allocated to a new life which you then lead, but with all memory of the past obliterated except for occasional uncanny, intuitive feelings.

I had the opportunity to interview this girl later as a visiting member to a team involved in the treatment of this patient in a unit where stress is placed on the very ill patients acquiring 'meaning' – the meaning in their mind of their behaviour and fantasies. I asked the patient who, apart from herself, she could think of among people important to her whom she would like to see receiving help. At first she looked perplexed, as if not understanding, and then said, 'My brother'. She explained that her brother was very ill, very similar to herself, even with regard to suicide; he badly needed help. This led to talk about people dying, and she described how since very early adolescence she had been preoccupied and obsessed with death. With some difficulty at first she proceeded to talk about her wish to destroy her father, which she had not been able to bring herself to do. She said he had been terrible to her, so terrible that she felt incapable now of talking about it. But most unexpectedly, soon afterwards she stated that he probably had reacted to her being a very bad girl, and as we proceeded she became increasingly insistent on her own badness.

This girl's history showed she had very persecutory feelings, borderline to paranoid feelings. She has two siblings also showing suicidal attempts, or intent. It is remarkable that in her early history the parents reported that after having been a very quiet and co-operative baby, bottle-fed, she became very unco-operative and difficult at the end of her first year, and was specially aggressive towards her father. Irrespective of all other very relevant factors in her case, what I want to stress is her preoccupation with keeping alive her objects at the point of developing a morbid interest in mortuary bodies and imparting her own life to them. In spite of her suicidal thoughts and attempts at suicide she had to keep herself alive in order to pass on her life (perhaps by dying); however, she had to believe in her own reincarnation so that the process could be repeated. In my interview she insisted the reincarnation was applied to herself. Towards the members of the therapeutic team she had shown increasing aggression and impatience at not being understood and helped sufficiently quickly. The urgency on this point appeared increasingly to become a matter of primary importance. It seems very clear that her problem was how to keep herself and thus her objects alive long enough, as explained, in order to achieve reparation before it was too late for her objects – and therefore too late for herself.

One more short example will illustrate how patients with a high degree of psychotic omnipotence can use this to keep objects they are supposed to have omnipotently killed; where they can get to them and resurrect them if needed. Thus, a psychotic man claimed to have killed more than thirty people (imaginary) and could talk about them quite freely, and without apparent guilt. However, he could also claim it did not matter because he could equally call them back to life, and in fact said he would probably do so when it would be judged necessary. When confronted with this God-like power to resurrect he agreed it was so, showing this remarkable need and capacity to be somehow in touch with non-psychotic reality, so frequently, if not always, found in these patients. He added they would not return completely to life but it would be more like a sort of existence on a screen. He also meant by this that they were not really dead and yet not really alive –

he could give them life up to a point. This again raises the question of death and dying in the unconscious.

An attempt was made with these five examples to illustrate the various levels at which the activity of keeping damaged objects alive within the inner space or inner world is carried out in the hope of putting them right, that is, doing reparation. Two of those patients were psychotics, showing different levels of suppression of reality; the 'mortuary' patient could be called 'borderline'; and the 'kidney' lady was a depressive, with marked hypochondria; the 'asthma' patient had quite a normal history until the death of her father.

These patients used a variety of methods and dynamic mechanisms to attain their goal, but they all failed to reach their real aim, which was to put right at a normal level of reality functioning what was wrong with their objects. They were thus being condemned themselves to a life of unreality and unhappiness.

DREAMS AND INNER OBJECTS

There is another very important aspect to be considered. It is the part played by the dream functions in this repairing activity. I have dealt in quite a detailed way with this question in two papers (see Chapters 2, 7). In the second of these I described in full how a young man of twenty-one, who had become psychotic, had completely split his life, which was spent on a farm until he left the countryside to live in town to go to university. When in town, any knowledge and memories of the farm life were totally abolished. This life had been a very traumatic one and could understandably have been suppressed from consciousness and experience. In the treatment he started dreaming and bringing back into the dream massive bits of his suppressed life in a way which could hardly be differentiated from somebody bringing conscious memories and experiences to treatment. The dreams were of very damaged parts of his life and, outstandingly, of damaged parents. Most striking was how the deadened parts of him and of his objects were brought to life with the intention of using my help to repair them. He had not known how to do this alone, and seemed, in the words of a patient of Melanie Klein, to have kept them in a state of 'suspended animation'. In a dream of that period ice and snow became ice-cream and he felt warmth inside. Then, I quote, 'following this [the ice-cream dream] there were dreams about funerals, about a hearse, about cemeteries and graves'. He consciously felt the woman part in him had to die. (He had had homosexual experiences.) Before that he had said he had killed the man in him. At this point the dreams were repetitively full of sexual themes, naked people, people going together into a room. Cars and farm tractors, as well as farm animals, began to appear as if there was resurrection of life everywhere. What he could not repair alone and had kept alive and hidden was reappearing in the treatment.

It is very instructive, I think, to understand what Freud thought about keeping objects alive or resurrecting them, by following some of his thoughts on such activities in dreams. His thoughts about death and dying in the unconscious have been referred to earlier. In his *Introductory Lectures* in 'Some Analyses of Sample Dreams' (XII), Freud writes:

> When anyone has lost someone near and dear to him, he produces dreams of a special sort for some time afterwards, in which knowledge of the death arrives at the strangest compromises with the need to bring the dead person to life again. In some of these dreams the person who had died is dead and at the same time still alive, because he does not know he is dead; only if he did know would he die completely. In others he is half dead and half alive, and each of these states is indicated in a particular way. We must not describe these dreams as simply nonsensical; for being brought to life again is no more inconceivable in dreams than it is, for instance, in fairy tales, in which it occurs as a very usual event. So far as I have been able to analyse such dreams, it has turned out that they are capable of a reasonable solution, but that the pious wish to bring the dead person back to life has been able to operate by the strangest means. (1916b, p. 187)

Freud then proceeds to an example of a dream dreamt by a man who had lost his father several years before: 'His father was dead, but had been exhumed and looked bad. He had been living since then and the dreamer was doing all he could to prevent him noticing it.' Because what follows is so relevant to the thesis of this paper, I will try to summarize what Freud says about the associations of the patient and his own interpretation of the dream, in a very condensed way.

Freud proceeds to say:

> His father was dead; we know that. His having been exhumed did not correspond to reality; and there was no question of reality in anything that followed. But the dreamer reported that after he had come away from his father's funeral, one of his teeth began to ache. He wanted to treat that tooth according to the precept of Jewish doctrine: 'If thy tooth offend thee, pluck it out!' And he went off to the dentist. But the dentist said: 'One doesn't pluck out a tooth. One must have patience with it, I'll put something in it to kill it; come back in three days and I'll take it out.' That 'take out', said the dreamer suddenly, 'that's the exhuming.' (1916b, p. 188)

From this Freud goes on analysing the dream and using further associations. For Freud, the patient had identified father with his tooth. According to Jewish law, he should pluck out what causes pain or offence. But according to the same law it should be just the opposite with regard to father. He should spare no expense or trouble to avoid hostile intentions or causing pain. We learn also that the father had been ill for a long time, causing his son a lot of expense for his nursing and treatment. And Freud then considers the working of the death wish against father, its being hidden, of course, and the guilt feelings associated with it.

But looked at from the point of view of reparation, something new appears. In the paragraph preceding the dream, Freud had described the bringing back to life of the dead ones. It seems obvious that an attempt was being made to bring father back to life as the patient felt responsible for his death. However, father was identified with the tooth, and the tooth was not dead. It had to be killed, presumably because it could not be repaired, and then pulled out. But the tooth was also the patient, or part of the patient, not solely representing father. Going to the dentist was, therefore, making sure that father was exhumed to be repaired. He looked bad like the tooth, and, although not dead, as nothing could be done he was to be killed like the tooth. This was also the fate of part of the patient, the part that had had a death-wish against father, and resented the efforts he had to make when father was still alive, and he resented the cost and effort of trying to repair father. The law of talion demanded similar punishment for him. There is a clear-cut case here of the failure of concrete repair, leading to failure of mourning and true psychic reparation. The identification with the dying, but not dead, tooth was an attempt to keep father, or part of father, alive in an attempt to repair him with the help of somebody else, the dentist. The illness of the tooth corresponded to the illness of father, too long to be tolerated, and the killing of the tooth to the death-wish of father. The bad tooth also corresponded to that part of the patient that could not be put right if father was not.

Here is a second short example from Freud:

One of my women patients lost her father in the course of the treatment. Since then, she has taken every opportunity of bringing him to life in her dreams. In one of these, her father appeared (in a particular connection of no relevance) and said: 'It's a quarter past eleven, it's half-past eleven, it's a quarter to twelve.' By way of interpretation of this oddity, all that occurred to her was that her father liked his grown-up children to appear punctually at the family meals. Among further associations the patient said a relative, before the dream, had remarked: 'The *Urmensch* (primal man) survives in all of us.' This seemed to provide us with the explanation. It had given her an excellent opportunity of bringing her dead father to life once again. She made him in the dream into an '*Uhrmensch*' (clockman) by making him announce the quarter-hours at midday. (1916c, pp. 234–5)

There is more evidence given by Freud of that which could make the mourning of father difficult, and his having to be brought back to life first.

Freud writes, 'There was a suspicion, based on the immediate situation in the treatment, that a carefully suppressed critical revolt against her beloved and honoured father played some part in the dream.' Thus, again, something had to be put right before his death, so he was returned to life, but only in the dream.

While writing this paper I became conscious that a new question was arising in my mind. When thinking about the Kleinian type of inner objects, concrete, feeling real and alive, and engaged in bewilderingly complex intra- and interpsychic relations, and using not only psychotic material but also dream material to describe this complex state of affairs, I thought about investigating more deeply and completely the relationship between inner objects and dream-objects.

In *The New Psychology of Dreaming*, Jones (1970) writes as follows:

> A dream can be characterized as a form of thought which is experienced as action. It thus occupies a unique place in the spectrum of symbolic functioning since it seems to be what it is not, i.e., action, and what it does not seem to be, i.e., thought. As a result of this we normally take a dream completely seriously while we are asleep, and tend to dismiss it when awake. Thus, dreams seem to exist outside the mainstream of adult experience in the form of either thought or action. (p. 146)

This would not be a bad description of inner objects at various levels of representation.

There is, it seems, a clear connection between inner objects and dream-objects. Scott (1988) writes:

> We learn about sleep and the place of dreams and the forgotten. We learn to place the I, the me, the self, within and put them to sleep and preserve them and wake to them. We may remember part of our dreaming and bring part of our dreams as 'dream residues' into our waking life. In the dream we remember part of our previous life (day residues). We sort out how all dreaming is not memory and that all memories are not dreams. We sort out day-dreams from night-dreams and facts from dreams or fancy. Perhaps fancy might be a good word for what we wake up to before we sort out facts from fancy.

Indeed, this thought of 'dream residues' in our waking life, so striking as a description of the unconscious in the conscious, and what Scott calls the 'place of dreams' in contrast with the place of external reality, seems to me also to apply to the place of inner objects and their levels of consciousness and unconsciousness. The place of our inner objects has its inhabitants, some of them always present and active and others being mere visitors, or visitors for a certain period in time. It is something of the sort that I have attempted to describe in my clinical examples.

DISCUSSION

In 1981, on the occasion of delivering the Clara Geroe Memorial Lecture to the Melbourne Psychoanalytic Society, I wrote:

> For my part I know of no greater experience, with the possibilities of the new knowledge, than to detect and come into contact with dying, but not dead, parts of the schizophrenic patient. To witness his incommensurable and hopeless efforts to protect those parts still precariously alive inside him, identified with and located in various parts of his body. Everything is concrete, he must not move or even think or wish, except to deny, project and hallucinate pseudo-repaired objects, but he fails to do reparation properly, and thus despairs. And I know of no deeper experience, of no greater achievement than to help them bring the dying parts to life, diminish their fear of damaging their loved objects, and help them to create less concrete inner objects, more symbols; experience more compassion, more humanity.

In the course of my work over the years I have become aware, especially with very ill patients, borderline and psychotic, but not exclusively so, that their internal objects were seldom if ever dead, but rather were kept dying and not dead by the patients. But it was only very slowly that one important reason for so doing became clearer to me, and this was that so long as the objects were kept alive there was a chance to repair them. However, as described in this paper, although wishing to do reparation, the knowledge of how to do it was lacking, and, so long as they were kept alive, there was hope that somebody would come who would know how, and would help to do it.

As mentioned previously, Melanie Klein's descriptions of the amazingly complex ways that dying bad and good inner objects (and external objects) are manipulated represent an enormously difficult task to master. Here are some quotations taken from her paper, 'A Contribution to the Psychogenesis of Manic-depressive States' (1935):

> It now becomes plain why, at this phase of development, the ego feels itself constantly menaced in its possession of internalized good objects. It is full of anxiety lest such objects should die. Both in children and adults suffering from depression, I have discovered the dread of harbouring dying or bad objects (especially the parents) inside one and an identification of the ego with objects in this condition.

> That is to say, the objects were killed but, since the subject was omnipotent, he supposed he could also immediately call them to life again. One of my patients spoke of this process as 'keeping them in suspended animation'. The killing corresponds to the defence-mechanism

(retained from the earliest phase) of destruction of the object; the resuscitation corresponds to the reparation made to the object.

The phantasy of keeping the kidney and the penis alive while they were being tortured expressed both the destructive tendencies against the father and the babies, and to a certain degree the wish to preserve them.

In my experience the paranoiac conception of a dead object within is one of a secret and uncanny persecutor. He is felt as not being fully bad and perhaps reappearing at any time in cunning and plotting ways, and seeming all the more dangerous and hostile because the subject tried to do away with him by killing him (the concept of a dangerous ghost).

People bring people other than themselves to be helped by doctors. For example, mothers bring children, husband, children and old parents. In order to help, people have to be alive and try to do something to help – cook, give medicines, bring money to buy necessities, and so on. Mothers must be alive to breastfeed or feed babies. One must keep alive to do all those things connected with maintenance and care of not only oneself but of one's objects. Compare the time-honoured hero behaviour – to give one's life for one's country or to save others. It does not seem it is by giving one's life that the good is achieved; it is better for a soldier to be alive to go on fighting than to die, as he is then lost to the 'good fight'. However, the risk of death is enormously increased and accepted, but it is still more useful to be alive, and first of all objects must be kept alive to be looked after. Martyrs for their religion do not consider death is final, but believe survival after death is essential to vindicate their behaviour. In 'sacrifice' the giving of life to give the good life-energy to other objects than self is a complex affair.

Putting something 'alive' into threatened objects to keep them alive is but a first step. But it is not enough simply to be alive; keeping alive is not 'curing' or 'repairing'. It is making possible the repair or reparation if one knows how to do it and has the means to do it. And if one cannot, maybe others know how and can. Therefore, one takes oneself and one's objects to the therapist, first to repair the objects, which means one is made free to live happily with objects being repaired. Second, the self may find out how to stop damaging objects and learning how to do reparation to one's objects. So often a short-cut is magically resorted to by premature identification with the therapist. Committing suicide is, among other things, giving up the possibility of doing reparation and, thus, continuing the destruction of objects by aggressive wishes and punishment of self, according to the law of talion. Even if it is to stop attacking the object, it leaves the object unrepaired from previous damage.

In religion, belief in survival after death can give a further chance to repair or to be punished. This need to keep alive may be seen in various behaviours, for example, reincarnation, care of dead bodies, resurrection, continuing to live in one's descendants. It is not possible in this paper to give an account of prehistoric religion, cult of the dead, rituals and other aspects of this subject. However, it is an amazing discovery to compare those rituals with those described by Melanie Klein with regard to the manipulations of inner objects: manoeuvres to keep the object safe: to prevent his or her return for revenge; attempts at ensuring that the object should be treated in such a way to ensure rites of passage; the site where the object is kept; the state in which it is kept; measures to re-insufflate life in the object; sacrifice to transfer life from a live object to the damaged or dead one.

However, one ritual is especially important for our purpose. It is what James (1957) has described as secondary burial. This refers to an extremely common custom of first preserving the body, or a part of it, for a certain period of time in certain conditions, and then proceeding to a final, secondary burial. This period preceding the secondary burial is considered as corresponding to a mourning period, a great deal of variation existing as to the ultimate fate of the person afterwards.

CONCLUSIONS

The present study is mostly based on the concept of an inner world, an inner space where inner objects exist, and also on the concept of reparation.

It has been suggested that the concept of the imago is too vague and theoretical to account for the clinical findings and concreteness of the structures met with in the deeper layers of the self and of the unconscious, which Klein called internal or inner objects. However, no doubt there is a correspondence between the two notions.

Inner objects are constructs of the subject partially based on the external objects of external reality and partially by the projections modifying the object through fantasies of the subject. They can be whole or part-objects. In a 'normal' person there is a kind of equilibrium between the inner world of inner objects and the external world of external objects. The more pathological the subject, the more distorted his views of the external world.

The aims of this paper were stated at the beginning. I have said little here about the many reasons for wanting to preserve and keep alive these inner objects, such as feelings of guilt, about which a great deal has been written, fear of internal persecution, fear of losing good and protective objects. I have rather chosen to emphasize the mechanisms used to keep the objects, especially the damaged and dying ones, alive in order to be able to do reparation and restore them as good objects, without which life cannot be normal, satisfying and worth living. One most important point about the failure of being able to do reparation is the difference between concrete repair and psychic reparation, a point of view extensively described previously (see Chapter 7).

Freud's views about death of oneself in the unconscious have been referred to. I do not know whether he made a distinction between death and dying in the unconscious anywhere in his writing with regard to oneself.

Freud did not write about displacement of objects, but of libido being withdrawn from the object, and in melancholia it was not displaced to another object, 'but served to establish an identification of the ego with the abandoned object. Thus the shadow of the object fell upon the ego, and the latter could henceforth be judged by a special agency, as though it were an object, the forsaken object'. Further on, writing about preliminary object choice and identification, he says, 'the ego wants to incorporate this object into itself, and in accordance with the oral or cannibalistic phase of libidinal development in which it is, it wants to do so by devouring it' (1917, pp. 249–50).

In this paper I have considered one of the possible fates of the forsaken or incorporated object, its being kept alive, possibly by identification and other ways, making others aware of its presence by self- and other types of recriminations, and thus asking for it to be repaired for the sake of the object and of the ego, and because the ego is unable to do it.

I have found the views of Melanie Klein concerning an inner world of inner objects to be essential in understanding and elaborating on the clinical findings I have reported here.

SUMMARY

In this paper it is suggested that patients bring to analysis their damaged inner objects, and not only themselves, to undergo reparation because they are unable to do it. Stress is put on the very complex mechanisms used to keep damaged and dying inner objects alive while waiting for help to come.

The contrast between concrete repair and psychic reparation appears to be very important, and the defences necessitated by failed reparation efforts are described. Failed reparative manoeuvres must not be confused with resulting defences.

Examples are given for various levels of personality organizations and pathology, including neurotic, borderline, psychotic, psychosomatic and hypochondriacal patients. A group of six neurotic patients is included.

15   ON IGNACIO MATTE-BLANCO

PART 1: A CRITICAL REVIEW OF THE UNCONSCIOUS AS INFINITE SETS: AN ESSAY IN BI-LOGIC

'This book is written for psychoanalysts as well as for mathematical philosophers.' This is the opening first sentence of the preface. It is important to make clear to those who might be tempted to read this book – and I hope they will be many – that psychoanalysts suspicious of the application of mathematical logic to psychoanalysis or worried because of their lack of basic knowledge in logico-mathematics and symbolic logic need not entertain such doubts. The book is written by a psychoanalyst with considerable clinical experience. His logico-mathematical treatment of psychoanalysis is made easy because every logico-mathematical concept used is simple and simply explained from first principles and clinical examples very clearly set out. Because of this double preoccupation of the author one could find some aspects of the book repetitive – as the author himself says – but in fact this is not really so. This method of presentation is very necessary because each renewed examination of the facts brings the emergence of new knowledge from old material of great interest to both the clinician and the theorist. In describing the ideas of the author, I have freely used quotations. Some of my descriptions are very nearly verbatim copies of the text.

Matte-Blanco states that some of the models used by psychoanalysis to contain, explain and classify new clinical findings and experiences are not sufficient any more and could be harmful in distorting the meaning of new observations by forcing them into old models.

He is also extremely concerned with the notion of the unconscious developed in Freud's writings and those of psychoanalysts. From being 'the unconscious', that is to say, a living aspect of the personality with activities governed by certain laws, it became demoted to merely the quality of being unconscious. Quoting Freud from *The Ego and the Id* (1923):

> When we find ourselves thus confronted by the necessity of postulating a third Ucs, which is not repressed, we must admit that the characteristic of being unconscious begins to lose significance for us. It becomes a quality which can have many meanings, a quality which we are unable to

make, as we should have hoped to do, the basis of far-reaching and inevitable conclusions.

Thus, that which is the greatest discovery of Freud, a once-in-a-lifetime discovery, was gradually turned to be a mere quality like any other. Matte-Blanco then makes a fine and careful analysis of what the concept 'the unconscious' was at first and what it has become. He also shows the contrast between the conscious and the unconscious.

In Matte-Blanco's own words:

> Freud's fundamental discovery is not that of the unconscious, not even in the dynamic sense (however important this may be) but that of a world – which he unfortunately called the unconscious – ruled by entirely different laws from those governing conscious thinking. He was not the first to speak of the unconscious, and much about it was known before him, but he was the first to make the fundamental discovery of this strange 'Realm of the Illogical', submitted, in spite of it being illogical, to precise laws which he found, in an extraordinary stroke of genius.

It is at this point that Matte-Blanco's own contribution may now be considered. He approaches and reformulates the 'precise laws' in the unconscious and contrasts them with the laws of bivalent or Aristotelian logic which characterize conscious functioning. Man lives simultaneously in two modes of 'being' governed by two sets of laws: the symmetrical or unconscious mode of being and the asymmetrical or conscious mode of being. The fundamental terms 'symmetrical' and 'asymmetrical' are used to denote the two systems of logic corresponding to the laws governing the two states of being. Hence the subtitle, *An Essay in Bi-Logic*.

The ideas of Matte-Blanco have evolved gradually in a series of papers from the mid-1950s and culminated in the present book. A schizophrenic woman who suffered from delusions complained, after blood had been taken from her arm and at other times, that her arm had been taken away. This was an expression of a well-known schizophrenic way of thinking, in developing the part and the whole. From the point of view of bivalent logic, this is a violation of well-established laws. What are the laws that apply here? Another example will help. When the analyst is interpreting to a patient that the latter is seeing the analyst as father or mother, he is implicitly establishing that, in terms of certain aspects or functions, the analyst is identical with the actual father or mother. In terms of symbolic logic this may be expressed by saying that the elements of a given class are equivalent between themselves with regard to the propositional function which defines the class: the three properties of reflexivity, symmetry and transivity are fulfilled. But the elements themselves are not identical; however, the unconscious treats them as identical.

Identity is a form of equivalence, but equivalence between members of a class is not identity. That is, within the class, defined by a certain characteristic or propositional function, all the other elements are treated as identical. Thus, for any class defined by a propositional function into which the analyst is put by the patient, it is applied with the same magnitude (mathematical) as that for the real person, the father or mother in this case.

As early as 1911 Freud had an amazing intuition of this, and Matte-Blanco quotes from the Schreber case: it shows us 'that in the patient's mind "Flechsigs" and "God" belonged to the same class. In one of his phantasies he overheard a conversation between Flechsig and his wife, in which the former asserted that he was "God Flechsig" so that his wife thought he had gone mad.' On the next page Freud adds that he views 'the decomposition of the persecutor into Flechsig and God as a paranoid reaction to a previously established identification of the two figures or their belonging to the same class.' As Matte-Blanco points out, Freud saw that the two figures belong to the same class but showed hesitance, as in the phrase 'identification of the two figures or their belonging to the same class'. Matte-Blanco then comments, 'for Schreber's madness consisted in affirming the identity, not the equivalence existing on account of the fact of their belonging to the same class'. The system *Ucs.* as defined by Freud has the following characteristics: absence of time; displacement; replacement of external by psychical reality; lack of mutual contradiction and condensation; absence of negation. These characteristics of the system *Ucs.* are analysed by Matte-Blanco in terms of the characteristics of the symmetrical system of functioning. There are two main principles, with a number of derived laws that have emerged from his studies:

First, the system *Ucs.* treats an individual thing (person, object, concept) as if it were a member or element of a set or class which contains other members; it treats this class as a subclass of a more general class, and this more general class as a subclass or subset of a more general class, and so on. This may be called the principle of generalization.

Second, the system *Ucs.* treats the converse of any relation as identical with the relation. In other words, it treats asymmetrical relations as if they were symmetrical. Example: if John is the brother of Peter, the converse is, Peter is the brother of John. It is a symmetrical relation because the converse is identical with the direct relation. However, if John is the father of Peter, the converse is, Peter is the son of John. Relation and converse are not identical but are called asymmetrical. The second principle states that the system *Ucs.* tends to treat any relation as if symmetrical. If John is the father of Peter, then Peter is the father of John, which is absurd in Aristotelian logic but normal in the system *Ucs.* This principle is therefore called the 'principle of symmetry'.

After fully considering the characteristics of the system *Ucs.* in the light of these principles Matte-Blanco concludes that, 'the special characteristics of the system unconscious described by Freud reveal the operation of a logic peculiar to this system, whose fundamental distinguishing mark is to treat as symmetrical, relations which in scientific logic are not so considered.'

It may be proper here to refer to the title of the book, *The Unconscious as Infinite Sets*, after having examined the reasons for its subtitle. The reader will have to grasp a certain characteristic of infinite sets; it is in connection with the part being equal to the whole. This appears in ordinary logic to be a very peculiar statement; however, a great and controversial mathematical discovery is that in certain conditions this is true. If the complete set of natural numbers is considered for each and every number 'n' of this set, there is always a number 2n of the same set. In other terms, there is a bi-univocal correspondence between each member of the two sets. That is, for 1, 2, 3, 4, etc., there is correspondingly 2, 4, 6, 8, etc. The set of even numbers is, however, obviously a subset only of the set of all complete numbers. So, the following definition was arrived at: a set is infinite when, and only when, it can be put in bi-univocal correspondence with a proper part of it. When he realized all this and its possible consequences, Cantor exclaimed: 'Je le vois, mais je ne le crois pas!' ('I see it, but can't believe it'.) Armed with logico-mathematical propositions and the concepts of infinite sets, Matte-Blanco proceeds to a systematic investigation of properties of the system *Ucs.* as described previously and of part-object psychology.

Using this new concept he is able to come to many understandings and new applications resulting from the reformulation of human experiences and object relations, that is, emotion, feeling and thinking. He states, 'the principle of symmetry explains or describes in the terms of simply bivalent logic, the violations of this logic which are observed in certain psychical manifestations'; 'the point to be considered is first whether such violations actually do take place and secondly whether their description in terms of the principle of symmetry is an accurate description of them.' The whole book is devoted to these questions.

It must be restated that those ideas and their application to psychoanalysis have slowly emerged in the author's mind in the course of psychoanalytical work. In the present volume they are put together and extended to practically every aspect of psychoanalytical theory. However, apart from throwing new light on specific problems there are also some fundamental conclusions that are of primary importance. Thus the unconscious is seen as a 'mode of being' which can be called 'symmetrical being', the other pole being conscious, logical or 'asymmetrical being'. The relationship between conscious and unconscious then can be seen to have a new meaning.

A thorough distinction can now be made between the unconscious proper and the repressed unconscious. The latter belongs to asymmetrical thinking while the former is truly the representative of symmetrical being. The quality of being conscious is to show the characteristics of asymmetrical thinking. It therefore stands to reason that the unconscious proper can never be apprehended as such but only through the distortions it creates in the asymmetrical mode of being. The two are incompatible. It follows, then, that what we know of and experience can only be a mixture of both. 'Mixture' is perhaps not a correct way of describing that state; the proportion of symmetry increases so that at the deepest levels there is pure symmetry and no space–time notions.

The notion of time, for instance, only emerges as a consequence of mental operations such as groupings, ordination, seriation, and so on, which are asymmetrical. Present in the book are not only 'mechanisms'; or mental operations; or concepts of psychoanalysis such as the id, ego and super-ego; or primary and secondary processes or problems relating to intro-jection, projection, projective identification; or the nature of object relations; schizophrenic thinking and other related problems. A large part of the book also deals with the problems of instinct, drives, emotions, sensation, feelings and their formulation in terms of symmetrical and asymmetrical logic, as well as their relation to thinking. Here the author shows his remarkable know-ledge of the problems relating to emotion when the attempt is made to try to recognize some laws relating to them. He is able to demonstrate the dual nature of emotional life and the participation of sensation-feeling in thinking. A possible method of quantitative measurement is suggested. The notion is put forward that the magnitudes of emotion are a function of the proportion between symmetrical and asymmetrical thinking. The more there is of the unconscious in a given manifestation, the greater will be the magnitude (in the mathematical sense) of emotion. This offers a new way of viewing the theory of affect and of cathexes. It is also very interesting to see how Matte-Blanco applies the concept of infinite sets not only to emotion but to the concepts of omnipotence, omniscience and idealization.

A most important aspect of the work is in connection with the concept of the unfolding or translating function. As Matte-Blanco points out, analysis is more and more concerned with the treatment of the whole personality and not symptoms. He considers therefore that this means not dealing only with the repressed unconscious, but with helping the unconscious to unfold itself. This he calls the translating function, that is, the way in which, confronted by the infinite set (the way, as we have described, that uncon-scious or symmetrical being appears to the conscious asymmetrical being), consciousness succeeds in selecting some asymmetrical functions which are a translation of some of the potentialities implicit in the unconscious or symmetrical mode of being. This bears some relation to the way Freud talks about word-presentations and the mnemic traces of words. Matte-Blanco writes,

> Symmetrical being can never in itself become asymmetrical, and hence can never enter human consciousness. In other words, the unconscious

can never be made conscious . . . What we can do instead, is to become (asymmetrically) conscious (aware) of some aspects of symmetrical being. Just as we cannot make our liver conscious but only become conscious of our liver.

It must be remembered here that Matte-Blanco refers to the unconscious and not the repressed unconscious. Thus just as aspects of the repressed unconscious can be made conscious by the lifting of repression, some indirect manifestations of the unrepressed unconscious, by establishment of connections with the asymmetrical conscious, can become translated and apprehended but not known as existing in the unconscious. Here the relationship of the two polarities symmetrical–asymmetrical can be seen to gain further meaning by considering the polarity homogeneous–indivisible and heterogeneous–divisible (see below). To become conscious, the first must undergo transformation into the second, thus losing an essential characteristic (homogeneous–indivisible) of the condition of being unconscious. Applying the concept of infinite sets, it follows that only: 'for a consciousness which can grasp an infinite number of relations the unconscious would be conscious'. It follows that in therapy increasing understanding means increasing the number of relations available to consciousness. But this means increasing the number of relations available at different moments in time and not simultaneously. Thus we have here an example of the problems attached to the translating function.

It has been mentioned at the beginning that this book has a dual purpose. It is written for psychoanalysts and logico-mathematical philosophers alike. One of the leading influences that inspired Matte-Blanco outside psychoanalysis itself is the philosophy of the Eleatic School, particularly that of Parmenides himself and his ideas on the continuous and the discontinuous, of two realities: a homogeneous–indivisible mode and a heterogeneous–dividing one. The author considers that many problems raised by the mathematical philosophers can be looked at from the new angle, the new conception derived by a combination of psychoanalytical observations and concepts put into bi-logical form. The ideas of a number of specialists on the subject are referred to and certain points analysed in the new perspective. Further, the all-important concepts of space, time and displacement are reviewed by the author in terms of bi-logic. The concept of multidimensional mental space is introduced as a possibility of solving problems that are of great importance to psychoanalysts and philosophers alike.

Never before has the data accumulated by psychoanalysts been offered to the logico-mathematical thinkers in a form that makes it so clearly available to them. This book could lead to the re-thinking of the fascinating controversy concerning Cantor's work which involved some of the greatest names in mathematics and philosophy: Kronecker, Wecstrass, Wedekind, Poincaré, Burali-Forte, Frege, Hilbert, Brouwer and Russell. However, it

represents above all a worthwhile new effort in symbolic logic and mathematical logic with data not yet analysed on such lines. Some brief references
are made to Wittgenstein, Sheffer, Whitehead and Russell, and Von Wright
as seen in terms of the present approach. There is a short special appendix
on Sartre.

It has not been an easy task to review this book, which is packed with
new and original ideas. Perhaps the best thing I can do is to give some of my
personal experiences when studying the book. I read it three times over,
returning to certain passages many a time. The fact that the author returns
to various aspects to look at them from different angles may at first sight
appear repetitive, but when I understood what it was about, I found it
extremely useful and necessary. I must also add that the problem of
symmetry and asymmetry had been one of my major preoccupations in my
studies throughout the years in chemistry, biology, art, folklore and then in
symbolism.

As a psychoanalyst with an interest in object relations theory, the idea of
a systematic approach to part-object psychology fascinated me. The problem
in science and philosophy of the continuous and discontinuous I felt to be
an absorbing one, and I had just started reflecting on Cantor's idea when I
came across Matte-Blanco's work. I then realized what I had failed to do,
which was to have transferred the concepts of physical symmetry and
asymmetry to the mind itself. Matte-Blanco has realized for the mind
something that had preoccupied others in the physical universe of science.
I have attempted to describe in the previous pages how he did it. I believe
that the way he restores the unconscious to its true position in man's
existence as a mode of being is a truly original achievement.

There is something I would like to say about asymmetrical thinking. As
the child becomes older, he becomes capable of more and more complex
mental operations. It is the genetic developmental psychology of Piaget
which has studied most completely this aspect of human thought. To solve
life problems or events the child has therefore a different battery of mental
operations, according to his level of intellectual development. The proportion of asymmetry increases as he grows. When the necessary asymmetrical
operations are not yet acquired, interpretations of life events and solutions
to various experiences and problems belong to another form of logic. One
realm of thought is this important one of the unconscious which Freud
discovered, and the rules of which Matte-Blanco has attempted to systematize.

For the practising psychoanalyst I think that it will prove most rewarding
to attempt to reinterpret for himself in terms of bi-logic what he has
interpreted already in his own choice of psychoanalytical models. What I
have attempted to do is to give a general description of the sort of ideas to
be found in this book. Even if the conclusions of the author were to be
disproved, which I doubt, this is the kind of work long overdue in psycho-

analysis. It fits well with current new ways of approaching psychoanalytical data. These many different ways may include, for instance, Lacan's efforts to restore the unconscious to its very essence, and his use of language; the work of Bion and his attempts to find a method to describe and deal with primary elements of knowledge and transformation processes; the applications of Piagetian psychology to psychoanalysis; the use of the classification activity of the mind to analytical data, theories of symbol-formation, metaphors by Rubinstein; the use of the psycholinguistics approach to dream function by Edelson.

With the help of simple logico-mathematical analysis Matte-Blanco has been able to approach and describe a world of living experiences and keep it alive as a world of emotion and feeling as well as a world of strange thinking. I am referring to this unconscious world the discovery of which constituted one of Freud's greatest contributions to the understanding of man. From the content and tone of many passages in this book and from direct comments by the author it is clear that he hopes to stimulate our imagination and intellectual curiosity and is well prepared for criticisms as well as constructive suggestions.

© 1975 Institute of Psycho-Analysis

PART 2: NOTES ON MATTE-BLANCO

For the practising psychoanalyst I think that it will prove most rewarding to attempt to use Matte-Blanco's ideas to reinterpret for himself in terms of bi-logic what he has interpreted already in his own choice of psychoanalytical models. I have tried to do so and it would seem appropriate to give a clinical example. It is the case of a young man showing extreme narcissistic and obsessional preoccupations. When he came to treatment, he had no emotional contact with anybody and did not work. Everything was extreme and total in what he did or attempted to do. He lived alone in a room and did not see anybody. When he went home he felt there was no room for both him and his father – it had to be one or the other. If they both stayed at home he expected a great and total catastrophe to happen. After a while, being very intelligent, he started at university. Work obsessed him; it had to occupy the totality of his time. An hour wasted meant total waste and that he had not worked at all. He made friends, but each friend had to consume the totality of his friendship. If he made friends with one person, then he had totally lost the other. In phantasy what he called sex was to imagine lying next to a young man whose qualities he liked, usually ultimate beauty. The reverse was also true, so that the other one was him and he the other one. His words always expressed totality and extremes as he filled the session with talk. He would never say something without saying its opposite.

When he started to dream it was about people who exerted total control. He described what he referred to as 'special dreams'. These were filled with mountains of infinite size, icebergs, snow, infinite skies, and total cata-strophes. Animals always appeared small but in such multitudes that they covered and filled everything. He had made good progress, but at the time I read Matte-Blanco, he was rather stuck, giving all his attention to his future final examination; all his attention to a future job; all to the analysis; all to his friends.

When I attempted to interpret the 'special dreams', he was very angry, saying I would destroy the incredible experience they were to him and reduce his dream experience to ordinary symbolic activity and ordinary relationships. His phantasies of how he related to people always implied a relationship where one party was totally superior to the other. Occasionally he reversed the position of who was superior and who was inferior. Sometimes he was filled with an enormous rage and indignation towards me and then he rushed out of the room. Although I had always interpreted his ambivalence and his tendency to extremes as possessiveness and jealousy, his mind was unable to proceed in any other way than by experiencing the part as tending to become the whole, and the whole as filling everything.

Then, after reading Matte-Blanco, I started the systematic interpretation of this with him, as well as pointing out his use of words. At first he took no interest in this. I persisted. After a gap of a few days he said that I was absolutely right. He always made things a totality, but it was not in the way I said. It was more like a vessel with two hulls connected together like an hour-glass, and the tiny tilt would make the whole shift to one role or another. I accepted this analogy, but after a while I came back to the part of his being transformed into an immensity that filled everything. Finally he got very pleasurably excited and told me that he had some two or three years earlier related dreams of childhood to me. They were about a tiny little sphere, the smallest that could be thought of, that became bigger and bigger, making the highest mountains look like nothing. It filled everything and he was petrified with awe. They were recurrent dreams, and after a while his fear gave way to a puzzled sense of interest. Some days later he told me that he had remembered that at school he had become fascinated by the infinite. I had never used the words 'the infinite' to him. He gestured with his hands making the sign of the infinite. He said that although he did not know anything about it, he knew there was a curve that came nearer and nearer to a line and never met it. He had been told something like that at school. His imagination was thrilled by this thought. Then he himself imagined triangles where sides would be made longer and longer at the vertex, but, although coming nearer and nearer, they never met. He thought that this was the process by which obsessions invaded his mind, but he could do nothing about it.

This patient demonstrates many of the points raised by Matte-Blanco. For example, 'The potentialities of the propositional function have unfolded until each one of them has come to be represented by an individual or an infinite number of individuals.' As soon as the patient deals with one item of emotional value to him, that item would tend to acquire the capacity to stand for all that existed and fill the whole of his existence. When he thought about another emotional item it proceeded to do the same. Instead of one item standing for all, there was also the reverse as well. He loved nature, and was also fascinated by very small animals and collected larvae. He had a dream where identical little alligators, the size of small lizards, would be poured on to the world covering everything until finally all of them in vast number would be the only thing there was. As mentioned before, this is a different process from his ambivalence and feelings of opposites. However, within ambivalence the process of infinite magnitude also applied, all black or all white. But all black did not only displace (say) all white; it extended at times to all other items, as previously described.

He attempted to make friends, but at the beginning of the treatment he could only choose them according to one proposition-function, beauty, which came to override every other aspect of a person. Then he had to become that person as described; then he felt there were not many persons, not two, but one. When in despair, he felt there was 'no other'; it was he and nobody else. He had come to represent an infinity of individuals.

But he then produced material to show that he himself stood for the phallus. He was unable to touch his penis. He also produced material showing how he stood for father. As he stood for all penises and all fathers, he could not logically relate to a father. In fact, he could not relate to his own father. Furthermore, his material showed that he had attempted to be his own mother and his own breast. It became clear that he was the breast that stood for all the breasts, the mothers, the penises and the fathers. Two sisters and a brother had become included in this method of treating all objects as being identical because of one propositional function – 'breastness' – grouping all those objects not as equivalent for that function but as identical.

But further still, the emotional magnitude attached to the propositional function became infinite, that is, the amount of 'breastness' became infinite or near-infinite. It contained all breastness. This was shown by the dreams in which mountains, icebergs and snow were in infinite proportions. The preoccupation with infinite activities was shown in his fascination with geometrical infinity and in his dream of the smallest, tiniest sphere developing into an all-space-occupying sphere. A twelfth-century manuscript, *Liber XXIV philosophium*, defines God as: *Deus est sphoera, cujus centrum ubique, circumferentia nusquam* ('God is a sphere whose centre is everywhere and circumference nowhere.') A second definition is also very relevant: 'God is in all his entirety present in any part of himself.'

The ambivalence and sense of the opposite was presumably a first attempt at classifying objects according to more than one propositional function, and a primitive step towards asymmetry. Proceeding from this first effort, normal asymmetrical thinking had taken place for a part of his thinking. There seemed to have been a further split between thinking and feeling, the latter having attained less asymmetry. Unfortunately, he could not prevent regression from more advanced asymmetry to less asymmetrical thinking, to ambivalence and, deeper still, to a situation where symmetry occupied a privileged position. His rages provide another example permitting bi-logical interpretation. For a long time he had repeatedly told me that he had intense rages at home and that his father also had terrible attacks of anger that terrified him. He had frequently become angry with me, on some occasions so angry that he had left the room with great trepidation. Years later, when talking about his angry feelings towards me, he mentioned I was very wrong to say that he got very angry at home and that his father could also get very angry. He said he had expressed his own anger only a few times in all his life, and this anger was 'piffling' compared to his anger against me. He also said that it was not true his father was always angry; he had not become angry more than three times.

I then started understanding what was happening. When in the room with me his anger was developing; it was like the sphere in the dream, and it became all of him and filled the room. He left before I was obliterated and there was no more me. Once he threw a book at me before going, but, because he classified father in the same class as himself, father also had such rages and so did it. This was another example of the principle of symmetry. He constantly accused me of being angry with him. Because of treating his penis as himself, he could not use it because of its anger. But the penis was also the breast that had frustrated him and caused his anger. Much of his material showed this, suggesting that bad or angry 'breastness' was the dominating propositional function encompassing all other functions.

In the introduction to my paper on 'The Schizoid Mode of Being' (see Chapter 2), I said of the patient similar to the one I have described:

> He is not ambivalent, he is pre-ambivalent. This is because of living a part-object psychology kind of life. In that way of life the part is equal to the whole, and sometimes it is one part which is the whole situation and sometimes another part. Such a person lives a split-off or partial kind of life. Presumably the stage of ambivalence is reached when two aspects of a situation are considered simultaneously, that is, that two propositional functions are allowed in a new kind of 'classification'.

It would seem that the 'infinite' magnitude of each aspect has diminished and allows the beginning of paying attention to another aspect. In treatment, one could postulate that it is an essential aspect of the transference. Thus my patient, transferring his overwhelming anger on to me, was able to compare it with his father's anger towards him or his towards his father. This is also the beginning of asymmetry because son, father and analyst cannot any more symmetrically be considered as the same. This allows the undoing of pathological structures and the formation of new ones. In the same text it is described thus:

Cohesion considered in structural terms must imply that two or more structures have ceased to have an autonomous activity but have combined into a totally new structure with a new activity and a new aim. This new aspect is the new propositional function or the function that will qualify the structure. Once that stage is achieved this more advanced structure cannot be easily disintegrated.

The importance of Matte-Blanco's ideas in understanding the therapeutic process can here be clearly seen. There are other very important aspects of the patient's experience to be considered. One of them is the claustro-agoraphobic structural organization; another is sado-masochistic behaviour; a third related to it (and to narcissism) is the question of big and small. In my paper, I have developed in detail the importance of the claustro-agoraphobic structuration of the personality as a basic organization, of which claustro-phobia and agoraphobia as symptoms, especially in anxiety states, are but the tip of the iceberg.

I have described how my patient, on occasion, would rush out of the room when getting angry. Clearly he was afraid of the consequence of his anger, perhaps in destroying me, and/or of me destroying him. He would thus put distance between him and me. However, this explanation alone would be missing the fact of his 'being' the anger and completely filling the room and obliterating me. By the principle of symmetry the reverse was true for him. This explains the overwhelming, uncontrollable, intolerable quality of claustrophobic anxiety in severe cases who have not 'distributed' the anxiety into a number of phobic objects.

However, a limited space with boundaries seems to offer a protection from the infinite magnitude of the anxiety, that is, a finite universe. In an open space the reverse becomes true and the absence of objects and boundaries renders the environment infinite in magnitude and the subject infinitely small. As is well known, there are many permutations and combinations of this phenomenon. Finally, it should be remembered that there is plenty of material to relate general space, personal space and internal space to the original situation in the womb; through displacement, representation and symbolization all sorts of situations stand for the original situation.

The patient left me in no doubt at all about this original situation, displaced on to many representational derivations. I will only mention some material necessary in order to pass on to the sado-masochistic organization and 'big and small'. He would always choose to study in places where there were other people. He went, especially when he was better, to small cafés, where he would take his books and writing materials. Later he started taking the bus and studying it. He would go right to the terminal, and then come back to his point of departure. He felt happy being contained and carried in the bus.

Then there was a baby that was himself. But he also had memories or phantasies of being in his cot and left alone. He would then press himself against the walls of the cot as if to obliterate the space between himself and the cot walls. He had similar phantasies about enveloping rubber suits or sensations on his cheek if something nice and soft were being put close against it. Those phantasies or experiences were related to the sado-masochistic phantasies which consisted mainly of being totally controlled and enslaved by somebody else, usually a man, but occasionally the situation would be reversed. Very occasionally, it would not be a man but a woman. He referred to his homosexuality, suggested by his phantasy of lying down next to a beautiful young man, then all the other man's beautiful character-istics would pass on to him. Occasionally there would be a reversal of the process. He had a younger brother towards whom he experienced sibling jealousy and a very complex relationship.

Gradually it emerged that in the absence of the mother he had phantasies of being contained inside her and never parted. This was the cot, the suit or any material closely touching or fitting him. This was the wished-for mother and the being inside her, possibly in the place of the younger brother. The real mother was mother *in absentia*, leaving him in the cot and possibly being with brother or father. This is the no-mother, the no-thing of Bion, as opposed to thing (mother) and nothing; i.e., neither thing (mother) nor no-thing (absent mother).

In sado-masochism, the actual object, ultimately always a substitute mother, is the no-thing or absent object. The sadistic attacks are in order to reduce the object to a no-object state by ultimate control so that the object, although physically existing, has no more a will of its own, personality of its own, and hardly a body of its own. The object is entirely replaced by the subject carrying on the sadism. There is no clearer description of this than in *The Story of O* (Réage, 1972), the pornographic novel in which the aim of all the sadistic and masochistic manoeuvres is to transform the object into the one in the mind of the subject. In an attempt to succeed, the sadistic state passes into the masochistic one, which is an attempt at fulfilling the wish of possessing the object forever and therefore making sure that the wish of the object is but the wish of the subject and nothing else. It can never succeed.

A deeper manoeuvre to succeed in this plan is in psychosis where an attempt is made to abolish external reality, that is, the mind of the object and possibly its body, while simultaneously replacing external reality with the subject's phantasies, which represents an attempt and a failure to achieve a control of infinite magnitude over the mother in the mind of the subject. In sado-masochism there is a total symmetry in which the mother is the child and the child is the mother. There is a conflict between the wish to create a mother as the subject wishes and a compulsion to repeat a situation, to re-create an absent mother, a no-thing (mother) with the object of the sado-masochism, whoever and whatever the sex is. The subject feels it is better, less painful to have a no-mother than to have nothing. When sado-masochism fails to relieve pain, sometimes the next attempt to succeed with this aim is psychosis. Perhaps, then, psychosis is among other things an attempt to restore to infinite magnitude and complete symmetry the homogeneous-continuous mode of being characteristic of the unconscious; psychosis attempts to reverse the impingement of external reality and logical thinking which created a heterogeneous, discontinuous state in the subject.

In the description of the patient's phantasies it has been shown how things were tiny or infinite in size, or very tiny with an infinite multitude of them. In a paper entitled 'Basic Schizoid Structures and Space-Time Factors' (see Chapter 9) analysing mental structures located at the stage where thought is spatially centred (Piaget), I mentioned the importance of the relative size of the subject and the object, and gave examples. Here is another one. In a group of patients who had all suffered serious psychotic episodes, one depressed patient, whose illness had taken the form of extremely manic episodes, at other times related how as a child he was terrified of facing his father. For instance, before he could even begin to obey an order such as to clean his shoes, he was shouted at immediately and hit for not having done as he was told. When asked what he could do in such a situation, he could only think of hiding or running away. A schizophrenic young man in the group, when suggesting one could try to be strong in facing father, suddenly said, 'Bigger and stronger than father'. At the early stages of natural development relative size plays a decisive role in the formation of mental structures and mechanisms of defence. I am firmly convinced that one of the most fundamental characteristics of the subject in the manic defence, but also in phobic anxieties, in narcissistic states and in sado-masochism, is getting bigger and making the object smaller.

In narcissism the subject takes all the importance and the object's importance is completely reduced. Narcissism can be a defence against the anxiety of being small and vulnerable. In sado-masochism the necessity is to control the object completely, leaving it no characteristics of its own. Similarly, in claustro-agoraphobic anxiety, the relative size of container and contained appears vital. Here again the conflict between symmetrical and asymmetrical relationships, and the part being equal to the whole, are very valuable concepts facilitating analysis of those states.

16 FEMININITY, SEXUALITY AND INNER SPACE

In the past few years so much ink has been poured on the subject of female sexuality that if one tries to write about it, one takes the risk of only adding to the immense ink-stain. I shall certainly avoid rewriting the history of the evolution of the concepts on this subject; this has been done so often already. It is understood; the woman is not a failed boy (*garçon manqué*). The question remains, What is she? What is her sexuality? As far as I am concerned, I shall choose a number of facts which I think contribute fundamentally to the understanding of female sexuality. It is possible to talk about sexuality only from a psychological point of view, but this implies that one deliberately accepts omitting all the biological aspects. One can, on the other hand, approach the subject at the frontier between the psychological and the biological. This is what I shall attempt to do.

First, considering the biological side of female sexuality, there are, among the findings, the studies of Jost (1947) in France. His studies on the sexuality of mammals suggest that every mammal from which one removes the gonads at a certain moment of its foetal evolution will develop into a female phenotype. This implies that a male, from which one has taken away the gonads early enough, will develop as a female phenotype. It seems the role of the sex chromosomes is to produce organizing substances which decide whether the gonads develop into ovaries or into testicles. The sexual hormones which are produced by these two organs decide on the sex of the foetus. So if one refers to the boy *manqué*, it is in fact more accurate to describe a male as a girl *manquée*. I shall come back to the immense importance of these facts later.

Second, there are the contributions of Masters and Johnson (1960), which describe the anatomy of the functional structure of the vagina. Their studies suggest that there is unity between the vagina–clitoris in producing the orgasmic capacity of the female genital organ and its right of existence as a developed and complete organ in itself. It is therefore not a boy *manqué* again.

Third, there is the menstrual cycle of the woman. In the psychoanalytic literature there are numerous references to the symbolism of the loss of blood and nearly none to the cycle itself. Yet from the psychological and biological point of view, the woman is a different being on each day of her cycle. After having spent twelve years studying the menstrual cycle from the biological point of view, as well as from the point of view of its corresponding phantasies, I think it is important, where certain aspects of female behaviour are concerned, to talk about a woman's experience specifying the moment in her cycle.

Fourth, there is the fact of the pregnancy, so important for the race. It is Helene Deutsch (1947) who first underlined the relationship between mother and foetus, and orgasm and birth, highlighting the narcissistic relationship possible between mother and child during the pregnancy.

Fifth, there is the period where the woman feeds her child. So much has been written on the period of pre-human biological evolution, where primates adopted an upright position, thus liberating the anterior limbs which could then be used to grasp. This is a change which led from *Homo erectus* to *Homo faber*. I have been struck by the importance of the period in mammals when the young could feed from a part of the body of the mother, her milk, without devouring the source of milk, the mother. There is taking from the mother but not destroying her. This is a precursor of the theory of part-objects and the depressive position, because of the implied respect for the object.

When one looks for the facts which play an important role in the formation of sexual identity of the man or the woman, it is quite easy as far as the man is concerned. He is a man because he possesses a penis. When a little girl is born I am not sure whether her sex is determined because one says, 'She has a vagina' or because one says, 'She has no penis.' I obviously speak not only of a conscious, objective statement, but also of what happens in the unconscious of the observer. The unconscious is something which one does not know in the same way as one knows the objective external facts. Hence we can already have an idea of why it is so difficult to know which is the positive factor analogous to the male factor which determines the female sex.

I would suggest that it is the inner space which determines for the woman her sexual identity and her sexual behaviour, and it is mainly of this factor which I shall be writing. As we know, space is something which is fashionable to talk about in all human sciences. In literature, in psychology, in psychoanalysis, there are descriptions of external space, internal space, cultural space, good and bad space, transitional space, the role of space in concrete thinking or in schizoid thinking, of ecological space. As far as external reality is concerned, the role of space and its structure reached its height with Piaget.

If we start from the penis we can see how it has allowed the male to adapt himself to the loss of conscious awareness of his inner space in so far as this inner space concerns his sexuality. In the field of object relations theory there is a concept of the internalization of the penis as an inner image or inner object, having a determining function in the establishment of sexual identity. The loss of the penis corresponds to a loss of sexual identity. The penis functions as a vital bridge between subject and object, and the loss of this bridging function leads inevitably to the loss of the object. The penis has a unique, magic role: a reparative or pseudo-reparative role in relation to depression. Depression equals a bad inner state, while mania, in identification with a magical penis, is its pseudo-reparation. Real reparation is different.

This is not the case with the woman, for whom the situation with regard to depression and mania is different from that of a man. The woman's genital organ is the 'entrance' to her cavity or inner space. The penis of the man invites him to forget the existence of his inner space and makes him search for the space of the other. In contrast, the genital organ of the woman reminds her all the time of her sexual inner space especially during the period before her menstruation. Here it is important to say *sexual* inner space because we have to consider the nature of this inner space.

Before being an adult genital reproductive space, the inner space of the woman has been many other things. Its first exit and entry is the mouth, but also the anus, the urethra and later the vagina.

I cannot resist giving wider consideration to the universality of the concept of inner space or inner cavity. By universality I mean the universe itself and the symbolic relationship of women with this universe. Melanie Klein talks about the womb of the mother being the universe of the child.

I should like to start with a description of the inner and outer space of the human being. The child is first contained within a container, the uterus, which is itself contained inside the body of the mother. The uterus equals a partial container in relationship to the body of the mother, the total container.

After birth the infant exists outside the mother, who, through her support, warmth and feeding recreates partially this uterine state for the baby. The maternal environment could be called a marsupial space. For a long time the baby cannot walk or displace himself freely. He is more or less limited to the space which contains him. He changes his personal space in relation to the outside space only when he is carried with his space within the external maternal space, like a marsupial in the pouch.

It is only after quite a while that he will move in relation to the marsupial space, that is, within his personal space. His space and the maternal space gradually increase, become structured and acquire mental representation. He will only cease to be contained in this container when the marsupial pouch and the space of the containing object will be the only and the same space. But in fact, I think that every subject retains a personal space and that its frontiers do not stop abruptly at those of this body. The supremely idealized object, God, possesses his own space, heaven.

I shall give you now another description of space, which I have also quoted elsewhere:

> Absolute motion is the translation of the body from one relative place into another. Thus in a ship under sail, the relative place of a body is that part of the cavity of the ship which the body fills and which therefore moves together with the ship; and the relative rest is the continuance of the body in that same part of that immovable space in which the ship itself, its cavity, and all it contains are really at rest. The body which relatively rests in the ship will really and absolutely move with the same velocity which the ship has on the earth . . . !

Who wrote this passage? Newton himself chose this image to explain the laws of relative motion in his *Philosophia Naturalis Principia Mathematica* (1687). Substitute for the ship the well-known symbol of the mother and the analogy is striking.

We also know that one of the analogies which Einstein has constantly and repeatedly used in order to illustrate his theory was that of a man in a box falling down a shaft. What would happen to objects which would fall out of his pockets, Einstein asked? Not satisfied with this, he was nearly obsessed with the question of what would happen to light travelling through the box. Further, since he was an adolescent, Einstein was fascinated by the idea of what he would find out if he could travel as fast as light. What he discovered was that he could never travel as fast as light – the secret had to remain a secret forever. God for him represented the field of knowledge into which he wanted to penetrate in order to know the secret of the Universe. He said that only this really interested him, not human beings.

If I quote these facts I am not in the least trying to describe the psychopathology of great men. On the contrary, it is to illustrate the universality of this experience. It is a fascinating thought that the birth of the baby and the experience of his world space may have something in common with the Big Bang Theory and that of the expanding universe.

Have these universal archetypes inspired the great thinkers? We have to go to the consideration of part-objects and part-subjects. The mouth, the primary/primordial cavity, as Spitz (1965) has called it, is the first place where the baby localizes his experiences. These consist of experiences coming from inside and outside. His object is the breast–nipple. The relation between the subject–mouth and the object–breast is confused. There is no distinct difference as to which part possesses which characteristics. It is also an enduring, nearly permanent relationship in the unconscious, an imprint. We know that some of these part-objects develop an equivalence and identification with each other through displacement and substitution. Mouth, anus, vagina, breast, faeces, penis, baby are exchangeable in their characteristics and functions; they can even become pathologically strictly identified.

It is obvious that satisfactory functioning of the vagina will have to be preceded by satisfactory functioning of the mouth and the anus in relation to their object. In this way the penis-as-breast will be well received by the vagina-as-mouth, and thus one could talk of a psychology of the vagina.

As Melanie Klein has so well put it, as I said before, the universe of the child is the womb of her mother. In this so important and mysterious inner place are all the good and bad objects of early childhood.

I have become more and more convinced that in every analysis one has to arrive at the body-self if one wants to achieve deep and enduring change. One of the various manifestations of this body-self is its relationship with claustrophobia and agoraphobia. Claustrophobic space is the result of projective identification of the body and its inner space into the outside world. Agoraphobic space is the space exterior to the body. It is therefore the child inside the mother's body who becomes claustrophobic inside the inner space of his mother projected into the outside world. The child becomes agoraphobic when he leaves the mother's womb. I am referring to the trauma of birth, relived in ordinary life in the containing spaces formed by projective identifications. When the child, and later the neurotic, psychotic or even the normal adult, sends objects out of his own inner space, such as a sound out of his mouth, or vomit, or faeces or urine, this exit of objects from his inner space will revive the person's experience of his own exit from his original container, the womb of mother. This experience of exit with his objects is probably projective identification with the departing objects. The phobic panic state arises from the time of the original (birth) anxiety when the ego was more or less non-existent. When there is regression to that phobic panic state, the functions of the adult ego are paralysed and are no longer at the disposal of the patient to help him to reflect on his anxiety. One could almost say that this is an organic memory or imprint of the birth experience and not only a psychological memory. It is in the psychoanalysis or psychotherapy of schizoid personalities and schizophrenics that claustrophobia and agoraphobia are found in their maximum manifestations.

After having understood this for years, it was with astonishment that I discovered the same link with introjected objects. In anorexia it is not only the breast of the mother or the penis of the father which is projected into the food and introjected, but also the baby itself. He becomes phobic in the mother – this means in her inner space – and in danger of persecution by bad inner objects. The state of the inner space and the good and bad objects which are inside it and the relationships developed between them are of central importance.

All these syndromes are doubtless more definite, more manifest, more spontaneously addressed in women than in men. But when he reaches the genital phase the man may not succeed in achieving complete denial of his pregenital inner space by the use of his penis. In this case he will experience the phobic anxiety of being in contact with the inner space of the woman made bad through projective identification of his own bad inner space, through the expulsion of his bad objects during orgasm into the inner space of the woman. In entering the woman's inner space in orgasm, he is identified with the baby–foetus and the contents of his own body, his faeces, for example.

I shall briefly consider the evolution of the concept of inner space in its progression from the pregenital to the genital. If everything goes well, the female inner space will be considered by the woman as satisfactory for introjection for her relationship with the foetus and with the penis. In the same way, the projection of her inner space into the outside world will enable the woman to move in a satisfying way in the outside world space. This woman will never be a phallic woman.

But if the woman's organization of the external world is based on a rigid projection of her internal world, feared and detested, full of bad objects, it will not be possible for her to create for herself or for others, whether for the family or her work, a milieu which is pleasant and facilitating. Even her appearance, her way of dressing, for example, is going to reflect these aspects of her internal world. Either there is an accord or mirroring between good or bad internal world and being well or badly dressed, or the woman makes an effort to be well dressed in order to hide the bad internal state, and thus she feels false and artificial. We know to what extent the mood of depressives can make itself felt by their way of dressing, by the state of their house or of their work.

A woman in treatment with me was obsessed with the bad state of her internal world. She had a series of dreams where she redecorated each room of the house, one by one, the last being the dining-room. Later her husband gave her a present of a magnificent fur coat. She then became very preoccupied with the necessity of transforming herself in order to be in keeping with her fur coat.

If, on the contrary, the bad inner space of a woman is dominating, then in a way similar to man she will try to deny the functions of this space through the phantasied possession of the penis. If the remaining bad inner space belongs to the paranoid-schizoid phase, the defence, using the phantasy penis, will be to avoid the anxiety of fragmentation and dissolution of the self. If the inner space belongs to the depressive position, the penis will be used as a manic defence against depression. Identification with the 'magic penis' may be the centre of a manic state. This state will be centred on the desire to possess a penis which permits denial of everything one cannot face. This is a pseudo-reparative penis which keeps the self from making use of the real functions of the penis, which are not only to provide pleasure but also to serve as a bridge between subject and object. These are the functions of a creative and truly reparative penis. A too-strong attachment, a too-deep fixation to the pseudo-penis does not allow the woman to resolve her Oedipus complex. When attachment to the pseudo-penis is vital, in view of her anxiety located in her bad inner space, the woman cannot develop an identification with the female functions.

Here I should like to allude to the importance of our third biological postulate, the menstrual cycle. If we consider the female cycle as a psycho-biological recapitulation of the period of female development, we can see how important it is not to ignore this factor. Unless a woman has attained a perfect psycho-homoeostatic balance, she will be at certain moments of her cycle more prone to some pregenital phantasies than at others. These cannot but influence her sexual and other behaviour. The phantasies during the premenstrual syndrome or menstruation illustrate how there are different phantasies at different times of the cycle.

We can now address the problem of the female orgasm. The point of departure of orgasm is a frontier zone between exterior and interior, between physical and mental. It would be absurd for psychoanalysts to ignore this fact. It needs the participation of the body and the mind in order to reach a satisfying orgasm. The physical female genital organ, the combination of the vagina–clitoris, needs to be capable of its functions as far as anatomy, physiology and hormones are concerned. In addition, the hormonal state can influence the fantasies of the moment, phantasies which themselves depend on the whole evolution of the phantasies of the person in question. Those phantasies in return can support or paralyse the functioning of the female organ.

We are still more or less at the same mysterious leap between the mental and the physical that Freud described. We have to explain what happens at the frontier between the physical and the mental when sexual tension increases locally. Let us take an example. A young pseudo-hermaphrodite has a dream where, in order to decide if she is male or female, she is going to toss a coin. She tosses the coin but it falls into a vertical position, neither heads nor tails. Here we have to consider all the possible solutions between the two extreme positions, heads or tails. One possibility is that the coin becomes fixed on the border or frontier between the two positions. On the other hand, we can imagine the coin endlessly oscillating between heads and tails, tails and heads, and the speed of the oscillation could be such that the coin could appear vertical while actually being in both states, both male and female, as an indicator of the identity choice.

A patient reported the following dream:

I am drinking with friends, I get up from the table. I am thirsty and I start drinking. I realize that the bottle I am drinking from has the neck of a feeding bottle; there is no teat but I can feel the rim which usually holds the teat. While thinking of this, I see the bottle more clearly. I hold it in

front of me and see that it has the shape of a baby's bottle. In the bottle I
see water. The level of the water falls and bubbles rise through the liquid.
I am aware that there is water which is becoming part of me; but this
something, which is part of me, I cannot feel. I am worried because I can
neither understand nor feel the water passing from being separate to
becoming an intimate part of me. As I am thinking this, the bottle becomes
bigger. Then I see that on the side of the bottle facing me, that is to say,
the internal bit, there is inscribed, in embossed letters on the surface,
instructions for weaning a baby.

This dream permits an analysis of certain aspects of frontier states, and I will
consider it only from this point of view. The person in the dream is having
three experiences; first, the liquid exterior to him, then the liquid which is
part of him, but also there is the experience of not having the experience,
that is to say, a non-experience, the frontier state between outside and inside,
between not-self and self, between the physical state and the mental state.
So we know what is missing: it is the experience in the mouth, the memory
or representation of water in the mouth, the primary cavity or frontier
between external space and internal space, yet part of both. The mouth is
also the frontier between sensation, that is to say, physical sensation and its
mental representation. The transformation, the bridge, is missing. This
evokes the idea of Winnicott's transitional experience, but it is missing.

If we translate such a mouth into a vagina and repeat the experience with
the penis, one can imagine the problems which follow from the sexual point
of view. It is also possible to imagine a series of permutations and combinations of what can happen in the mouth, that is, sensation without transformation into the area of phantasy; or the reverse, phantasy but deception in the
area of sensation.

Now we must not neglect the domain of part-states, or the psychology of
part-states and the problem of the 'magnitudes' and of the relation of the
part to the whole. The concept of part-objects, which originated with Freud,
even if indirectly, had been developed further by Karl Abraham and finally
achieved its peak with Melanie Klein. Here I want to consider the consequences of the equation: the part is equal to the whole.

Part of the body-self, the mouth, considered as a nucleus of the self, is a
centre which can expand and join up with the circumference, that is to say,
with the boundary, of all the self. The whole self is contained in the mouth
and, by displacement and projective identification, with other part-centres,
such as the anus and vagina. The mouth contains the whole self at a certain
stage of development.

When a child, or the unconscious, or the neurotic, or the psychotic treats
a part as being equal to the whole, he may be applying the laws of infinite
sets. There are many examples. For the baby, the mouth at a certain moment
can be his whole self in becoming identical with the infinite whole, that is

to say, identical with all that there is. Similarly the breast becomes a whole mother, and the inner space becomes the whole universe. Applying this to orgasm we now have the best way of describing the build-up of sexual tension expanding into the whole being and finally replacing everything while acquiring an infinite magnitude. Narcissistic anger is another example. The pre-orgasmic state of sexual tension is made up of a number of components; a localized sensation which expands and irradiates, a consciousness of the sexual object or partner, and the phantasy system which contributes to the creation of tension. This is a frontier or borderline state. But at a certain moment there is no orgasmic state, that is to say, a part occupies the whole. There is no longer any boundary, any separate part, but only a whole.

Here is an example which relates to the female orgasm, the space in which it takes place and its relationship with the child and the mother. A young mother of twenty-eight who had been married for five and a half years, felt criticized by everyone, whatever the circumstances and whoever it was. She often had attacks of extreme tension when she felt that she was going to expel from herself everything that caused this internal tension. She felt herself ready to scream, to attack someone and in reality to knock that person flat out.

Her father was a schizophrenic, and her parents had violent quarrels caused by her father's violence and by his eccentricities. Yet she loved him greatly because he was good and kind to her on occasions, and she spoke of him nostalgically. One day when she was eight years old her mother told her without explanation that her father had gone and that she would never see him again. In fact, she never saw him again.

She felt that her explosive tensions, even if not caused, at least had been made conscious and magnified, by the fact that she thought her husband, because of his studies, had made her delay fulfilling her wish to have a baby. It was him who was the object of these explosions. For a year they had been trying to conceive, and she thought that their lack of success was due to her state of mind, her resentment of her husband. This was very unfavourable for conception, she said. We were talking of her sexual relationship with her husband; she said that it was excellent but that since she had been having these feelings it sometimes happened that she had excellent sex with an extremely satisfying orgasm and that on other occasions she provoked him sexually and then lost all interest, perhaps in order to punish him.

As we proceeded, I asked her, 'When you want to make love and to have an orgasm, have you any thoughts or phantasies which help?' She smiled – she had a very sweet, nostalgic smile – and said, 'I am in a place; the ideal of a place comes to mind.' I asked for a few more details. 'No, there is nothing except a place; yes, a place.' Then she reflected and said, 'A place, perhaps there is someone there, but in any case I never find anyone. It is a place like Greenwich, you know, the Cutty-Sark' (the Cutty Sark is one of the most famous English sailing ships from the time of grain and tea trading, and which is in dry dock and available for visiting.) I indicated that I understood.

A little later I asked her how she was sleeping and if there were any ideas which helped her to get to sleep. Smiling, she said, 'The same thoughts.' I asked, does she dream? She said yes. She told this dream: she is facing a tunnel and is holding a knife and looking for her grandmother but she never attacks her. For the second time the symbolism of the mother-ship returned. I should add that in her attacks of mad tension she wanted the presence of someone who will calm and reassure her. Narcissistic rage equals separation; orgasm equals reunion with the mother, dissolution of the object and universal unity.

Here is now the case in more detail of a woman who illustrates the fundamental role of her phantasies about her inner space, the state of its objects, its role, its badness and its goodness. Her parents were immigrants and she came with them to Britain as a little girl. She was a highly intelligent woman, with extremely high ideals, but at the same time convinced and despairing of the terrible state of her own inner space and its relation to that of her mother. Her efforts to repair that state at the same time met with horror at the incapacity to do so. It will be seen how in the course of her analysis she experienced immense distress connected with primitive processes of destructive and intrusive identification into the mother's body, of whom she was herself part of its content.

By the end of the analysis she had made such remarkable progress that she became able to undertake considerable responsibility in her work life and since then has been very successful. It was only her courage and high intelligence that enabled her to make contact with these powerful destructive phantasies that had marred her life. That patient's life was dominated by an extraordinary desire to penetrate her mother's body, not only to find herself there but also to discover something in her mother's body, without knowing what that something might be.

She hated her mother and would have wanted to be completely different from her, but she thought, with rage, shame and despair, that she was becoming more and more like her mother. From the beginning of the analysis she wanted to know everything about the analyst's private life, to penetrate into it completely both emotionally and physically. She roamed night and day round his home trying to see inside by looking through the keyhole. She would intrude in another way by telephoning without speaking. In addition, when there was no reply she would let the telephone ring, falling asleep while listening to it ringing in his house.

She was totally ashamed of herself. If anything humiliated her, she would then become immensely enraged. If her main thought was threatened, she would humiliate anyone she thought had humiliated her. Each session was for her a humiliation because she felt the analyst threw her out without any more ado at the end of the session. Despite being extremely intelligent, she wanted to be not only mentally part of him, but to be physically inside him as well. She stated that she and her analyst should become one being, body and spirit.

Her father, who was dead, had been a very angry and violent man. Although she hated her father, it was really her mother who was her *bête noire*. The mother increasingly came to her mind. Although she would have wanted to see her disappear, the patient could not leave her mother alone for long. When she visited her mother she had the obsessive idea of rummaging through her drawers, sideboards, chests, from which she would take out everything she could find. She would then clean them and put them back, putting the objects in order while looking for something she never found.

All that activity humiliated her deeply, but she could not stop herself from doing it. She felt humiliated by everyone, lived in shame and wished unendingly to revenge herself by trying to shame others and by highlighting their faults and errors. She did the same thing with other people with whom she had had anything to do, for example people at work.

Although she was a pretty woman, quite normal physically, she felt dirty, repugnant, nauseous. She had made a split in her body image, speaking at times of the horrible state of her interior, disgusting, full of bad things, polluted and polluting, then, almost simultaneously, she would say that she was pure, that she had absolutely no natural needs, and demanded that I believe her.

She felt her genitals were disgusting, as was the sexual act. The penis was experienced as the giver of shame. She was married, but was refusing to have a child. For her, being pregnant was a shameful state – to become pregnant would be to proclaim that she had committed a shameful act. There was no difference between being pregnant and being full of something horrible.

The opposite of this state was the state of original purity and union with the mother. The loss of this state of purity was for her terrible. She said nothing would prevent her from finding that state of union again through forcing herself into others in order to retrieve what she had lost. For her, knowledge meant knowing the interior of the body of the mother, but through her intuitive curiosity she could find nothing good, only repugnant objects.

It was difficult to understand why she always had the same way of responding to the analyst's interpretations. If something she had said was interpreted she would always say that she had not said it. Then the analyst repeated what she had said, and then she was in agreement that he had understood well. He would then say to her that what she had just said also had another meaning which he interpreted. She would then inevitably respond that she had not made the original statement. It was only much later and after different interpretations of this behaviour that the analyst understood what was happening. When he repeated what she said then she and the analyst became one sole person. When he did not repeat her words exactly and instead interpreted, that made them two persons. At this moment she would reproach him vehemently for not loving her, for not letting her penetrate into him in order to stay and live in total love, in a perfect union.

It was after many years of analysis that she remembered that she had slept in the same room as her parents until the age of at least three or four. The reverse of her frantic search to know the interior of her mother was a morbid fear and a terrible shame that one could know her own interior, be it the sordidness contained in her body, be it the interior of her flat, or be it the interior of her thoughts. She saw eyes everywhere which penetrated within and without, and she thought that she could hide nothing from anyone, to her great shame and humiliation. Very probably she experienced a primitive identification with the interior of the mother in a bad state, for which she felt responsible.

There was a similarity in the pattern of the woman's phantasies of her own internal space, of that of her mother and probably of that of the majority of women. Only some women came up to her ideal of purity and dignity. If they did, she admired them and then felt the need enviously to attack them. This vicious humiliating–humiliated circle forced her into a completely sado-masochistic form of reparation.

Her only possibility of feeling alive was when another was being humiliated, shamed, incompetent, hopeless. At this moment she, by contrast, was able to feel complete, whole, capable and even compassionate. She could then care for and repair the victim.

From the beginning she decided that the analyst was incapable, incompetent, in a state of depression, helpless, homosexual, desperate. She then became the one who was going to transform him, introduce him to life. The non-realization of her wishes and phantasies made her feel inferior, good for nothing, hopeless. At this point, in a narcissistic rage, she sought revenge. She also used the feeling of shame and humiliation in order to deny her feelings of guilt.

However, as was mentioned at the beginning of describing her treatment, this woman had an immense determination to achieve reparation of herself and of her objects. There was a constant conflict between her bad and good impulses. At the start of the treatment every impulse met with its opposite, and it was too often the destructive impulse that won. But as the treatment proceeded she became more and more conscious of her phantasies and behaviour. Also her determination to change showed her courage and determination to succeed, which she did. The description of this powerful task is evident of the struggle and, happily, of its good ending.

In view of the fact that the mechanisms and structures which underpin female sexuality described in this paper are confined to the preverbal stage, it is possible that their relationship with adult femininity is not at first evident. Yet if we accept that the exterior world and the interior world influence each other reciprocally, it becomes clear that the manner in which the woman behaves in the external world will depend on the objects in the internal world with which she identifies and projects into the external world. The pattern of her external world relationships also determines to a certain degree the fixedness and immutability of this inner world. In order to be a woman, it is necessary to find pleasure in being penetrated and in containing an object sexually and maternally within her own body. She must feel pleasure in feeding and giving. In the symbolic world this will then generate the possibility of feeling that the qualities arising from her primitive structures are intrinsic, valuable and desirable outside in her social context.

Intelligence will be intelligence in its own right, feminine or masculine; feminine creativity will have its own rights alongside masculine creativity; male/female relationships will not depend any more on the axis superior-inferior; and differences will be able to be accepted as both desirable and complementary.

SUMMARY

Here is a short summary of what I have presented to you. Sexuality is essentially a frontier state between the biological and psychological. The internal space, the primordial inner space, continues existing at the frontier of psychic representation, perhaps one could say the preconscious. It almost retains three-dimensional characteristics. This space possesses entry and exit; mouth, anus, vagina.

The development of inner space varies in men and women. The mouth and the anus have in part the same relationships with the inner space and its objects in both sexes during the pregenital phase. But with the boy the penis – the exterior object – among its different functions serves fundamentally to obliterate the importance of his own personal inner space as far as adult genital functioning is concerned. He does have to contend, however, with the inner space of the woman as well as that of his internal mother. In contrast, the woman's inner space acquires increasing importance from the genital point of view. The genital organ, vagina–clitoris, replaces the mouth as entry point to the inner space. The penis replaces the breast, the foetus replaces food in its various forms.

In an intermediate phase, anus and excrement as well as the urethra and urine have played their role as transitional elements. Fixation at the anal stage and the urinary function will give a special excremental sense to the menstrual loss of blood, to pregnancy and to birth.

If her inner space continues existing as a bad space with bad inner objects, the woman's fear of castration will remain dominant. The need for a 'magic penis' will arise, and hence envy of the penis will be a necessity. Vaginal–clitoral sensations will be felt as being bad, dangerous and undesirable because the pleasure could invite and encourage an encounter with the bad inner space and its bad objects. Orgasm would have an expelling quality towards the pregenital inner objects. Confusion of orifices and sphincters would bring a fear of a simultaneous discharge from all the orifices, as in an epileptic fit.

In addition, pregenital conflicts such as oral, anal, urethral, muscular aggression would be stimulated and would endanger the life of the loved object. Feelings of shame and guilt would be exacerbated. The potential dissolving capacity of orgasm in regard to the ego, instead of being ecstasy would become a loss of the ego/self, with resulting panic. Loss of feeling and frigidity then become an essential defence. Masturbation becomes the only possible substitute, a total renunciation of all sexual experiences with a partner.

It would seem that splitting must play an important role in male and female sexuality because it is almost impossible to predict whether a schizoid person will be orgasmic, impotent or frigid. The same applies to the obsessional or the hysteric. In contrast, for the schizoid person, whether impotent or orgasmic, sexual identity will inevitably present problems of indetermination, doubts and confusion.

The bad state of the inner space in certain conditions corresponds to the depressive state and to the introjection of objects in a bad state. The penis can then play a role which is either manic, involving denial and pseudo-reparation, or the penis can have a role that is truly creative and reparative.

I have mainly talked about the first months of the life of the infant, of this preverbal period when the infant, with the unconscious structures that Freud has discovered, constructs his inner world with the given facts of his body and those of his external world. The woman who has added to the great discovery of this man of genius is Melanie Klein. It is sometimes a terrifying world, this infantile world which the infant creates with the good and bad experiences of the environment. One could say he creates his heaven and his hell, his angels and his devils. But it is not only a sadistic and frightening world but also one that has strength in its compassion. This compassion comes with the depressive position and will continue to develop during life if all goes well, that is to say, if the processes that we have described are not too disrupted at the beginning of life.

17 Awake, Going to Sleep, Asleep, Dreaming, Awaking, Awake: Comments on W. Clifford M. Scott

PART I

These are a few thoughts that came to mind on reading Clifford Scott's paper on 'Repairing broken links between the unconscious, sleep and instinct; and conscious, waking and instinct' (1988). It is not intended to take up his thoughts, but just to give way to some free associations – perhaps not so free.

Scott wishes to consider the consequences of approaching sleep as an instinct. He discovers after many years of having such preoccupations that the thought had come to Freud in his eighty-second year, as expressed in his *An Outline of Psycho-Analysis* (1940). What I wish to daydream about are principally the relations he makes between 'becoming conscious and waking', 'becoming unconscious and going to sleep'; and modern views of 'partly awake', 'partly asleep'.

However, I would like in the first place to consider what kind of ideas come to mind when trying to define sleep as an instinct. There is an admirable summing-up in a few paragraphs of the present status of instinct theory by Tinbergen, Nobel Laureate in physiology, in *The Fontana Dictionary of Modern Thought* (1988). However, they are not views that take into account psychological necessities. I shall therefore consider what Lawrence Kubie has to say in his no-less admirable paper on 'Instincts and homeostasis' (1958). In that paper Kubie suggests that an instinct or drive (Scott prefers instinct) consists of a biochemical substrate, a neuronal net and a psychological superstructure in search of an object that satisfies the need of the 'instinctual drive'. (In all my researches on psychophysical relationships this formulation has been the most helpful and guiding principle to co-ordinate data referring to behaviour belonging to both the physiological and the representational world, conscious and unconscious, including the phantasy world and the world of inner and external objects. At one end of the spectrum physiological needs will dominate instinctual activity, and at the other end it will be the psychological needs.)

I would like to give a few thoughts to some of the activities of sleeping and waking in this model. Sleeping is necessary from the physiological point of view in order to repair a large number of body activities. There is no need to pinpoint them except as to the brain, since the psychological aspects are directly related to the brain's good maintenance. Thus, the instincts maintain physiological aims, that is, objects in good order in sleep. And now, in sleep, what is it that happens to a person's psychological aims or objects? Due to Freud's genius we know that psychological aims, objects of the instinct, are most active in sleep but they are of a different kind from the object-seeking activity of the waking state. Objects of the waking state and of the sleeping state, though not totally different, do differ in important aspects.

It may be interesting to see if one can apply ideas of waking and sleeping to dream-objects and inner objects. The rest of these reflections will be devoted to those very points. Before that, there is a most controversial consideration to mention. It is that of primary narcissism. That implies a phase of existence at the beginning of life where the subject has no psychological object except him- or herself. There are no 'others'. Sleep is given as an example. If in sleep the dreamer can return to a state of primary narcissism, it would have to be in a phase of sleep where dream content contains no object other than the dreamer. Awaking people in all phases of sleep shows dream-objects existing. Only if the dreamer in the dream cannot distinguish between himself and his dream-objects could one talk of fusion, but this is not primary narcissism.

A few considerations must be introduced here before going further. There can be no doubt that the immense progress made in the observation of the newborn and of the infant in its first days, weeks and months has demonstrated unequivocally that the infant is endowed with unthought-of capacities for being aware of objects of the external world (for instance, Stern, 1985). However, if one talks of 'fusion' between the infant and external objects, then I think it would be far better to go on applying to the problem the ideas of falling asleep and waking up. Scott mentions in his paper that 'sleep–wake problems' relate to 'descriptions of being partly awake' when asleep; and partly asleep while awake. Partly awake means partly obeying the laws of the system *Cs.*, that is, for Freud, secondary processes, and partly asleep means partly obeying the laws of the system *Ucs.*, that is, primary processes. As Freud has remarked, it would be difficult to imagine a human being living only according to primary processes. In a recent book, Matte-Blanco (1988) has considered the problem in all sorts of mental states in terms of the proportion of what he calls 'symmetrical' (system *Ucs.*) and 'asymmetrical' (system *Cs.*) thinking. That would eliminate the controversy about objectless states, primary narcissism and fusion states, for it would mean considering how much of the one or the other is present.

It is not possible to leave that subject without considering what, in terms of object relationships and in terms of an instinct, leads a person to go to sleep and to wake up.

At a most basic level one can say that one cannot survive without waking up because of the need for the help of the external world. Thus newborn babies could go on sleeping for ever if they did not have to drink or eat. They have no access to fluid or food except through an external object. And to take milk, for instance, they have to be sufficiently awake to be able to suck. In order to function to survive when awake, babies must go to sleep to repair all sorts of processes needed to be awake. It is remarkable that, although not having to feed through the mouth *in utero*, the foetus sucks or learns to suck his thumb and to swallow some meconium, presumably to be ready to do so when severed from the placenta and the uterine mother. I unfortunately do not know when the foetus sucks his thumb in relationship to sleep cycles *in utero*, that is, at what stage of pregnancy.

At *no time*, including *in utero*, is there only *one* kind of object relationship. There seems to be, rather, a varying proportion of whatever waking and sleeping object relationships are considered to be.

Still on the subject of sleep as instinct, there is yet to be considered one of the possible 'aims' of the wish for and satisfaction from sleep. Freud considered dreaming as wish-fulfilment, the Freudian wish. This has been the subject of innumerable discussions and arguments. Some dreams, in spite of a lot of intellectual gymnastics, will not fit in. Perhaps, then, they are failed attempts at wish-fulfilment? However, the very title of Scott's paper possibly gives a clue! 'Repairing broken links . . .' In the paper on reparation (see Chapter 13) I have considered the problem of reparation in dreams, as well as in other papers. Perhaps the wish for us to reflect upon is the wish to repair, for that is the function of sleep as instinct – biological, concrete repair. It follows that its psychic counterpart is the function of psychic reparation, at least so it could be thought from Scott's use of the word 'repairing'.

In the state of dreaming in the REM phase, the brain is neither in the fully asleep state nor fully in the waking state. There is a tendency nowadays to consider this paradoxical phase as belonging more to the waking state (Freud's *Pcs.*). Dreaming activity belongs to the representational function although it gives an experience of external perceptual quality to the dreamer. Could one say 'virtual' perceptual quality?

The dream uses information received from the external world during the waking state – at least in part. Then the dream functions (dream-work?) use this information – or day residues – and transform it into a scenario that is dream imagination or unconscious phantasy. Thus a piece of the external world has been taken in, or introjected and assimilated, that is, transformed into a phantasy system of the inner world.

Similarly, after waking up, night-dream or sleep residues find their way into the waking phantasies and information from the external world. They influence the way the external information is interpreted (Scott's 'night residues'). Thus we have here the basis for the more or less exact way that introjective and projective identification work.

This also sheds some light not only on how inside is *transferred* outside and vice versa. During certain phases of sleep, external perceptual information being abolished, memories of those external bits of information can be considered, because of lack of external reality-testing, as material that can be manipulated, used, transformed by certain mechanisms and according to the laws of the system *Ucs*. After being thus transformed and having acquired a sense of perceptual reality, the dream information, as dream or sleep residue, influences and becomes part of the system through which the information from the external world is interpreted in the waking state by the 'conscious mind'.

It may be necessary here to define in one way or another Kleinian inner objects. They are successors to the imago concept but have become endowed with life, sensation, activity and other characteristics of living objects, although also representations. They are nuclei of memories, affective, sensory and structural, distinguishable from other such nuclei, and between themselves they have intrapsychic relationships. I myself consider that such 'nuclei' have a structure that possesses a biochemical substrate, a neuronal net and a psychological superstructure.

They can be affected at all three levels. It would be necessary to compare the above definition with the question of how to define a dream-object. In part the same consideration applies but there is the engima with regard to the source of the images used by the dreamer of the dream, which can be totally different from all that we know of in the external world of perception. Where do they come from? There is no answer. Freud writes: 'Where do all the patients get the frightful perverse details which are often as remote from their experiences as from their knowledge!' (1895).

If we start with dream-objects, could we say that they seem to awaken when a person goes to sleep? So when a person goes to sleep a part of his mind awakes. During that 'dreaming-awakeness', dream-objects are liberated from the laws of consciousness or of the external world, or of physics, for example, laws of time or of gravity. Then they can indulge in elaborate scenarios or even in a kind of science fiction, but according to the laws that Freud describes. When the dreamer awakes to the external world can one say that dream-objects go to sleep? And when asleep do they dream?

Do they dream? A question of a rhetorical nature and probably impossible to answer. But we know what might be Freud's answer. The relationship between sleeping, dream-objects and waking dream-objects should be a dynamic one. That means that their respective activity is maintained in various proportions, which implies a tendency, as for all living structures, to attempt to teach their aims. Therefore there must be either a struggle or, vice versa, a cohesion of efforts between dream-objects awake and dream-objects asleep. Those levels of activity of dream-objects awake and dream-objects asleep must therefore reach and influence, through the concept of sleep residues, consciously awake relationships of the subject with the external world but at different levels. This is the opposite condition from that described by analogy to a static theory of non-dynamic schemata made visible by a ray of light illuminating this area, or that other view rejected by Piaget (the metaphor is his) in connection with his idea of how structures move to a higher, more sophisticated level of functioning. (The schemata of Piaget are more static than Freudian ones, but they nevertheless imply a dynamic restructuration from one level to another.)

How are we to begin to deal with internal objects awake and asleep? I think that a great deal of what has been said about dream-objects applies to internal objects. However, there are also differences. It seems that internal objects do not have those mysterious qualities and appearances mentioned earlier and coming from nowhere we know, which dream-objects have. They are much more dependent on characteristics of external-world objects for their make-up, although, as mentioned before, by projective identification they contain contributions from the mysterious inner images, themselves strongly modified in turn by the images or bits of information coming from the external world. The correspondences and similarities between internal and external objects are much more powerful than those between external objects and dream-objects. The internal objects contain more of the external world data and information.

So when the external world goes to sleep it is possible that the external-world part of the internal object also goes to sleep, and the internal object takes on a greater resemblance to the dream-object. It is difficult to say if it becomes the dream-object. When the dreamer awakes, then the internal object regains the influence of its external-object part and function. Thus the relationship between internal objects and dream-objects is a very complex one and made more complicated by the waking–sleeping–waking cycle.

And now, what is it that happens to ego, super-ego and id in that sleep–waking cycle? In some way all three structures are internal objects to the self but they constitute the I, the me; all the other internal objects are external to them, though within the self. The problem as to what introjects, or characteristics of introjects, go to contribute to the construction of ego and super-ego, respectively, has always been most perplexing to psycho-analysts (Heimann, 1952). However, at least ego and super-ego must have similarities with the characteristics of inner objects and dream-objects just described when we come to consider ego and super-ego going to sleep and waking up. The ego, being the self-structure in charge of assessing the relationship of self to the external world, contains in its make-up more of the information about the external world and has the greatest epistemophilic drive. When one goes to sleep it would seem that the dream-ego 'awakes' or becomes dominant and then treats the material available to it according to what are called the laws of the system *Ucs*. However, as mentioned earlier, Freud has pointed out that it is not possible to imagine anybody existing on the primary processes only. Thus, even the dream-ego asleep uses a mixture of primary and secondary processes, or internal and external worlds, in varying proportions. (Within his own terminology, as mentioned earlier, Matte-Blanco has dealt extensively with the varying proportions of the two systems in psychic activity in terms of 'symmetry' and 'asymmetry' in feeling and thinking.)

Similar considerations apply to the super-ego; however, the super-ego, being a structure that differs fundamentally from the ego as to the epistemophilic function, probably has a different sleep–waking cycle. I do not know quite how to tackle the problem. When the part of the super-ego deriving from the external world goes to sleep, what kind of super-ego is left?

Freudian and Kleinian answers must be very different, and only a close study of super-ego function during dreaming can provide material for an answer. However, if we consider the primitive super-ego of Klein, we know that she considers the role of early good and bad introjects, or good and bad internal objects, as playing a fundamental role in super-ego functions. It may be that, when the structures belonging to the later super-ego – that part which is more conscious, more external-reality adapted, if not more reasonable – go to sleep, then the primitive super-ego, good and bad inner objects, remain or become awake, and thus reveal the primitive aspects of the super-ego. There must be, therefore, not only a struggle between super-ego and ego, but also between parts of the super-ego in its hierarchical organization. Somewhere the id is in contact with the somatic processes from which it derives instinctual urges and to which it gives mental expression. This has been dealt with in this essay using Kubie's model (1958). Becoming aware of instinctual needs can only be via the phantasy systems while awake and asleep; and the concept has been thoroughly developed earlier. Needless to add here that Freud's structural model implies a varying kind of relationship between id, ego and super-ego in the varying proportions of their characteristics that will be present and active in the partly awake, partly asleep, states.

Then, considering the Kleinian model of the paranoid-schizoid and depressive positions, it has long been the way of thinking of Kleinian analysts to consider how much a piece of behaviour or mental state is influenced by each system respectively. So, applying Scott's thinking, we have to assess how much paranoid-schizoid thinking is nearer to partly asleep and dreaming-thinking than is that of the depressive position. Many comparative references have been made in the literature to paranoid-schizoid mechanisms and primary processes. All this cannot be dealt with here, but what has been written here about inner objects and dream is fully relevant to this question.

I have dealt extensively, theoretically and clinically, with the problem of how much of the paranoid-schizoid and of the depressive position structures were present in the dreams of a schizophrenic patient, how these related to his internal interpretation of the external world, and, above all, how the working through from the paranoid-schizoid position to the depressive position was carried on in the patient's dreams.

However, I wish to stress the fact that, since reading Scott's thorough investigation of sleep and waking and going to sleep in his 1975 paper, I have systematically investigated the technique of first finding out how patients prepare to go to sleep, how they wake up and behave subsequently, and how, in between, they have slept and dreamt. It is simply amazing how much more one learns that way; abundant information comes to light about behaviour and phantasy and dream-life. This is the way, *par excellence*, to use Scott's terminology: broken links between awake, asleep, dreaming and awaking are repaired; continuity of meaning is restored.

I will give a short example of a patient whom I saw in an interview many years ago, only once, but who has remained in my mind ever since. I am quoting from memory. He was a young man of about twenty and said to be a brilliant medical student. He was found lying in snow, in the midst of a snowstorm, some miles outside Quebec City. He was taken to hospital and diagnosed as living a schizophrenic episode. He felt inspired by God to undertake a religious mission that demanded that he walk from Quebec to Montreal in the freezing weather, lightly dressed, but protected by the divine power. I was asked to interview him. I will relate only the following. The patient was a nice young man and he had no difficulty in talking. As part of the interview, at one point I asked him to tell me how he prepared to go to bed and to sleep. He said that he undressed and went to bed without clothes. I then asked in what position he waited for sleep to come. He said it was on the side (I cannot remember which side) with the knees bent. As he said that, he had a little, gentle, nostalgic smile on his face and he added, 'just like a foetus'. Asked how he slept, he said he remembered one dream. There was a lovely blue sky and a nice warm sun. Then I said, 'How do you wake up, and with what thoughts?' Again the nostalgic little smile, and then he said, 'I go straight to have an ice-cold bath.' I do not remember what was said about his thoughts just before going to sleep and those when waking up, but I think that what I have related is sufficiently clear. In a short moment, in a few words, perhaps the most important aspects of his life had been revealed, and the links between his thoughts and actions repaired and restored.

There remains now to deal with the ultimate point, the ultimate question raised by Dr Scott: the sleep from which no one wakes up. Scott writes:

> This sequence [sleep–dream–waking, etc.] . . . is constantly repeated, until – we hope – we reach a second childhood when, ideally, sleeping and dying become more nearly the same thing, just as we used to feel they were before we discovered that sleep and death could be so different.

Hamlet could not work it out: 'To die, to sleep, perchance to dream.'

There is a good deal of literature nowadays about what children phantasize about death, children who know they are going to die. I am going to mention only death in the unconscious, death in dreams.

I understand that Freud had doubts about being able to dream about one's own death as opposed to the death of others. The death of others is an experience we have in the external world, but not our own. I do not know what difference there is in the mind of an infant, or of a very young child, between absence of an important object in the external world and its reappearance, as compared to the disappearance of such an object for ever. Neither do I know what he feels about the reappearance of an object when he wakes up, or about its absence; or again, for how long a dream-object continues to exist after waking up. I know that babies who do not yet talk are often extraordinarily suspicious when facing somebody not very familiar just after waking up, although they had previously smiled at that person and even played with him. Even then, if the baby is aware of a permanent absence of the 'other', can he imagine his own permanent absence?

And what about the person he or she was in the dream and who has disappeared on waking up? And when he or she falls asleep, what are the thoughts just pre-sleep about who it is one will be in the dream and what objects will be met and in what circumstances and with what consequences? Good dreams, sweet dreams or horrifying nightmares?

I believe I read somewhere that Klein did not agree with Freud about not being able to dream of one's own death. I am not sure. However, as I have pointed out elsewhere, she nearly always says 'dead or dying' about the dream-object. Whatever the answer to this perplexing question, it is certain that someone who is 'dead' at one moment in a dream can be alive at another moment in the same dream. How is all that related to ideas of survival after death?

The above considerations are extremely important with regard to reparation drives; Scott might say *reparation instinct*. In a paper on reparation and one on 'That Which Patients Bring to Analysis' (see Chapters 13, 14), I have stressed again and again the tremendous efforts made by patients (and I suppose by all human beings) to keep alive their internal objects needing and awaiting repair. Are they considered to be asleep and hoping to wake up to salvation and a better life, or for the end to come and to be mourned? The end of all dreams.

POSTSCRIPT

In my presentation to the British Society of 'That Which Patients Bring to Analysis' (1988), I considered analogies between 'tablet potentials', such as sleeping pills and their consequences; an ovum as inner object unfolding; and the potentials of inner objects and dream-objects. I am becoming more and more unable to dismiss thoughts about considering inner objects and dream-objects as a kind of *gene*, as psychic genes, unfolding on another occasion . . .

PART II

Scott writes:

> The polarities of life and death as instincts, and the polarities of waking and sleeping as instincts, were brought home to me a few years ago when I developed cancer of a lung and was lucky to have it successfully removed.

This encourages me to relate a personal experience that I think is relevant to the problem of life and death and of going to sleep, sleeping and waking.

A few years ago I too underwent a very serious heart operation. The risks were very kindly explained to me, and the fact that the statistics were overwhelmingly on the side of success, but I had to consider the possibility that I might die. I underwent the operation, which involved the stopping of the heart and artificial blood circulation. Due to a complication, I had to be returned to the operating theatre before I had recovered from the anaesthetic. When I woke up I was feeling well, and subsequently my heart did very well. However, something else happened. After a day or two I started getting extremely anxious and disturbed when having to go to sleep. Losing 'awakeness', sleeping was no longer resting and then waking to a new day, it was like sinking into darkness and never waking up. I started not wanting to take the usual, traditional sleeping pill at night.

About darkness, I must explain a most important point. Throughout my life I had been used to going to sleep in complete darkness; the slightest light disturbance to the darkness would interfere with sleep. I was born in the tropics where the passage from day to night and vice versa is very, very sharp and quick. And at night, then, in the ward, I was hanging on to the slightest light. Light had come to mean being alive and saved from whatever night, darkness, sleep were.

After a while I noticed something else. There were three patients in the same ward who had kidney trouble, and each of them was on dialysis with a pump working to ensure kidney circulation. More and more my anxiety became linked to the pumps. Finally, I could not bear it any longer and went to the doctor in charge of the ward and said, 'I don't know the explanation, but those pumps are putting me in an awful state; please move me to another ward.' At that point the doctor exclaimed, 'Oh, you are suffering from the heart-pump syndrome.' Leaving many details out, this meant that when my heart was kept stopped for several hours and circulation maintained by a pump, some sort of memory at a most primitive level had been formed and was revived by the kidney pumps when I was falling asleep or knew that I was going into the state of sleep. The reverse of this had happened when I had awoken from the operation: waking meant I was alive. I tested my brain functions to make sure they were preserved and not damaged.

Now, the task is to make some sort of analysis of those experiences. To my knowledge I was not particularly anxious previous to the operation and anaesthetic. During the operation there were two new 'states of body and mind' that have to be considered. One was the absence of sensation, whatever it is, of the beating heart and the other the new sensation of the pump. Whether it was the one or the other or both that were at work in the state of anxiety I do not know. Did the kidney pumps revive the heart-pump experience, or revive the absence of the heartbeat or both? It must be an amazing experience to be without a beating heart, alive and awake. Of course I was asleep with an anaesthetic, not ordinarily sleep, but apparently sufficiently awake – Scott's 'partly awake, partly asleep' – to record the absent heart. Did I also record the darkness in some sort of mysterious way because, later, as I related, I had to cling to some sort of light to help put up with the horrible anxiety? And this for a few months afterwards even when the anxiety had practically disappeared. Now I can sleep with varying degrees of darkness and light (not more than a small degree of light).

I have remembered that round about the 1960s Dr Salk (brother of the poliomyelitis Salk) introduced the metronome to calm anxious babies and send them to sleep. The idea was to re-introduce the mother's heartbeat rhythm by the metronome. Had I not only been deprived of my lifelong comfort, my introjected mother heartbeat, but had it been replaced by a poor substitute mother (although intellectually life-saving), the pump? Further, my new heart, or rather repaired heart, was not beating at the same rate as the old one. I always had a very slow pulse; now my pulse was very fast by comparison. Later, with medication, there was major improvement.

At this point it is time to raise the question of the role of inner objects in the maintenance of normal psychic life. Looked at according to the structure I have suggested for what is called an inner object – biochemical substrate, neuronal net and psychological superstructure, the last level being a nucleus of highly cathected memories – a very important inner object had been disturbed in me, not only at the two physiological levels, biochemical and neuronal, but mightily so at the psychodynamic level.

Since nobody experiences death before dying, and it is only from the death of others that one can try and imagine one's own death, anxiety about death is about what? One aspect at least must or could be about what we imagine is the fate of those who have died. Can one avoid projecting being-alive into the dead and therefore imagining that they could still experience after death what we, being alive, could imagine about dreadful circumstances? Other phantasies, of course, could exist, good ones. But those relevant to anxiety and fear cannot be about a blissful situation. Many thoughts have come to my mind, and out of many considerations I want to choose one which I think is most relevant to psychoanalysis and to treatment.

In several papers I have described claustro- agoraphobia and claustro-agoraphilia as a fundamental, primitive, universal 'position' (for want of a better term, and in no competition with Klein). I refer the reader to those papers. All human beings (and most, if not all, that is alive) come to being from an enclosed space. With birth one escapes, whether wishing it or not, from the original enclosing space. We live in another space then, from which we also come out with death. There is no escape from death; it is the ultimate claustrophobic state for some, and for others (how many?) the ultimate claustro-agoraphiliac state. As described in the above-mentioned papers, all sorts of situations in life acquire symbolically the claustrophobic characteristics. What we project into death must be very dependent on experiences and phantasies about those states. It has been customary for humankind in general and psychoanalysts in particular to phantasize the return to the womb as a state of bliss. I wonder about the origin of this golden-age phantasy. To return to Scott, who quotes Freud: 'We are justified in saying there arises at birth an instinct to return to the intra-uterine life which has been abandoned – an instinct to sleep' (Freud, 1940, p. 166).

Judging from innumerable dreams of innumerable patients, those that are commonly interpreted as return to the womb are, in my view, overwhelmingly claustrophobic and anxiety dreams. Supposing, then, that these could be retrospective projections of later situations, that still leaves the possibility of the original uterine bliss.

I quoted earlier the dream of the young schizophrenic patient, one of the very few dreams of that kind I have come across. There are just as many reasons to think of the discomfort of intra-uterine life as of its bliss.

We will never know for sure what the foetus feels and thinks, but we know he wants to get out and participates actively in the move towards this from the days he starts to kick and to make a space for himself in the uterine wall; to be born he takes up the right position to come out. Thus the 'instinct' to come out of the 'claustro' situation is stronger than the staying in. Further, now that it is known that there is a foetal sleep cycle and a REM phase, with or without dream content, a question without an answer, we have to phantasize the state from which the foetus falls asleep and the state to which he 'wakes up'. I guess it is the beginning of consciousness. But it is dark inside. Outside it is light. Darkness and light, unconscious–conscious, awake, asleep, dreaming, awake. Being born? Re-born? Re-re-born?

18   THE SCAPEGOAT MOTIF IN SOCIETY AND ITS MANIFESTATIONS IN A THERAPEUTIC GROUP

(with F.K. Taylor)

The persecution and massacre of scapegoats have often assumed such epidemic proportions, in both ancient and modern history, that one is tempted to speak of a psychosocial disease with a potentially high mortality rate. Such a disease warrants attention even when it appears in an abortive and relatively harmless form.

In this paper we intend to consider briefly, in the first part, some aspects of the psychological and sociological implications of scapegoat phenomena. In the second part we shall describe the observation of such phenomena in a therapeutic group.

THE PSYCHOGENESIS OF THE NEED FOR SCAPEGOATS

The word 'scapegoat' derives from a religious ceremony which was designed to transfer the guilt of the Jewish people to an animal; in this case, a goat. Other religious cults have known similar practices. Often a human being was chosen as the recipient of the displaced guilt. Anthropologists, moreover, have described many superstitious customs in primitive people which had a similar purpose. The essence of all these procedures was the transfer of guilt by means of a magic rite.

Such procedures have always been closely associated with aggressive and extra-punitive attitudes. In some ancient societies scapegoat ceremonies ended in sacrificial death. It is possible that the notoriety of these homicidal ceremonies has tended to distort the original meaning of the term 'scapegoat'. At least the term is today often loosely applied to denote no more than a whipping-boy on whom angry feelings can be vented when the person who is the legitimate target of anger cannot be openly attacked. A scapegoat, in this truncated sense, is merely the butt of displaced aggression. It is more in keeping with the original purport of the term to define a scapegoat as a person who is made to suffer as a carrier of displaced guilt.

The need for scapegoat victims seems to arise particularly in individuals who are predisposed by an inclination to adopt extra-punitive attitudes to others who are disturbed by an unacknowledged sense of guilt and self-dissatisfaction.

Guilt feelings by themselves are not sufficient to cause desires for a scapegoat victim. They may be resolved in other ways: for example, by repentant acts of reparation and expiation, by increased exertion to overcome failure and incapacity, or by a resigned curbing of aspirations to keep them within attainable bounds. When guilt feelings are combined, however, with extra-punitive propensities, the individual is likely to prefer a self-deceptive projection of guilt to the more painful task of a soul-searching and self-denying ordinance.

The guilt feelings which can give rise to a need for scapegoats in predisposed individuals need not be conscious. Psychoanalytical investigations have acquainted us with the many harmful effects that can spring from the Pandora's Box of unconscious guilt; the need for scapegoat victims can be one of them.

The victim cast for the role of a scapegoat may be an innocent person, who, by misfortune, becomes the target of paranoid vilification; he may be a criminal whose guilt is mainly by the contrivance of others who manoeuvred them into committing wrongs. We might term them 'engineered scapegoats', to have a short label for them. They are made to act as understudies in place of those who dare not assume the role of sinners themselves. Unconscious machinations of this kind on the part of parents may be the cause of some delinquent and criminal careers, as was suggested, for instance, by Ruth S. Eissler (1949).

The scapegoat, whether actually guilty or innocent, whether fully or partially culpable, may be punished with a ferocious severity which only fits the enormity of the projected guilt. But the presence or absence of scapegoat phenomena should not be judged by the degree of vindictiveness manifested in the persecution of the victim. Activities which appear relatively innocuous fall into the same category. The most widespread scapegoat-baiting activity is perhaps the popular pastime of scandalmongering and the gleeful gossip which pillories the real or imagined follies of social superiors. The victims of these activities need suffer no more than the indignity of being judged and found guilty *in absentia*, though their fate may be at times far more painful.

The scapegoat motif may also appear in a form which betrays an awareness of the essential innocence of the victim. Such scapegoats are viewed as martyrs who, while free from guilt, accept the punishment for it. This motif has attained sublime expression in the worship of Jesus as the Redeemer of the guilt of mankind.

The appeal of scapegoat-hunting rests, however, not only on the self-deceptive relief it affords through the callous shifting of a burden of personal guilt and suffering on to other shoulders. It holds out other, and perhaps even more tempting, attractions. The indignation with which the guilt of the scapegoat is condemned inflates narcissistic feelings of self-righteousness and moral superiority. The ego, acting in smug alliance with the super-ego, is furnished with an opportunity of abreacting accumulated spite without the fear of self-condemning scruples. Moreover, under the guise of denouncing sin, the individual can act like a voyeur, probe with scoptophilic eagerness the depravity of the scapegoat's guilt, and perhaps, with a thrill of abhorrence, add embellishments to it in fantasy.

The persecution of scapegoats thus not only frees the predisposed person from an oppressive mood of self-dissatisfaction, it also provides him or her with narcissistic and scoptophilic gratifications, and with opportunities for the self-righteous discharge of aggression and the vicarious savouring of forbidden fruit.

INDIVIDUAL VARIATIONS OF THE NEED FOR SCAPEGOATS

The ease with which individuals resort to the persecution of scapegoats may be presumed to vary according to their extra-punitive tendencies and their degree of unacknowledged self-dissatisfaction. Some indication of this variability seems to be contained in recent studies of 'social attitudes', such as those carried out by Adorno *et al.* in America (1950), and by Eysenck in England (1947, 1951).

The American group of investigators were particularly concerned with the study of a personality type prone to a special kind of scapegoat-formation: the authoritarian, ethnocentric personality characterized by social prejudice against members of other groups, by hostility towards 'moral minorities' (for example, criminals, perverts), and by contempt for the masses. From this American research it appears that the social attitudes of people can be ranged along an 'ethnocentric-liberal' continuum, with scapegoat-baiting tendencies clustering round the ethnocentric pole.

Eysenck's studies of social attitudes seem to supplement the American findings. Using a factor-analytical approach, he obtained two general factors by which social attitudes appear to be independently characterized. One of these factors he termed 'Conservatism-Radicalism'. It has some relation to the 'ethnocentric-liberal' factors of the American authors, though it is less exclusively weighted with scapegoat-baiting tendencies at its conservative pole. The second factor was labelled 'Tendermindedness-Toughmindedness', and it distinguishes those who express hostility to other ethnic groups, and advocate the extinction of life by euthanasia, abortion and compulsory sterilization.

The results of these investigations throw some light on the distribution of scapegoat-baiting propensities in large communities. The American studies were, however, too exclusively concentrated on the characteristics of ethnocentric individuals with their fascist, anti-Semitic, and Negro-baiting leanings.

Eysenck's findings suggest that scapegoat-baiting tendencies are associated primarily with 'toughmindedness', and that the form of scapegoat phenomena may differ according to the 'conservative' or 'radical' attitudes of toughminded people.

It should be noted, however, that these attitude studies were carried out in two democratic communities and with reference to the political and socioeconomic problems of these countries. The question arises whether a comparable investigation of attitudes in population groups of different size, organization, and ideological milieu would have yielded similar attitude factors. It seems to us that the answer should be yes, provided the attitude tests used had a comparable relevance to the problems and ideologies of the particular group under investigation. One would expect to find that the members of any established group differ in their degree of loyalty to the ideals and traditions of their group, so that they could also be ranged along a conservative–radical continuum. Some members will be comparable to those of Eysenck's subjects, who believed in the excellence of the maxim 'My country, right or wrong'; they would stand for the defence and conservation of a stereotyped group concept which they have idealized and idolized. The attitudes of other people will display an iconoclastic bias to tilt against the tyranny of routine conditions and traditional beliefs.

Thus we may assume that in every social group a factor comparable to the 'conservative–radical' factor may be found, indicating varying degrees of loyalty to group ideals. Similarly, the 'tenderminded–toughminded' factor is likely to be present as people are bound to differ with regard to the aggressive and extra-punitive spirit of their social opinions.

These factors would, of course, have validity only with reference to the groups examined. A person belonging to two groups of divergent standards and aims is likely to differ in his or her respective social attitudes to the ideals of either group.

THE SOCIO-GENESIS OF THE NEED FOR SCAPEGOATS

Differences in social attitudes will influence the choice of scapegoat victims. The loyalist or 'conservative' party will tend to select those who deviate from familiar conventions and appear to threaten their group fetish. They will thus be inclined to turn against fellow members who default in their observance of ideal group codes; against those who violate traditional customs and are therefore regarded as odd, immoral, or criminal; and against the stranger, outsider and foreigner whose behaviour is *outré*. The 'radical' party, on the other hand, will tend to find scapegoats among the loyalist defenders and privileged upholders of traditions which are regarded by this party as outmoded and iniquitous.

But conditions of social life do not equally favour these two kinds of scapegoat persecutions. All members of a society are linked by bonds of loyalty to common ideals, even if the fervour and range of their loyalties differ. The most rebellious citizens still obey most of the dictates of the customs and conventions of their society, and therefore share, to some extent, the loyalists' suspicions of non-conforming offenders and of outsiders. Moreover, should the rebellious faction attempt to follow their seditious bent and challenge the entrenched powers which guard the *status quo*, they are likely to be thwarted and fobbed off with puppet scapegoats on whom they can vent their exasperation without harm to the authorities.

For these reasons scapegoat persecutions in human societies have been generally directed against deviants, outsiders, and underprivileged minorities. History is full of blatant and savage examples of persecutions in which authority and populace joined forces in hunting down a common quarry, variously denounced and abused as witch or criminal, heretic or saboteur, traitor or enemy, or by whatever scapegoat synonym happened to be fashionable.

But the notoriety of these examples cannot hide the fact that even the most devoted group loyalty is never unconditional or free from the taint of potential rebelliousness. A close scrutiny of social life will always detect a grumbling undercurrent of seditious discontent from which the most partisan and orthodox factions are by no means exempt. It can be noted in the caricatures of prominent people, in the onerous ceremonials which elevate and encumber royalty, in the mobbing of celebrities, the stories of Damocles' sword and Polycrates' ring, the Robin Hood tales of chivalrous banditry, the appeal of Gilbertian satire, the sporting support of David against Goliath, the interest in the decline and fall of powerful empires or patriarchal families (*The Forsyte Saga*, *Buddenbrooks*), and in numerous other examples. At times the submerged desires for insurrection erupt into an open challenge to authority which may sweep the governing powers away with revolutionary violence, or change them, with democratic etiquette, by an election swing.

These signs of rebellious inclinations are generally subdued and held in check, not only because their open expression would be punished by the guardians of law and order, but because each citizen has to buttress his law-abiding conduct by the repression of desires to mutiny against the restraint of social discipline. Unconsciously these repressed desires are, in part, linked with the guilt of parricidal urges which had been roused in infancy by oedipal jealousies and the yoke of parental supremacy. The projection of this unconscious guilt fans the violence of scapegoat persecutions. The very crimes with which the victim is charged reflect the repressed desires for murderous revolt.

History provides striking evidence for the parricidal components of the scapegoat motif. In times of social calamity, for instance, public clamours will be heard demanding the sacrifice of a highly placed scapegoat who can be accused of incompetence, irresponsibility, or worse. In cruder ages, some communities sanctioned ceremonial occasions on which parricidal urges could be collectively and openly satisfied. The 'scapegoat kings' of these communities were slain when they grew too old and feeble, or when their term of office expired, or perhaps even annually as Frazer assumed. In time, however, the scapegoat king, to quote Frazer (1913), 'contrived by force or craft to extent his reign and sometimes to procure a substitute who, after a short and more or less nominal tenure of the crown, was slain in his stead.'

These substitutes often had to establish their temporary title by enacting aspects of the regal role which had an undisguised oedipal significance. The mock king of the Persian Sacaea, for instance, was required to perform sexual intercourse (publicly, as some authors presume) with the women of the king's harem. The festivals of Astarte, Aphrodite, Cybele, and Isis provided similar public spectacles in which a chosen scapegoat was 'allowed, or rather required, to enjoy the embraces of a woman who played the Goddess of Love' (Frazer), before he was put to death. The Roman Saturnalia were originally presided over by a mock king who was given 'full licence to indulge his passions and to taste of every pleasure, however base and shameful' (Frazer), but he forfeited his life at the end of his brief spell as chartered libertine.

It is obvious that the heroes of these scapegoat dramas suffered death not only to pacify the parricidal passions of the populace, but also as the arch-criminals who had openly dared to gratify forbidden oedipal desires. They were 'engineered' scapegoats, victims who were exploited by the community to act as understudies in a tabooed role. The spirit of levity and irresponsibility thus engendered, and enhanced by emotional resonance to the spectacle witnessed, tended to overflow into public revelries. Orgiastic festivities, therefore, often accompanied the sacrifice of these scapegoats, though the licence thus socially sanctioned was never without its limits and restraints.

In the course of centuries, the stark crudities of these ancient festivities gradually disappeared. The barbarous scapegoat drama took on a burlesque form. The tragic figure of the King of the Saturnalia became, in medieval times, a buffoon who officiated at the Feast of Fools, or a King of the Bean, Lord of Misrule, or Abbot of Unreason. The last symbol of his sacrifice and its deeper parricidal meanings may have been, as Jones (1951) suggests, the ceremony of the boar's head at the Christmas banquet – a sign of the close unconscious connections between parricidal desires and totem feasts which Freud had pointed out in his *Totem and Taboo* (1913). Today only a faint and demure echo of saturnalian revelries remains. It can still be observed in the holiday spirit of Christmas-time with its good cheer and special fare, its modest licence of a kiss under the mistletoe, and its last relics of customs symbolizing the overthrow of authority, such as the army and navy tradition which prescribes that officers serve the lower ranks on Christmas Day.

But, as the ancient scapegoat drama thus lost its pungency, other spectacles appeared on the social scene to serve as outlets for the need for scapegoat victims. The Middle Ages had their Inquisition and the *Malleus Maleficarum*, which ensured a plentiful supply of female scape-goats, stigmatized as witches, who were forced by torture to admit vile and lecherous associations with the forces of Evil. In modern times the appeal of the scapegoat drama is exploited by the popular press in their sensational reports of murder trials, by the cinema with its 'crime does not pay' entertainment, and by political propaganda which imputes malevolence and atrocity to the opponent, and perhaps stages a limelight trial of political offenders who have to prove their guilt through public confession.

It has also been said that our present-day society engineers scapegoat criminals by other and more subtle means. Eissler, for instance, has given examples of the subterfuge with which rational measures of crime preven-tion are evaded by turning a blind eye on living conditions which are known to breed lawlessness, by favouring a regime in many delinquency institutions which is more likely to foster antisocial tendencies than to cure them, and by many other methods which unwittingly frustrate the well-intentioned policies to which public lip-service is paid. She compared our society to Dorian Gray, whose picture reflected his dissolute life, whereas he himself preserved the appearance of innocence.

THE SCAPEGOAT MOTIF IN A THERAPEUTIC GROUP

GROUP COMPOSITION

The group, which met once-weekly for treatment sessions, consisted of seven female patients who had been suffering from neurotic symptoms of depersonalization for many years. Two members were relative newcomers, and their influence on ongoing events was limited. We shall therefore concern ourselves mainly with the nucleus of five patients who had jointly started their treatment six months before the two newcomers had been added to the group.

The ages of the five patients ranged from twenty-nine to thirty-nine. They were all timid and self-conscious, and led a very restricted social life. Two were married but childless. The group composition was unbalanced in one respect: four of the five members were outpatients and came from respect-able middle-class homes; their occupations had been those of temporary typists and civil servants; their sexual life had been without obvious blemish.

The fifth member, Miss S, differed, however, in all these aspects from the others. She was an inpatient with a working-class background, and had in the past been employed as housemaid or factory-hand. She was the only member who had lost both parents, and the only member with a history of illicit sexual affairs.

The group prestige of Miss S was low. At first she had found it difficult to take part in the conversation. She generally sat there, tense and silent, uncrossing her legs in anxious discomfort. In later sessions, when she began to talk, she was either aggressive or complained of feeling inferior and rejected. Some of her early contributions shocked the group. She spoke of homo- and heterosexual desires at a time when the other patients shied away from such embarrassing topics. She frequently roused the jealousy of her fellow members by asking for extra interviews with the therapist.

GROUP EVENTS

During the first few months of treatment the group achieved only poor cohesion because of the strong egocentric preoccupations of the patients. The conversation was generally slow and halting: it was reminiscent of the kind of pseudo-conversation which Piaget (1924) has described in young children before the age of seven, and has characterized as 'monologue collectif'.

The introduction of two new patients, after six months of treatment, welded the group temporarily into a semblance of solidarity. All but one of the old members united in grumbling dissatisfaction with this intrusion of strangers into a familiar group environment.

A similar and equally short-lived episode of improved solidarity occurred, some weeks later, when the patients began to show signs of being disturbed by their ambivalent transference feelings for the therapist, which they were reluctant to admit and discuss openly. They turned to a related topic instead. They levelled an attack against a figment of their imagination, that of the sexually domineering male. Their discussions livened up as they eagerly aired their aggressive fantasies.

But the rather nebulous shape of this figment was only a poor substitute for the male therapist, their real target. It was not possible to keep up for long the pretence of completely disregarding the part he played in their dilemma. A timidly daring note of rebellion against his authority was sounded, but its poignancy was disguised by an affectation of playful banter. He was told facetiously that his presence prevented free discussions; would he please leave the room or, at least, turn his back on them?

With this change of target from the figment, which they could collectively revile, to the living and responsive figure of the therapist, for whom they harboured ambivalent desires, the phalanx of feminine solidarity was broken. Individual voices were now heard in defence of the therapist, dreams were reported which clearly indicated erotic transference feelings, signs of jeal-ousy appeared among the members (especially between Miss S and Miss F, who later formed a close relationship), and the appeal for private therapeutic interviews became more frequent.

COLLECTIVE LIBIDINAL MOTIVATIONS

At this stage the group was very agitated. They could no longer blind themselves to the realization that group treatment had stirred up sexual conflicts in them. They were still not ready to face openly the transference origin of their emotional upset, or the incestuous guilt which was uncon-sciously linked with it. Three group members, however, were prepared now to consider, at least, those sexual fears and conflicts which had disturbed them in the past or were a cause of anxiety outside the group. The other two members remained in opposition; yet they betrayed their erotic animation by the eagerness with which they prompted others to be frank about embarrassing sexual data and by a temporary aggravation of their neurotic symptoms (one of them developed a new symptom in the form of a writer's cramp, at that time).

The group was thus divided on the issue of sexual self-revelations. Previously they had collectively avoided these topics, apart from the initial brazen infringement of this tacit group taboo by Miss S. But there had been for some time an undercurrent of stirred-up erotic feelings in the group, which was not vented in open discussion.

This undercurrent was most clearly demonstrated in the response of Mrs D, who occupied a 'leader' position in the group – as had been established by a method of socio-metric investigation, described elsewhere by one of us (Taylor, 1951) – which accorded her highest scores in dominance and popularity. It has often been found that such group leaders take the initiative in revealing suppressed group motivations either openly or in disguised form. Mrs D, who in two years of married life had remained averse to intercourse, had reported to the group some months before that there had been a change in her attitude to sex. She had decided to have a baby, and had been able to submit to intercourse more often in spite of her repugnance. But when she became pregnant, she again tended to refuse physical intimacy.

The pregnancy of Mrs D may be considered both as an acting out of motivations aroused by the group sessions, and as a non-verbal disclosure of these motivations to the group.

When the group eventually reached the stage of sharply dividing the members on the issue of frank revelations of erotic feelings and fantasies, Mrs D joined with Miss S and Miss F in accepting the necessity of candid discussion. But, as the group was not united and the group climate not too favourable, Miss S and Miss F could not discuss their emotional problems openly during sessions. They also began to show an inclination to act out their erotic difficulties. At first, they formed a conspiratorial friendship to exchange sexual secrets privately and outside the group. When the therapist interpreted their evasive behaviour, acrimonious recriminations between the two opposing group factions ensued.

The group atmosphere at this stage is best illustrated by a brief excerpt from the record of a therapeutic session:

Miss S: I think I know why I can talk in front of Miss F and Mrs D. It's because they're the only ones who can talk about sex.

Miss A: If I don't talk about it, it's because I have nothing to say.

Mrs B: Sex has no bearing on my problems.

Miss S (angrily): Why do you say sex has no bearing on your problems? Your married life isn't satisfactory.

Mrs B: It is satisfactory. That's all. And I don't think it has anything to do with my symptoms.

Miss S: It must have. You have no children. That's not normal.

Mrs B: I can't afford children.

Miss A: I've had dreams about sex. I might talk about that. But I don't want to get married. That doesn't interest me.

Miss S, as this quotation shows, had at this time lost her original fear of talking in the group, and had consequently gained in dominance. She made some disclosures about her past sex life, and mentioned in particular that the partners of her illicit affairs had always been married men.

The division of the group into two opposing camps was, however, not a constant feature. At times the members united in a common resistance against candid self-revelations, and denied that they were stirred by libidinal conflicts. They shifted the blame on to the therapist. It was not they who were interested in sex, it was the therapist who prompted them to discuss it and who read sexual meanings into their most innocent slips.

The group discussions thus alternated between half-daring disclosures and anxious attempts at camouflaging the signs of their increased sexual conflicts. On the whole, the sessions began to fail in their therapeutic task of providing an opportunity for the verbal ventilation of emotional difficulties. Often the discussions contained sexual innuendoes which were, however, not elaborated during the meetings, though they seemed to lead to whispered exchanges afterwards.

There were also signs that some members desired to indulge in erotic experimentations outside the group. The therapist repeatedly interpreted this desire to act out, and warned the group against this eventuality. But in spite of these precautions it soon transpired that the friendship between Miss S and Miss F was cemented by an exchange of confidential information about flirtations they had started with married men.

When the other members learned about this, their curiosity was aroused. They wanted to know details. How far had they been able to go? And what

prevented them from going further? A prurient game of wheedling information from Miss S and Miss F developed, and the eagerness of the group seemed
to act as a spur on the two members to risk acts of greater daring. This, for
instance, is an excerpt of a group discussion at this stage:

> Miss A: I would love to know what Miss F is thinking about.
> Miss F: Hm – I ought to have a lot to say.
> Miss S: You ought to – from what you told me.
> Miss F (to Miss S with a coy smile): Keep quiet.
> Miss A (to Miss F): Did you go out with this man?
> Miss F: No.
> Miss A: Why not?
> Miss F: He's changed his mind.
> Miss S: But you told me that he asked you to go out with him.
> Miss F: Yes, but I refused. It's always the same with me. I back out.
> Miss S: But you're disturbed. You told me that you can't sleep.
> Miss F (laughingly): I'm not saying any more. Today I . . . No, I won't talk.
> Miss S: What happened today?
> Miss F: Nothing . . . I want to go out with him, but I can't.
> Miss A: Because he's married?
> Miss F: No. (turning to Miss S): Come on. You talk now.
> Miss S (after some hesitation): I'm still going out with my boyfriend. He
> wanted me to stay in a hotel with him.
> Miss F: And now you're in a fix.

At the end of this session the therapist reiterated that these erotic ventures
were neurotic reactions to the group's inability to have frank discussions,
and that such reactions were likely to impede their therapeutic progress.

Miss S Acts as Understudy Scapegoat

The therapist's endeavours to re-establish a more favourable therapeutic
atmosphere proved fruitless. The stage was already set and the actors
determined on their course. Three weeks after the session just reported,
Miss S succumbed to the temptation and had intercourse. In the following
group sessions she was very disturbed and refused to take part in the
discussion. She merely asked for a private interview with the therapist. To
him she confessed what had taken place. She was afraid of pregnancy, and
felt very guilty that she had let the doctor and the group down. She was asked
to inform the group so that the reasons for her acting out could be discussed.
    In the next session, Miss S was still extremely agitated. The group made
several unsuccessful attempts to get her to talk, but it was only after the
therapist had intervened and encouraged her that she was able to muster
sufficient determination to make a public confession:

Miss S: I'm ashamed of myself. I can't talk. I could talk to Miss F and Mrs D, but not to the others.
Miss A: Is it something that happened over the weekend?
Miss S: Yes . . . A compulsion made me do it. I should only have done it, if I'd been married.
Miss A: Did you have intercourse?
(Miss S nods. Then she apologizes for having disgraced the group, and having slept with a man she did not even love.)
Miss A: I've always thought Miss S would do it.

The group did not hide their disapproval. They condemned Miss S, and also blamed Miss F, her friend, because she too was guilty of a liaison with a married man.

The censure of the group stung Miss S. Her remorse changed into an aggressive outburst: she had only done what the others had not even dared to talk about; and she felt none the worse for it – on the contrary, all her symptoms had disappeared.

This defiant attitude of Miss S and her denial of guilt were still present in the subsequent group session:

Miss F (to Miss S): Do you still have pangs of conscience?
Miss S: What do you mean?
Miss F: Your guilty conscience about the weekend.
Miss S: I'm only afraid that I might have a baby.
Miss A: Have your symptoms come back?
Miss S: Funnily enough, no.

To everybody's surprise, Miss S went on to say that she felt very pleased with herself. When the group tried to elicit the reason for this peculiar self-satisfaction, Miss S gave an apparently incongruous explanation, which, however, contained a significant clue to her behaviour. She told the group that during the week nurses had been instructed on her ward in the application of bandages, and she had been asked to serve as a model for them. She had felt glad to have this opportunity of being of service to others. She had had none of her usual feelings of tongue-tied inferiority on that occasion.

In the week following this group session Miss S menstruated. She lost her fear of being pregnant, yet she felt disappointed and all her previous neurotic symptoms reappeared. She expressed this paradoxical reaction by saying, 'Instead of feeling happy and relieved, I feel I have lost something.'

In subsequent sessions Miss S's defiance of the group mellowed, and the tension which had alerted the patients eased. It then became clear that Miss S had not only served as a model for nurses, but also for the group members, who had vicariously rehearsed their inhibited sexual desires by using Miss S as an understudy.

The scapegoat performance of Miss S proved to have a beneficial effect on subsequent group proceedings. The split between the two opposing group factions was, at least partially, healed, and the patients were able to discuss sexual topics with greater freedom, candour and liveliness. They talked about their fears and conflicts concerning nakedness, childbirth, breastfeeding, masturbation, and even about their fantasies concerning the sexual intimacy between their parents.

The coaxing of Miss S to risk sexual ventures outside the group had disappeared. The libidinal group tensions now found a more adequate discharge in group discussions and the tendencies to act out proved less disturbing during the subsequent course of treating this group.

DISCUSSION OF GROUP EVENTS

Before considering the genesis of the scapegoat phenomena which this group had presented, it seems advisable to outline some of the characteristics of therapeutic groups which are conducted on analytical lines. These groups have a unique task which differentiates them from other social groups. The patients are required to speak candidly about those personal feelings and fears which cannot be disclosed in other social environments. A similar task of intimate self-exposure is, of course, characteristic of individual psychotherapy as well, but there it takes place in a very private and confidential setting. In a therapeutic group, on the other hand, the disclosures are made publicly, not only to the therapist, but to the whole group audience.

In the course of group treatment the resistance against this task of self-revelation undergoes a gradual but significant change. In the beginning of treatment the patients have to overcome their reluctance about the disagreeable task of confessing, in a semi-public situation, very intimate and embarrassing data about themselves. These data, however, have their origin and relevance in the patients' past and present life outside the group.

As treatment progresses and the patients form closer interpersonal ties in the group, a new form of resistance against the task of candid self-revelation makes itself felt. It becomes increasingly disconcerting to disclose certain emotional responses because the disclosure had to be made to the very persons who may have evoked responses because the disclosure has to be made to the very persons who may have evoked the emotions, and certainly have become involved in them. In so far as these emotions stir up emotional conflicts, they may not even gain conscious awareness, and manifest themselves merely in an aggravation or change of neurotic symptoms. This result is analogous to the well-known phenomenon in individual psychoanalysis that the neurosis changes into a transference neurosis, with its attendant transference resistances. In group treatment it is, however, not only the relationship to the therapist but also that to fellow group members which causes this reaction.

It is at this stage, when the interactions in the group have acquired poignant personal meanings in the minds of the participants, that events make their appearance which are comparable to those occurring on the vaster stage of community life. The group may then mirror in miniature some of the social and political crosscurrents which agitate the life of human societies. The immediacy of observation and the candour of self-revelation in the therapeutic group provide us with an opportunity for observing and evaluating these social occurrences to an extent which is not feasible in other social settings.

The first scapegoat phenomena which we observed in our group made their appearance at a time when the patients had become disturbed by their transference feelings for the therapist, and were reluctant to disclose them. In their common resistance to the task of candidly revealing these feelings they turned, first, against an imaginary scapegoat: the figment of the sexually domineering male. But this attempt to find a scapegoat solution for their emotional insecurity was short-lived. The patients could not escape the realization that the true culprit responsible for their predicament was the therapist, yet they lacked the temerity to rebel openly against him as they depended on his authority and guidance. Only a caricature of their seditious desires appeared in the form of facetious remarks that his presence was undesired. At a later stage there were occasional incidents when the group members succeeded in being more outspoken about some of their negative feelings towards the therapist. On such occasions they treated him as a scapegoat who could be blamed for upsetting them unduly by a disconcerting interest in their sexual conflicts, which they tried to hide and deny. But the frank disclosure of either positive or negative transference feelings towards the therapist presupposed a reliance on group unity and the support of fellow members; and such group unity was achieved only very occasionally.

Theoretically, four principal methods of reducing the libidinal tensions roused by group events were open to the patients.

First, they could employ repressive and allied defence mechanisms to escape awareness of their emotional conflicts. This is essentially a neurotic solution and tends to aggravate clinical symptoms. It also encourages a search for scapegoats who could be made to serve as targets for the projection of unconscious guilt. Patients with a predisposition in this direction may react in one of four ways: they may blame the therapist and his methods of conducting treatment; they may accuse leading group members of introducing irrelevant and disturbing topics into the conversation; they may condemn as immoral those fellow-members who can be more candid in disclosing their sexual difficulties; or they may tempt other patients to commit an act of sexual licence so that they are able to turn on them in self-righteous indignation.

Second, the libidinal conflicts may be partially accepted, but not frankly revealed to the group. Under these circumstances patients may indulge in some form of erotic experimentation outside the group to find out how far they can overcome their emotional handicaps. This acting out may lead to unpleasant consequences, but it does constitute a form of confession to the group, though often a disguised and non-verbal one. In this category belongs the behaviour of Mrs D, the group leader, who became pregnant in the course of treatment, and also the conduct of Miss S and Miss F, who started flirtations with male acquaintances. The guilt feelings stirred by this acting out may lead to an exacerbation of neurotic symptoms, and to attempts to unload the burden of guilt on to a scapegoat, such as the group as a whole or certain stigmatized members of it.

Third, the libidinal conflicts may be freely discussed in the group, but shorn of all indications that the group and its members have been instrumental in activating the conflicts, and have become directly involved in them. The best-known example of this defence mechanism is the conscious resistance of the disclosure of erotic feelings for the therapist. But an equally strong resistance exists in a group against the disclosure of such feelings for fellow-members. This was demonstrated in a group experiment performed by one of us. The amalgamation of a male and female group after months of separate treatment led to a conspicuous increase in the discussion of homosexual topics. This response was interpreted as indicating a release of motivations which had been repressed in the homo-erotic atmosphere of one-sex groups, but found overt expression when the libidinal field milieu had been changed and heterosexual conflicts had become more poignant in the presence of members of the opposite sex. It is also of interest that in both these groups, which for a while met alternatively as one- and two-sex groups, there were signs that the leading members were treated as scapegoats. These members had become excessively perturbed by their homosexual fears and conflicts, and their companions had banded together to belittle them by sarcastic remarks.

Fourth, the ideal method of reducing libidinal conflicts in a therapeutic group is to ventilate them freely and without censorship of past events or of relevant links with the present group situation. The adoption of this method is the ideal aim of group therapy – an aim which is for the most part utopian rather than practically attainable.

These four methods of solving libidinal tensions in group treatment are not independently and exclusively employed by the patients. All of them are constantly utilized to some extent and in varying degrees. In our group there was, however, a sharp division among members in the methods they chiefly adopted. Three patients were prepared to acknowledge and discuss their libidinal fears and guilt feelings in accordance with the principles and norms for which the therapeutic group stood. They may be regarded as a 'loyalist' faction – a right-wing party in the unique atmosphere of a therapeutic group and in contrast to the prevailing standards of our society, discussions and confessions. But the loyalist members had only the slender majority of one over the opposing and dissenting faction, which adhered to a Potemkin programme of deceiving the group public and themselves by concealing their defects.

The almost-even balance between the two group factions prevented a candid ventilation of the libidinal tensions in the group. As a result, tendencies appeared in the loyalist party to resolve their emotional difficulties outside the group by acting them out in erotic experimentation instead of bringing them to the group for a clarification and readjustment through discussion under therapeutic guidance.

At that stage, however, a spurious unity of purpose was established among the group members. They united in a stealthy endeavour, of which they were hardly aware, to induce one of their number to understudy them and act the part of their own inhibited erotic desires which had been stimulated by group treatment, but for which no adequate outlet was found in the group sessions.

This endeavour of the group to engineer a scapegoat proved successful. The most vulnerable member succumbed to the pressure of these group manoeuvres. She committed an illicit sexual act. But when the group censured her, she defiantly exposed the hypocrisy of her companions.

The similarity of this group episode to some of the ancient scapegoat ceremonies is apparent. In either case a person is induced to violate a taboo that has been set up by a society which guiltily repudiates the unconscious appeal of the tabooed act. The scapegoat shoulders the guilt of his or her companions and becomes the victim of their unconscious envy. His punishment absolves the companions from the sin they secretly desired.

In our group, the scapegoat drama was, however, not completed. The group member who had been cast for the scapegoat role, though accepting her guilt, denied the right of her companions to blame her, and even called the bluff of the group manoeuvres designed to make her the butt of projected accusations. Thus, instead of purging the guilt of her fellow-members, she forced them to deal with their disowned libidinal urges in a more candid and self-searching manner.

The social effect of the ancient scapegoat drama was, however, not limited to the catharsis of guilt feelings. Other emotions were roused in the spectators who, though they dared not imitate the crime of the scapegoat, were incited to follow his lead part of the way; to relax at least some of the inhibitions of social discipline and decorum. The scapegoat drama thus had a seductive effect on the community, and it is therefore not surprising that orgiastic festivities were frequently associated with scapegoat ceremonies. Society sanctioned, at such times, a moderate degree of collective licence, which varied with the moral milieu of the society concerned.

A similar process of social seduction has been noticed by Redl (1942) in certain groups of adolescent children which form around a 'central person', who dares to commit a forbidden initiatory act and thereby enables his less audacious companions to shed some of their inhibitory fears.

It seems that the scapegoat episode in our group also had a seductive effect of this kind. The resonance of libidinal desires awakened in the group members could, however, find a legitimate outlet in verbal activities only, as this is the only licence permitted, and even encouraged, in the therapeutic group setting. The scapegoat certainly had a liberating effect on group discussions, and enabled the patients to reveal subsequently many of their libidinal conflicts. The frequency of oedipal topics at that time was also noteworthy, as it may have indicated that the scapegoat episode had been initiated by the transfer of unconscious oedipal wishes into the group setting, and particularly into the relationships between patients and therapist.

The group member who enacted the scapegoat role did so not only because of the pressure exerted on her by the companions, but also in compliance with her own unconscious inclinations. She belonged to that class of socially maladjusted patients who translate masochistic fantasies into life experiences. In her past life there had been several episodes when she had invited misfortune by infringing social codes in such a way that she was bound to suffer disapproval and punishment. She displayed the same behaviour pattern in the group. She was disliked by most of her fellow patients, whom she often shocked by needlessly provocative sexual self-disclosures. At the same time she took a delight in self-pitying emphasis of her social inferiority; she even went to the length of pretending, without truth, that she had no relatives in the world, that she was a lonely deserted orphan for whom nobody cared. It is of interest in this respect that we have noticed similar manoeuvres to engineer a scapegoat in another female group; the patient singled out for the scapegoat role there also presented the picture of the masochistic character neurosis.

SUMMARY

Some of the psychological and sociological implications of the scapegoat motif have been considered.

It has been argued that scapegoat-baiting tendencies occur particularly in individuals with an extra-punitive or 'toughminded' social attitude who are inclined to shift the burden of personal guilt and self-dissatisfaction on to other shoulders. This self-deceptive device affords them not only relief from guilt feelings, whether conscious or unconscious, but also provides them with opportunities for narcissistic and scoptophilic gratifications, and for the self-righteous discharge of aggression.

Reference has been made to some recent studies on social attitudes. The kind of scapegoat chosen by people with different social attitudes may vary according to their 'conservative–radical' bias. Those with 'conservative' or 'ethnocentric' social attitudes tend to turn against people who deviate from cherished group ideals; those with 'radical' social tendencies tend to find scapegoats among the loyalist defenders of traditions.

Social conditions do not favour these two kinds of scapegoat choice equally. The 'conservative' tendencies to persecute deviants are more readily manifested as they accord with the interests of the guardians of orthodoxy. 'Radical' desires, on the other hand, to heap scapegoat-blame on social superiors, though they seem to be equally common in societies, can, in general, achieve only muffled expression because their rebellious implications rouse the resistance of entrenched authority.

Ancient societies provided ceremonially regulated outlets for these, usually inhibited, seditious desires to remove and supplant persons in privileged and responsible social positions. The typical ceremony seems to have been one in which a person was made to enact a temporary role of regal power and sexual licence, and thus to commit the crime ambivalently desired and repudiated by the community, of usurping the prerogatives of sovereignty. A scapegoat was thus 'engineered' who, by serving as understudy for the mutinous, though disowned, desires of his fellow citizens, purged their secret guilt and suffered punishment, ostensibly in redemption of his enacted crime, but covertly also as the mock representative of authority. The oedipal aspect and parricidal theme of the scapegoat drama was often clearly displayed in these ancient ceremonies.

The 'engineering' of scapegoats has not disappeared in modern communities, though the manoeuvrers by which persons are inveigled into committing wrongs, as the understudies of intriguing companions, are often less crude and obvious.

A relevant observation of 'engineering' a scapegoat which occurred in an all-female therapeutic group has been described. The members of the group all suffered from symptoms of depersonalization, were socially very inhibited, and had great difficulty in discussing, during group sessions, their personal conflicts, particularly those of a sexual nature or their transference feelings for the therapist. In an attempt to resolve their anxieties and guilt feelings they resorted eventually to clandestine manoeuvres which aimed at staging a scapegoat drama.

The victim chosen was a half-willing one. She was a group member who suffered from a masochistic character neurosis, and who differed from her companions in several respects. She had a lower social and educational background, and was the only group member with a past history of illicit sexual affairs. In the beginning of treatment she was so disturbed that she could hardly participate in group discussions. When she did, she was provocative by deliberately disclosing sexual material which shocked her companions.

When the group had reached an impasse, caused by their inability to ventilate emotional conflicts freely, stealthy and unacknowledged machinations appeared in the behaviour of the group which seemed designed to induce the chosen victim to indulge in a sexual venture, and thus to act out vicariously the inhibited and illicit libidinal desires of her companions. The group succeeded, and the victim began to enact her scapegoat role. She started a flirtation with a married man, a casual acquaintance, and the group members evinced their scoptophilic pleasure by a marked interest in the progress of this affair. But when the sexual venture was consummated, the group turned away and voiced their condemnation and disapproval. The scapegoat, however, though feeling very guilty, denied her companions the right to blame her, and defiantly exposed their hypocrisy.

The 'crime' of the scapegoat thus did not absolve the group from their guilt. The episode, however, had the result of liberating group discussions, and of initiating a more candid and therapeutically beneficial ventilation of the patients' guilt-charged libidinal conflicts.

BIBLIOGRAPHY

Place of publication is London unless otherwise noted.

Adorno, T.W., Frenkel-Brunswick, E., Levinson, D.J., and Sanford, R.N. (1950) *The Authoritarian Personality*. New York: Harper Bros.

Battro, M. (1973) *Piaget: A Dictionary of Terms*, eds E. Ritschverimann and S.F. Campbell. Oxford: Pergamon.

Bion, W.R. (1962) *Learning from Experience*. Heinemann Medical.

—— (1963) *Elements of Psycho-Analysis*. Heinemann Medical.

—— (1965) 'Transformations', in *Seven Servants: Four Works* New York: Jason Aronson, 1977.

Bronowski, J.S. and Bellugi, V. (1970) 'Language, name and concept', *J. Science* 168: 699.

De Swart, S.H. (1972) 'A possible theory of language acquisition within the framework of Piaget's developmental theory', in ed. P. Adams *Language in Thinking*. New York: Penguin.

Deutsch, H. (1947) *The Psychology of Women*. Research Books.

Edelson, M. (1973) 'Language and dreams', in eds R.S. Eissler *et al.*, *The Psychoanalytic Study of the Child*. New York: Quadrangle, pp. 203–87.

Eissler, R.S. (1949) 'Scapegoats of society', in ed. K.R. Eissler, *Searchlights on Delinquency*. Imago.

Eliot, T.S. (1944) *Four Quartets*. Faber and Faber, 1959.

Eysenck, H.J. (1947) 'Primary social attitudes: I. The organisation and measurement of social attitudes', *Int. J. Opin. Attit. Res.* 1: 49–84.

—— (1951) 'Primary social attitudes and the "social insight test"', *Brit. J. Psych.* 42:114–22.

Frazer, Sir J.G. (1913) *The Golden Bough*. Macmillan.

Freud, S. (1895) 'Project for a scientific psychology', in ed. J. Strachey, *The Standard Edition of the Complete Psychological Works of Sigmund Freud*, 24 vols. Hogarth, 1953–74. vol. 1.

—— (1897) Letter 70 from the Fliess Papers. *S.E.* 1.

—— (1900) *The Interpretation of Dreams*, *S.E.* 5.

—— (1909) 'Notes upon a case of obsessional neurosis'. *S.E.* 10, pp. 153–318.

—— (1911) 'Psycho-analytic notes on an autobiographical account of a case of paranoia'. *S.E.* 12, pp. 12–82.

—— (1913) *Totem and Taboo*. *S.E.* 13.

—— (1914) 'The Moses of Michelangelo'. *S.E.* 13.

—— (1915a) 'Instincts and their vicissitudes'. *S.E.* 14.

—— (1915b) 'Thoughts for the times on war and death'. *S.E.* 14.

—— (1916a) 'Some character-types met with in psycho-analytic work'. *S.E.* 14.

—— (1916b) 'Some analyses of sample dreams'. *S.E.* 15.

—— (1916c) 'Uncertainties and criticisms'. *S.E.* 15.

—— (1917) 'Mourning and melancholia'. *S.E.* 14.

—— (1918) 'From the history of an infantile neurosis'. *S.E.* 17.

—— (1923) *The Ego and the Id. S.E.* 19.

—— (1924) 'Loss of reality in neurosis and psychosis'. *S.E.* 19.

—— (1930) *Civilization and its Discontents. S.E.* 21.

—— (1940) *An Outline of Psycho-Analysis. S.E.* 23.

Glick, J. (1988) *Chaos.* New York: Penguin.

Greenberg (1970) *Universals of Language.*

Guntrip, H. (1968) *Schizoid Phenomena, Object Relations and the Self.* Hogarth.

Heimann, P. (1952) in eds M. Klein, P. Heimann, S. Isaacs and J. Rivière, *Developments in Psycho-Analysis.* Hogarth.

Hewes, G. (1974) in ed. E. Linden, *Apes, Men and Language.* New York: Penguin.

Isaacs, S. (1952) in eds M. Klein, P. Heimann, S. Isaacs and J. Rivière, *Developments in Psycho-Analysis.* Hogarth.

Jakobson, R. (1968) *Child Language, Aphasia and Phonological Universals.* The Hague: Mouton.

James, E. O. (1957) *Prehistoric Religion.* Thames and Hudson.

Jones, E. (1951) *Essays in Applied Psychoanalysis.* Hogarth.

Jones, R.M. (1970) *The New Psychology of Dreaming.* New York: Grune & Stratton.

Joseph, B. (1989) *Psychic Equilibrium and Psychic Change: Selected Papers of Betty Joseph*, eds M. Feldman and E. Bott Spillius. Tavistock/ Routledge.

Jost, A. (1947) *Arch. Anat. Micr. Morph.* 36: 271.

—— (1953) *Recent Program Hormone Res.* 8: 379.

Klein, M. (1921) 'The development of a child', *Int. J. Psycho-Anal.* 4. Also in *Writings 1*, pp. 1–53.

—— (1923) 'The role of the school in libidinal development', *Writings 1*, pp. 59–76.

—— (1927) 'Criminal tendencies in normal children', *Br. J. Med. Psych.* 7. Also in *Writings 1*, pp. 170–85.

—— (1928) 'Early stages of the Oedipus conflict', *Int. J. Psycho-Anal.* 9. Also in *Writings 1*, pp. 186–98.

—— (1929) 'Infantile anxiety-situations reflected in a work of art and the creative impulse.' *Int. J. Psycho-Anal.* 10. Also in *Writings 1*, pp. 210–18.

—— (1930) 'The importance of symbol-formation in the development of the ego', *Int. J. Psycho-Anal.* 11. Also in *Writings 1*, pp. 219–32.

—— (1931) 'A contribution to the theory of intellectual inhibition', *Int. J. Psycho-Anal.* 12. Also in *Writings 1*, pp. 236–47.

—— (1932) *The Psychoanalysis of Children*, trans. A. Strachey. Hogarth. Also as *Writings 2*.

—— (1935) 'A contribution to the psychogenesis of manic-depressive states', *Int. J. Psycho-Anal.* 16. Also in *Writings 1*, pp. 262–89.

—— (1940) 'Mourning and its relation to manic-depressive states', *Int. J. Psycho-Anal.* 21. Also in *Writings 1*, pp. 344–69.

—— (1945) 'The Oedipus conflict in the light of early anxieties', *Int. J. Psycho-Anal.* 26. Also in *Writings 1*, pp. 370–419.

—— (1946) 'Notes on some schizoid mechanisms', *Int. J. Psycho-Anal.* 27. Also in *Writings 3*, pp. 1–24.

—— (1952) 'Some theoretical conclusions regarding the emotional life of the infant', in eds M. Klein, P. Heimann, S. Isaacs and J. Rivière, *Developments in Psycho-Analysis*. Hogarth. Also in *Writings 3*, pp. 61–93.

—— (1957) *Envy and Gratitude*. Tavistock. Also in *Writings 3*, pp. 176–235.

—— (1975) *The Writings of Melanie Klein*. vol. 1: *Love, Guilt and Reparation and Other Works 1921–1945*; vol. 2: *The Psycho-Analysis of Children*; vol. 3: *Envy and Gratitude and Other Works 1946–1963*. Hogarth/Institute of Psycho-Analysis.

Kubie, L. (1958) 'Instincts and homeostasis', *Psych. Med.* 10: 15–30.

Laplanche, J. and Pontalis, J.B. (1973) *The Language of Psycho-Analysis*, trans. D. Nicholson-Smith. New York: Norton.

Lorenz, E. Lecture quoted in Glick (1988).

Marais, E. (1969) *The Soul of the Ape*. Anthony Blond.

—— (1973) *The Soul of the White Ant*. New York: Penguin.

Masters, W.H. and Johnson, W.E. (1960) *Human Sexual Response*. Boston: Little, Brown.

Matte-Blanco, I. (1975) *The Unconscious as Infinite Sets: An Essay in Bi-Logic*. Duckworth.

—— (1988) *Thinking, Feeling and Being*. Routledge.

Meltzer, D. (1967) *The Psychoanalytic Process*. Heinemann Medical.

Moerck, E.L. (1977) *Pragmatic and Semantic Aspects of Early Language Development*. Univ. Park Press.

Pétot, J.M. (1979a) *Melanie Klein 1919–1932: Premières Découvertes et premiers systèmes*. Paris: Dunod.

—— (1979b) *Melanie Klein 1932–1960: Le Moi et le bon objet*. Paris: Dunod.

Piaget, J. (1924) 'Les Traits principaux de la logique de l'enfant', *J. psych. norm. et path.* 21: 48–101.

—— (1945) *La Formation du symbole chez l'enfant*. Neuchatel et Paris: Delachaux-Niestle.

—— (1947) *The Psychology of Intelligence*. Kegan Paul.

—— (1950) *Introduction à l'épistémologie génétique*. 3 vols. Paris: Presses Univ. de France.

—— (1972) *Problèmes de psychologie génétique*. Denoël Ed.

Proust, M. (1982) *Remembrance of Things Past*, trans. C.K. Scott Moncrieff and T. Kilmartin. vol. 1, *Swann's Way*. New York: Vintage Press.

Réage, P. (1972) *The Story of O*. Transworld: Corgi, 1985.

Redl, F. (1942) 'Group emotion and leadership', *Psychiatry*, 5: 592–6.

Rivière, J. (1937) *Love, Hate and Reparation*. Hogarth.

Rouah, A. (1980) 'Anorexia nervosa', *Psychotherapia* 6: 17–25.

Rubinstein, B.D. (1972) 'On metaphor and related phenomena', in eds R.R. Holt and E. Peterfreund, *Psychoanalysis and Contemporary Science*. vol. 1. New York: Int. Univ. Press.

Scott, W.C.M. (1975) 'Remembering sleep and dreams', *Int. Rev. Psycho-Anal*. 2: 253–354.

—— (1988) 'Repairing broken links between the unconscious, sleep and instinct; and conscious, waking and instinct', *Free Assoc*. no. 12: 84–91.

Segal, H. (1973) *Introduction to the Work of Melanie Klein*. Hogarth.

—— (1981) *The Work of Hanna Segal: A Kleinian Approach to Clinical Practice*. New York: Aronson.

Solie, P. (1988) *Le Sacrifice*. Albri Michel.

Sokolov, A.N., ed. (1972) *Inner Speech and Thought*. New York: Plenum.

Spitz, R.A. (1965) *The First Year of Life*. New York: Int. Univ. Press.

Stern, D.N. (1985) *The Interpersonal World of the Infant*. New York: Basic.

Taylor, F.K. (1949) 'Experimental investigation of collective social and libidinal motivations in therapeutic groups', *Br. J. Med. Psych*. 22: 169–82.

—— (1951) 'Quantitative evaluation of psychosocial ·phenomena in small groups,' *J. Ment. Sc*. 97: 690–717.

Thom, R. (1973) 'Sur la typologie des langues naturelles. Essai d'interprétation psycholinguistique', in eds M. Gross, M. Halle and M.P. Schutzenberger, *The Formal Analysis of Natural Languages*. Proc. First Inter. Conf. The Hague: Mouton.

—— (1975) *Structural Stability and Morphogenesis*. New York: W.A. Benjamin.

Tinbergen, N. (1988) 'Instinct', *The Fontana Dictionary of Modern Thought*. Fontana Press, p. 313.

LIST OF PUBLICATIONS OF HENRI REY

(1949) (with D. Pond and C. Evans) 'Clinical and electroencephalographic studies in temporal lobe function', *Proc. R. Soc. Med.* 42: 891.

(1953) (with F.K. Taylor) 'The scapegoat motif in society and its manifestations in a therapeutic group', *Int. J. Psycho-Anal.* 34: 1–12.

(1955) (with Naidoo) 'Response of 5-Nucleotidase in the brain to estrogen administration in the growing rat', *Int. J. Endoc.* 12: 231.

(1957) (with U. Nicholson-Lailey and A. Trappl) 'Endocrine activity in psychiatric patients with menstrual disorders', *Br. Med. J.* 843.

—— 'Metabolism in recurrent schizophrenic illness', *Somatic Aspects.* Pergamon Press.

—— 'Amenorrhoea in psychiatric states'. *Proc. R. Soc.* 48.

(1959) (with A. J. Coppen) 'Distribution of androgyny in mental patients', *Br. Med. J.* 11: 1445-7.

—— (with U. Nicholson-Bailey and A. Trappl) 'Endocrinal activity in psychiatric patients with menstrual disorders', *Br. Med. J.* 11: 1445.

—— 'Biological role of depression in neurosis and its use in psychotherapy', *Congressus Psychiatricus Bohemo Slovenicus* 253.

(1961) 'Serial biochemical and endocrine investigations in recurrent mental illness', Rey *et al. J. Psych. Res.* V: 165-9.

—— 'A study in the relationship of hormones, brain activity and behaviour in women suffering from mental illness', *Proc. Third World Cong. Psychiatry*, Montreal, Canada 2: 830.

(1962) 'Psychotherapy with schizophrenics – a review', *Int. J. Psycho-Anal.* 43: 471.

(1963) 'Freud and Jung – a critical review', *Int. J. Anal. Psych.*

(1975) 'Liberté et process de pensée psychotique', *La Vie médicale au Canada français* 4.

(1975) 'Intrapsychic object relations: the individual and the group', in ed., Wolberg, *Group Psychotherapy*. New York: Aronson.

—— 'A critical review of Matte-Blanco's *The Unconscious as Infinite Sets*', *Int. J. Psycho-Anal.* 49.

(1979) 'Schizoid phenomena in the borderline', in eds J. LeBoit and A. Capponi, *Advances in the Psychotherapy of the Borderline Patient*, New York: Aronson, pp. 449–84.

(1981) 'Psycholinguistics, object relations theory and the therapeutic process'. Lecture given April 1980 to the Br. Psych-Anal. Soc. [see below, 1986]

(1986) 'The psychodynamics of psychoanalytic and psycholinguistic structures', *J. M. Klein Soc.* 4.

—— 'The schizoid mode of being and the space–time continuum (beyond metaphor)', *J. M. Klein Soc.* 4: 53.

—— 'Psycholinguistics, object relations theory and the therapeutic process', *J. M. Klein Soc.* 4: 53-73.

—— 'Féminité, sexualité et espace intérieur', *Cahiers pédagogiques* V: 88–111.

—— 'Basic structures and space–time factors', *Cahiers pédagogiques* V, Univ. Montréal.

—— 'Reparation', *J. M. Klein Soc.* 4: 5–36.

—— 'The psychodynamics of depression', *J. M. Klein Soc.* 4: 93–104.

(1988) 'That which patients bring to analysis', *Int. J. Psycho-Anal.* 69: 457.

—— 'The schizoid mode of being', in ed. E. Spillius, *Melanie Klein Today*, vol. 1. Routledge.

(1992) 'Awake, going to sleep, asleep, dreaming, awaking, awake: comments on W. Clifford M. Scott', *Free Associations* no. 27: 439–54.

INDEX

Abraham, Karl 270
acting out 64–5, 302; dreams, sensori-motor activity, change and 37–8
Adorno, T.W. *et al.* 290
agoraphobia *see* claustro-agoraphobia
anorexia nervosa 47–85, 174, 267; body image and 64, 65, 67; clinical example 47–62 (discussion 63–6); clinical example of therapeutic group 76–85 (discussion 83–5); comparison with manic-depressive psychosis 133–4; double identification and 64, 67; foetus and 64–6, 68, 69, 70, 74, 83; food and 65, 66–7, 84–5; pseudo-pregnancy and 64, 66, 70, 73; relation to bulimia 74–5; space-centred thought in 65, 69, 70–1, 72; theoretical considerations 69–74; transference love and 68; treatment 66–9
auto-erotic phase 33–4, 166–7, 168

Battro, M. 22, 165–6
Bellugi, V. 179
bi-logic 249–56; clinical example reinterpreted in terms of 256–62; *see also* Matte-Blanco, Ignacio
Bion, Wilfred 11, 16, 139, 164, 256, 261
birth 25, 168, 221–2, 267
Book of the Dead 207
borderline states 2–3, 8–20, 143; clinical example of therapeutic group 39–46; space–time continuum and displacement in 20–30; *see also* schizoid patients
brain as support in depression 190–1
Bronowski, J.S. 179
bulimia 65, 195; relation to anorexia nervosa 76–85

Cantor, G. 252, 254, 255
catatonia 14, 173
chaos theory 6
Chomsky, N. 32, 37, 38, 177
claustro-agoraphobia 3, 221, 260, 267, 287; in schizoid/borderline states 9, 21, 24–6, 169; in schizophrenics 10, 25–6, 171
claustro-agoraphobia-philia 3, 83, 84, 287
combined parents 70, 71, 147, 217, 218
conservative–radical factor in social attitudes, scapegoats and 290–2
constructional activity, early, and primitive intrapsychic groups 32–4

death 168; belief in life after 246–7; and dying in unconscious 236–7, 241, 248, 283–4; sleep and 285–7
death instinct 1–2, 210, 211, 236
depression 16, 17–18, 85, 209; anaclitic 34, 193–4; depersonalized 9, 169; masked 198; psychodynamics of 190–8; reversibility of, and therapeutic process 199–206 (clinical example 205–6);

depression *(cont.)*, symptoms of 195-6, 203; *see also* manic-depressive psychosis

depressive position 5-6, 19, 35, 139-40, 144, 194; dream function and 137-8, 147, 149, 282-3; reparation and 209, 215

despair and reparation 226

De Swart, S.H. 178

Deutsch, Helene 264

dissolution-reconstruction process: depression and 196; dreams and 188-9; psychoanalysis and 137, 177, 178-80

domains 167-8, 171; of words 183, 184

double identification 64, 67, 129

dreams 4, 147-50, 188-9, 191-2, 277-87; inner objects and 241-4, 280-1, 284-5; reparation and 224-6, 241, 243, 279; sensori-motor activity, change, acting out, and 37-8; *see also under* Freud

drives, theory of 4, 199, 210-11, 277

drug treatment 134, 135, 192

Edelson, Marshall 164, 177, 256; 'Language and Dreams' 37, 166

ego and sleep-waking cycle 281-2

Einstein, A. 22, 266

Eissler, Ruth S. 289, 294

Eleatic School of philosophy 254

Eliot, T.S. 28

environmental and genetic factors 6, 72-3, 134-5

ethnocentric-liberal continuum in social attitudes, scapegoats and 290-1

Eysenck, H.J. 290-1

female sexuality and inner space 263-76; clinical example 272-5

foetus 5; anorexia nervosa and 64-6, 68, 69, 70, 74, 83; birth and 25, 168, 221-2, 267; sleep and 167, 279, 287

forgiveness 226-7

Frazer, Sir J.G. 293

Freud, S. 11, 35, 37, 71, 73, 165, 176, 177, 189, 248, 253, 269, 282, 293; on developmental stages 33-4, 166-7; on dreams 36, 163, 166, 191, 214, 224, 242-4, 277, 279, 280, 284; on forgiveness 226-7; on life and death instincts 1-2, 210, 211; on melancholia 196, 203, 209, 212, 236; on primary and secondary processes 32, 38, 143, 278, 281; on reparation 17, 207, 208, 209, 210, 214, 226-7, 236; Schreber case 5, 70, 251; on sleep 277, 278; structural theory 23, 166; on unconscious 15, 236, 249-50, 251-2, 255, 256

genetic and environmental factors 6, 72-3, 134-5

Gödel's Theorem 6, 177

Greenberg 181, 182

groups, primitive intrapsychic, and early constructional activity 32-4

groups, psychotherapeutic: characteristics of 300-1; clinical example for anorexia nervosa and bulimia 76-85 (discussion 83-5); clinical example for chronic schizophrenia 151-62 (commentary 159-62);

groups, psychotherapeutic:
    characteristics of *(cont.)*,
    clinical example of role of
    therapist 38-46; clinical
    example of scapegoat motif in
    294-304 (discussion 300-4);
    clinical example of that which
    patients bring to analysis
    229-36; intrapsychic object
    relations and 31-46; libidinal
    tensions in 296-8, 301-3;
    space in 164
groups, social, scapegoats and
    291-4
Guntrip, H. 9

heart-pump syndrome 285-6
Heimann, P. 281
hero behaviour 246
Hewes, G. 179-80
hierarchical organization of
    structures 138-40, 183
hierarchies, evolutionary 34-5
hierarchy of object loss,
    depression and 192-4
hierarchy of organic and psychic
    supports, depression and
    190-5
hypochondria and failed
    reparation: clinical example
    238-9

identity disorders in
    schizoid/borderline states 8-9,
    13, 26-7, 168-9, 276
idioglossias 186-7
id and sleep-waking cycle 282
infant, spatial development in
    21-30
infinite sets 270-1; unconscious
    as 175, 249-62

inner objects 286; damaged and
    dying 229-48; defined 280;
    dream-objects and 244, 281,
    284-5; group psychotherapy
    and 31, 32, 39, 46
inner space and female sexuality
    263-76; clinical example
    272-5
inner speech 180-1
instincts, theory of 4, 199,
    210-11, 277
Isaacs, Susan 33

Jakobson, R. 142
James, E.O. 247
Johnson, W.E. 263
Jones, E. 293
Jones, R.M. 187-8; *The New
    Psychology of Dreaming* 37,
    244
Joseph, Betty 69
Jost, A. 5, 199, 263

Klein, M. 2, 34, 70, 73, 136-7,
    148, 172, 218, 265, 270, 276,
    282; on depressive position
    138, 139, 140, 194, 215; on
    dreams 224-5, 284; on inner
    objects 245-6, 247, 248, 280;
    on paranoid-schizoid position
    138, 139, 140, 215, 224; on
    reparation 4, 17, 196, 210,
    211, 212-17, 218, 220-1, 222,
    223, 224-6, 227; on sadism
    212-13
Kubie, Lawrence 4, 199, 210,
    277, 282

Lacan, J. 5, 72, 166, 256
language *see* psycholinguistics
Laplanche, J. 11, 33-4, 167
law of talion 17, 19, 67, 133, 197,
    204
Liber XXIV philosophium 258

logico-mathematical philosophy and unconscious 249–62
Lorenz, E. 6

McDougall, Patsy 74
manic defence 17–19, 219, 225
manic-depressive psychosis 6, 224–5; verbatim account 86–135 (commentary on treatment 126–35; history 86–7, 126–7); comparison with anorexia nervosa 133–4; physical factors in 134–5
manic state 29, 173, 197; dynamics of 209–10; identification with penis and 18–19, 130–1, 134, 219–21, 265, 268–9
Marais, Eugène: *The Soul of the Ape* 35, 192; *The Soul of the White Ant* 34–5
marsupial space 21, 167, 265
martyrs 246, 289
Masters, W.H. 263
Matte-Blanco, Ignacio 4, 71, 164, 217, 278, 282; *The Unconscious as Infinite Sets: An Essay in Bi-Logic* 175, 249–62
Maudsley Hospital, as 'brick mother' x
Meltzer, D. 174
menstrual cycle 264, 265, 269
metasystems 5–6, 38, 176–7
Moerck, E.L. 141
mourning 138, 150, 196, 209, 243
movement: in depression and mania 29, 173; and displacement 27–9, 173–4; in infant development 27–8, 29; and life 221–3; in schizoid states 28–9, 174

narcissism 167, 256, 262
Nash, Professor E. 47
Newton, I. 22; *Philosophia Naturalis Principia Mathematica* 266

object(s): clinical example of life and death of in manic-depressive psychosis 128–9; domain of 167–8; lost and damaged, reparation and 209, 212, 213, 219; words as 183, 184; *see also* inner objects; part-objects
object relations, intrapsychic, in individual and group 31–46; dreams, sensori-motor activity, change and acting-out 37–8; early constructional activity and primitive intrapsychic groups 32–4; evolutionary hierarchies 34–5; role of therapist 38–46 (clinical example 39–46); space and sensori-motor schemas 35–7
object relations theory 23–4, 32–3, 171, 183, 208, 265, 278–9; psycholinguistics, therapeutic process and 136–50 (clinical examples 142–3, 144–50)
Oedipus complex 4–5
orgasm, female, problem of 269–71; clinical example 271–2

paranoid-schizoid position 5–6, 237, 282–3; psycholinguistics and 137–8, 139–40, 142–3, 147, 149; reparation and 209, 215, 217, 218, 219, 224
Parmenides 254
parricidal urges and scapegoats 292–3

part-objects 4, 9–10, 23, 174, 216, 217, 252, 255
penis 5; identification with *see under* manic state; reparation and 18, 217–18, 219–21, 264–5
personal space 21, 167, 265–6
Pétot, J.M. 211, 215
Piaget, J. 2, 15, 32, 164, 211, 255, 295; on becoming conscious 143–4; on hierarchical organization of thought 138–9, 140, 164–5; on language and thought 136–7, 186, 189; on object permanence 29–30, 193; on reversibility 200–1, 206; on schemas 22–3, 34, 35–8, 165, 180, 188, 281; on sensori-motor stage 22–3, 35–7, 165, 200–1; on spatial development 20–1, 22, 35–7, 264; on time concept 28, 29, 165
Pontalis, J.B. 11, 33–4, 167
pregnancy 264; anorexia nervosa and pseudo- 64, 66, 70, 73
principle of generalization 251
principle of symmetry 251, 252, 260
projective identification 9–10, 11, 138, 185; clinical example in manic-depressive psychosis 127–8
Proust, M. 30
psychoanalysis:
    logico-mathematical treatment of 249–62; that which patients bring to 229–48 (clinical examples in a group 229–36; clinical examples in individuals 237–41); universals of 1–7
psychoanalytic and psycholinguistic structures, psychodynamics of 176–89

psycholinguistic(s) 3; object relations theory, therapeutic process and 136–50 (clinical examples 142–3, 144–50); and psychoanalytic structures, psychodynamics of 176–89
psychosis 160, 261–2

Redl, F. 303
relative size of subject and object 175, 262
reparation 4, 138, 207–28, 264–5, 279, 284; attempted, clinical example of in manic-depressive psychosis 131–3; defences and 215, 218, 228, 237; depression and 196–7, 203, 204–5, 209; schizoid mode of being and 12, 17, 18, 44, 211–12, 215–23; that which patients bring to analysis and 229–48
reversibility of depression, therapeutic process and 199–206; clinical example 205–6
Rivière, Joan 33, 211
Rouah, A. 47
Rubinstein, Benjamin D. 164, 178, 256

sadism 213–13, 214, 215
sado-masochism 260–1, 262
Salk, Dr 286
saturnalian revelries 293–4, 303
scapegoat motif in society 288–306; ancient scapegoat dramas 293–4, 303; clinical example of in therapeutic group 294–304; engineered scapegoats 289, 293, 305;

scapegoat motif in society *(cont.)*,
individual variations of need
for 290–1; psychogenesis of
need for 288–90; socio-genesis
of need for 291–4
schizoaffective disorders 6, 16,
193
schizoid patients 143, 276; basic
schizoid structures and
space–time factors 163–75,
211–12, 220; characteristics of
8–9, 168–9; clinical example
of therapeutic group 39–46;
depressive position and 19;
manic defence and 17–19;
mode of being 8–20;
reparation and 12, 17, 18, 44,
211–12, 215–23;
schizophrenic breakdown and
14–15, 19–20; space–time
continuum and displacement
in 20–30; transformation,
representation and
symbolization in 15–17
schizophrenia 11–12, 15–16,
175, 217–19; chronic, clinical
example of therapeutic group
in 151–62 (commentary
159–62); claustro-agoraphobia
and 10, 25–6, 171; disorders of
verbal thought and 3, 5, 19,
144–9; hearing voices and
160–1; interference with
thoughts and 160, 161; from
schizoid states to 14–15, 19–20
Scott, W. Clifford M. 4, 244;
'Repairing broken links
between the unconscious,
sleep and instinct; and
conscious, waking and
instinct' 277–87
secondary burial 247
Segal, Hanna 225
semantic density concept 181–2

sensori-motor activity, dreams,
change and acting out 37–8
sensori-motor schemas and space
22–3, 35–7, 71, 72, 165
sexual identity problems in
borderline and schizoid
patients 8–9, 13, 168–9, 276
sexuality, female, inner space and
263–76; clinical example
272–5
sexuality, male, development of
264–5
sleep: paradoxical phase of
191–2, 193, 279; and waking
277–87; *see also* dreams
social attitudes and scapegoats
290–1
Sokolov, A.N. 180
space: in groups 164; inner,
female sexuality and 263–76
(clinical example 272–5);
marsupial ix, 21, 167, 265;
personal 21, 167, 265–6;
sensori-motor schemas and
22–3, 35–7, 71, 72, 165;
universal 22, 27, 167
space-centred thought in anorexia
nervosa 65, 69, 70–1, 72
space–time continuum and
displacement in borderline
state 20–30
space–time factors and basic
schizoid structures 163–75,
211–12, 220
spatial development of infant and
his world 21–30
Spitz, R.A. 34, 193, 266
splitting 11–12, 138, 276; clinical
example in manic-depressive
psychosis 127, 134
Steiner, John 170
Stern, D.N. 278
Story of O, The 261

structures: defined 23; ghost 189; hierarchical organization of 138–40, 183; psychoanalytic and psycholinguistic, psychodynamics of 176–89; role in psychoanalysis 166; space–time factors and basic schizoid 163–75, 211–12, 220

super-ego and sleep–waking cycle 282

symmetrical and asymmetrical modes of being 250, 252–3, 254, 255, 258–9, 278

Tallemant des Réaux, G. 174

Taylor, F.K. 296

tenderminded–toughminded factor in social attitudes, scapegoats and 290–1

therapeutic process: object relations theory, psycholinguistics and 136–50 (clinical examples 142–3, 144–50); reversibility of depression and 199–206 (clinical example 205–6)

therapist, role of 202; in therapeutic groups 38–46 (clinical example 39–46)

Thom, René 3, 73–4, 181–3

time: concept of 27–8, 29, 36, 165, 172–3, 253; see also space–time continuum; space–time factors

Tinbergen, N. 277

translating function 253–4

unconscious: death and dying in 236–7, 241, 248, 283–4; as infinite sets 175, 249–62; role in reparation 224; system Ucs. 15, 251–2, 278

universal space 22, 27, 167

vagina–clitoris 263, 267, 270, 275

Voltaire, F. 27

Winnicott, D. 36, 128, 270

womb, return to 221–2, 287

words: 'basin of attraction' of 183, 184; meaning and 184–7; as objects 183, 184